The Concise Cengage Handbook

KIRSZNER

& MANDELL

2020 APA Update Edition

8 Use technology.

Being tech-savvy is essential to success in college. You probably already have most of the skills you need but if you don't, it's important to make an effort to become fluent in the following:

- ✔ Composing in word-processing programs such as *Microsoft Word* or *Google Drive*
- ✔ Sending emails and attaching files to them
- ✔ Using the Internet and evaluating websites **(See Chapter 43)**
- ✔ Using your library's electronic resources **(See Chapter 42)**
- ✔ Scanning and inserting documents that contain images as well as text
- ✔ Using technology to enhance a project—for example, learning how to use *PowerPoint* or *Keynote* for a presentation or *Google Sheets* to make a table **(See Chapter 11)**
- ✔ Syncing information among various devices (phone, computer, tablet, etc.)
- ✔ Knowing when to use technology —and when not to **(See Chapters 11–12)**

FIGURE 10 Sample notes on a journal article in the *ZotPad* app.

Notetaking apps like *ZotPad* can be useful both in and out of the classroom.

Be aware of the online services your school offers.

Many campuses rely on customizable information-management systems called **portals**. You can use your user ID (or school email) and password to access services such as locating and contacting your advisor and viewing your class schedule and grades. Portals may also be connected to individual course websites.

Make contacts.

Classmates

Be sure you have the phone numbers and email addresses of at least two students in each of your classes. These will come in handy if you miss class, need help understanding notes, or want to form a study group.

FIGURE 11 Student talking with instructor.

Jack Hollingsworth/Digital Vision/Getty Images

Friends from Activities or Work-Study Jobs

Build relationships with students who participate in college activities with you. They are likely to share your goals and interests, and you may want to discuss decisions like choosing a major, considering further education, and making career choices.

Instructors

Develop a relationship with your instructors, particularly those in the areas of study that interest you most.

One of the things cited most often in studies of successful students is the importance of **mentors**, experienced academic and professional individuals whose advice you trust. Long after you leave college, you will find these contacts useful.

 Be a lifelong learner.

- ✔ Get in the habit of reading local and national newspapers.
- ✔ Make connections outside the college community to keep in touch with the larger world.
- ✔ Attend plays and concerts sponsored by your school or community.
- ✔ Go to lectures offered at your local library or bookstore.

FIGURE 12 Students at a performance.

Rawpixel/Shutterstock.com

Never miss an opportunity to learn.

Think about the life you will lead after college. Think about who you want to be and what you have to do to get there. This is what successful students do.

The Concise Cengage Handbook

KIRSZNER & MANDELL

Fifth Edition

2020 APA Update Edition

Laurie G. Kirszner
University of the Sciences, Emeritus

Stephen R. Mandell
Drexel University

 CENGAGE

Australia • Brazil • Canada • Mexico • Singapore • United Kingdom • United States

CENGAGE

The Concise Cengage Handbook, Fifth Edition
2020 APA Update Edition
Laurie G. Kirszner,
Stephen R. Mandell

Product Director: Monica Eckman

Product Team Manager:
Nicole Morinon

Product Manager: Laura Ross

Senior Content Developer:
Leslie Taggart

Content Developer: Karen Mauk

Associate Content Developer:
Karolina Kiwak

Associate Content Developer:
Rachel Smith

Product Assistant:
Claire Branman

Senior Managing Content
Developer: Cara Douglass-Graff

Marketing Director:
Stacey Purviance

Senior Content Project Manager:
Rosemary Winfield

Senior Art Director:
Marissa Falco

Manufacturing Planner:
Betsy Donaghey

IP Analyst: Ann Hoffman

IP Project Manager: Farah Fard

Production Service and
Compositor: Karen Stocz,
Cenveo® Publisher Services

Text and Cover Designer:
Cenveo® Publisher Services

Cover Image: James Weinberg

Library of Congress Control Number: On file.

Student Edition:
ISBN: 978-1-337-27996-3

Loose-leaf Edition:
ISBN: 978-1-337-27994-9

Cengage
200 Pier 4 Boulevard
Boston, MA 02210
USA

Cengage is a leading provider of customized learning solutions with employees residing in nearly 40 different countries and sales in more than 125 countries around the world. Find your local representative at **www.cengage.com.**

To learn more about Cengage platforms and services, register or access your online learning solution, or purchase materials for your course, visit **www.cengage.com.**

Printed in the United States of America
Print Number: 05   Print Year: 2021

How to Use This Book

As writers, you already know that to express your ideas clearly, you need to understand the basic principles of grammar, mechanics, and style. And, as writers in the digital age, you also know that you need to use a variety of electronic tools to compose and design documents and to navigate the Internet and find information in the library. We wrote *The Concise Cengage Handbook* with these needs in mind. The result is a book that you can depend on to give you useful, no-nonsense, practical advice about writing.

Despite its compact size, *The Concise Cengage Handbook* is a complete reference for the college writer. Not only does it explain and illustrate the writing process, but it also offers guidance on grammar, style, punctuation, and mechanics and includes extensive sections on research and MLA and APA documentation styles. In addition, a unique section—Part 2, "Composing in Various Genres"—includes chapters on writing essay exams, writing in the workplace, designing effective documents, and composing in digital environments.

We have worked hard to make *The Concise Cengage Handbook* inviting, useful, clear, and—most of all—easy to use. To achieve these goals, we incorporated distinctive design features—icons, close-up boxes, checklists, and marginal cross-references and navigational aids—throughout the text to help you locate information quickly. Familiarizing yourself with the following page, which explains these design features, will help you get the most out of this book.

Throughout *The Concise Cengage Handbook* we have made every effort to address the challenges that real writers face in the twenty-first century and to provide you with clear explanations and sound advice. The result is a book that you can rely on—and one that you will use with ease and, perhaps, even with pleasure.

Laurie Kirszner
Steve Mandell
January 2016

The Concise Cengage Handbook: Design Features

- **New planning guides** throughout the text help you plan and organize a range of documents in various genres.
- **Collaborative writing icons** appear alongside sections and exercises that emphasize peer review and other collaborative work.
- **Numerous checklists** summarize key information that you can quickly access as needed.
- **Close-up boxes** provide an in-depth look at some of the more perplexing writing-related issues you will encounter.
- **Chapter 47**, "MLA Documentation Style," includes the updated documentation guidelines put forth in the eighth edition of the *MLA Handbook* (2016). **Chapter 48, "APA Documentation Style,"** includes the most up-to-date documentation and format guidelines from the American Psychological Association. In addition, color-coded and annotated diagrams of sample works-cited entries clearly illustrate the elements of proper documentation.
- **Marginal cross-references** throughout the book allow you to go directly to other sections that treat topics in more detail.
- **Marginal multilingual cross-references** (designated by **ml**) throughout the book direct you to sections of Part 8, "Composing for Multilingual Writers," where concepts are presented as they apply specifically to multilingual writers.
- **Multilingual tips** are woven throughout the text to explain concepts in relation to the unique experiences of multilingual students.
- **Numerous exercises** throughout the text allow you to practice at each stage of the writing, revising, and editing processes. Answers are provided in the back of the book for items marked with a ▶.
- **An extensive writing-centered treatment of grammar, punctuation, and mechanics,** including hand-edited examples, explains and illustrates specific strategies for improving your writing.
- **A new "Ten Habits of Successful Students" foldout** illustrates and helps you apply the strategies of successful students both in and out of college.

Acknowledgments

We would like to take this opportunity to thank Anne Stameshkin for her work on the new "Ten Habits of Successful Students" foldout and on the documentation updates; Kelly Cannon, Muhlenberg College, for his research advice; and Sherry Rankins-Robertson, University of Arkansas at Little Rock, for her digital writing advice.

We would also like to thank the following reviewers for their advice, which helped us develop the fifth edition:

Negussie Abebe, *Lone Star College, University Park*
Christine Barr, *Lone Star College, University Park*

Christina Bisirri, *Seminole State College of Florida*
Woodward Bousquet, *Shenandoah University*
William Carney, *Cameron University*
James Crooks, *Shasta College*
Michael Duffy, *Moorpark College*
Christopher Ervin, *Western Kentucky University*
Daniel Fitzstephens, *University of Colorado Boulder*
Ginger Fray, *Lone Star College, Greenspoint Center*
Hillary Gallego, *North Lake College*
Andrew Green, *University of Miami*
Rebecca Hoff, *West Virginia University Parkersburg*
John Hyman, *American University*
Parmita Kapadia, *Northern Kentucky University*
Laura Knight, *Mercer County Community College*
Bobby Kuechenmeister, *University of Toledo*
Laura La Flair, *Belmont Abbey College*
Angela Laflen, *Marist College*
Meredith Love-Steinmetz, *Francis Marion University*
Walter Lowe, *Green River Community College*
Cassie Plott, *Rowan-Cabarrus Community College*
Chrishawn Speller, *Seminole State College of Florida*
Mary Tripp, *University of Central Florida*
Isera Tyson-Miller, *State College of Florida*
Martha Vertreace-Doody, *Kennedy-King College*
Alex Vuilleumier, *Portland Community College*
Ann Westrick, *Bowling Green State University*
Karen Wilson, *Lakeland Community College*

At Cengage, we are grateful to Nicole Morinon, Product Team Manager; Laura Ross, Product Manager; Leslie Taggart, Senior Content Developer; Rachel Smith, Associate Content Developer; and Claire Branman, Product Assistant, for keeping the project moving along, and to Rosemary Winfield, Senior Content Project Manager, for her careful attention to detail. Our biggest thanks go to Karen Mauk, our wonderful Content Developer; as always, it has been a pleasure to work with her.

The staff of Cenveo did its usual stellar job, led by our talented Project Manager and Copyeditor Karen Stocz. James Weinberg's cover design is the icing on the cake.

We would also like to thank our families for being there when we needed them. And, finally, we each thank the person on the other side of the ampersand for making our collaboration work one more time.

Teaching and Learning Resources

Online Instructor's Manual and Answer Key

The Online Instructor's Manual and Answer Key contains an abundance of instructor materials, including sample syllabi, activities, and answers to the book's exercises. To download or print the manual, log on to login .cengage.com with your faculty account.

MindTap

MindTap® English for Kirszner and Mandell's *The Concise Cengage Handbook*, fifth edition, engages your students to become better thinkers, communicators, and writers by blending your course materials with content that supports every aspect of the writing process.

- Interactive activities on grammar and mechanics promote application in student writing
- Easy-to-use paper management system helps prevent plagiarism and allows for electronic submission, grading, and peer review
- A vast database of scholarly sources with video tutorials and examples supports every step of the research process
- Professional tutoring guides students from rough drafts to polished writing
- Visual analytics track student progress and engagement
- Seamless integration into your campus learning management system keeps all your course materials in one place

MindTap lets you compose your course, your way.

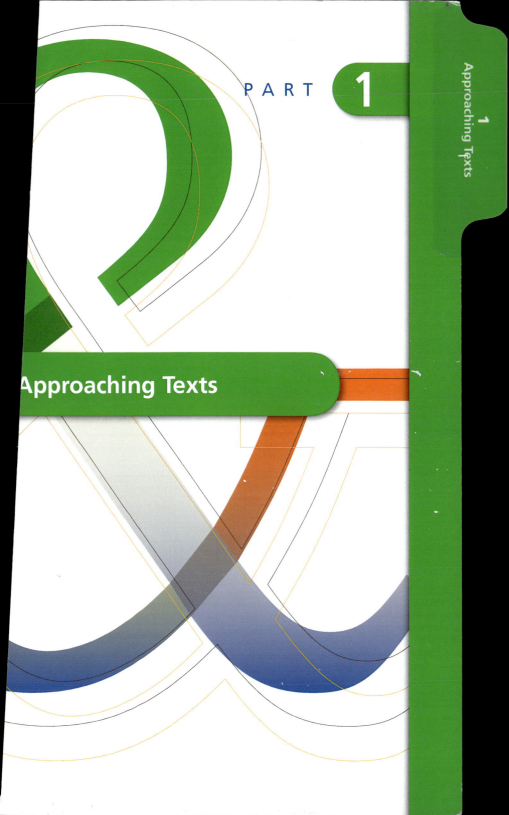

Approaching Texts

P A R T

Approaching Texts

CHAPTER 1

Reading to Write

Reading is an essential part of learning. Before you can become an effective writer and a successful student, you need to know how to get the most out of the texts you read.

Central to developing effective reading skills is learning the techniques of **active reading**. Being an active reader means being actively involved in the text: marking the text in order to identify parallels, question ambiguities, distinguish important points from not-so-important ones, and connect causes with effects and generalizations with specific examples. The understanding you gain from active reading prepares you to think (and write) critically about a text.

> **MULTILINGUAL TIP**
>
> When you read a text for the first time, don't worry about understanding every word. Instead, just try to get a general idea of what the text is about and how it is organized. Later on, you can look up any unfamiliar words.

1a Previewing a Text

Before you begin reading a text, you should **preview** it—that is, skim it to get a sense of the writer's subject and emphasis.

When you preview a **periodical article**, skim the introductory and concluding paragraphs for summaries of the writer's main points. (Journal articles in the sciences and social sciences often begin with summaries called **abstracts**.) Thesis statements, topic sentences, repeated key terms, transitional words and phrases, and transitional paragraphs can also help you to identify the key points a writer is making. In addition, look for the **visual cues**—such as headings and lists—that writers use to emphasize ideas.

See 11b–c

When you preview a **book**, start by looking at its table of contents; then, turn to its index. A quick glance at the index will reveal the amount of coverage the book gives to subjects that may be important to you. As you leaf through the chapters, look at pictures, graphs, or tables and the captions that appear with them.

CHECKLIST

Previewing a Text

When you preview a text, try to answer these questions:

❑ What is the text's general subject?

❑ What are the writer's key points?

---

continued

Previewing a Text *(continued)*

❑ How much space does the writer devote to topics relevant to your interests or research?

❑ What other topics are covered?

❑ Who is the author of the text? What do you know about this writer?

❑ Is the text current? Is its information up-to-date?

❑ Does the text strike you as interesting, accessible, and useful?

1b   Highlighting a Text

When you have finished previewing a work, photocopy relevant sections of books and articles, and print out useful material from online sources. Then, **highlight** the pages, using a system of graphic symbols and underlining to identify the writer's key points and their relationships to one another.

CHECKLIST
Using Highlighting Symbols

When you read a text, use strategies such as the following to help you understand the material:

❑ Underline to indicate information you should read again.

❑ Box or circle key words or important phrases.

❑ Put question marks next to confusing passages, unclear points, or words you need to look up.

❑ Draw lines or arrows to show connections between ideas.

❑ Number points that are discussed in sequence.

❑ Draw a vertical line in the margin to set off an important section.

❑ Star especially important ideas.

1c   Annotating a Text

After you have read through your material once, read it again—this time, more critically. At this stage, you should **annotate** the content, recording your responses to what you read. This process of recording notes in the margins or between the lines will help you to better understand the writer's ideas and your own reactions to those ideas.

Some of your annotations may be relatively straightforward. For example, you may

MULTILINGUAL TIP
You may find it useful to use your native language when you annotate a text.

define new words, identify unfamiliar references, or jot down brief summaries. Other annotations may reflect your personal reactions to the text. For example, you may identify a parallel between an experience of your own and one described in the text, or you may note your opinion of the writer's position.

As you start to **think critically** about a text, your annotations may identify points that confirm (or challenge) your own ideas, question the appropriateness or accuracy of the writer's support, uncover the writer's biases, or even question (or dispute) the writer's conclusion.

See
Ch. 6

The following passage illustrates a student's highlighting and annotations of a passage from Michael Pollan's book *The Omnivore's Dilemma*.

People drank 5x as much as they do today

In the early years of the nineteenth century, Americans began drinking more than they ever had before or since, embarking on a collective bender that confronted the young republic with its first major public health crisis—the obesity epidemic of its day. Corn whiskey, suddenly superabundant and cheap, became the drink of choice, and in 1820 the typical American was putting away half a pint of the stuff every day. That comes to more than five gallons of spirits a year for every man, woman, and child in America. The figure today is less than one.

‼

As the historian W. J. Rorabaugh tells the story in *The Alcoholic Republic*, we drank the hard stuff at breakfast, lunch, and dinner, before work and after and very often during. Employers were expected to supply spirits over the course of the workday; in fact, the modern coffee break began as a late-morning whiskey break called "the elevenses." (Just to pronounce it makes you sound tipsy.) Except for a brief respite Sunday morning in church, Americans simply did not gather—whether for a barn raising or quilting bee, corn husking or political rally— without passing the whiskey jug. Visitors from Europe—hardly models of sobriety themselves—marveled at the free flow of American spirits.

?

"Come on then, if you love toping," the journalist William Cobbett wrote his fellow Englishmen in a dispatch from America. "For here you may drink yourself blind at the price of sixpence."

✳

Did the gov't take action?

The results of all this toping were entirely predictable: a rising tide of public drunkenness, violence, and family abandonment, and a spike in alcohol-related diseases. Several of the Founding Fathers— including George Washington, Thomas Jefferson, and John Adams— denounced the excesses of "the Alcoholic Republic," inaugurating an American quarrel over drinking that would culminate a century later in Prohibition.

Why?

✳

But the outcome of our national drinking binge is not nearly as relevant to our own situation as its underlying cause. Which, put simply, was this: American farmers were producing far too much corn. This was particularly true in the newly settled regions west of the Appalachians, where fertile, virgin soils yielded one bumper crop after another. A

Examples from contemporary US farming?

mountain of surplus corn piled up in the Ohio River Valley. <u>Much as today, the astounding productivity of American farmers proved to be their own worst enemy, as well as a threat to public health.</u> For when yields rise, the market is flooded with grain, and its price collapses. What happens next? The excess biomass works like a vacuum in reverse:

This is his point

<u>Sooner or later, clever marketers will figure out a way to induce the human omnivore to consume the surfeit of cheap calories.</u>

EXERCISE 1.1

Find an article that interests you in a newspaper or magazine (or online). Read it carefully, highlighting it as you read. When you have finished, annotate the article.

1d   Reading Electronic Texts

Even when electronic documents physically resemble print documents (as they do in online newspaper articles), the way they present information can be very different. Print documents are **linear**; that is, readers move in a straight line from the beginning of a document to the end. Print documents are also self-contained, including all the background information, explanations, supporting details, and visuals necessary to make their point.

Electronic documents, however, are usually not linear. They often include advertising, marginal commentary, and graphics, and they may also include sound and video. In addition, links embedded in the text encourage readers to go to other sites for facts, statistical data, visuals, or additional articles that supplement the discussion. For example, readers of the electronic discussion of gun control pictured in Figure 1.1 could link to FBI data about the connection between "concealed carry laws" and violent crime. Once they access this material, they can choose to read it carefully, skim it, or ignore it.

The format of electronic texts presents challenges to readers. First, because links to other material interrupt the document's flow, it may be hard for readers to focus on a writer's main idea and key points or to follow an argument's logic. In addition, pages may be very busy, crowded with distracting marginalia, visuals, and advertisements. For these reasons, it makes sense to use a slightly different process when you apply active reading strategies to an electronic text.

Previewing During the previewing stage, you will probably want to skim the text online, doing your best to ignore visuals, marginal commentary, advertising, and links. If the text looks like something you will want to read more closely, you should print it out (taking care to print the

Link to related book

Links to related articles

Request for email comments

Link to related web page

Link to FBI data

FIGURE 1.1 Excerpt from "Do More Guns Mean Less Crime?" A *Reason Online* Debate. Reprinted by permission of *Reason*.

"printer-friendly" version, which will usually omit the distracting material and enable you to focus on the text's content).

Highlighting and Annotating Once you have hard copy of an electronic text, you can proceed to highlight and annotate it just as you would a print text. Reading on hard copy will enable you to follow the writer's main idea instead of clicking on every link. However, you should be sure to circle any links that look promising so you can explore them later on.

Note: You can also highlight and annotate web-based texts by using a program such as *Diigo*, which makes it possible for you to highlight and write self-stick notes on electronic documents.

EXERCISE 1.2

Find an essay online that interests you. Print the essay, and then highlight and annotate it, paying special attention to the features discussed in **1d**.

1e   Writing a Critical Response

Once you have previewed, highlighted, and annotated a text, you should have the understanding (and the material) you need to write a **critical**

response that *summarizes, analyzes,* and *interprets* the text's key ideas and perhaps *evaluates* them as well. It can also *synthesize* the ideas in the text with ideas in other texts.

CHECKLIST

Elements of a Critical Response

When you write a critical response, you may include some or all of the following elements.

❏ **Summary:** What is the writer saying?

❏ **Analysis:** What elements is the text made up of?

❏ **Interpretation:** What does the text mean?

❏ **Synthesis:** How is the text like and unlike other texts? How are its ideas like and unlike ideas in other texts?

❏ **Evaluation:** Is the text accurate and reliable? Do its ideas seem reasonable?

The following is a student's critical response to the passage from *The Omnivore's Dilemma* on pages 5–6.

Author and title identified

Summary

Analysis and interpretation

Evaluation

In an excerpt from his book *The Omnivore's Dilemma*, Michael Pollan discusses the drinking habits of nineteenth-century Americans and makes a connection between the cause of this "national drinking binge" and the factors behind our twenty-first-century unhealthy diets. In both cases, he blames the overproduction of grain by American farmers. He links nineteenth-century overproduction of corn with "a rising tide of public drunkenness, violence, and family abandonment, and a spike in alcohol-related deaths," and he also links the current overproduction of grain with a "threat to public health." Although there are certainly other causes of our current problems with obesity, particularly among young children, Pollan's analogy makes sense. As long as farmers need to sell their overabundant crops, consumers will be presented with a "surfeit of cheap calories"—with potentially disastrous results.

CHECKLIST

Writing a Critical Response

As you first read a text, keep the following questions in mind:

❏ Does the text provide any information about the writer's background? If so, how does this information affect your reading of the text?

❏ What is the writer's purpose? How can you tell?

❑ What audience is the text aimed at? How can you tell?

❑ What is the text's most important idea? What support does the writer provide for that idea?

Then, as you look more closely at the text, think about these questions:

❑ What information can you learn from the text's introduction and conclusion?

❑ What information can you learn from the thesis statement and topic sentences?

❑ Does the writer make any statements that suggest a particular bias?

See 6c

❑ How would you characterize the writer's tone?

❑ Are there parallels between the writer's experiences and your own?

❑ Where do you agree with the writer? Where do you disagree?

EXERCISE 1.3

Write two critical responses: one reacting to the newspaper article in Exercise 1.1 and one reacting to the electronic text you worked with in Exercise 1.2. When you have finished, write a few sentences summarizing the similarities and differences between the two articles.

CHAPTER 2

Understanding the Rhetorical Situation

Everyone who sets out to write confronts a series of choices. In the academic, professional, public, and private writing that you do in school, on the job, and in your personal life, your understanding of the rhetorical situation is essential—influencing the choices you make about content, emphasis, organization, format, style, and tone.

Before you begin to write, you should try to answer the following questions:

- What is my **rhetorical situation**, or context for writing?
- What is my **purpose** for writing?
- Who is my **audience**?
- What **genre** should I use in this situation?

2a Considering the Rhetorical Situation

Begin by considering the **rhetorical situation**, the set of conventions that are associated with a particular writing assignment. By keeping this rhetorical situation in mind throughout the writing process, you make sure that your writing keeps its focus.

In college, the rhetorical situation is often identified by your assignment. For example, if your assignment asks you to write about an event, such as a family tradition, you will need to identify a specific occurrence, such as a family beach trip, to focus on. In personal, civic, and professional writing, the rhetorical situation is often determined by a particular event, interest, or concern that creates the need for this writing. For example, you may write a proposal to your boss to request funding for a project or to suggest a better way of performing a particular task.

2b Determining Your Purpose

In simple terms, your **purpose** for writing is what you want to accomplish. Sometimes your purpose is to **reflect**, to express feelings or look back on your thinking. Or, your purpose may be to **inform**, to convey factual information as accurately and as logically as possible. At other times, your purpose may be to **persuade**, to convince your readers. Finally, your purpose may be to **evaluate**, to make a judgment about something, as in a book or film review, a recommendation report, or a comparative analysis.

1 Writing to Reflect

In journals, writers are often introspective, exploring ideas and emotions to make sense of their experiences; in autobiographical memoirs and personal blog posts, writers communicate their emotions and reactions to others. Another type of reflective writing is **metacognitive writing**, in which writers explain what they have learned and consider the decisions made throughout the writing process.

> At the age of five, six, well past the time when most other children no longer easily notice the difference between sounds uttered at home and words spoken in public, I had a different experience. I lived in a world magically compounded of sounds. I remained a child longer than most; I lingered too long, poised at the edge of language—often frightened by the sounds of *los gringos*, delighted by the sounds of Spanish at home. I shared with my family a language that was startlingly different from that used in the great city around us. (Richard Rodriguez, *Aria: Memoir of a Bilingual Childhood*)

2 Writing to Inform

In news articles, writers report information, communicating factual details to readers. In reference books, instruction manuals, and textbooks, as well as on websites sponsored by nonprofit organizations and government agencies, writers provide definitions and explain concepts or processes, trying to help readers see relationships and understand ideas.

> Most tarantulas live in the tropics, but several species occur in the temperate zone and a few are common in the southern U.S. Some varieties are large and have powerful fangs with which they can inflict a deep wound. These formidable-looking spiders do not, however, attack man; you can hold one in your hand, if you are gentle, without being bitten. Their bite is dangerous only to insects and small mammals such as mice; for man it is no worse than a hornet's sting. (Alexander Petrunkevitch, "The Spider and the Wasp")

Note: In your personal writing, you may convey information informally in *Facebook* updates, text messages, tweets, and instant messages.

3 Writing to Persuade

In proposals and editorials, as well as in advertising and on political websites and blogs, writers try to convince readers to accept their positions on various issues.

> America must make sure the melting pot continues to melt: immigrants must become Americans. Seymour Martin Lipset, professor of political science and sociology at the Hoover Institution, Stanford University, observes: "The history of bilingual and bicultural societies that do not assimilate are histories of turmoil, tension and tragedy. Canada, Belgium, Malaysia, Lebanon—all face crises of national existence in which minorities press for autonomy, if not independence. Pakistan and Cyprus have divided. Nigeria suppressed an ethnic rebellion. France faces difficulties with its Basques, Bretons and Corsicans." (Richard D. Lamm, "English Comes First")

4 Writing to Evaluate

In reviews of books, films, or performances and in reports, critiques, and program evaluations, writers assess the validity, accuracy, and quality of information, ideas, techniques, products, procedures, or services. Sometimes they assess the relative merits of two or more things.

> Review of *A Dance with Dragons* by George R. R. Martin. Random House, 2011. May 16, 2015.
>
> I am a fan of the HBO series *Game of Thrones*, so I was looking forward to the release of *A Dance with Dragons*, the fifth book in the series *A Song of Ice and Fire*. Although I found the fourth book in the series slightly disappointing, *A Dance with Dragons* is a great read. Westeros, the world created by George R. R. Martin, has a complex history that stretches back thousands of years. The characters who inhabit Westeros are interesting and believable. Their various motives, flaws, and morals drive their actions in compelling ways with surprising and far-reaching consequences. It was easy to get lost in this faraway world and wrapped up in its people and history. I'm looking forward to seeing how this latest volume comes to life on the screen in *Game of Thrones*.

Close-Up PURPOSE AND CONTENT

Your purpose for writing determines the material you choose and the way you organize and express your ideas.

- A memoir might *reflect* on the negative aspects of summer camp, focusing on mosquitoes, poison ivy, homesickness, institutional food, and so on.
- A magazine article about summer camps could *inform*, presenting facts and statistics to show how camping has changed over the years.
- An advertising brochure designed to recruit potential campers could *persuade*, enumerating the benefits of the camping experience.
- A nonprofit camping association's website could *evaluate* various camps, assessing facilities, costs, staff-to-camper ratios, and activities in order to assist parents in choosing a camp.

Although writers write to reflect, to inform, to persuade, and to evaluate, these purposes are certainly not mutually exclusive, and writers may have other purposes as well. The checklist below lists some specific purposes for writing.

CHECKLIST
Determining Your Purpose

Before you begin to write, you need to determine why you are writing. Your purposes can include any of the following:

❏ to reflect	❏ to draw comparisons	❏ to take a stand
❏ to inform	❏ to make an analogy	❏ to identify problems
❏ to persuade	❏ to define	❏ to suggest solutions
❏ to evaluate	❏ to criticize	❏ to identify causes
❏ to explain	❏ to motivate	❏ to predict effects
❏ to amuse or entertain	❏ to satirize	❏ to interpret
❏ to discover	❏ to speculate	❏ to instruct
❏ to analyze	❏ to warn	❏ to inspire
❏ to debunk	❏ to reassure	

As you begin to write, determining your purpose for writing is critical. As you consider the requirements of your assignment, your rhetorical situation and purpose work together. Later, identifying and considering the needs of your audience will help you shape the content, organization, tone, and style of your writing.

EXERCISE 2.1

The primary purpose of the following article from the *New York Times* is to present information. Suppose you were using the information in an orientation booklet aimed at students entering your school, and your purpose was to persuade students of the importance of maintaining a good credit rating. How would you change the original article to help you achieve this purpose? Would you reorder any details? Would you add or delete anything?

What Makes a Credit Score Rise or Fall?

By Jennifer Bayot

Your financial decisions can affect your credit score in surprising ways. Two credit-scoring simulators can help consumers understand the potential impact.

The Fair Isaac Corporation, which puts out the industry-standard FICO scores, offers the myFICO simulator. A consumer with a score of 707 (considered good) and three credit cards would be likely to add or lose points from his score by making various financial moves. Following are some examples:

- By making timely payments on all his accounts over the next month or by paying off a third of the balance on his cards, he could add as many as 20 points.
- By failing to make this month's payments on his loans, he could lose 75 to 125 points.
- By using all of the credit available on his three credit cards, he could lose 20 to 70 points.
- By getting a fourth card, depending on the status of his other debts, he could add or lose up to 10 points.
- By consolidating his credit card debt into a new card, also depending on other debts, he could add or lose 15 points.

The other simulator, the What-If, comes from CreditXpert, which designs credit management tools and puts out its own, similar credit score. A consumer with a score of 727 points (also considered good) would be likely to have her score change in the following ways:

- Every time she simply applied for a loan, whether a credit card, home mortgage or auto loan, she would lose five points. (An active appetite for credit, credit experts note, is considered a bad sign. For one thing, taking on new loans may make borrowers less likely to repay their current debts.)
- By getting a mortgage, she would lose two points.
- By getting an auto loan or a new credit card (assuming that she already has several cards) she would lose three points.
- If her new credit card had a credit limit of $20,000 or more, she would lose four points, instead of three. (For every $10,000 added to the limit, the score drops a point.)
- By simultaneously getting a new mortgage, auto loan and credit card, she would lose seven or eight points.

2c   Identifying Your Audience

When you are in the early stages of a writing project and staring at a blank screen, it is easy to forget that you are writing for an audience. However, most of the writing you compose is directed at a specific **audience**, a particular reader or group of readers. Sometimes your audience is indicated by your assignment; at other times, you must decide for yourself who your readers are.

1 Writing for an Audience

At different times, in different roles, you address a variety of audiences. Before you write, you should think about the characteristics of the audience (or audiences) that you will be addressing.

See 2d

- **In your personal life,** you may send notes, emails, or text messages to friends and family members. You may find yourself writing on social media and for special occasions in a variety of formats or **genres**.
- **In your public life,** as a citizen, a consumer, or a member of a community, you may respond to social, economic, or political issues by writing letters or emails to newspapers, public officials, or representatives of special interest groups. You might also be called on to write media releases, brochures, flyers, or newsletters for civic, political, or religious organizations.
- **As an employee,** you may write emails, memos, proposals, and reports to your superiors, to staff members you supervise, or to coworkers; you may also be asked to address customers or critics, board members or stockholders, funding agencies or the general public.
- **As a student,** you will likely write reflective statements and responses as well as essays, reports, and exams in various academic disciplines. You may also participate in peer review sessions, writing evaluations of classmates' drafts as well as written responses to classmates' comments about your own work-in-progress.

As you write, you shape your writing according to what you think your audience needs and expects. Your assessment of your readers' interests, educational level, biases, and expectations determines not only the information you include, but also what you emphasize and how you arrange your material.

2 The College Writer's Audience

As a student, you may be asked to write for a specific audience, or you may be asked to select an audience. Often, college writers assume they are writing for an audience of one: the instructor who assigns the essay; however, this is not always the case because many instructors want students to address real-life rhetorical situations.

When writing for your instructors, you need to demonstrate your knowledge of the subject; instructors want to see whether you can express your ideas clearly and accurately. They assign written work to encourage you to **think critically**, so the way you organize and express your ideas can be as important as the ideas themselves.

See Ch. 6

Instructors expect accurate information, standard grammar and correct spelling, logically presented ideas, and a reasonable degree of stylistic sophistication. They also expect you to define your terms and to support your generalizations with specific examples. Finally, instructors expect you to draw your own conclusions and to provide full and accurate **documentation** for ideas that are not your own.

See Chs. 47–48

If you are writing in an instructor's academic field, you can omit long overviews and basic definitions. Remember, however, that outside their areas of expertise, most instructors are simply general readers. If you think you may know more about a subject than your instructor does, be sure to provide background and to supply the definitions, examples, and analogies that will make your ideas clear.

Even though all academic fields of study—or **disciplines**—share certain values, instructors in different disciplines emphasize different aspects of writing. For example, they expect your writing to conform to discipline-specific formats, conventions, and citation systems. Keep in mind that their requirements will often be different from those you will learn in your composition classes.

MULTILINGUAL TIP

Instructors are available outside of class during office hours, which are typically listed on your course syllabi. Keep in mind that instructors are available throughout the semester to help you succeed in your courses. It is a good idea to contact your instructors during the first week of school to introduce yourself and to explain what you hope to learn in your courses. You can email them to set up appointments or stop by during office hours.

③ Writing for Other Students

Before you submit an essay to an instructor, you may have an opportunity to participate in **peer review**, sharing your work with your fellow students and responding in writing to their work. When you participate in peer review, it is helpful to think of your classmates as an audience whose needs you should take into account.

See 5c2

● **Writing Drafts** If you know that other students will read a draft of your essay, consider how they might react to your ideas. For example, are they likely to disagree with you? To be confused, or even mystified, by any of your references? To be shocked or offended by your essay's language or content? You should not assume that your fellow students will automatically share your values, political opinions, or cultural frame of reference. For this reason, it is important to maintain a neutral tone and use moderate language in your essay and to explain any historical, geographical, or cultural references that you think might be unfamiliar to your audience.

• **Making Comments** When you respond to another student's writing, you should take into account how your classmate will react to your comments. Your tone is important. You want to be as encouraging (and as polite) as possible. In addition, keep in mind that your purpose is to offer insightful comments that can help your classmate write a stronger essay. (Your instructor may have specific response prompts that you should use to provide feedback.) Remember, when you respond to another student's essay, your goal is to be constructive, not critical or negative.

CHECKLIST
Writing for an Academic Audience

Before you respond to an assignment in your college courses, you need to identify the audience you are writing for. The following questions can help you understand what your audience expects:

❑ What discipline are you writing for?

❑ What kinds of assignments are typical of this discipline?

❑ What expectations do instructors in this discipline have?

❑ What style considerations are important in this discipline?

❑ What writing conventions are used in this discipline?

❑ What formats are used in this discipline?

❑ What research sources are used in this discipline?

❑ What documentation style is used in this discipline?

EXERCISE 2.2

Look again at the article in Exercise 2.1 on page 13. This time, try to decide what audience or audiences it seems to be aimed at. Then, consider what (if anything) might have to be changed to address the needs of each of the following audiences:

• College students
• Middle-school students
• The elderly
• People with limited English skills
• People who do not live in the United States

2d Selecting a Genre

In your college courses, you will compose many different kinds of texts—for example, academic essays, book reviews, research reports, proposals, lab reports, and case studies. These different types of texts—with their distinctive characteristics and conventions—are referred to as **genres**. In simple terms, a genre is a way of classifying a text according to its style, structure, and format.

A writer's choice of the genre, structure, and medium for writing is based on the intended message and audience. For example, if a writer seeks to inform an audience about an upcoming sales event, an *Instagram* post might be appropriate for college students, but a newspaper advertisement might be better for a more mature audience.

Most college writing assignments specify a particular genre. For example, your composition instructor might ask you to write an essay about a personal experience, to evaluate a novel or a film, or to take a position on an issue that you feel strongly about. In these cases, your familiarity with the conventions of the narrative essay, the book or film review, and argumentative writing, respectively, would help you decide how to approach and develop the assignment. (For detailed discussions of the genres most frequently used in various disciplines, **see Part 2.**)

CHAPTER 3

Planning

3a Understanding the Writing Process

Writing is a constant process of decision making—of selecting, reconsidering, deleting, and rearranging material as you plan, shape, draft and revise, and edit and proofread your work.

The Writing Process

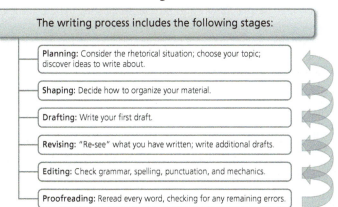

The writing process includes the following stages:

Planning: Consider the rhetorical situation; choose your topic; discover ideas to write about.

Shaping: Decide how to organize your material.

Drafting: Write your first draft.

Revising: "Re-see" what you have written; write additional drafts.

Editing: Check grammar, spelling, punctuation, and mechanics.

Proofreading: Reread every word, checking for any remaining errors.

Of course, the neatly defined stages listed above do not communicate the reality of the writing process. In practice, this process is neither a linear series of steps nor an isolated activity. (In fact, in a digital environment, a significant part of the writing process can take place in full view of an online audience.) Writing is also often interactive: the writing process can be interrupted (and supplemented) by emailing, blogging, chat room discussions, or exploring the Internet.

Moreover, the stages of the writing process actually overlap: as you look for ideas, you begin to shape your material; as you shape your material, you begin to compose; as you develop a draft, you reorganize your ideas; as you revise, you continue to discover new material. These stages may be repeated again and again throughout the writing process. In this sense, the writing process is cyclical. During your college years and in the years that follow, you will develop your own version of the writing process and use it whenever you write, adapting it to the audience, purpose, and writing situation at hand.

& Close-Up COLLABORATIVE WRITING PROJECTS

In school—and particularly in the workplace—you will find that writing is increasingly a collaborative effort. On a regular basis, you will work with others to plan projects, do research, draft different sections of a single document (or different components of a larger project), and offer suggestions for revision. Software such as *Google Drive* allows users to compose documents synchronously and, with the History feature, to view changes made in a file or revert to an earlier version of the file.

3b Computers and the Writing Process

See Ch. 10

Computers are essential for writing and communicating in both academic and workplace settings. In addition to using word-processing applications for typical writing tasks, writers may rely on programs such as *PowerPoint*® or *Prezi* for giving presentations; *Publisher*® or an Adobe application, such as *Photoshop*, *Illustrator*, or *InDesign*, for creating customized résumés or brochures; and web-page authoring software such as *Dreamweaver*® or Web 2.0 technologies, such as *Wix*, *Weebly*, or *WordPress*, for creating Internet-accessible documents that include images, movies, and a wide range of visual effects.

With the prominent role of the Internet in professional, academic, and personal communication, it is increasingly likely that the feedback you receive on your writing will be electronic. For example, if your instructor uses course management software such as *Blackboard*™ or *Canvas*, you may receive an email from your instructor about a draft that you have submitted to a digital drop box. Or, you may use discussion boards for attaching or sharing your documents with other students. Chat room and Net meeting software also allow you to discuss ideas collaboratively and to offer and receive feedback on drafts.

Although the specific tools you use may be course- or workplace-specific, you will still have to develop an efficient writing process. **Chapter 12** provides more comprehensive information on the options available to you as you compose in digital environments.

3c Understanding Your Assignment

Planning your essay—thinking about what you want to say and how you want to say it—begins well before you actually start recording your thoughts in any organized way. This planning is as important a part of the writing process as the writing itself. During this planning stage, you determine your **purpose** for writing and identify your **audience**. Then, you go on to focus on your assignment, choose and narrow your topic, and gather ideas.

Before you start to write, be sure you understand the exact requirements of your **assignment**. Ask questions if necessary, and be sure you understand the answers.

CHECKLIST

Understanding Your Assignment

To help you understand your assignment, consider the following questions:

❏ Has your instructor assigned a specific topic, or can you choose your own?

❏ Has your instructor indicated what genre you are to use?   *See 2d*

❏ What is the word or page limit?

❏ How much time do you have to complete your assignment?

❏ Will you get feedback from your instructor? Will you have an opportunity to participate in peer review?   *See 5c2*

❏ Does your assignment require research, and, if so, how many and what types of sources should you use?

❏ What format (for example, MLA) are you supposed to follow? Do you know what its conventions are?   *See Ch. 47*

❏ If your assignment has been given to you in writing, have you read it carefully and highlighted key words?

❏ Have you reviewed (and do you understand) your instructor's grading criteria?

Rebecca James, a first-year composition student, was given the following assignment prompt.

Wikipedia has become a common starting point for students seeking information on a research topic. Because anyone can alter articles in this database, the reliability of *Wikipedia* as a valid source of information has been criticized by members of the academic community. In an essay of about three to five pages, evaluate the benefits and drawbacks of using *Wikipedia* in college research. To support your assessment, focus on a *Wikipedia* entry related to one of your courses.

The class was given three weeks to complete the assignment. Students were expected to do some research and to have the instructor and other students read and comment on at least one draft.

3d   Finding a Topic

Sometimes your instructor will assign a specific topic, but most of the time you will be given a general, structured assignment, which you will have to narrow to a **topic** that suits your purpose and audience.

From Assignment to Topic

Course	Assignment	Topic
American History	Analyze the effects of a social program on one segment of American society	The effects of the GI Bill of Rights on American service-women
Sociology	Identify and evaluate the success of one resource available to the homeless population of one major American city	The role of the Salvation Army in meeting the needs of Chicago's homeless
Psychology	Write a three- to five-page essay assessing one method of treating depression.	Animal-assisted therapy for severely depressed patients

& **Note:** If your instructor permits you to do so, you can work with other students to narrow your topic.

Rebecca had no trouble thinking of ways she used *Wikipedia* to find general information, but she knew that the site was controversial in the academic community because several of her instructors discouraged her from using it as a research source. As she composed her essay, she knew she would have to find a balance between the usefulness of *Wikipedia* on the one hand and its lack of reliability on the other.

Because her assignment was so specific, Rebecca was easily able to restate it in the form of a topic.

Topic: *Wikipedia* and college research

EXERCISE 3.1

College campuses across the United States are working to achieve sustainability, making an effort to be more sensitive to environmental concerns and to become more "green."

With this exercise, you will begin the process of writing a three- to five-page essay in which you consider how your school is working toward this goal, what more it needs to do in the future, and how your suggestions for improvement will benefit your school.

Begin by looking up the word *sustainability* on the Internet. Think about this issue as it applies to your school, and (with your instructor's permission), talk to your friends and classmates about it. When you think you understand what is being done (and what is not being done) to make your campus more "green," list five specific environmental issues you could write about. Then, choose one of these areas of concern as the topic for your essay, and write a few sentences explaining why you selected this topic.

Your purpose in this essay will be to make recommendations for changes that could be adopted at your school. Your audience will be your composition instructor, members of your peer review group, and, possibly, a wider campus audience—for example, readers of your campus newspaper.

3e Finding Something to Say

Once you have a topic, you can begin to collect ideas for your essay, using one (or several) of the strategies discussed in the following pages.

1 Reading and Observing

As you read textbooks, magazines, and newspapers and explore the Internet, be on the lookout for ideas that relate to your topic. Films, television programs, interviews, letters, emails, and questionnaires can also provide material. But be sure your instructor permits such research—and remember to **document** ideas that are not your own. If you do not, you will be committing plagiarism.

> **MULTILINGUAL TIP**
>
> Don't use all your time making sure you are writing grammatically correct sentences. Remember, the purpose of writing is to communicate ideas. If you want to write an interesting, well-developed essay, you will need to devote plenty of time to the activities described in this section. You can then edit your work once you have determined and refined your ideas.

When students in Rebecca's composition class were assigned to read *Wikipedia*'s policy statement, "Researching with *Wikipedia*," in preparation for their See Ch. 46 essay assignment, she learned about the problems of using *Wikipedia* in college-level research. This reading assignment gave her a wider perspective on her topic and encouraged her to look beyond her own experience with *Wikipedia*.

2 Keeping a Journal

Many professional writers keep print or electronic **journals** (sometimes in the form of blogs), writing in them regularly whether or not they have a specific project in mind. Journals, unlike diaries, do more than simply record personal experiences and reactions. In a journal, you explore ideas, ask questions, reflect on your thinking and the information you are processing, and draw conclusions. You might, for example, analyze your position on a political issue, try to solve an ethical problem, or trace the evolution of your ideas about an academic assignment.

One of Rebecca's journal entries appears below.

Journal Entry

I use *Wikipedia* all the time, whenever something comes up that I want to know more about. Once my roommate and I were talking about graffiti art, and I started wondering how and where it began. I went to *Wikipedia* and found a long article about graffiti's origins and development as an art form. Some of my instructors say not to use *Wikipedia* as a research source, so I try to avoid going to the site for essay assignments. Still, it can be really helpful when I'm trying to find basic information. A lot of business and financial terms come up in my accounting class, and I can usually find simple explanations on *Wikipedia* of things I don't understand.

3 Freewriting

When you **freewrite**, you write nonstop about anything that comes to mind, moving as quickly as you can. Give yourself a set period of time—say, five minutes—and don't stop to worry about punctuation, spelling, or grammar, or about where your freewriting takes you. This strategy encourages your mind to make free associations; thus, it helps you to discover ideas you probably aren't even aware you have. When your time is up, look over what you have written, and underline, circle, bracket, star, boldface, or otherwise highlight the most promising ideas. You can then use one or more of these ideas as the center of a focused freewriting exercise.

When you do **focused freewriting**, you zero in on your topic. Here, too, you write without stopping to reconsider or reread, so you have no time to be self-conscious about style or form, to worry about the relevance of your ideas, or to count how many words you have (and panic about how many more you think you need). At its best, focused freewriting can suggest new details, a new approach to your topic, or even a more interesting topic.

Excerpts from Rebecca's freewriting and focused freewriting exercises appear below.

Freewriting (Excerpt)

I'm just going to list a bunch of things from my accounting class notes that I've recently looked up in *Wikipedia*: shareholder, stakeholder, strategic management, core competency, certified public accountant, certified management accountant, financial accounting, profit and loss. Not really sure which entry to focus on for this assignment. All the entries have strengths and weaknesses. I guess that's the point, but some *Wikipedia* articles are better than others. Maybe I'll choose an article that's sort of in the middle—one that provides some good basic info but could also be improved in some ways.

Focused Freewriting (Excerpt)

I think I'm going to use the "Financial Accounting" article as my focus for this essay. It explains this accounting field pretty clearly and concisely, which is good. However, it does have some problems, which are identified at the top of the article: specifically, a lack of cited sources. This article seems to represent a good balance of *Wikipedia*'s benefits and drawbacks. I hope I can think of enough things to say about the article in my essay. I could start off with some background info on *Wikipedia* and then lead into the financial accounting example. That way, I can use the financial accounting article to support my points about *Wikipedia* in general.

4 Brainstorming

One of the most useful ways to collect ideas is by brainstorming (either on your own or in a group). This strategy enables you to recall bits of information and to see connections among them.

When you **brainstorm**, you list all the points you can think of that seem pertinent to your topic, recording ideas—comments, questions, single words, symbols, or diagrams—without considering their relevance or trying to understand their significance.

Close-Up   COLLABORATIVE BRAINSTORMING

In addition to brainstorming on your own, you can also try **collaborative brainstorming**, working with other students to think of ideas to write about. If you and your classmates are working with similar but not identical

(continued)

COLLABORATIVE BRAINSTORMING *(continued)*

topics—which is often the case—you will have the basic knowledge to help one another, and you can share your ideas without concern that you will all wind up focusing on the same few points.

Typically, collaborative brainstorming is an informal process. It can take place in person (in class or outside of class), on the phone, in a chat room, or on a class discussion board. Some instructors lead class brainstorming sessions; others arrange small-group brainstorming discussions in class.

Whatever the format, the exchange of ideas is likely to produce a lot of material that is not useful (and some that is irrelevant), but it will very likely also produce some ideas you will want to explore further. (Be sure you get your instructor's permission before you brainstorm with other students.)

An excerpt from Rebecca's brainstorming notes appears below.

Brainstorming Notes (Excerpt)

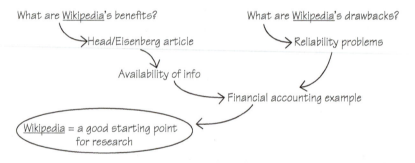

Topic: <u>Wikipedia</u> and College Research

What are <u>Wikipedia</u>'s benefits?

→Head/Eisenberg article

Availability of info

What are <u>Wikipedia</u>'s drawbacks?

→Reliability problems

→ Financial accounting example

<u>Wikipedia</u> = a good starting point
for research

Close-Up   FINDING IDEAS

You can use the following computer strategies to help you find material to write about:

- When you **freewrite**, try turning down the brightness of the monitor, leaving the screen dark to eliminate distractions and encourage spontaneity. When you reread what you have written, you can boldface or underline important ideas (or highlight them in color).
- When you **brainstorm**, type your notes randomly. Later, after you print them out, you can add more notes and graphic elements (arrows, circles, and so on) to indicate connections between ideas.

5 Clustering

Clustering—sometimes called *webbing* or *mapping*—is similar to brainstorming. However, clustering encourages you to explore your topic in a more systematic (and more visual) manner.

Begin your cluster diagram by writing your topic in the center of a sheet of paper. Then, surround your topic with related ideas as they occur to you, moving outward from the general topic in the center and writing down increasingly specific ideas and details as you move toward the edges of the page. Following the path of one idea at a time, draw lines to create a diagram (often lopsided rather than symmetrical) that arranges ideas on spokes or branches radiating out from the center (your topic).

Rebecca's cluster diagram appears below.

Cluster Diagram

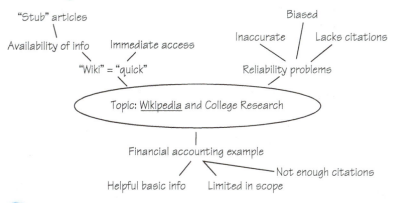

6 Asking Journalistic Questions

Journalists ask the **questions** *Who? What? Why? Where? When?* and *How?* to ensure that they have explored all angles of a story, and you can use these questions to make sure you have considered all aspects of your topic. Asking these basic questions is an orderly, systematic strategy for finding material to write about.

Rebecca's list of journalistic questions appears below.

Questions

- <u>Who</u> uses *Wikipedia*, and for what purposes?
- <u>What</u> is a wiki? <u>What</u> are *Wikipedia's* benefits? <u>What</u> are its drawbacks?

MULTILINGUAL TIP

Using your native language for planning activities has both advantages and disadvantages. On the one hand, if you do not have the pressure of trying to think in English, you may be able to come up with better ideas. Also, using your native language may help you record your ideas more quickly and keep you from losing your train of thought. On the other hand, using your native language while planning may make it more difficult for you to move from the planning stages of your writing to drafting. After all, you will eventually have to write your essay in English.

- When was *Wikipedia* created? When did it become so popular among college students?
- Where do people go for more information after reading a *Wikipedia* article?
- Why are people drawn to *Wikipedia*? Why do some instructors discourage students from using it as a research source?
- How can *Wikipedia* be used responsibly? How can *Wikipedia* be improved?

7 Asking In-Depth Questions

If you have time, you can search for ideas to write about by asking a series of more focused questions about your topic. These **in-depth questions** can give you a great deal of information, and they can also suggest ways for you to eventually shape your ideas into paragraphs and essays.

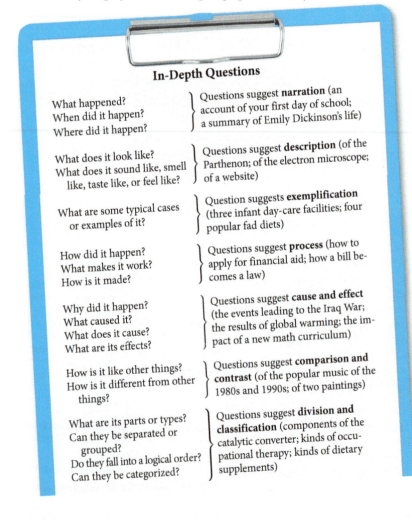

In-Depth Questions

What happened?
When did it happen?
Where did it happen?
} Questions suggest **narration** (an account of your first day of school; a summary of Emily Dickinson's life)

What does it look like?
What does it sound like, smell like, taste like, or feel like?
} Questions suggest **description** (of the Parthenon; of the electron microscope; of a website)

What are some typical cases or examples of it?
} Question suggests **exemplification** (three infant day-care facilities; four popular fad diets)

How did it happen?
What makes it work?
How is it made?
} Questions suggest **process** (how to apply for financial aid; how a bill becomes a law)

Why did it happen?
What caused it?
What does it cause?
What are its effects?
} Questions suggest **cause and effect** (the events leading to the Iraq War; the results of global warming; the impact of a new math curriculum)

How is it like other things?
How is it different from other things?
} Questions suggest **comparison and contrast** (of the popular music of the 1980s and 1990s; of two paintings)

What are its parts or types?
Can they be separated or grouped?
Do they fall into a logical order?
Can they be categorized?
} Questions suggest **division and classification** (components of the catalytic converter; kinds of occupational therapy; kinds of dietary supplements)

> What is it?
> How does it resemble other members of its class? How does it differ from other members of its class?
>
> } Questions suggest **definition** (What is Marxism? What is photosynthesis? What is a wiki?)

An excerpt from Rebecca's list of in-depth questions appears below.

In-Depth Questions (Excerpt)

What are the elements of a helpful *Wikipedia* article? Comprehensive abstracts, internal links, external links, coverage of current and obscure topics.

What are the elements of an unreliable *Wikipedia* article? Factual inaccuracy, bias, vandalism, lack of citations.

Note: Many college assignments require research. **See Part 7** for information on composing with sources.

EXERCISE 3.2

List all the potential sources you can think of for the essay you are writing: specific newspapers and magazines (including your school's publications), websites focusing on the environment, textbooks in related fields, newsletters and flyers, personal observations of your campus, and so on. Exchange lists with a classmate, and add two sources to your classmate's list.

EXERCISE 3.3

Make a cluster diagram and brainstorming notes for the topic you selected in Exercise 3.1. If you have trouble thinking of material to write about, try freewriting. Then, write a journal entry assessing your progress and evaluating the different strategies for finding something to say. Which strategy worked best for you? Why?

EXERCISE 3.4

Using the two question strategies described and illustrated on pages 25–28 to supplement the work you did in Exercises 3.2 and 3.3, continue generating material for your essay-in-progress.

EXERCISE 3.5

Consider what kinds of visual images might enhance your essay-in-progress. For example, would a photograph of a particular person or place be helpful? List several possibilities, and write a few sentences explaining what each visual might add to your essay.

EXERCISE 3.6

Go to *Google Images*, and find a visual to use in your essay. Using the visual as a focus, brainstorm to find additional ideas to write about.

CHAPTER **4**

Shaping

Now it is time to start sifting through your ideas to choose those you can use. As you do this, you begin to **shape** your material into a thesis-and-support essay.

4a　Understanding Thesis and Support

Your **thesis** is the main idea of your essay, the central point or claim that your ideas support. The concept of **thesis and support**—stating the thesis and then supplying information that explains and develops it—is central to much of the writing you will do in college and beyond.

PLANNING GUIDE

THESIS-AND-SUPPORT ESSAY

Your **assignment** will ask you to write an essay that supports a thesis.
Your **purpose** will be to present ideas and support them with specific reasons, examples, and so on.
Your **audience** will usually be your instructor or other students in your class.

INTRODUCTION	
• Begin by introducing readers to your subject. • Use a specific introductory strategy to create interest. • State your essay's thesis.	**Thesis statement templates:** • Although..., ... • Because..., it seems likely that... • Many people believe...; however, ...
BODY PARAGRAPHS	
• Begin each paragraph with a topic sentence that states the paragraph's main idea. • In each paragraph, support the topic sentence with facts, details, reasons, examples, and so on.	**Topic sentence templates:** • The first (second, third) cause is... • One (another, the final) example is...
• Arrange material in each paragraph according to a specific pattern of development: narration, cause and effect, comparison and contrast, and so on. • Include transitional words and phrases to connect ideas within and between paragraphs.	**Templates for introducing support:** • For example,... • As...points out,... • According to...,...
CONCLUSION	
• Begin with a restatement of your thesis (in different words) or a review of your essay's main points. • Use a specific concluding strategy to sum up your ideas. • Try to close with a memorable sentence.	**Closing statement templates:** • All in all,... • All things considered,... • For all these reasons,...

4b   Developing an Effective Thesis Statement

An effective **thesis statement** has four characteristics:

1. **An effective thesis statement clearly communicates your essay's main idea.** It tells readers what your essay's topic is and suggests what you will say about that topic. In other words, the thesis statement is not just the topic of your essay but a specific claim you make about that topic. Thus, your thesis statement reflects your essay's purpose.

2. **An effective thesis statement is more than a general topic, a statement of fact, or an announcement of your intent.**

Topic	Statement of Fact	Announcement
The environment	The environmental movement has had an impact on many college campuses.	In this essay, I will discuss the impact of the environmental movement on college campuses.

Effective Thesis Statement
By encouraging sustainability, organizing conferences to raise awareness
of environmental issues, and offering courses that educate students
about the need to protect the planet, colleges and universities can bring
the environmental movement to their campuses.

3. **An effective thesis statement is carefully worded.** Because it communicates your essay's main idea, your thesis statement should be clearly
   and accurately worded. Your thesis statement—usually expressed in a
   single concise sentence—should be direct and straightforward. It should
   not include abstract language, overly complex terminology, or unnecessary details that might confuse or mislead readers.

   Be particularly careful to avoid vague, wordy phrases—*centers on,
   deals with, involves, revolves around, has a lot to do with, is primarily concerned with*, and so on.

   The real problem in our schools ~~does~~ *is* not ~~revolve around~~ the
   absence of nationwide goals and standards; the problem is ~~primarily
   concerned with~~ the absence of resources.

   Finally, an effective thesis statement should not include words or
   phrases such as *personally, I believe, I hope to demonstrate*, and *it seems
   to me*, which weaken your credibility by suggesting that your conclusions are tentative or are based solely on opinion rather than on reading,
   observation, and experience.

4. **An effective thesis statement suggests your essay's direction, emphasis,
   and scope.** Your thesis statement should not make promises that your
   essay will not fulfill. It should suggest where you will place your emphasis
   and indicate in what order your major points will be discussed, as the
   following thesis statement does.

Effective Thesis Statement
Widely ridiculed as escape reading, romance novels are important as
a proving ground for many never-before-published writers and, more
significantly, as a showcase for strong heroines.

This thesis statement is effective because it tells readers that the essay
to follow will focus on two major roles of the romance novel: providing
markets for new writers and (more important) presenting strong female
characters. It also suggests that the essay will briefly treat the role of the
romance novel as escapist fiction. As the following diagram shows, this
effective thesis statement also indicates the order in which the various
ideas will be discussed.

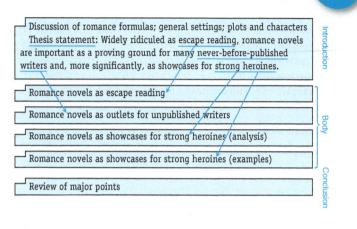

Introduction

Discussion of romance formulas; general settings; plots and characters
Thesis statement: Widely ridiculed as escape reading, romance novels are important as a proving ground for many never-before-published writers and, more significantly, as showcases for strong heroines.

Body

Romance novels as escape reading

Romance novels as outlets for unpublished writers

Romance novels as showcases for strong heroines (analysis)

Romance novels as showcases for strong heroines (examples)

Conclusion

Review of major points

Close-Up   DEVELOPING AN EFFECTIVE THESIS STATEMENT

Here are some other problems to watch out for when you draft a thesis statement.

Thesis Statement Too General

Plagiarism is a serious problem.

Effective Thesis Statement

Instituting an honor code can reduce plagiarism and other forms of academic cheating on our campus.

Thesis Statement Too Narrow

Plagiarism is a form of academic cheating.

Effective Thesis Statement

Plagiarism, a form of academic cheating, undermines the educational process.

Wordy Thesis Statement

To address and curb the serious problem of the incidence of plagiarism on our college campus, I think steps must be taken by all different members of the college community, working together not only to establish but also to maintain certain mutually agreed-upon standards of academic integrity.

Effective Thesis Statement

To solve the problem of plagiarism on our campus, all members of the college community need to work to establish and maintain standards of academic integrity.

As she tried to decide on a thesis statement for her essay about *Wikipedia* and college research, Rebecca James reviewed her freewriting, brainstorming, and other prewriting material and also talked with friends, most of whom shared her own positive opinion of *Wikipedia*. To stress the value of *Wikipedia* in college research yet still acknowledge the drawbacks her instructors had pointed out, Rebecca drafted the following thesis statement.

Thesis Statement: Despite its limitations, *Wikipedia* can be a valuable tool for locating reliable research sources.

4c Revising Your Thesis Statement

At this point, your thesis statement is only **tentative**. As you write and rewrite, you will think of new ideas and see new connections. As a result, you may change your essay's direction, emphasis, and scope, and if you do so, you must reword your thesis statement to reflect these modifications.

As Rebecca revised her essay, her emphasis changed, and so did her thesis statement. Because most of her research suggested that *Wikipedia* should be used with caution, she decided in her revised thesis statement to emphasize the site's usefulness not as an authoritative source but rather as a starting point for further research. Compare her tentative thesis statement above with her revised thesis statement in her essay's final draft in **5e**.

Close-Up USING A THESIS STATEMENT TO SHAPE YOUR ESSAY

The wording of your thesis statement often suggests not only a possible order and emphasis for your essay's ideas, but also a specific pattern of development—*narration, description, exemplification, process, cause and effect, comparison and contrast, division and classification*, or *definition*. (These familiar patterns of development may also shape individual paragraphs of your essay.)

See 13d

Thesis Statement	Pattern of Development
As I grew more involved with the developmentally delayed children at the Learning Center, I came to see how important it is to treat every child as an individual.	Narration
Looking around the room where I spent my childhood, I realized that every object I saw told me I was now an adult.	Description

The risk-taking behavior that has characterized recent years is illustrated by the increasing interest in high-risk sports such as mountain biking, ice climbing, and sky diving.	Exemplification
Armed forces basic training programs take recruits through a series of tasks designed to build camaraderie as well as skills and confidence.	Process
The gap in computer literacy between rich and poor has significant social and economic consequences.	Cause and Effect
Although people who live in cities and people who live in small towns have some similarities, their views on issues such as crime, waste disposal, farm subsidies, and educational vouchers tend to be very different.	Comparison and Contrast
The section of the proposal that recommends establishing satellite health centers is quite promising; unfortunately, however, the sections that call for the creation of alternative educational programs, job training, and low-income housing are seriously flawed.	Division and Classification
Many people once assumed that rape was an act perpetrated by a stranger, but today's definition is much broader.	Definition

EXERCISE 4.1

Working in a group of three or four students, analyze each of the following items, and explain why none of them qualifies as an effective thesis statement.

1. In this essay, I will examine the environmental effects of residential and commercial development on the coastal regions of the United States.
2. Residential and commercial development in the coastal regions of the United States
3. How to avoid coastal overdevelopment
4. Coastal Development: Pro and Con
5. Residential and commercial development of America's coastal regions benefits some people, but it has a number of disadvantages.
6. The environmentalists' position on coastal development
7. More and more coastal regions in the United States are being overdeveloped.
8. Residential and commercial development guidelines need to be developed for coastal regions of the United States.

9. Coastal development is causing beach erosion.
10. At one time I enjoyed walking on the beach, but commercial and residential development ruined the experience for me.

EXERCISE 4.2

Review all the notes you have accumulated so far, and use them to help you develop a thesis for an essay on the topic you chose in Chapter 3, Exercise 3.1.

4d Constructing a Scratch Outline

Once you have a tentative thesis statement, you may want to construct a scratch outline to guide you as you write. A **scratch outline** is a brief, informal organizational plan that arranges your essay's main points (and perhaps its major supporting ideas) in an orderly way.

Rebecca's scratch outline appears on below.

Scratch Outline

Thesis statement: Despite its limitations, *Wikipedia* can be a valuable tool for locating reliable research sources.

- Definition of *wiki* and explanation of *Wikipedia*
- *Wikipedia*'s benefits
  - Links
  - Comprehensive abstracts
  - Current and popular culture topics
  - "Stub" articles
- *Wikipedia*'s potential
- *Wikipedia*'s drawbacks
  - Not accurate
  - Bias
  - Vandalism
  - Not enough citations
- Financial accounting example: benefits
- Financial accounting example: drawbacks

At this stage of the writing process, Rebecca decided that her scratch outline was all she needed to guide her as she wrote a first draft. (Later on, she might decide to construct a more formal outline to check her essay's logic and organization.)

Although you may be used to constructing outlines for your written work by hand, a number of software applications and formatting features can help in this process, including the outlining feature in some desktop publishing and word-processing programs (such as *Microsoft Word*). Another useful tool for outlining (particularly for presentations) is *Microsoft PowerPoint*, presentation software that enables you to format information on individual slides with major headings, subheadings, and bulleted lists.

Close-Up FORMAL OUTLINES

Sometimes—particularly when you are writing (or revising) a long or complex essay—a scratch outline is not enough to guide you. In these cases, you will need to construct a **formal outline**, which indicates both the exact order and the relative importance of all the ideas you will explore. A formal outline can be either a sentence outline or a topic outline. (For information on how to construct a formal outline and for an example of a complete **sentence outline, see 5c4.** For an example of an excerpt from another sentence outline, **see 41k3.** For an example of a formal **topic outline, see 41i.**)

EXERCISE 4.3

Find an editorial on your essay's topic in a newspaper or on the Internet. Then, prepare a scratch outline of the editorial that includes the writer's key points and major supporting ideas.

EXERCISE 3.4

Prepare a scratch outline for the essay you have been developing in Chapters 3 and 4.

CHAPTER **5**

Drafting and Revising

5a Writing a Rough Draft

Once you are able to see a clear order for your ideas, you are ready to write a rough draft of your essay. A **rough draft** usually includes false starts, irrelevant information, and unrelated details. At this stage, though, the absence of focus and order is not a problem. You write your rough draft simply to get your ideas down so that you can react to them. You should expect to add or delete words, reword sentences, rethink ideas, and reorder paragraphs as you write. You should also be open to discovering some new ideas—and even to taking an unexpected detour.

CHECKLIST

Drafting Strategies

The following suggestions can help you as you draft and revise:

❑ **Prepare your work area.** Once you begin to write, you should not have to stop because you need better lighting, important notes, or anything else.

❑ **Fight writer's block.** An inability to start (or continue) writing, writer's block is usually caused by fear that you will not write well or that you have nothing to say. If you really don't feel ready to start drafting, take a short break. If you decide that you really don't have enough ideas to get you started, use one of the strategies for finding something to say.

See 3e

❑ **Get your ideas down on paper as quickly as you can.** Don't worry about sentence structure, spelling and punctuation, or finding exactly the right word—just write. Writing quickly helps you uncover new ideas and new connections between ideas. You may find that following a scratch outline enables you to move smoothly from one point to the next, but if you find this structure too confining, go ahead and write without consulting your outline.

See 4d

❑ **Write notes to yourself.** As you type your drafts, get into the habit of including bracketed, boldfaced notes to yourself. These comments, suggestions, and questions can help you when you write subsequent drafts.

❑ **Take regular breaks as you write.** Try writing one section of your essay at a time. When you have completed a section—for example, one paragraph—take a break. Your mind will continue to focus on your assignment while you do other things. When you return to your essay, writing will be easier.

❑ **Leave yourself enough time to revise.** All writing benefits from revision, so be sure you have time to reconsider your work and to write as many drafts as you need.

MULTILINGUAL TIP

Using your native language occasionally as you draft your essay may keep you from losing your train of thought. However, writing most or all of your draft in your native language and then translating it into English is generally not a good idea. This process will take a long time, and the translation into English may sound awkward, especially if it comes from a translation tool located online or in your word-processing program.

When you write your rough draft, concentrate on the body of your essay, and don't waste time mapping out an introduction and conclusion. (These paragraphs are likely to change substantially in subsequent drafts.) For now, focus on drafting the support paragraphs of your essay.

Using her scratch outline to guide her, Rebecca James wrote the following rough draft. Notice that she included boldfaced and bracketed notes to remind herself to add or check information when she revised her draft.

Rough Draft

Wikipedia and College Research

When given an assignment, students often turn first to *Wikipedia*, the popular free online encyclopedia that currently includes over 26,000,000 articles. Despite its limitations, *Wikipedia* can be a valuable tool for locating reliable research sources. **[Add more here]**

A wiki is an open-source website that allows users to edit or alter its content. Derived from a Hawaiian word meaning "quick," the term *wiki* conveys the swiftness and ease with which users can access information on such sites. **[Do I need to document this? Definition from *Encyclopaedia Britannica*]** *Wikipedia* is the most popular wiki. It includes a range of topics, such as **. . . . [Include a couple of examples here]** *Wikipedia*'s editing tools make it easy for users to add new entries or edit existing ones.

The site offers numerous benefits to its users. One benefit of *Wikipedia* over traditional print encyclopedias is its "wikilinks," or internal links to other content within *Wikipedia*. **[Use info from Head and Eisenberg article]** *Wikipedia* articles also often include external links to other sources as well as comprehensive abstracts. *Wikipedia* articles are constantly being updated and provide unmatched coverage of popular culture topics and current events. **[Make sure this is correct]** Finally, the site includes "stub" articles, which provide basic information that may be expanded by users.

Wikipedia claims that its articles "are never considered complete and may be continually edited and improved. Over time, this generally results in an upward trend of quality and a growing consensus over a neutral representation of information." **["About" page—need full citation]** *Wikipedia* ranks its articles according to the criteria of accuracy, neutrality, completeness, and style, letting users know which articles are among the site's best. In fact, some of *Wikipedia*'s best articles are comparable to those found in professionally edited online encyclopedias, such as *Encyclopaedia Britannica*. **[Check on this to make sure]** Although there's no professional editorial board to oversee the development of content within *Wikipedia*, experienced users may become editors, and this role allows them to monitor the process by which content is added and updated. Users may also use the "Talk" page to discuss an article's content and make suggestions for improvement.

Wikipedia's popularity has also stimulated emergent technologies. For example, the free open-source software *MediaWiki* runs numerous wiki websites. Other companies are also trying to capitalize on *Wikipedia*'s success by enhancing users' experience of the site. The online service *Pediaphon*, for instance, converts *Wikipedia* articles into MP3 audio files.

Wikipedia concedes, "not everything in *Wikipedia* is accurate, comprehensive, or unbiased." **["Researching with *Wikipedia*" page— need full citation]** Because anyone can create or edit *Wikipedia* articles, they can be factually inaccurate, biased, and even vandalized. Many *Wikipedia* articles also lack citations to the sources that support their claims, revealing a lack of reliability. **[Need more here]**

Personally, I have benefited from using *Wikipedia* in learning more for my accounting class. For example, the *Wikipedia* article "Financial Accounting" defines this field in relation to basic accounting concepts. The article contains several internal links to related *Wikipedia* articles and some external links to additional resources and references. **[Compare this article to similar articles on sites like *Encyclopaedia Britannica*]**

Although the *Wikipedia* article on financial accounting provides helpful, general information on this accounting field, it is limited in terms of reliability and scope. **[Explain more here. Add a visual?]** The limitations of the financial accounting article suggest possible problems with *Wikipedia*.

Wikipedia articles are a good starting point for research and link to more in-depth sources. *Wikipedia* users should understand the current shortcomings of this popular online tool. **[Add more!]**

EXERCISE 5.1

Write a rough draft of the essay you began planning in Chapter 3.

5b Moving from Rough Draft to Final Draft

As you revise successive drafts of your essay, you should narrow your focus from larger elements, such as overall structure and content, to increasingly smaller elements, such as sentence structure and word choice.

1 Revising Your Drafts

After you have developed a rough draft, set it aside for a day or two if you can. When you return to it, focus on only a few areas at a time. As you review this first draft, begin by evaluating your essay's thesis-and-support structure and general organization. Once you feel satisfied that your thesis statement says what you want it to say and that your essay's content supports this thesis and is logically arranged, you can turn your attention to other matters. For example, you can make sure that you have included all the **transitional words and phrases** that readers will need to follow your discussion.

See 13b2

As you review your drafts, you may want to look at the questions in the "Revising Your Essay" checklists on pages 51–52. If you have the opportunity for **peer review** with classmates or a visit to the writing center, consider your readers' comments carefully. At this stage of the process, you should also try to arrange a **conference** with your instructor.

See 5c2–3

Because it can be more difficult to read text on the computer screen than on hard copy, you may want to print out your draft. This will enable you to make revisions by hand on printed pages and then return to the computer to type these changes into your document. (As you type your draft, you may want to leave extra space between lines. This will make any errors or inconsistencies more obvious and at the same time give you plenty of room to write questions and add new material.)

If you write your revisions by hand on hard copy, you may find it helpful to develop a system of symbols. For instance, you can circle individual words or box groups of words (or even entire paragraphs) that you want to relocate, using an arrow to indicate the new location. You can also use numbers or letters to indicate the order in which you want to rearrange ideas. When you want to add words, use a caret like *this*.

An excerpt from Rebecca's rough draft, with her handwritten revisions, appears below.

Draft with Handwritten Revisions (Excerpt)

The article contains several internal links to related *Wikipedia* articles and some external links to additional resources and references. *In comparison, the wiki Citizendium doesn't contain an article on financial accounting, and the "Financial Accounting" article in the professionally edited Encyclopaedia Britannica consists only of a link to a related EB article.*

Close-Up MANAGING FILES

As you revise, it is important to manage your files carefully, following these guidelines:

- First, be sure to save your drafts. Using the Save option in your word processor's file menu saves only your most recent draft. If you prefer to save every draft you write (so you can return to an earlier draft to locate a different version of a sentence or to reconsider a section you have deleted), use the Save As option instead.
- Also, be sure to label your files. To help you keep track of different versions of your essay, label every file in your project folder by content and date (for example, **First Draft, Nov 5**).
- Finally, be very careful not to delete material that you may need later; instead, move this material to the end of your document so that you can reassess its usefulness later on and retrieve it if necessary.

2 Adding Visuals

As you write and revise, you should consider whether one or more **visuals** might strengthen your essay by providing support for the points you are making. Sometimes you may want to use a visual that appears in one of your sources; at other times, you may be able to create a visual (for example, a photograph or a chart) yourself; at still other times, you may need to search *Google Images* or another image database to find an appropriate visual.

CHECKLIST

Adding Visuals to Your Essay

To add a visual to your essay, follow these steps:

- ❑ Find an appropriate visual.
- ❑ Place the image in a suitable location in your essay.
- ❑ Format the image, and make sure it is clearly set off from the written text.
- ❑ Introduce the visual with a sentence (or refer to it in the text).
- ❑ Label the visual.
- ❑ Always document a borrowed visual.

Once you have decided to add a particular visual to your essay, the next step is to determine where to insert it. (In general, you should place the visual in the part of the essay where it will have the greatest impact in terms of conveying information or persuading your audience.) Then, you need to format the visual. (Within *Microsoft Word*, you can double-click on an image to call up a picture-editing menu that allows you to alter the size, color, and position of the image within your essay and even enables you to wrap text around the image.) Next, you should make sure that the visual stands out in your essay: surround it with white space, add ruled lines, or enclose it in a box.

After you have inserted the visual where you want it, you need to integrate it into your text. You can include a sentence that introduces the visual (**The following table illustrates the similarities between the two health plans**), or you can refer to it in your text (**Figure 1 shows Kennedy as a young man**) to give it some context and explain why you are using it. You should also identify the visual by labeling it (**Fig. 1. Photo of John F. Kennedy, 1937**). In addition, if the visual is not one you have created yourself, you must document it. In most academic disciplines, this means including full source information directly below the image and sometimes in the list of references as well. (To see how Rebecca James integrated a visual into her essay, see **5e.**)

See Chs. 47–48

EXERCISE 5.2

Look carefully at the visual you chose in Chapter 3, Exercise 3.6. In one sentence, state the main idea that this visual communicates to its audience. Then, list the individual elements in the visual that support this main idea. Does this visual help to support or clarify a point you are trying to make in your essay? If it does not, look for one that does. Finally, decide where to place the visual in your essay.

5c Using Specific Revision Strategies

Everyone revises differently, and every writing task calls for a slightly different process of revision. Five strategies in particular can help you revise at any stage of the writing process.

1 Using Word-Processing Tools

Your word-processing program includes a variety of tools designed to make the revision process easier. For example, *Microsoft Word*'s **Track Changes** allows you to make changes to a draft electronically and to see the original version of the draft and the changes simultaneously. Changes appear in color as underlined or crossed-out text (or as balloons in the margin), and you can view the changes on the screen or in print. This feature also allows you to accept or reject all changes or just specific changes.

Another useful tool is **Compare Documents**. Whereas Track Changes allows you to keep track of changes to a single document, Compare Documents allows you to analyze the changes in two completely separate versions of a document, usually an original and its most recent update. Changes appear in color as highlighted text.

Rebecca used Track Changes as she revised her rough draft. An excerpt from her draft, along with her changes, follows.

Draft with Track Changes (Excerpt)

A wiki is an open-source website that allows users to edit and add to ~~or alter~~ its content. Derived from a Hawaiian word meaning "quick," the term *wiki* conveys the swiftness and ease with which users can access information on such sites as well as contribute content ("Wiki"). Since its creation in 2001 by Jimmy Wales, *Wikipedia* has grown into a huge database of articles on ~~is the most popular wiki. It includes a range of~~ topics ~~, such as . . . .~~ ranging from contemporary rock bands to obscure scientific and technical concepts. In accordance with the site's policies, users can edit existing articles and add new articles using *Wikipedia*'s editing tools, which do not require specialized programming knowledge or expertise. ~~make it easy for users to add new entries or edit existing ones.~~

Close-Up TRACK CHANGES VS. COMPARE DOCUMENTS

Where you are in the writing process can help you decide whether to track your changes or to compare one complete version of your document with another. **Track Changes** is especially useful in helping you follow sentence-level changes as you draft and revise; it can also be helpful later on, when you edit words and phrases. **Compare Documents** is most helpful when you are comparing global changes, such as paragraph unity and thesis-and-support structure, between one draft and another.

---

2 Participating in Peer Review

Peer review—a collaborative revision strategy that enables you to get feedback from your classmates—is another useful activity. With peer review, instead of trying to imagine an audience for your essay, you address a real audience, exchanging drafts with classmates and commenting on their writing. Such collaborative work can be formal or informal, conducted in person or electronically. For example, you and a classmate may email drafts back and forth, using *Word*'s Comment tool (see page 44), or your instructor may conduct the class as a workshop, assigning students to work in groups to critique each other's essays. Students can also comment on classmates' drafts posted on a course discussion board or listserv.

CHECKLIST

Guidelines for Peer-Review Participants

To get the most out of a peer-review session, keep the following guidelines in mind:

- ❑ **Know the material.** To be sure you understand what the student writer needs and expects from your comments, read the essay several times before you begin writing your response.

- ❑ **Focus on the big picture.** Try not to get bogged down in minor problems with punctuation or mechanics or become distracted by an essay's proofreading errors.

- ❑ **Look for a positive feature.** Try to zero in on what you think is the essay's greatest strength.

- ❑ **Be positive throughout.** Try to avoid words such as *weak, poor,* and *bad;* instead, try using a compliment before delivering the "bad news": "Paragraph 2 is very well developed; can you add this kind of support in paragraph 4?"

- ❑ **Show respect.** It is perfectly acceptable to tell a student that something is confusing or inaccurate, but don't go on the attack.

- ❑ **Be specific.** Avoid generalizations such as "needs more examples" or "could be more interesting"; instead, try to offer helpful, focused suggestions: "You could add an example after the second sentence in paragraph 2"; "Explaining how this process operates would make your discussion more interesting."

- ❑ **Don't give orders.** Ask questions, and make suggestions.

- ❑ **Include a few words of encouragement.** In your summary, try to emphasize the essay's strong points.

Close-Up   ELECTRONIC PEER REVIEW

Some software is particularly useful for peer-review groups. For example, *Word*'s **Comment** tool allows several readers to insert comments at any point or to highlight a particular portion of the text they would like to comment on and then insert annotations. Comments are identified by the initials of the reviewer and by a color assigned to the reviewer.

Other online programs also facilitate the peer-review process. For example, *InSite* is a web-based application that allows students to respond to each other's drafts with a set of peer-review questions, as shown on page 44.

(continued)

ELECTRONIC PEER REVIEW *(continued)*

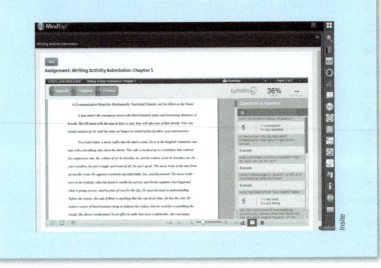

An excerpt from Rebecca's rough draft with peer reviewers' comments appears below. (Note that her classmates used *Word*'s Comment tool to insert comments.)

Draft with Peer Reviewers' Comments (Excerpt)

Personally, I have benefited from using *Wikipedia* in learning more for my accounting class. For example, the Wikipedia article "Financial Accounting" defines this field in relation to basic accounting concepts. The article contains several internal links to related *Wikipedia* articles and some external links to additional resources and references. In comparison, the wiki *Citizendium* doesn't contain an article on financial accounting, and the "Financial Accounting" article in the professionally edited *Encyclopaedia Britannica* consists only of a link to a related *EB* article.

Comment [KL1]: It's also helpful for other classes outside my major.

Comment [KL2]: Why is this imp.? Maybe explain more?

Comment [BR3]: Yes! This is one of my fav. features of *Wikipedia*.☺

Comment [CB4]: But sometimes these links don't lead to the best sources either. . . .

CHECKLIST

Questions for Peer Review

The following questions can help guide you through the peer-review process:

❏ What is the essay about? Is the topic appropriate for the assignment?

❏ What is the essay's main idea? Is the thesis clearly worded? If not, how can the wording be improved?

❏ Is the essay arranged logically? Do the body paragraphs appear in an appropriate order?

❏ What ideas support the thesis? Does each body paragraph develop one of these ideas?

❏ Is any necessary information missing? Identify any areas that seem to need further development. Is any information irrelevant? If so, suggest possible deletions.

❏ Can you think of any ideas or examples from your own reading, experience, or observations that would strengthen the writer's essay?

❏ Can you follow the writer's logic? If not, would clearer connections between sentences or paragraphs be helpful? Where are such connections needed?

❏ Is the introductory paragraph interesting to you? Would another opening strategy be more effective?

❏ Does the conclusion leave you with a sense of closure? Would another concluding strategy be more effective?

❏ Is anything unclear or confusing?

❏ What is the essay's greatest strength?

❏ What is the essay's greatest weakness?

For information on audience concerns for peer-review participants, **see 2c3**.

3 Using Instructors' Comments

Instructors' comments—in conjunction with correction symbols, in marginal comments, or in conferences—can also help you revise.

Correction Symbols Your instructor may indicate concerns about style, grammar, mechanics, or punctuation by using the correction symbols listed at the end of this book. Instead of correcting a problem, the instructor will simply identify it and supply the number of the section in this handbook that deals with the error. After reading the appropriate pages, you should be able to make the necessary corrections on your own. For example, the symbol and number noted within the following sentence referred a student to **19e2**, the section in this handbook that discusses sexist language.

Instructor's Comment: Equal access to jobs is a desirable goal for all
Sxt—see 19e2
~~mankind.~~

After reading the appropriate section in the handbook, the student made the following change.

Revised: Equal access to jobs is a desirable goal for everyone.

Marginal Comments Instructors frequently write marginal comments on your essays to suggest changes in content or structure. These comments may ask you to add supporting information or to arrange paragraphs differently within the essay, or they may recommend stylistic changes, such as more varied sentences. Marginal comments may also question your logic, suggest a more explicit thesis statement, ask for clearer transitions, or propose a new direction for a discussion. In some cases, you can consider these comments to be suggestions rather than corrections. You may decide to incorporate these ideas into a revised draft of your essay, or you may not. In all instances, however, you should take your instructor's comments seriously.

An excerpt from Rebecca's rough draft, along with her instructor's comments, follows. (Note that her instructor used *Microsoft Word*'s Comment tool to insert comments.)

Draft with Instructor's Comments (Excerpt)

Personally, I have benefited from using *Wikipedia* in learning more for my accounting class. For example, the *Wikipedia* article "Financial Accounting" defines this field in relation to basic accounting concepts. The article contains several internal links to related *Wikipedia* articles and some external links to additional resources and references. In comparison, the wiki *Citizendium* doesn't contain an article on financial accounting, and the "Financial Accounting" article in the professionally edited *Encyclopaedia Britannica* consists only of a link to a related *EB* article.

Comment [JB1]: Revise to eliminate use of "personally" and the first person ("I") in this essay. Use this ¶ to talk about *Wikipedia*'s benefits to college students, using the accounting article as an example.

Comment [JB2]: In your final draft, edit out all contractions. (Contractions are too informal for most college writing.) See 32b1.

Conferences Many instructors require or encourage one-on-one conferences, and you should certainly schedule a conference if you can. During a conference, you can respond to your instructor's questions and ask for clarification of marginal comments. If a certain section of your essay presents a problem, use your conference time to focus on it, perhaps asking for help in sharpening your thesis or choosing more accurate words.

Getting the Most Out of a Conference

To make your conference time as productive as possible, follow these guidelines:

❑ **Make an appointment.** If you are unable to keep your appointment, be sure to call or email your instructor to reschedule.

❑ **Review your work carefully.** Before the conference, reread your notes and drafts, and go over all your instructor's comments and suggestions. Make all the changes you can on your draft.

❑ **Bring a list of questions.** Preparing a list in advance will enable you to get the most out of the conference in the allotted time.

❑ **Bring your work-in-progress.** If you have several drafts, you may want to bring them all, but be sure you bring any draft on which your instructor has commented.

❑ **Take notes.** As you discuss your essay, write down any suggestions that you think will be helpful so you won't forget them when you revise.

❑ **Participate actively.** A successful conference is not a monologue; it should be an open exchange of ideas.

Close-Up WRITING CENTER CONFERENCES

If you are unable to meet with your instructor—and, in fact, even if you are—it is a good idea to make an appointment with a tutor in your school's writing center. A writing tutor (who may be either a professional or a student) is likely to know a good deal about what your instructor expects and is trained to help you produce an effective essay.

What a writing tutor can do is help you find ideas to write about and develop a thesis statement, identify parts of your essay that need more support (and help you decide what kind of support to include), and coach you as you revise your essay. What a tutor will *not* do is write your essay for you or act as a copyeditor or a proofreader.

When you meet with a tutor, follow the guidelines in the checklist above—and always bring a copy of your assignment as well as your latest draft (including any instructor comments).

Conferences can also take place online—most often, through email. If you send emails to your instructor, to your writing center tutor, or to members of your peer-review group, include a specific subject line that clearly identifies the message as coming from a student writer (for example, "question about assignment" or "comments on my essay"). This is especially important if your email address does not include your name. When you attach a document to an email and send it for comments, mention the attachment in your subject line (for example, "first draft—see attachment")—and be sure your name appears on the attachment itself, not just on the email.

Note: Your instructor may also require conferences through course management software or through collaborative software such as *Google Drive*.

Close-Up　COLLABORATION AND THE REVISION PROCESS

In a sense, the feedback you get from your instructor (or from a writing center tutor)—in conference, by email, or in written comments on a draft—opens a dialogue that is a form of collaboration. Like the comments you get from your classmates during peer review, these comments present ideas for you to react to, questions for you to answer, and answers to questions you may have. As you react to these comments, you engage in a collaboration that can help you revise your work.

4　Using a Formal Outline

Outlining can be helpful early in the revision process, when you are reworking the larger structural elements of your essay, or later on, when you are checking the logic of a completed draft. A formal outline reveals at once whether points are irrelevant or poorly placed—or, worse, missing. It also reveals the hierarchy of your ideas—which points are dominant and which are subordinate.

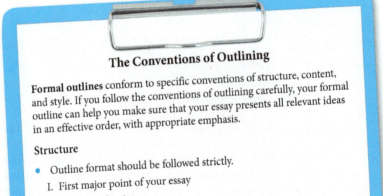

The Conventions of Outlining

Formal outlines conform to specific conventions of structure, content, and style. If you follow the conventions of outlining carefully, your formal outline can help you make sure that your essay presents all relevant ideas in an effective order, with appropriate emphasis.

Structure
- Outline format should be followed strictly.
  - I. First major point of your essay
    - A. First subpoint

B. Next subpoint
  1. First supporting example
  2. Next supporting example
    a. First specific detail
    b. Next specific detail
II. Second major point

- Headings should not overlap.
- No heading should have a single subheading. (A category cannot be subdivided into one part.)
- Each entry should be preceded by an appropriate letter or number, followed by a period.
- The first word of each entry should be capitalized.

Content

- The outline should include the essay's thesis statement.
- The outline should cover only the body of the essay, not the introductory or concluding paragraphs.
- Headings should be concise and specific.
- Headings should be descriptive, clearly related to the topic to which they refer.

Style

- Headings of the same rank should be grammatically parallel.
- A **sentence outline** should use complete sentences, with all verbs in the same tense.
- In a sentence outline, each entry should end with a period.
- A **topic outline** should use words or short phrases, with all headings of the same rank using the same parts of speech.
- In a topic outline, entries should not end with periods.

As part of her revision process, Rebecca made the following sentence outline of her rough draft (shown on pages 37–38) to help her check her essay's organization.

Sentence Outline

<u>Thesis statement</u>: Despite its limitations, *Wikipedia* can be a valuable tool for locating reliable research sources.

I. A wiki is an open-source website that allows users to edit or alter its content.

A. *Wikipedia* is the most popular wiki.

B. *Wikipedia* includes a range of topics.

II. *Wikipedia* offers numerous benefits to its users.

    A. Many *Wikipedia* articles contain internal links.

    B. Many *Wikipedia* articles contain external links.

    C. Many *Wikipedia* articles contain comprehensive abstracts.

    D. Many *Wikipedia* articles cover current and popular culture topics.

    E. Site includes "stub" articles.

III. *Wikipedia* is making efforts to improve the quality of its content.

    A. *Wikipedia* ranks its articles using the criteria of accuracy, neutrality, completeness, and style.

    B. Users may serve as editors of the site's content.

    C. Users may use the "Talk" page to make suggestions for improvement.

IV. *Wikipedia*'s popularity has stimulated emergent technologies.

    A. The free open-source software *MediaWiki* runs numerous wiki websites.

    B. The online service *Pediaphon* converts *Wikipedia* articles into MP3 audio files.

V. *Wikipedia* also has several drawbacks.

    A. *Wikipedia* articles may be factually inaccurate.

    B. *Wikipedia* articles may be biased.

    C. *Wikipedia* articles may be vandalized.

    D. Many *Wikipedia* articles lack sufficient citations.

VI. The *Wikipedia* article "Financial Accounting" offers certain benefits.

    A. It defines the field in relation to basic accounting concepts.

    B. It offers a visual breakdown of the key terms within the discipline.

    C. It provides internal and external links to additional resources and references.

VII. *Wikipedia*'s "Financial Accounting" article is limited in the information it offers.

    A. It is unreliable.

    B. It is limited in scope.

This outline revealed some problems in Rebecca's draft. For example, she saw that point IV was not relevant to her discussion, and she realized that she needed to develop the sections in which she discussed the benefits and drawbacks of the specific *Wikipedia* entry that she selected for this assignment. Thus, the outline helped her to revise her rough draft.

Close-Up FORMATTING AN OUTLINE

If you use your computer's word-processing program to construct a formal outline, the Bullets and Numbering feature and the AutoFormat feature will help you to format it properly. Usually found in the Format menu, Bullets and Numbering allows you to select the format type of your outline, including styles that use roman numerals, letters, and/or numbers. Once you have selected your outline style, AutoFormat will arrange what you type in the selected format and allow you to customize the formatting further.

EXERCISE 5.3

Outline the most recent draft of your essay, and use this outline to help you check the arrangement of your essay's ideas. Make any structural revisions you think are necessary. (Try not to worry at this point about stylistic issues, such as sentence variety and word choice.)

5 Using a Revision Checklist

The revision checklists below (and the editing checklists on pages 54–55) are keyed to sections of this text. Moving from global to specific concerns, they parallel the actual revision process. As your understanding of the writing process increases and you become better able to assess the strengths and weaknesses of your writing, you may want to add items to (or delete items from) these checklists. You can also use your instructors' comments to tailor the checklists to your own needs.

CHECKLISTS
Revising Your Essay
The Whole Essay

❑ Do you understand your essay's purpose? (**See 2b.**)

❑ Have you taken your audience's needs into account? (**See 2c.**)

❑ Are thesis and support logically related, with each body paragraph supporting your thesis statement? (**See 4a.**)

❑ Is your thesis statement clearly and specifically worded? (**See 4b.**)

❑ Have you discussed everything promised in your thesis statement? (**See 4b.**)

❑ Have you presented your ideas in a logical sequence? Can you think of a different arrangement that might be more appropriate for your purpose? (**See 4c.**)

Paragraphs

❏ Does each body paragraph have just one main idea? (**See 13a.**)

❏ Are topic sentences clearly worded and logically related to your thesis? (**See 13a1.**)

❏ Does each body paragraph have a clear organizing principle? (**See 13b1.**)

❏ Are the relationships between sentences within your paragraphs clear? (**See 13b2–4.**)

❏ Are your body paragraphs developed fully enough to support your points? (**See 13c.**)

❏ Does your introductory paragraph arouse reader interest and prepare readers for what is to come? (**See 13e2.**)

❏ Are your paragraphs arranged according to familiar patterns of development? (**See 13d.**)

❏ Have you provided transitional paragraphs where necessary? (**See 13e1.**)

❏ Does your concluding paragraph sum up your main points? (**See 13e3.**)

Sentences

❏ Have you used correct sentence structure? (**See Chs. 24 and 25.**)

❏ Have you avoided potentially confusing shifts in tense, voice, mood, person, or number? (**See 28a1–4.**)

❏ Are your sentences constructed logically? (**See 28b–d.**)

❏ Have you placed modifiers clearly and logically? (**See Ch. 27.**)

❏ Are your sentences varied? (**See Ch. 15.**)

❏ Have you combined sentences where ideas are closely related? (**See 15a.**)

❏ Have you used emphatic word order? (**See 16a.**)

❏ Have you used sentence structure to signal the relative importance of clauses in a sentence and their logical relationship to one another? (**See 16b.**)

❏ Have you strengthened your sentences with repetition, balance, and parallelism? (**See 16c–d, 18a.**)

❏ Have you eliminated nonessential words and unnecessary repetition? (**See 17a–b.**)

❏ Have you avoided overloading your sentences with too many words, phrases, and clauses? (**See 17c.**)

Words

❏ Is your level of diction appropriate for your audience and your purpose? (**See 19a.**)

❏ Have you selected words that accurately reflect your intentions? (**See 19b1.**)

❏ Have you chosen words that are specific, concrete, and unambiguous? (**See 19b3–4.**)

❏ Have you enriched your writing with figures of speech? (**See 19c.**)

❏ Have you eliminated jargon, neologisms, pretentious diction, clichés, and offensive language from your writing? (**See 19d–e.**)

EXERCISE 5.4

Review the most recent draft of your essay, this time focusing on paragraphing, topic sentences, and transitions and on the way you structure your sentences and select your words. (Use the appropriate items in the checklists on pages 51–52 as a guide.)

EXERCISE 5.5

Using the revision checklists on pages 51–52 as a model, create a ten-item customized checklist—one that reflects the specific concerns that you need to consider when you revise an essay. Then, use this checklist to help you in your revision.

Close-Up CHOOSING A TITLE

When you are ready to decide on a title for your essay, keep these criteria in mind:

- A title should be descriptive, giving an accurate sense of your essay's focus. Whenever possible, use a key word or phrase that is central to your essay.
- A title can echo the wording of your assignment, reminding you (and your instructor) that you have not lost sight of it.
- Ideally, a title should arouse interest, perhaps by using a provocative question or a quotation or by taking a controversial position.

Assignment: Write about a problem on college campuses today.

Topic: Free speech on campus

Possible Titles:

Free Speech: A Problem for Today's Colleges (echoes wording of assignment and includes key words of essay)

How Free Should Free Speech on Campus Be? (provocative question)

The Right to "Shout 'Fire' in a Crowded Theater" (quotation)

Hate Speech: A Dangerous Abuse of Free Speech on Campus (controversial position)

5d Editing and Proofreading

Once you have revised your drafts to your satisfaction, two final tasks remain: **editing** and **proofreading**.

1 Editing

When you **edit**, you concentrate on grammar and spelling, punctuation and mechanics. (You can use the checklists below to guide you.) Although you have dealt with these issues as you revised previous drafts of your essay, editing is now your primary focus. As you proceed, read each sentence carefully, consulting the items on the editing checklist below. Keep your preliminary notes and drafts and your reference books (such as this hand-book and a dictionary) nearby as you work. Some reference works (such as *Dictionary.com* and *Merriam-Webster.com*) are available online.

CHECKLISTS

Editing Your Essay

Grammar

❑ Do subjects and verbs agree? (**See 26a.**)

❑ Do pronouns and antecedents agree? (**See 26b.**)

❑ Are verb forms correct? (**See 22a.**)

❑ Are tense, mood, and voice of verbs logical and appropriate? (**See 22b–d.**)

❑ Have you used the appropriate case for each pronoun? (**See 21a–b.**)

❑ Are pronoun references clear and unambiguous? (**See 21c.**)

❑ Are adjectives and adverbs used correctly? (**See Ch. 23.**)

Punctuation

❑ Is end punctuation used correctly? (**See Ch. 29.**)

❑ Are commas used correctly? (**See Ch. 30.**)

❑ Are semicolons used correctly? (**See Ch. 31.**)

❑ Are apostrophes used correctly? (**See Ch. 32.**)

❑ Are quotation marks used where they are required? (**See Ch. 33.**)

❑ Are quotation marks used correctly with other punctuation marks? (**See 33e.**)

❑ Are other punctuation marks—colons, dashes, parentheses, brackets, slashes, and ellipses—used correctly? (**See Ch. 34.**)

Spelling and Mechanics

❑ Are all words spelled correctly? (**See Ch. 35.**)

❑ Is capitalization consistent with standard English usage? (**See Ch. 36.**)

❑ Are italics used correctly? (**See Ch. 37.**)

❑ Are hyphens used where required and placed correctly within and between words? (**See Ch. 38.**)

❑ Are abbreviations used where convention calls for their use? (**See Ch. 39.**)

❑ Are numerals and spelled-out numbers used appropriately? (**See Ch. 40.**)

2 Proofreading

After you have completed your editing, print out a final draft and **proofread**, rereading every word carefully to make sure neither you nor your computer missed any typos or other errors.

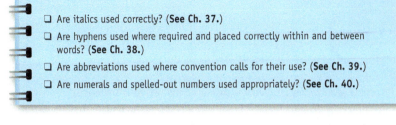

Close-Up PROOFREADING STRATEGIES

To help you proofread more effectively, try using these strategies:

• Read your essay aloud, listening for places where you stumble or hesitate.

• Have a friend read your essay aloud to you.

• Read silently word by word, using your finger or a sheet of paper to help you keep your place.

• Read your essay's sentences in reverse order, beginning with the last sentence.

Use the Search or Find command to look for usage errors you commonly make—for instance, confusing *it's* with *its*, *lay* with *lie*, *effect* with *affect*, *their* with *there*, or *too* with *to*. You can also uncover sexist language by searching for words such as *he*, *his*, *him*, or *man*.

See 19e2

Keep in mind that neatness does not equal correctness. The clean text that your computer produces can mask flaws that might otherwise be apparent; for this reason, it is up to you to make sure no spelling errors or typos slip by.

When you have finished proofreading, check to make sure the final typed copy of your essay conforms to your instructor's format requirements.

EXERCISE 5.6

Using the checklists on 54–55 as a guide, edit your essay. Then, proofread it carefully, give it an appropriate title, and print out your final draft.

Close-Up USING SPELL CHECKERS AND GRAMMAR CHECKERS

Although spell checkers and grammar checkers can make the process of editing and proofreading your work easier, they do have limitations.

- **Spell Checkers** A spell checker simply identifies strings of letters it does not recognize; it does not distinguish between homophones or spot every typographical error. For example, it does not recognize *there* in "They forgot there books" as incorrect, nor does it identify a typo that produces a correctly spelled word, such as *word* for *work* or *thing* for *think*. Moreover, a spell checker may not recognize every technical term, proper noun, or foreign word you may use.

- **Grammar Checkers** A grammar checker scans documents for certain features (the number of words in a sentence, for example); however, it is not able to read a document to see if it makes sense. As a result, a grammar checker is not always accurate. For example, it may identify a long sentence as a run-on when it is, in fact, grammatically correct, and it generally advises against using passive voice—even in contexts where it is appropriate. Moreover, a grammar checker does not always supply answers; often, it asks questions—for example, whether *which* should be *that* or whether *which* should be preceded by a comma—that you must answer. In short, a grammar checker can guide your editing and proofreading, but you must be the one who decides when a sentence is (or is not) correct.

5e Preparing a Final Draft

The annotated essay that follows is the final draft of Rebecca James's essay, which you first saw on pages 37–38. It incorporates the suggestions that her peer reviewers and her instructor made on her rough draft.

This final draft is very different from the rough draft of the essay. As she revised, Rebecca shifted her emphasis from her own largely positive view of *Wikipedia* to a more balanced, more critical view, and she revised her thesis statement accordingly. She also provided more examples, adding specific information from sources to support her points, and she included paren-thetical documentation and a works-cited list conforming to MLA docu-mentation style. Finally, she added a visual (accompanied by a caption) to illustrate the specific shortcomings of the *Wikipedia* article she selected for the assignment.

See Ch. 47

See 5b2

Rebecca James

Professor Burks

English 101

14 March 2016

Wikipedia: Friend or Foe?

Introduction

When given a research assignment, students often turn first to *Wikipedia*, the popular free online encyclopedia. With over 26,000,000 articles, *Wikipedia* is a valuable source for anyone seeking general information on a topic. For college-level research, however, *Wikipedia* is most valuable when it is used not as an authoritative source but as a gateway to more reliable research sources.

Thesis statement

A wiki is an open-source website that allows users to edit and add to its content. Derived from a Hawaiian word meaning "quick," the term *wiki* conveys the swiftness and ease with which users can access information on such sites as well as contribute content ("Wiki"). Since its creation in 2001 by Jimmy Wales, *Wikipedia* has grown into a huge database of articles on topics ranging from contemporary rock bands to obscure scientific and technical concepts. In accordance with the site's policies, users can edit existing articles and add new articles using *Wikipedia*'s editing tools, which do not require specialized programming knowledge or expertise.

Background on wikis and *Wikipedia*

Wikipedia offers several benefits to researchers seeking information on a topic. Longer *Wikipedia* articles often include comprehensive abstracts that summarize their content. Articles also often include links to other *Wikipedia* articles. In fact, *Wikipedia*'s internal links, or "wikilinks," are so prevalent that they significantly increase *Wikipedia*'s web presence. According to Alison J. Head and Michael B. Eisenberg, college

Benefits of *Wikipedia*

James 2

students conducting a *Google* search often click first on the *Wikipedia* link, which usually appears on the first page of *Google*'s list of search results. Head and Eisenberg quote a student from their study as saying, "I don't really start with *Wikipedia*; I *Google* something and then a *Wikipedia* entry usually comes up early on, so I guess I use both in kind of a two-step process." In addition, many *Wikipedia* articles contain external links to other online and print sources, including reliable peer-reviewed sources. Finally, because its online format allows users to update its content at any time from any location, *Wikipedia* offers up-to-the-minute coverage of political and cultural events as well as information on popular culture topics that receive little or no attention in other reference sources. Even when the available information on a particular topic is limited, *Wikipedia* allows users to create "stub" articles, which provide basic information that other users can expand over time. In this way, *Wikipedia* offers an online forum for a developing bank of information on a range of topics.

Benefits of *Wikipedia*

Another benefit of *Wikipedia* is that it has the potential to become a reliable and comprehensive database of information. As *Wikipedia*'s "About" page explains, the site's articles "are never considered complete and may be continually edited and improved." This ongoing editing improves quality and helps to ensure "a neutral representation of information." Using the criteria of accuracy, neutrality, completeness, and style, *Wikipedia* classifies its best articles as "featured" and its second-best articles as "good." In addition, *Wikipedia*'s policy statements indicate that the information in its articles must be verifiable and must be based on documented, preexisting research. Although no professional editorial board oversees

James 3

the development of content within *Wikipedia*, experienced users may become editors, and this role allows them to monitor the process by which content is added and updated. Users may also use the "Talk" page to discuss an article's content and make suggestions for improvement. With these control measures in place, some *Wikipedia* articles are comparable to articles in professionally edited online resources.

Despite its numerous benefits and its enormous potential, *Wikipedia* is not an authoritative research source. As the site's "Researching with *Wikipedia*" page concedes, "not everything in *Wikipedia* is accurate, comprehensive, or unbiased." Because anyone can create or edit *Wikipedia* articles, they can be factually inaccurate or biased—and they can even be vandalized. Many *Wikipedia* articles, especially those that are underdeveloped, do not supply citations to the sources that support their claims. This absence of source information should lead users to question the articles' reliability. Of course, many underdeveloped *Wikipedia* articles include labels to identify their particular shortcomings—for example, poor grammar or missing documentation. Still, users cannot always determine the legitimacy of information contained in the *Wikipedia* articles they consult.

Limitations of Wikipedia

For college students, *Wikipedia* can provide useful general information and links to helpful resources. For example, accounting students will find that the *Wikipedia* article "Financial Accounting" defines the field in relation to basic accounting concepts and offers a visual breakdown of the key terms within the discipline. This article can help students in accounting classes to understand the basic differences between

Strengths of "Financial Accounting" Wikipedia *article*

James 4

this and other types of accounting. The article contains several internal links to related *Wikipedia* articles and some external links to additional resources and references. In comparison, the wiki *Citizendium* does not contain an article on financial accounting, and the "Financial Accounting" article in the professionally edited *Encyclopaedia Britannica* consists only of a link to a related *EB* article.

Weaknesses of "Financial Accounting" *Wikipedia* article

Although the *Wikipedia* article on financial accounting provides helpful general information about this accounting field, it is limited in terms of its reliability and scope. The top of the article displays a warning label that identifies the article's shortcomings. As fig. 1 illustrates, the article's problems include a lack of cited sources. The limitations of the financial accounting article reinforce the sense that *Wikipedia* is best used not as a source but as a path to more reliable and comprehensive research sources.

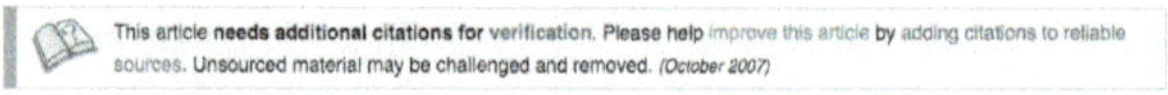

This article **needs additional citations for** verification. Please help improve this article by adding citations to reliable sources. Unsourced material may be challenged and removed. *(October 2007)*

Fig. 1. "Financial Accounting." *Wikipedia*, 14 Mar. 2016, 15:04, en.wikipedia.org/wiki/Financial_accounting.

Conclusion

Like other encyclopedia articles, *Wikipedia* articles should be used only as a starting point for research and as a link to more in-depth sources. Moreover, users should keep in mind that *Wikipedia* articles can include more factual errors, bias, and inconsistencies than professionally edited encyclopedia articles. Although future enhancements to the site may make it more reliable, *Wikipedia* users should understand the current shortcomings of this popular online tool.

James 5

Works Cited

"About *Wikipedia*." *Wikipedia*, 8 Mar. 2016, 15:07,
en.wikipedia.org/wiki/Wikipedia:About.

Head, Alison J., and Michael B. Eisenberg. "How College
Students Use the Web to Conduct Everyday Life Research."
First Monday, vol. 16, no. 4, 2011. *Google Scholar*, papers.
ssrn.com/sol3/papers.cfm?abstract_id=2281533.

"Researching with *Wikipedia*." *Wikipedia*, 8 Mar. 2016,
15:25, en.wikipedia.org/wiki/Wikipedia: Researching_
with_Wikipedia.

"Wiki." *Encyclopaedia Britannica*, 2014, www.britannica.com/
topic/wiki.

5f Creating a Writing Portfolio

A **writing portfolio**, a collection of written work in print or electronic form,
offers a unique opportunity for you to present your intellectual track record,
showing how you have developed as a writer in response to the **learning
outcomes** (what you are expected to learn) set by your instructor or your
school. Increasingly, colleges have been using portfolios as a way not only to
assess individual students' performance but also to see if the student body as
a whole is meeting the school's standards.

The purpose of a writing portfolio is to demonstrate a writer's skill sets,
knowledge, and achievements. Portfolios allow writers to collect a body of
writing in one place and to organize and present it in an effective, attractive format, offering a view of a student's writing that focuses more on the
complete body of work than on individual assignments. While compiling
individual items (sometimes called **artifacts**) to include in their portfolios,
students reflect on their work and measure their progress; as they do so,
they may improve their ability to evaluate their own work.

1 Assembling Your Portfolio

The first step in collecting artifacts for your portfolio is making sure you
understand your purpose and your instructor's requirements.

Many academic disciplines are moving toward electronic portfolios because, when posted on the Internet, they are immediately accessible to peers and instructors (as well as to prospective employers). However, not all material lends itself to an electronic format. You may need to supplement your electronic portfolio with print documents if they cannot be easily scanned.

CHECKLIST

Suggested Content for Portfolios

The following material might be included in a portfolio:

See 5f2

- ❏ **Internal hyperlinks within a table of contents or home page** to help readers navigate artifacts in the portfolio
- ❏ Reflective statement in the form of a cover memo, letter, or essay, with internal hyperlinks to portfolio content
- ❏ **Writing projects** that provide context for portfolio content
- ❏ **Planning material**, such as journal or blog entries and brainstorming notes
- ❏ **Shaping material**, such as thesis statements and outlines
- ❏ **Rough drafts with comments** made by peer reviewers, instructors, and writing center tutors
- ❏ **Revised drafts**, showing revisions made with Track Changes
- ❏ **Photocopies of source material**
- ❏ **Final drafts**
- ❏ **External hyperlinks** to online source material and other websites that support the portfolio
- ❏ **Visuals** that enhance your documents
- ❏ **Audio and video clips of presentations**
- ❏ *PowerPoint* **slides**
- ❏ **Collaborative work**, with your own contributions clearly marked
- ❏ **A résumé**, if the portfolio will be submitted to a prospective employer

---

EXERCISE 5.7

List the specific items you might include in a portfolio for one of your classes. Then, discuss your proposed portfolio content with a group of two or three other students, and consider whether you could add any of your classmates' suggested items to your list.

2 Writing a Reflective Statement

Instructors usually require students to introduce their portfolios with a **reflective statement**—a memo, letter, or essay in which students assess their writing improvement and achievements over a period of time. An instructor often wants you to respond in this statement to the course learning outcomes and provide evidence, or an artifact, to show you understand each particular outcome. Reflective statements allow students to see themselves as writers and to discover their strengths as well as the areas in which there is still room for improvement. Keep in mind that a reflective statement is not merely a summary of your completed work; it is an opportunity for you to look closely and analytically at your writing and thus to gain insights about your development as a writer.

CHECKLIST
Writing a Reflective Statement

In your reflective statement, try to answer the following questions:

❑ What skills or knowledge does each item in your portfolio demonstrate? How do these skills and knowledge relate to your instructor's goals? How do they relate to your own academic or professional goals?

❑ How are the individual items in your portfolio related? What have you learned about each project in the context of your entire portfolio? How do the projects illustrate your skills and knowledge?

❑ How have comments made by peer reviewers and by your instructor helped you revise your work? Keep in mind that you may choose to refer to or even include written feedback from your instructor; however, you are not required to include graded work, which is confidential under the Family Educational Rights and Privacy Act (FERPA).

❑ How, specifically, has your writing changed throughout the course? What skills will you continue to work on?

❑ Which items in your portfolio best represent your development as a writer? Now that you have some distance from this work, do you have new insights about your writing that you didn't have before?

Following is an excerpt from the reflective statement for a student's writing portfolio, in which Rebecca James discusses her essay about *Wikipedia*.

Excerpt from Reflective Statement

What has always scared me even more than staring at a blank computer screen is working hard on an essay only to have it returned full of red comments. The step-by-step *Wikipedia* essay assignment helped me to confront my fear of revision and realize that revision—including outside feedback—is essential to writing.

Comments I received in peer review showed me that feedback could be constructive. I was relieved to see my classmates' comments were tactful and not too critical of my essay's flaws. I think the electronic format was easier for me than face-to-face discussions would have been because I tend to get discouraged and start apologizing when I hear negative comments.

EXERCISE 5.8

Write a few paragraphs of a reflective statement in which you discuss what you learned during the process of writing your essay.

CHAPTER **6**

Thinking Critically

See Ch. 7

As you read and write essays, you should carefully consider the ideas they present. This is especially true in **argumentative essays**—those that take a stand on a debatable issue.

Although some writers try their best to be fair, others attempt to manipulate readers by using emotionally charged language, by unfairly emphasizing certain facts over others, and by using flawed logic. For this reason, it is particularly important that you think critically when you read and write. **Thinking critically** means learning to distinguish fact from opinion, evaluate supporting evidence, detect bias, evaluate visuals, and use principles of logic to arrive at valid conclusions.

See 6e

6a   Distinguishing Fact from Opinion

A **fact** is a verifiable statement that something is true or that something happened. An **opinion** is a personal judgment or belief that can never be substantiated beyond any doubt and is, therefore, debatable. In other words, a fact is something that is *known* to be true or have happened, and an opinion is something that is believed to be true or have happened.

Fact: Measles is a potentially deadly disease.

Opinion: All children should be vaccinated against measles.

An opinion may be **supported** or **unsupported**.

> **Unsupported Opinion:** I think that all children in Pennsylvania should be vaccinated against measles.

> **Supported Opinion:** Despite the fact that an effective measles vaccine is widely available, several unvaccinated Pennsylvania children have died of measles each year since 1992. States that have instituted vaccination programs have had no deaths in the same time period. For this reason, all children in Pennsylvania should be vaccinated against measles.

As the examples above show, supported opinion is much more convincing than unsupported opinion. Remember, however, that support can only make an opinion more convincing; it cannot turn an opinion into a fact.

Opinions can be supported with **examples, statistics**, or **expert opinion**.

Examples

The American Civil Liberties Union is an organization that has been unfairly characterized as left wing. It is true that it has opposed prayer in the public schools, defended conscientious objectors, and challenged police methods of conducting questioning and searches of suspects. However, it has also backed the antiabortion group Operation Rescue in a police brutality suit and presented a legal brief in support of a Republican politician accused of violating an ethics law.

Statistics

A recent National Institute of Mental Health study concludes that mentally ill people account for more than 30 percent of the homeless population (Young 27). Because so many homeless people have psychiatric disabilities, the federal government should seriously consider expanding the state mental hospital system.

Expert Opinion

Clearly no young soldier ever really escapes the emotional consequences of war. As William Manchester, noted historian and World War II combat veteran, observes in his essay "Okinawa: The Bloodiest Battle of All," "the invisible wounds remain" (72).

Note: Remember that all words and ideas that you borrow from a source must be **documented**.

See Chs. 47–48

EXERCISE 6.1

Some of the following statements are facts; others are opinions. Identify each fact with the letter *F* and each opinion with the letter *O*. Then, consider what kind of information, if any, could support each opinion.

► 1. The incidence of violent crime fell in the first six months of this year.
► 2. Tougher gun laws and more police officers led to a decrease in crime early in the year.

3. The television rating system uses a system similar to the familiar movie rating codes to let parents know how appropriate a certain show might be for their children.
4. The television rating system would be better if it gave specifics about the violence, sexual content, and language in rated television programs.
5. Affirmative action laws and policies have helped women and minority group members advance in the workplace.
6. Affirmative action policies have outlived their usefulness.
7. Women who work are better off today than they were twenty years ago.
8. The wage gap between men and women in similar jobs is smaller now than it was twenty years ago.
9. The Charles River and Boston Harbor are less polluted than they were ten years ago.
10. We do not need to worry about environmental legislation anymore because we have made great advances in cleaning up our environment.

6b Evaluating Supporting Evidence

See
7b1

The examples, statistics, or expert opinion that a writer uses to support a statement is called **evidence**. The more convincing the supporting evidence, the more willing readers will be to accept a statement.

All evidence, however—no matter what kind—must be *reliable, sufficient, representative,* and *relevant.*

- Evidence is **reliable** if it meets commonly accepted standards of truth or correctness. Evidence is likely to be reliable if it comes from a trustworthy source— one whose author is recognized as an expert in a particular field. Such a source quotes accurately and does not present remarks out of context. It also does not contain factual, grammatical, or typographical errors. It also presents examples, statistics, and expert testimony fairly, drawing them from other reliable sources. Finally, it includes documentation to help readers evaluate both the writer and evidence. (See **Chapters 47 and 48** for more information on documentation.)
- Evidence is **sufficient** if a writer presents enough information to justify a statement or conclusion. It is not enough, for instance, for a writer to cite just one example in an attempt to demonstrate that most poor women do not receive adequate prenatal care. Similarly, the opinions of a single expert, no matter how reputable, would not be enough to support this position.
- Evidence is **representative** if it reflects a fair range of viewpoints. Writers should not choose evidence that supports just their position and ignore evidence that does not. In other words, they should not permit their biases to govern their choice of evidence.
- Evidence is **relevant** if it is on topic and specifically applies to the case being discussed. For example, a writer cannot support the position that increased airport security in the United States has discouraged terrorist

attacks by citing only examples from European airports. To be relevant, evidence must also be current. Statistics on terrorism that are several years old are not likely to be relevant for an essay about present-day security practices at airports.

EXERCISE 6.2

Read the following student paragraph, and evaluate its supporting evidence.

> The United States is becoming more and more violent every day. I was talking to my friend Gayle, and she mentioned that a guy her roommate knows was attacked at dusk and had his skull crushed by the barrel of a gun. Later she heard that he was in the hospital with a blood clot in his brain. Two friends of mine were walking home from a party when they were attacked by armed men right outside the A-Plus Mini Market. These two examples make it very clear to me how violent our nation is becoming. My English professor, who is in his fifties, remembers a few similar violent incidents occurring when he was growing up, and he was even mugged in London last year. He believes that if more London police carried guns, the city would be safer. Two of the twenty-five people in our class have been the victims of violent crime, and I feel lucky that I am not one of them.

6c Detecting Bias

Bias is the tendency to base conclusions on preconceived ideas or on emotions rather than on evidence. Keep in mind that bias is not necessarily a bad thing. To one extent or another, everyone is biased. It becomes a problem, however, when bias gets in the way of clear thinking. As a critical reader, you should be aware that bias may sometimes lead writers to see what they want to see and to ignore evidence that contradicts or challenges their own points of view.

Close-Up DETECTING BIAS

When you read, look for the following kinds of bias:

- **The Writer's Stated Beliefs** If a writer expresses skepticism about the benefits of increasing the minimum wage, you should be alert to the possibility that the writer may not present an accurate (or balanced) view of the subject.

(continued)

DETECTING BIAS (continued)

- **Sexist or Racist Statements** A writer who assumes that all engineers are male or all nurses are female reflects a clear bias. A researcher who assumes that certain racial or ethnic groups are inherently superior to others is very likely to present a biased view.
- **Slanted Language** Some writers use **slanted language**—language that contains value judgments—to influence readers' reactions. For example, a newspaper article that states "The politician gave an impassioned speech" gives one impression; the statement "The politician delivered a diatribe" gives another.
- **Biased Tone** The tone of a piece of writing indicates a writer's attitude toward readers or toward the subject. For example, an angry or sarcastic tone might suggest that the writer is not presenting a case fairly; a dismissive tone might suggest that the writer is ignoring opposing points of view.
- **Biased Choice of Evidence** Frequently, the examples or statistics cited in a piece of writing reveal the writer's bias. For example, a writer may include only examples that support a point and leave out examples that may contradict it. Or, the writer may cite a single study that supports his or her point but ignore several others that do not.
- **Biased Choice of Experts** A writer should cite experts who represent a cross section of opinion. If, for instance, a writer assessing a state's policy on fracking includes only statements by experts who vehemently oppose the policy, the writer is presenting a biased case.

EXERCISE 6.3

Read the following essay about home schooling, a movement supported by parents who have abandoned traditional schools in favor of teaching their children at home. After evaluating the quality of the writer's supporting evidence, identify her biases, and decide if these biases undercut her argument in any way.

Questioning the Motives of Home-Schooling Parents

America's most famous home-schooling parents at the moment are Andrea Yates and JoAnn McGuckin. Yates allegedly drowned her five children in a Houston suburb. McGuckin was arrested and charged with child neglect in Idaho. Her six kids barricaded themselves in the family's hovel when child-care workers came to remove them.

The intention here is not to smear the parents who instruct 1.5 million mostly normal children at home. But a social phenomenon that isolates children from the outside world deserves closer inspection.

The home-schooling movement runs an active propaganda machine. It portrays its followers in the most flattering terms—as bulwarks against the moral decay found in public, and presumably private, schools. Although now associated with conservative groups, modern home-schooling got its start among left-wing dropouts in the '60s.

Home-schooled students do tend to score above average on standardized tests. The most likely reason, however, is that most of the parents are themselves upper income and well educated. Students from those backgrounds also do well in traditional schools.

Advocates of home-schooling have become a vocal lobbying force in Washington, D.C. Children taught at home may be socially isolated, but the parents have loads of interaction. Membership in the anti-public-education brigade provides much comradeship.

The mouthpiece for the movement, the Home School Legal Defense Association (*www.hslda.org*), posts articles on its Web site with headlines like, "The Clinging Tentacles of Public Education." Trashing the motivations of professional teachers provides much sport.

Perhaps the time has come to question the motives of some home-schooling parents. Are the parents protecting their children from a cesspool of bad values in the outside world? Or are the parents just people who can't get along with others? Are they "taking charge" of their children's education? Or are they taking their children captive?

Yates and McGuckin are, of course, extreme cases and probably demented. But a movement that insists on parents' rights to do as they wish with their children gives cover for the unstable, for narcissists and for child-abusers.

In West Akron, Ohio, reporters would interview Thomas Lavery on how he successfully schooled his five children in their home. The kids all had top grades and fine manners. They recalled how their father loved to strut before the media.

Eventually, however, the police came for Lavery and charged him with nine counts of child endangerment. According to his children, Lavery smashed a daughter over the head with a soda can after she did poorly in a basketball game. Any child who wet a bed would spend the night alone, locked in the garage.

A child who spilled milk had to drop on his or her knees and lick it up from the floor. And in an especially creepy attempt to establish himself as master, Lavery would order his children to damn the name of God.

The best way to maintain the sanctity of a family madhouse is to keep the inmates inside. Allowing children to move about in the world could jeopardize the deal.

In some cases, it might also prevent tragedy. Suppose one of Andrea Yates' children had gone to a school and told a teacher of the mother's spiraling mental state. The teacher could have called a child-welfare officer and five little lives might have been saved.

Putting the horror stories aside, there's something sad about home-schooled children. During the New Hampshire presidential primary race, I attended an event directed at high-school and college students. The students were a lively bunch, circulating around the giant room, debating and arguing. Except for my table.

About four young people and a middle-aged woman were just sitting there. The teenagers were clearly intelligent and well behaved. I tried to chat, but they seemed wary of talking with strangers. The woman proudly informed me that they were her children and home-schooled.

The Home School Legal Defense Association condemns government interference in any parent's vision of how a child might be educated. The group's chairman, Michael Farris, says things like, "We just want to say to the government: We are doing a good job, so leave us alone."

Could that be where JoAnn McGuckin found her twisted sense of grievance? "Those are my kids," she said as Idaho removed her children from their filthy home. "The state needs to mind its own business." (Froma Harrop, *Seattle Times*)

6d Understanding Inductive Reasoning

See Ch. 7

Argumentative essays rely primarily on **logic**—the study of the principles of reasoning. Logical reasoning enables you to construct arguments that reach valid conclusions in a systematic and persuasive way. Before you can evaluate (or write) arguments, you need to understand the basic principles of inductive and **deductive** reasoning.

See 6e

1 Moving from Specific to General

Inductive reasoning moves from specific facts, observations, or experiences to a general conclusion. Writers use inductive reasoning when they address a skeptical audience that requires a great deal of evidence before it will accept a conclusion. You can see how inductive reasoning operates by studying the following list of specific statements that focus on the relationship between SAT scores and admissions at one particular liberal arts college.

- The SAT is an admission requirement for all applicants.
- High school grades and rank in class are also examined.
- Nonacademic factors, such as sports, activities, and interests, are taken into account as well.
- Special attention is given to the applications of athletes, minorities, and children of alumni.
- Fewer than 52 percent of applicants for a recent class with SAT verbal scores between 600 and 700 were accepted.
- Fewer than 39 percent of applicants with similar math scores were accepted.
- Approximately 18 percent of applications with SAT verbal scores between 450 and 520 and about 19 percent of applicants with similar SAT math scores were admitted.

After reading the statements above, you can use inductive reasoning to reach the general conclusion that although they are important, SAT scores are not the single factor that determines whether or not a student is admitted to this college.

2 Making Inferences

No matter how much evidence you present, an inductive conclusion is never certain, only probable. The best you can do is present a convincing case to readers. You arrive at an inductive conclusion by making an **inference**, a statement about the unknown based on the known.

In order to bridge the gap that exists between your specific observations and your general conclusion, you have to make an **inductive leap**, which enables you to make a reasonable inference from the available information. If you have presented enough specific evidence, this gap will be relatively small and your readers will readily accept your conclusion. If the gap is too big, your readers will accuse you of making a <u>hasty generalization</u> and will not accept your conclusion.

See 6f

6e Understanding Deductive Reasoning

1 Moving from General to Specific

Deductive reasoning moves from a generalization believed to be true or self-evident to a more specific conclusion. Writers use deductive reasoning when they address an audience that is more likely to be influenced by logic than by evidence. The process of deduction has traditionally been illustrated with a **syllogism**, a three-part set of statements or propositions that includes a **major premise**, a **minor premise**, and a **conclusion**.

Major Premise: All high-fat foods are unhealthy.

Minor Premise: French fries are a high-fat food.

Conclusion: Therefore, french fries are unhealthy.

The **major premise** of a syllogism makes a general statement that the writer believes to be true. The **minor premise** presents a specific example of the belief that is stated in the major premise. If the reasoning is sound, the **conclusion** should follow from the two premises. (Note that the conclusion introduces no terms that have not already appeared in the major and minor premises.) The strength of a deductive argument is that if readers accept the premises, they must grant the conclusion.

When you write an <u>argumentative essay</u>, you can use a syllogism during the planning stage (to test the validity of your points), or you can use it as a revision strategy (to test your logic). In either case, the syllogism enables you to express your deductive argument in its most basic form and to see whether it makes sense.

See Ch. 7

2 Constructing Sound Syllogisms

A syllogism is **valid** (or logical) when its conclusion follows from its premises. A syllogism is **true** when it makes accurate claims—that is, when the information it contains is consistent with the facts. To be **sound**, a syllogism must be both valid and true. However, a syllogism may be valid without being true or true without being valid. The following syllogism, for example, is valid but not true.

Major Premise: All politicians are male.

Minor Premise: Senator Mazie Hirono is a politician.

Conclusion: Therefore, Senator Mazie Hirono is male.

As odd as it may seem, this syllogism is valid. In the major premise, the phrase *all politicians* establishes that the entire class *politicians* is male. After Mazie Hirono is identified as a politician, the conclusion that she is male automatically follows—but, of course, she is not. Because the major premise of this syllogism is not true, no conclusion based on it can be true. Even though the logic of the syllogism is correct, its conclusion is not. Therefore, the syllogism is not sound.

3 Recognizing Enthymemes

An **enthymeme** is a syllogism in which one of the premises—often the major premise—is unstated. Enthymemes often occur as sentences containing words that signal conclusions—*therefore, consequently, for this reason, for, so, since,* or *because.*

Melissa is on the Dean's List; therefore, she is a good student.

The preceding sentence contains the minor premise and the conclusion of a syllogism. The reader must fill in the missing major premise in order to complete the syllogism and see whether the reasoning is logical.

Major Premise: All those on the Dean's List are good students.

Minor Premise: Melissa is on the Dean's List.

Conclusion: Therefore, Melissa is a good student.

Bumper stickers often take the form of enthymemes, stating just a conclusion ("Eating meat is murder") and leaving readers to supply the major and minor premises. Careful readers, however, are not so easily fooled. They supply the missing premise (or premises), and then determine if the resulting syllogism is sound.

MULTILINGUAL TIP

In many cultures, people present arguments in order to persuade others to believe something. However, the rules for constructing such arguments are different in different cultures. In US academic settings, writers are discouraged from using the types of arguments listed in the box on pages 73–74 because they are not considered fair.

6f   Recognizing Logical Fallacies

Fallacies are flawed arguments. A writer who inadvertently uses logical fallacies is not thinking clearly or logically; a writer who intentionally uses them is dishonest and is trying to deceive readers. It is important that you learn to recognize fallacies so that you can challenge them when you read and avoid them when you write.

Logical Fallacies

- **Hasty Generalization** Drawing a conclusion based on too little evidence
  The person I voted for is not doing a good job in Congress. Therefore, voting is a waste of time. (One disappointing experience does not warrant the statement that you will never vote again.)

- **Sweeping Generalization** Making a generalization that cannot be supported no matter how much evidence is supplied
  Everyone should exercise. (Some people, for example those with severe heart conditions, might not benefit from exercise.)

- **Equivocation** Shifting the meaning of a key word or phrase during an argument
  It is not in the public interest for the public to lose interest in politics. (Although clever, the shift in the meaning of the term *public interest* clouds the issue.)

- **Non Sequitur (Does Not Follow)** Arriving at a conclusion that does not logically follow from what comes before
  Kim Williams is a good lawyer, so she will make a good senator. (Kim Williams may be a good lawyer, but it does not necessarily follow that she will make a good senator.)

- **Either/Or Fallacy** Treating a complex issue as if it has only two sides
  Either we institute universal health care, or the health of all Americans will be at risk. (Good health does not necessarily depend on universal health care.)

- **Post Hoc** Establishing an unjustified link between cause and effect
  The United States sells corn to Russia. This must be what caused the price of corn to rise. (Other factors, unrelated to the sale, could have caused the price to rise.)

- **Begging the Question (Circular Reasoning)** Stating a debatable premise as if it were true
  Stem-cell research should be banned because nothing good can come from something so inherently evil. (Where is the evidence that stem-cell research is "inherently evil"?)

(continued)

Logical Fallacies (*continued*)

- **False Analogy** Assuming that because things are similar in some ways, they are similar in other ways

  When forced to live in crowded conditions, people act like rats. They turn on each other and act violently. (Both people and rats might dislike living in crowded conditions, but unlike rats, most people do not necessarily resort to violence in this situation.)

- **Red Herring** Changing the subject to distract readers from the issue

  Our company may charge high prices, but we give a lot to charity each year. (What does charging high prices have to do with giving to charity?)

- **Argument to Ignorance** Saying that something is true because it cannot be proved false, or vice versa

  How can you tell me to send my child to a school where there is a child whose mother might have been exposed to Ebola? After all, doctors can't say for sure that my child won't catch Ebola, can they? (Just because a doctor cannot prove the speaker's claim to be false, it does not follow that the claim is true.)

- **Bandwagon** Trying to establish that something is true because everyone believes it is true

  Since most people believe in global warming, it must be a genuine threat. (Where is the evidence to support this claim?)

- **Argument to the Person** (*Ad Hominem*) Attacking the person and not the issue

  Of course the former vice president supports drilling for oil in the Arctic. He once worked for an oil company. (By attacking his opponent, the writer attempts to sidestep the issue.)

- **Slippery Slope** Suggesting, without justification, that one thing will inevitably lead to another, usually undesirable, thing

  We have to do something about tuition increases. This semester, my school increased tuition by 8 percent. Soon they'll be charging $100,000 a year. Where will it stop? (Tuition may be rising, but supposing such an extreme increase, without proof, is simply a scare tactic.)

EXERCISE 6.4

& Working in a group of three students, identify the logical fallacies in the following statements. In each case, name the fallacy, and then rewrite the statement to correct the problem. Finally, select one person in each group to present the results to the class.

1. Membership in the Coalition Against Pornography has more than quadrupled since the 1990s. Convenience stores in many parts of the country have limited their selection of pornography and, in many cases, taken pornography off the shelves. In 1995, the defense appropriations bill included a ban on the sale of pornography on military installations. The American public clearly believes that pornography has a harmful effect on its audience.

2. With people such as Larry Flynt and Hugh Hefner arguing that pornography is harmless, you know that pornography is causing its readers to live immoral lifestyles.

3. The Republican Party and conservative thinkers are all for the free market when the issue is the environment, but they will be the first ones to call for a limit to what can be shown on movies, television, and the Internet.

4. Television is out of control. There is more foul language, sex, and sexual innuendo on television than there has ever been before. The effects of this obscene and pornographic material have been documented in studies that suggest that serial killers and other criminals are very likely to be regular consumers of pornographic materials.

5. We know that television causes children to be more violent. So what can we use to control television? More governmental control of television content will help us reduce violence.

6. Study after study has been completed, and none of the researchers has presented incontrovertible evidence that rap music causes an increase in violent behavior among its listeners.

7. A boy in Idaho set fire to his family's home after watching a television stunt show. From this incident, we can conclude that television has a negative influence on children's behavior.

8. We want our children to grow up in safe neighborhoods. We would like to see less violence in the schools and on the playgrounds. We would like to be less fearful when we have to go out at night. If we stop polluting our culture with violent images from television and popular music, we can reclaim our communities and our children.

9. Ted Bundy and Richard Ramirez, two serial killers, both viewed pornography regularly. Pornography caused them to kill women.

10. Some people believe that violent content on the Internet affects children and want the government to limit it. Others believe that children are unaffected by violent Internet content. I do not think that violence on the Internet causes children to become violent.

CHAPTER 7

Composing an Argumentative Essay

For many students, the true test of their critical thinking skills comes when they write an **argumentative essay**, an essay that takes a stand on an issue and uses logic and evidence to convince readers. When you write an argumentative essay, you follow the same process you use when you write any essay. However, because the purpose of an argument is to influence the way readers think or to move them to action, you need to use some additional strategies to present your ideas to your audience.

See Chs. 3–5

7a · Planning an Argumentative Essay

1 · Choosing a Topic

As with any type of essay, choosing the right topic for your argumentative essay is important. You should choose a topic that interests and challenges you, one in which you have an emotional and intellectual stake. It stands to reason that the more you care about a topic, the more enthusiastically you will pursue it. You should also choose a topic that you know something about. The more you know about your topic, the easier it will be to gather the information you need to write about it. Even though you care about your topic, you should be willing to consider other people's viewpoints—even those that contradict your own beliefs. If the situation warrants—for example, if the evidence goes against your position—you should be willing to change your position. If you find that you cannot be open-minded, you should choose another topic. Remember, in order to be persuasive, you will have to demonstrate to readers that your position is fair and that you have considered both the strengths and the weaknesses of opposing arguments.

You should also consider other factors when choosing a topic. Your topic should be narrow enough so that you can write about it within your page limit. If your topic is too broad, you will not be able to treat it in enough detail. In addition, your topic should be interesting to your readers. Keep in mind that some topics—such as "The Need for Gun Control" or "The Fairness of the Death Penalty"—have been discussed and written about so often that you may not be able to say anything new or interesting about them. Instead of relying on an overused topic, choose one that enables you to contribute something to the debate.

2 Developing a Thesis

After you have chosen a topic, your next step is to take a stand—to summarize your position in a <u>thesis statement</u>. Properly worded, this thesis statement lays the foundation for the rest of your argument. A thesis statement for an argumentative essay challenges readers to consider your points and to think in ways that they may not have anticipated. It almost always raises questions that have no easy or pat answers. When you develop your thesis statement, make sure that it is *clearly stated* and that it is *debatable*.

See 4b

- Your argumentative thesis should be **clearly stated.** A good thesis statement leaves no doubt in readers' minds about what you intend to discuss or what direction your argument will take. It is a good idea to write a preliminary draft of your thesis statement. If you write down this tentative thesis, you will be able to make sure that it says exactly what you want it to say.
- Your argumentative thesis should also be **debatable**—that is, it should take a stand on an issue. Because your thesis statement determines the direction your argumentative essay will take, you should make sure that it accurately presents your position. For this reason, a **factual statement**—a verifiable assertion about which reasonable people do *not* disagree—is not suitable as a thesis statement for an argumentative essay.

Fact: First-year students are not required to purchase a meal plan from the university.

Thesis Statement: First-year students should not be required to purchase a meal plan from the university.

One way to make sure that your thesis statement is actually debatable is to formulate an **antithesis**, a statement that takes the opposite position. If you can state an antithesis, you can be certain that your thesis statement is debatable.

Thesis Statement: Term limits would be beneficial because they would bring in people with fresh ideas every few years.

Antithesis: Term limits would not be beneficial because elected officials would always be inexperienced.

3 Defining Your Terms

You should always define the key terms you use in your argument; after all, the soundness of an entire argument may hinge on the definition of a word that may mean one thing to one person and another thing to someone else. For example, in the United States, *democratic* elections involve the selection of government officials by popular vote; in other countries, the same term may be used to describe elections in which only one candidate is running or in which all candidates represent the same party. For this reason, if your argument hinges on a key term like *democratic*, you should make sure that your readers know exactly what you mean by it.

Close-Up DEFINING YOUR TERMS

Be careful to use precise terms in your thesis statement. Avoid vague and judgmental words, such as *wrong*, *bad*, *good*, *right*, and *immoral*.

Vague: Censorship of the Internet would be wrong.

Clearer: Censorship of the Internet would unfairly limit free speech.

---

4 Considering Your Audience

See 2c

As you plan your essay, keep a specific **audience** in mind. Are your readers unbiased observers or people deeply concerned about the issue you plan to discuss? Can they be cast in a specific role—concerned parents, victims of discrimination, irate consumers—or are they so diverse that they cannot be categorized? If you cannot be certain who your readers are, direct your argument to a general audience.

Always assume a **skeptical audience**—one that is likely to question or even challenge your assumptions. Even sympathetic readers will need to be convinced that your argument is logical and that your evidence is solid. Skeptical readers will need reassurance that you understand their concerns and that you are willing to concede some of their points. However, no matter what you do, you may never be able to convince hostile readers that your conclusion is valid or even worth considering. The best you can hope for is that these readers will acknowledge the strengths of your argument even if they reject your conclusion.

5 Refuting Opposing Arguments

As you develop your argument, you should briefly summarize and then **refute**—that is, argue against—opposing arguments by showing that they are untrue, unfair, illogical, unimportant, irrelevant, inaccurate, or misguided. (If an opponent's position is so strong that it cannot be refuted, concede the point, and then identify its limitations.) In the following paragraph, a student refutes the argument that Sea World should keep whales in captivity.

> Of course, some will say that Sea World wants to capture only a few whales, as George Will points out in his commentary in *Newsweek*. Unfortunately, Will downplays the fact that Sea World wants to capture a hundred whales, not just "a few." And, after releasing ninety of these

whales, Sea World intends to keep ten for "further work." At hearings in Seattle last week, several noted marine biologists went on record as condemning Sea World's research program.

Note: When you acknowledge an opposing view, be careful not to distort or oversimplify it. This tactic, known as creating a **straw man**, can seriously undermine your credibility. **See 6f** for coverage of logical fallacies.

7b Using Evidence Effectively

1 Supporting Your Argument

Most arguments are built on **assertions**—statements that you make about your topic—backed by <u>evidence</u>—supporting information in the form of examples, statistics, or expert opinion. (Keep in mind that all information—words and ideas—that you get from a source requires <u>documentation</u>.)

See
6b

See
Chs.
47–48

Common knowledge—assertions that are **self-evident** ("All human beings are mortal"), **true by definition** (2 + 2 = 4), or **factual** ("The Atlantic Ocean separates Europe and the United States")—needs no proof. All other kinds of assertions require support.

Note: Remember that you can never prove a thesis conclusively—if you could, there would be no argument. The best you can do is to provide enough evidence to establish a high probability that your thesis is reasonable or valid.

2 Establishing Credibility

Clear reasoning, compelling evidence, and strong refutations are necessary components of an argument. But these elements in themselves are not sufficient to create a convincing argument. In order to convince readers, you have to satisfy them that you are someone they should listen to—in other words, that you have **credibility**.

Establishing Common Ground When you engage in argument, it is tempting to go on the attack, emphasizing the differences between your position and those of your opponents. Writers of effective arguments, however, know they can gain a greater advantage by establishing common ground between their opponents and themselves.

One way to establish common ground is to use the techniques of **Rogerian argument**, based on the work of the psychologist Carl Rogers. According to Rogers, you should consider your readers colleagues with whom you must collaborate to find solutions to problems. Instead of verbally assaulting them, you should emphasize points of agreement. In this way, rather than taking a confrontational stance, you establish common ground and work toward a resolution of the problem you are discussing.

Demonstrating Knowledge Including relevant personal experiences in your argumentative essay can show readers that you know a lot about your subject; demonstrating this kind of knowledge gives you authority. For example, describing what you observed at a National Rifle Association convention can give you authority in an essay arguing for (or against) gun control.

You can also demonstrate knowledge by showing that you have done research into a subject. By referring to important sources of information and by providing accurate **documentation** for your information, you show readers that you have done the necessary background reading.

See
Chs.
47–48

Maintaining a Reasonable Tone Your tone is almost as important as the information you present. Talk *to* your readers, not *at* them. If you lecture your readers or appear to talk down to them, you will alienate them. Remember that readers are more likely to respond to a writer who seems sensible than to one who is strident or insulting. For this reason, you should use moderate language, qualify your statements, and avoid words and phrases such as *never*, *all*, and *in every case*, which can make your claims seem exaggerated and unrealistic.

Presenting Yourself as Someone Worth Listening To Present your argument in positive terms, and don't apologize for your views. For example, do not rely on phrases—such as "In my opinion" and "It seems to me"—that undercut your credibility. Be consistent, and be careful not to contradict yourself. Finally, limit your use of the first person ("I"), and avoid slang and colloquialisms.

3 Being Fair

Because argument promotes one point of view, it is seldom objective. However, college writing requires that you stay within the bounds of fairness and avoid **bias**. To be sure that the support for your argument is not misleading or distorted, you should take the following steps.

See
6c

Avoid Distorting Evidence You **distort** evidence when you misrepresent it. Writers sometimes intentionally misrepresent their opponents' views by exaggerating them and then attacking this extreme position, but you should avoid this unfair tactic in your college writing.

Avoid Quoting Out of Context You **quote out of context** when you take someone's words out of their original setting and use them in another. When you select certain statements and ignore others, you can change the meaning of what someone has said or suggested.

Avoid Slanting You **slant** an argument when you select only information that supports your case and ignore information that does not. Slanting also occurs when you use **inflammatory language**—language calculated to arouse strong emotions—to create bias.

Avoid Using Unfair Appeals Traditionally, writers of arguments try to influence readers by appealing to their sense of reason. Problems arise when writers attempt to influence readers unfairly. For example, writers can use **fallacies** to fool readers into thinking that a conclusion is logical when it is not. Writers can also employ inappropriate emotional appeals—to prejudice or fear, for example—to influence readers. These unfair appeals are unacceptable in college writing.

See 6f

7c Organizing an Argumentative Essay

In its simplest form, an argument consists of a thesis statement and supporting evidence. However, argumentative essays frequently use **inductive** and **deductive reasoning** and other specialized strategies to win audience approval and overcome potential opposition.

See 6d–e

PLANNING GUIDE

ARGUMENTATIVE ESSAY

Your **assignment** will ask you to take a stand on an issue.
Your **purpose** will be to convince readers to accept your position on the issue.
Your **audience** will be your instructor or other students in your class or school.

INTRODUCTION

- Begin by presenting a brief overview of your subject.
- Show readers how your subject concerns them.
- State your thesis. (If your thesis is very controversial, you may want to delay stating it until later in the essay.)

Thesis statement templates:
- The idea that…is popular, but…
- Recent studies, however, suggest that…
- The following actions are necessary because…
- In my opinion,…

BACKGROUND

- Briefly review the basic facts of the controversy.
- Provide definitions of key terms or an overview of others' opinions on the issue.

Topic sentence templates:
- One (another) way is…
- The first (second, third) reason is…
- One advantage (another advantage) is…

ARGUMENTS IN SUPPORT OF THE THESIS

- Begin with your weakest argument and work up to the strongest.
- If your arguments are equally strong, begin with the one with which your readers are most familiar and most likely to accept.
- Support your arguments with evidence—facts, examples, and expert opinion.

Templates for introducing support:
- As…mentions in his/her article, "…"
- According to…,…
- In his/her book,…says, "…"

continued

PLANNING GUIDE: Argumentative Essay (continued)

REFUTATION OF OPPOSING ARGUMENTS

Refutation templates:
- Of course, not everyone agrees that...; however,...
- Although it is true that..., it is not necessarily true that...
- On the one hand,...; on the other hand,...

- Refute opposing arguments by demonstrating that they are untrue, unfair, illogical, or inaccurate.
- If an opposing argument is particularly strong, concede its strength, and point out its limitations.

CONCLUSION

Closing statement templates:
- For these reasons,...
- The current situation can be improved by...
- Let us hope that...
- In conclusion,...

- Reinforce the stand you are taking.
- Remind readers of the weaknesses of opposing arguments, or underscore the logic of your position.
- End with a strong concluding statement, such as a memorable quotation or a call to action.

7d Writing and Revising an Argumentative Essay

The following student essay includes many of the elements discussed in this chapter. The student, Samantha Masterton, was asked to write an argumentative essay on a topic of her choice, drawing her supporting evidence from her own knowledge and experience as well as from other sources.

Masterton 1

Samantha Masterton

Professor Egler

English 102

14 April 2016

The Returning Student: Older Is Definitely Better

After graduating from high school, young people must decide what they want to do with the rest of their lives. Many graduates (often without much thought) decide to continue their education uninterrupted, and they go on to college. *Introduction* This group of teenagers makes up what many see as typical first-year college students. Recently, however, this stereotype has been challenged by an influx of older students, including myself, into American colleges and universities (Holland). Not only do these students make a valuable contribution to the schools they attend, but they also offer an alternative to young people who go to college simply because they do not know what else to do. A few years off between high school *Thesis statement* and college can give many students the life experience they need to appreciate the value of higher education and to gain more from it.

The college experience of an eighteen-year-old is quite *Background* different from that of an older "nontraditional" student. The typical high school graduate is often concerned with things other than studying—for example, going to parties, dating, and testing personal limits. However, older students—those who are twenty-five years of age or older—are serious about the idea of returning to college. Although many high school students do not think twice about whether or not to attend college, older students have much more to consider when they think about returning to college. For example, they must decide how much time they can spend getting their degree and consider the impact that attending college will have on their family and their finances.

In the United States, the makeup of college students is changing. According to the US Department of Education report *Pathways to Success*, the percentage of students who could be classified as "nontraditional" is continually increasing (2–3). So, despite the challenges that older students face when they return to school, more and more are choosing to make the effort.

Most older students return to school with clear goals. Getting a college degree is often a requirement for professional advancement, and older students are therefore more likely to take college seriously. In general, older students enroll in college with a definite course of study in mind. For older students, college is an extension of work rather than a place to discover what they want to be when they graduate. An influential study by psychologists R. Eric Landrum, Je T'aime Hood, and Jerry M. McAdams concluded, "Nontraditional students seemed to be more appreciative of their opportunities, as indicated by their higher enjoyment of school and appreciation of professors' efforts in the classroom" (744).

Older students also understand the actual benefits of doing well in school; as a result, they take school seriously. The older students I know rarely cut classes or put off studying. This is because older students are often balancing the demands of home and work and because they know how important it is to do well. The difficulties of juggling school, family, and work force older students to be disciplined and

Masterton 3

focused—especially concerning their schoolwork. This pays off: older students tend to spend more hours per week studying and tend to have a higher GPA than younger students do (Landrum et al. 742-43).

My observations of older students have convinced me that many students would benefit from delaying entry into college. Eighteen-year-olds are often immature and inexperienced. They cannot be expected to have formulated definite goals or developed firm ideas about themselves or about the world in which they live. In contrast, older students have generally had a variety of real-life experiences. Most have worked for several years, and many have started families. Their years in the "real world" have helped them become more focused and more responsible than they were when they graduated from high school. As a result, they are better prepared for college than they would have been when they were younger.

Of course, postponing college for a few years is not for everyone. Certainly some teenagers have a definite sense of purpose and these individuals would benefit from an early college experience. Charles Woodward, a law librarian, went to college directly after high school, and for him the experience was positive. "I was serious about learning, and I loved my subject," he said. "I felt fortunate that I knew what I wanted from college and from life." Many younger students, however, are not like Woodward; they graduate from high school without any clear sense of purpose. For this reason, it makes sense for them to postpone college until they are mature enough to benefit from the experience.

Granted, some older students have difficulties when they return to college. Because they have been out of school

Argument in support of thesis

Refutation of opposing argument

Refutation of opposing argument

Masterton 4

so long, these students may have problems studying and adapting to academic life. As I have seen, though, most of these problems disappear after a period of adjustment. Of course, it is true that many older students find it difficult to balance the needs of their family with college and to deal with the financial burden of tuition. However, this challenge is becoming easier with the growing number of online courses, the availability of distance education, and the introduction of governmental programs, such as educational tax credits (Agbo 164-65).

Conclusion

All things considered, higher education is often wasted on the young, who are either too immature or too unfocused to take advantage of it. Taking a few years off between high school and college would give these students the time they need to make the most of a college education. The increasing number of older students returning to college seems to indicate that many students are taking this path. According to a US Department of Education website, *Fast Facts*, eight million students enrolled in American colleges in 2012 were twenty-five years of age or older. Older students such as these have taken time off to serve in the military, to gain valuable work experience, or to raise a family. In short, they have taken the time to mature. By the time they get to college, these students have defined their goals and made a firm commitment to achieve them.

Concluding statement

Masterton 5

Works Cited

Agbo, Seth. "The United States: Heterogeneity of the Student
    Body and the Meaning of 'Nontraditional' in U.S. Higher
    Education." *Higher Education and Lifelong Learners:
    International Perspectives on Change*, edited by Hans G.
    Schuetze and Maria Slowey, Routledge, 2000, pp. 149-69.

Holland, Kelley. "Back to School: Older Students on the Rise in
    College Classrooms." *NBCNews.com,* 28 Aug. 2014, www.
    nbcnews.com/business/business-news/back-school-older-
    students-rise-college-classrooms-n191246.

Landrum, R. Eric, et al. "Satisfaction with College by
    Traditional and Nontraditional College Students."
    Psychological Reports, vol. 89, no. 3, 2001, pp. 740-46.

United States, Department of Education, Institute of
    Educational Sciences. *Fast Facts.* National Center for
    Educational Statistics, 2014.

---. ---. *Pathways to Success: Integrating Learning with Life
    and Work to Increase National College Completion*. By the
    Advisory Committee on Student Financial Assistance,
    2012.

Woodward, Charles B. Interview. 8 Mar. 2016.

Works-cited list begins new page

Two sets of three unspaced hyphens indicate that *United States* and *Dept. of Educ.* are repeated from the previous entry

CHECKLIST

Writing Argumentative Essays

☐ Is your topic debatable?

☐ Does your essay have an argumentative thesis?

☐ Have you adequately defined the terms you use in your argument?

☐ Have you considered the opinions, attitudes, and values of your audience?

☐ Have you summarized and refuted opposing arguments?

☐ Have you supported your points with evidence?

☐ Have you documented all information that is not your own?

☐ Have you established your credibility?

☐ Have you been fair?

☐ Have you constructed your arguments logically?

☐ Have you avoided logical fallacies?

☐ Have you provided your readers with enough background information?

☐ Have you presented your points clearly and organized them logically?

☐ Have you written an interesting introduction and a strong conclusion?

Close-Up   USING TRANSITIONS IN ARGUMENTATIVE ESSAYS

Argumentative essays should include transitional words and phrases to indicate which paragraphs are arguments in support of the thesis, which are refutations of arguments that oppose the thesis, and which are conclusions.

Arguments in Support of Thesis

accordingly	given
because	generally
for example	in general
for instance	since

Refutations

although	in all fairness
admittedly	naturally
certainly	nonetheless
despite	of course
granted	

Conclusions

all things considered	in summary
as a result	therefore
in conclusion	thus

CHAPTER 8

Composing a Literary Analysis

Learning to read, respond to, and write about literature are important skills that can serve you while you are a college student as well as later in your life beyond the classroom.

8a Reading Literature

When you read a literary work you plan to write about, you use the same critical thinking skills and **active reading** strategies you apply to other works you read: you preview the work and highlight it to identify key ideas and cues to meaning; then, you annotate it carefully.

See Ch. 1

As you read and take notes, focus on the special concerns of **literary analysis**, considering elements such as a short story's plot, a poem's rhyme or meter, or a play's staging. Look for *patterns*, related groups of words, images, or ideas that run through a work. Look for *anomalies*, unusual forms, unique uses of language, unexpected actions by characters, or original treatments of topics. Finally, look for *connections*, links with other literary works, with historical events, or with biographical or cultural information.

Note: Before you begin planning your essay, review **Chapter 46** to be sure you understand exactly what **plagiarism** is and how to avoid it.

8b Writing about Literature

When you have finished your reading and annotating, you develop a topic; then, you follow the writing process outlined in **Chapters 3–5**. First, you **freewrite** and **brainstorm** to find ideas to write about; after that, you decide on a **thesis** and use it to help you organize your material. As you arrange your material, you will begin to see a structure emerging. At this point, you are ready to start drafting your essay.

See 3e4

See 4a–c

When you write about literature, your goal is to make a point and support it with appropriate references to the work under discussion or to related works or secondary sources. As you write, you observe the conventions of literary criticism, which has its own specialized vocabulary and formats. You also respond to certain discipline-specific assignments. For instance, you may be asked to **analyze** a work, to take it apart and consider one or more of its elements—perhaps the plot or characters in a story or the use of language in a poem. Or, you may be asked to **interpret** a work, to explore its possible meanings. Finally, you may be called on to **evaluate** a work, to assess its strengths and weaknesses.

More specifically, you may be asked to trace the critical or popular reception to a work, to compare two works by a single writer (or by two different writers), or to consider the relationship between a work of literature and a literary movement or historical period. You may be asked to analyze a character's motives or the relationship between two characters or to comment on a story's setting or tone.

When you write an essay about literature, you will often be asked to use sources to support the points you are making about a particular work of fiction, poetry, or drama. Sometimes, however, you may be asked to analyze, interpret, or evaluate a literary work solely on the basis of your own reactions. Whatever the case, understanding exactly what you are expected to do will make your writing task easier.

CHECKLIST

Conventions of Writing about Literature

When you write about a literary work, keep the following conventions in mind:

❑ Use present-tense verbs when discussing works of literature (**The character of Mrs. Mallard's husband is not developed**).

❑ Use past-tense verbs only when discussing historical events (**Owen's poem conveys the destructiveness of World War I, which at the time the poem was written was considered to be . . .**); when presenting historical or biographical data (**Her first novel, published in 1811 when Austen was thirty-six, . . .**); or when identifying events that occurred prior to the time of the story's main action (**Miss Emily is a recluse; since her father died she has lived alone except for a servant**).

❑ Support all points with specific, concrete examples from the work you are discussing, *briefly* summarizing key events, quoting dialogue or description, describing characters or setting, or paraphrasing ideas.

❑ Combine paraphrase, summary, and quotation with your own interpretations, weaving quotations smoothly into your essay (**see 44d1**).

❑ Be careful to acknowledge all the sources you use, including the literary work or works under discussion. Introduce the words or ideas of others with a reference to the source, and follow borrowed material with appropriate parenthetical documentation (**see 47a1**). Be sure you have quoted accurately and enclosed the words of others in quotation marks.

❑ Include a works-cited list (**see 47a2**) in accordance with MLA documentation style.

❑ When citing a part of a short story or novel, supply the page number (**168**). For a poem, give the line numbers (**2-4**) if they are included in the text; in your first reference, include the word *line* or *lines* (**lines 2-4**). For a classic verse play, include act, scene, and line numbers (**1.4.29-31**). For other plays, supply act and/or scene numbers. (When quoting more than four lines of prose or more than three lines of poetry, follow the guidelines outlined in **33b**.)

❏ Avoid subjective expressions such as *I feel, I believe, it seems to me*, and *in my opinion*. They weaken your essay by suggesting that its ideas are "only" your opinion and have no validity in themselves.

❏ Avoid unnecessary plot summary. Your goal is to draw a conclusion about one or more works and to support that conclusion with pertinent details. If a plot development supports a point you wish to make, a *brief* summary is acceptable, but plot summary is no substitute for analysis.

❏ Use literary terms accurately. For example, be careful not to confuse *narrator* or *speaker* with *writer*. Feelings or opinions expressed by a narrator or character do not necessarily represent those of the writer. You should not say, **In the poem's last stanza, Frost expresses his indecision** when you mean the poem's *speaker* (not the poet) is indecisive.

❏ Italicize titles of books and plays (**see 37a**); enclose titles of short stories and poems in quotation marks (**see 33c**). Book-length poems are treated as long works, and their titles should be italicized.

8c Sample Literary Analysis (without Sources)

Daniel Johanssen, a student in an introductory literature course, wrote an essay about Delmore Schwartz's 1959 poem "The True-Blue American," which appears on the next page. Daniel's essay, which begins on page 93, includes annotations that highlight some conventions of writing about poetry.

THE TRUE-BLUE AMERICAN

Jeremiah Dickson was a true-blue American,

For he was a little boy who understood America, for he felt that he must

Think about *everything*; because that's *all* there is to think about,

Knowing immediately the intimacy of truth and comedy,

Knowing intuitively how a sense of humor was a necessity   5

For one and for all who live in America. Thus, natively, and

Naturally when on an April Sunday in an ice cream parlor Jeremiah

Was requested to choose between a chocolate sundae and a banana split

He answered unhesitatingly, having no need to think of it

Being a true-blue American, determined to continue as he began: 10

Rejecting the either-or of Kierkegaard,[1] and many another European;

Refusing to accept alternatives, refusing to believe the choice
    of between;

Rejecting selection; denying dilemma; electing absolute
    affirmation: knowing

        in his breast   15

            The infinite and the gold

            Of the endless frontier, the deathless West.

"Both: I will have them both!" declared this true-blue American

In Cambridge, Massachusetts, on an April Sunday, instructed

        By the great department stores, by the Five-and-Ten,   20

Taught by Christmas, by the circus, by the vulgarity and grandeur
    of Niagara Falls and the Grand Canyon,

Tutored by the grandeur, vulgarity, and infinite appetite gratified and

        Shining in the darkness, of the light

On Saturdays at the double bills of the moon pictures,   25

The consummation of the advertisements of the imagination
    of the light

Which is as it was—the infinite belief in infinite hope—of Columbus,
    Barnum, Edison, and Jeremiah Dickson.

---

[1]Søren Kierkegaard (1813–1855)—Danish philosopher who greatly influenced
twentieth-century existentialism. *Either-Or* (1841) is one of his best-known works.

Johanssen 1

Daniel Johanssen

Professor Stang

English 1001

8 April 2016

Irony in "The True-Blue American"

  The poem "The True-Blue American," by Delmore
Schwartz, is not as simple and direct as its title suggests.
In fact, the title is extremely ironic. At first, the poem
seems patriotic, but actually the flag waving strengthens
the speaker's criticism. The poem may seem to support and
celebrate America, but it is actually a bitter critique of the
negative aspects of American culture.

  According to the speaker, the primary problem with
America is that its citizens falsely believe themselves to be
authorities on everything. The following lines introduce the
theme of the "know-it-all" American: "For he was a little
boy who understood America, for he felt that he must /
Think about *everything*; because that's *all* there is to think
about" (lines 2-3). This theme is developed later in a series of
parallel phrases that seem to celebrate the value of immediate
intuitive knowledge and a refusal to accept or to believe
anything other than what is American (4-6).

  Americans are ambitious and determined, but these
qualities are not seen in the poem as virtues. According
to the speaker, Americans reject sophisticated "European"
concepts such as doubt and choices and alternatives and
instead insist on "absolute affirmation" (13)—simple solutions
to complex problems. This unwillingness to compromise
translates into stubbornness and materialistic greed.
This tendency is illustrated by the boy's asking for *both* a

Title of poem
is in quotation
marks

Thesis
statement

Slash separates
lines of poetry
(space before
and after slash)

Parenthetical
documentation
indicates line
numbers (the
word *line* or
lines is included
only in the first
reference to the
poem)

chocolate sundae *and* a banana split at the ice cream
parlor—not "either-or" (11). Americans are characterized
as pioneers who want it all, who will stop at nothing to
achieve "The infinite and the gold / Of the endless frontier,
the deathless West" (16–17). For the speaker, the pioneers
who seek this "endless frontier" are not noble or self-
sacrificing; they are like greedy little boys at an ice cream
parlor.

   According to the speaker, the greed and materialism
of America began as grandeur but ultimately became mere
vulgarity. Similarly, the "true-blue American" is not born
a vulgar parody of grandeur; he learns from his true-blue
fellow Americans, who in turn were taught by experts:

> By the great department stores, by the Five-and-Ten,
>
> Taught by Christmas, by the circus, by the
>
> > vulgarity and grandeur of Niagara Falls and
> >
> > the Grand Canyon,
>
> Tutored by the grandeur, vulgarity, and infinite
>
> > appetite gratified. . . . (20-22)

Among the "tutors" the speaker lists are such American
institutions as department stores and national monuments.
Within these institutions, grandeur and vulgarity coexist; in
a sense, they are one and the same.

   The speaker's negativity climaxes in the phrase
"Shining in the darkness, of the light" (24). This
paradoxical statement suggests that negative truths are
hidden beneath America's glamorous surface. All the grand
and illustrious things of which Americans are so proud are
personified by Jeremiah Dickson, the spoiled brat in the ice
cream parlor.

Annotations (left margin):

More than 3 lines of poetry are set off from text and introduced by a colon. Quotation is indented 1/2" from left margin; no quotation marks are used.

Documentation is placed one space after final punctuation

Johanssen 3

Like America, Jeremiah has unlimited potential. He   Conclusion
has native intuition, curiosity, courage, and a pioneer spirit.
Unfortunately, however, both America and Jeremiah Dickson
are limited by their willingness to be led by others, by their
greed and impatience, and by their preference for quick,
easy, unambiguous answers rather than careful philosophical
analysis. Regardless of his—and America's—potential, Jeremiah
Dickson is doomed to be hypnotized and seduced by glittering
superficialities, light without substance, and to settle for
the "double bills of the moon pictures" (25) rather than the
enduring truths of a philosopher such as Kierkegaard.

Johanssen 4

Work Cited

Schwartz, Delmore. "The True-Blue American." *Selected Poems:
Summer Knowledge*, New Directions, 1967, p. 163.

8d Excerpts from Sample Literary Analysis (with Sources)

Tim Westmoreland, a student in an introductory literature course, was
asked to write a source-based analysis of John Updike's short story "A&P."
Excerpts from this essay, which uses MLA documentation style, follow.

See 47a

Note: For an example of a complete source-based essay that uses MLA
documentation, **see 47c**.

Tim Westmoreland

Professor Adkins

Literature 2101

25 April 2016

"A&P": A Class Act

John Updike's "A&P," like many of his other works, is a
"profoundly American" story about social inequality and an
attempt to bridge the gap between social classes (Steiner).
The story is told by an eighteen-year-old boy who is working
as a checkout clerk in an A&P in a small New England town
five miles from the beach. The narrative is delivered in a
slangy, colloquial voice that tells of a brief but powerful
encounter with a "beautiful but inaccessible girl" from
another social and economic level (Wells 128). Sammy, the
narrator, is working his cash register on a slow Thursday
afternoon when, as he says, "In walks these three girls in
nothing but bathing suits" (Updike, "A&P" 239). Lengel, the
store's manager—a Sunday school teacher and "self-appointed
moral policeman"—confronts the girls, telling them that they
should be decently dressed (Wells 131). It is a moment of
embarrassment and insight for all parties concerned, and in an
apparently impulsive act, Sammy quits his job. Although the
plot is simple, what is at the heart of the story is complex: a
noble gesture that serves as a futile attempt to cross social
and economic boundaries.

Through Sammy's eyes, we see the class conflict that
defines the story. The privileged young girls in bathing suits
are very different from the few customers who are shopping
in the store. Sammy refers to the customers as "sheep"
(Updike, "A&P" 240) and describes one of them as "a witch

Introduction (combines paraphrase, summary, and quotation)

Title included in parenthetical citation because essay cites two sources by Updike

Thesis statement

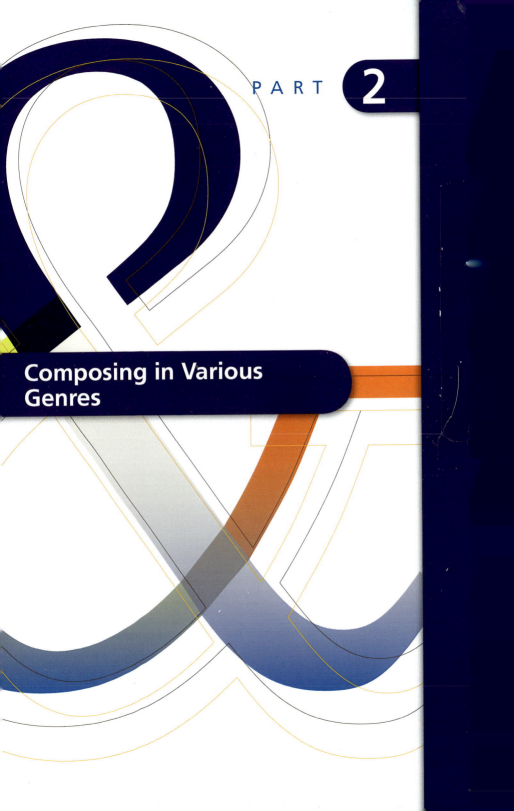

PART 2

Composing in Various Genres

Composing in Various Genres

CHAPTER **9**

Writing Essay Exams

To write an essay examination, or even a paragraph-length answer, you must do more than memorize facts; you must see the relationships among them. In other words, you must **think critically** about your subject.

See
Ch. 6

9a   Planning an Essay Exam Answer

Because you are under time pressure during an exam, you may be tempted to skip the planning and revision stages of the writing process. But if you write in a frenzy and hand in your exam without a second glance, you are likely to produce a disorganized or even incoherent answer. With careful planning and editing, you can write an answer that demonstrates your understanding of the material.

1   Review Your Material

Be sure you know beforehand the scope and format of the exam. How much of your text and class notes will be covered—the entire semester's work or only the material presented since the last exam? Will you have to answer every question, or will you be able to choose among alternatives? Will the exam be composed entirely of fill-in, multiple-choice, or true/false questions, or will it call for sentence-, paragraph-, or essay-length answers? Will the exam test your ability to recall specific facts, or will it require you to demonstrate your understanding of the course material by drawing conclusions?

All exams challenge you to recall and express in writing what you already know—what you have read, what you have heard in class, what you have reviewed in your notes. Before you take any exam, then, you must study: reread your text and class notes, highlight key points, and perhaps outline particularly important sections of your notes.

Different kinds of exams, however, require different strategies. When you prepare for a short-answer exam, you may memorize facts without analyzing their relationship to one another or their relationship to a body of knowledge as a whole: the definition of pointillism, the date of Queen Victoria's death, or the formula for a quadratic equation, for example. When you prepare for an essay exam, however, you must do more than remember bits of information; you must also make connections among ideas.

See
foldout

When you are sure you know what to expect, see if you can anticipate the essay questions your instructor might ask. Try out likely questions on classmates in a **study group,** and see whether you can do some collaborative brainstorming to outline answers to possible questions. (If you have time, you might even practice answering one or two in writing.)

2 Consider Your Audience and Purpose

See
Ch. 2

The **audience** for an exam is the instructor who prepared it. As you read the questions, think about what your instructor has emphasized in class. Keep in mind that your **purpose** is to demonstrate that you understand the material, not to make clever remarks or introduce irrelevant information. Also, try to use the vocabulary of the particular academic discipline and to follow any discipline-specific stylistic conventions your instructor has discussed.

3 Read through the Entire Exam

Before you begin to write, read the questions carefully to determine your priorities and your strategy. First, be sure that your copy of the test is complete and that you understand exactly what each question requires. If you need clarification, ask your instructor or proctor for help. Then, plan carefully, deciding how much time you should devote to answering each question. Often, the point value of each question or the number of questions on the exam indicates how much time you should spend on each answer. If an essay question is worth fifty out of one hundred points, for example, you will probably have to spend at least half (and perhaps more) of your time planning, writing, and proofreading your answer to that particular question.

Next, decide where to start. Responding first to questions whose answers you are sure of is usually a good strategy. This tactic ensures that you will not become bogged down in a question that baffles you and left with too little time to write a strong answer to a question that you understand well. Moreover, starting with the questions that you are sure of can help build your confidence.

4 Read Each Question Carefully

To write an effective answer, you need to understand the question. As you read any essay question, you may find it helpful to underline key words and important terms.

Sociology: Distinguish among Social Darwinism, instinct theory, and sociobiology, giving examples of each.

Music: Explain how Milton Babbitt used the computer to expand Schoenberg's twelve-tone method.

Philosophy: Define existentialism and identify three influential existentialist works, explaining why they are important.

Look carefully at the wording of each question. If the question calls for a comparison and contrast of two styles of management, an analysis of *one* style, no matter how comprehensive, will not be acceptable. If the question asks for causes and effects, a discussion of causes alone will not do.

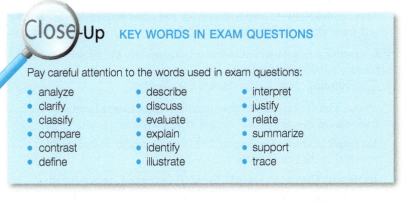

Close-Up **KEY WORDS IN EXAM QUESTIONS**

Pay careful attention to the words used in exam questions:

- analyze
- clarify
- classify
- compare
- contrast
- define
- describe
- discuss
- evaluate
- explain
- identify
- illustrate
- interpret
- justify
- relate
- summarize
- support
- trace

The wording of a question suggests what you should emphasize. For instance, an American history instructor would expect very different answers to the following two exam questions:

- Give a detailed explanation of the major <u>causes</u> of the Great Depression, noting briefly some of the effects of the economic collapse on the United States.
- Give a detailed summary of the <u>effects</u> of the Great Depression on the United States, briefly discussing the major causes of the economic collapse.

Although the two questions above look alike, the first calls for an essay that stresses *causes*, whereas the second calls for one that stresses *effects*.

5 Brainstorm to Find Ideas

Once you think you understand the question, you need to <u>find something to say</u>. Begin by **brainstorming**, quickly listing all the relevant ideas you can remember. Then, identify the most important points on your list, and delete the others. A quick review of the exam question and your supporting ideas should lead you toward a workable thesis for your essay answer.

See 3e

9b Shaping an Essay Exam Answer

Like an essay, an effective exam answer has a <u>thesis-and-support</u> structure.

See 4a–b

1 Stating a Thesis

Often, you can answer the exam question in the form of a **thesis statement**. For example, the American history exam question "Give a detailed summary of the effects of the Great Depression on the United States, briefly discussing the major causes of the economic collapse" suggests the following thesis statement:

Effective Thesis Statement: The Great Depression, caused by the American government's economic policies, had major political, economic, and social effects on the United States.

This effective thesis statement addresses all aspects of the question but highlights only relevant concerns.

The following thesis statements are not effective:

Vague Thesis Statement: The Great Depression, caused largely by irresponsible spending, had a number of very important results.

Incomplete Thesis Statement: The Great Depression caused major upheaval in the United States.

Irrelevant Thesis Statement: The Great Depression, caused largely by America's poor response to the 1929 stock market crash, had more important consequences than World War II did.

2 Constructing a Scratch Outline

See 4c

Because time is limited, you should plan your answer before you write it. Therefore, once you have decided on a suitable thesis, you should make a scratch outline that lists your major points. Once you have completed your outline, check it against the exam question to make certain it covers everything the question calls for—and *only* what the question calls for. Then, you can consult your outline as you draft your essay.

9c Writing and Revising an Essay Exam Answer

PLANNING GUIDE

ESSAY EXAM

Your **assignment** will be to write an essay that answers a specific question.
Your **purpose** will be to demonstrate that you understand the course material and can use this information to answer the exam question.
Your **audience** will be your instructor.

INTRODUCTION

Opening statement templates:
- In class this semester, ...
- To give an overview of the situation, ...
- Some background information can put things in perspective; for example, ...

- Begin by providing background to establish the context for your discussion.
- State your thesis (in the form of an answer to the exam question).

BODY PARAGRAPHS

- Provide specific support for your thesis, referring to your reading and the course materials.
- Arrange material in each paragraph according to the specific pattern (or patterns) of development suggested by the exam question.
- Include as many specific examples and details as possible.
- Include clear topic sentences and transitions.
- Use parallel sentence structure and repeat key words and terms.
- Refer to the exam question to keep yourself (and your reader) on track.

Thesis statement templates:
- Although some sources suggest that…, it makes more sense to conclude that …
- Because of …, it is obvious that …

Topic sentence templates:
- One (another, the most important) reason is …
- The first (second, another) example is …
- One (the next, a final) cause (or effect) is …

CONCLUSION

- Restate your thesis (in different words).
- Summarize your key points.
- End with a strong concluding statement.

Templates for introducing support:
- For example,…
- As our textbook makes clear,…
- Several of the readings support the idea that…

Concluding statement templates:
- For all these reasons,…
- As these examples show,…

Although essay answers should be complete and detailed, they should not contain irrelevant material. Every unnecessary fact or opinion increases your chance of error, so don't repeat yourself or volunteer unrequested information, and don't express your own feelings or opinions unless such information is specifically asked for. In addition, be careful to support all your general statements with specific examples.

Be sure to leave enough time to revise what you have written. If you suddenly remember something you want to add, you can insert a few additional words with a caret ($\wedge$). Neatly insert a longer addition at the end of your answer, box it, and label it so your instructor will know where it belongs.

Finally, don't forget to leave a few minutes to proofread your essay to spot misspellings and typos.

MULTILINGUAL TIP

Because of time pressure, it is difficult to write in-class essay exam answers that are as polished as your out-of-class writing. You should do your best to convey your ideas as clearly as you can, but keep in mind that instructors are usually more concerned with your content than with your writing style. Therefore, instead of wasting time searching for the "perfect" words or phrases, use words and grammatical constructions that are familiar to you. You can use any remaining time to check your grammar and mechanics. Finally, don't waste time recopying your work unless what you have written is illegible.

In the one-hour essay exam answer that appears below, notice how the student restates the question in her thesis statement and keeps the question in focus by repeating key words such as *cause*, *effect*, *result*, *response*, and *impact*.

Effective Essay Exam Answer

Question: Give a detailed summary of the effects of the Great Depression on the United States, briefly discussing the major causes of the economic collapse.

Introduction—thesis statement rephrases exam question

The Great Depression, caused by the American government's economic policies, had major political, economic, and social effects on the United States.

Policies leading to Depression (¶ 2 summarizes causes)

The Depression was precipitated by the stock market crash of October 1929, but its actual causes were more subtle: they lay in the US government's economic policies. First, personal income was not well distributed. Although production rose during the 1920s, the farmers and other workers got too little of the profits; instead, a disproportionate amount of income went to the richest 5 percent of the population. The tax policies at this time made inequalities in income even worse. A good deal of income also went into development of new manufacturing plants. This expansion stimulated the economy but encouraged the production of more goods than consumers could purchase. Finally, during the economic boom of the 1920s, the government did not attempt to limit speculation or impose regulations on the securities market; it also did little to help build up farmers' buying power. Even after the crash began, the government made mistakes: instead of trying to address the country's deflationary economy, the government focused on keeping the budget balanced and making sure the United States adhered to the gold standard.

Transition from causes to effects

The Depression, devastating to millions of individuals, had a tremendous impact on the nation as a whole. Its political, economic, and social consequences were great.

Early effects (¶s 4–8 summarize important results in chronological order)

Between October 1929 and Roosevelt's inauguration on March 4, 1933, the economic situation grew worse. Businesses were going bankrupt, banks were failing, and stock prices were falling. Farm prices fell drastically, and hungry farmers were forced to burn their corn to heat their homes. There was massive unemployment, with millions of workers jobless and humiliated, losing skills and self-respect. President Hoover's Reconstruction Finance Corporation made loans available to banks, railroads, and businesses, but Hoover thought state and local funds (not the federal government) should finance public works programs and relief. Confidence in the president declined as the country's economic situation worsened.

One result of the Depression was the election of Franklin Delano Roosevelt. By the time of his inauguration, most American banks had closed, thirteen million workers were unemployed, and millions of farmers were threatened by foreclosure. Roosevelt's response was immediate: two days after he took office, he closed all the remaining banks and took steps to support the stronger ones with loans and to prevent the weaker ones from reopening. During the first hundred days of his administration, he kept Congress in special session. Under his leadership, Congress enacted emergency measures designed to provide "Relief, Recovery, and Reform." *Additional effects: Roosevelt's emergency measures*

In response to the problems caused by the Depression, Roosevelt set up agencies to reform some of the conditions that had helped to cause the Depression in the first place. The Tennessee Valley Authority, created in May 1933, was one of these. Its purposes were to control floods by building new dams and improving old ones and to provide cheap, plentiful electricity. The TVA improved the standard of living of area farmers and drove down the price of power all over the country. The Agricultural Adjustment Administration, created the same month as the TVA, provided for taxes on basic commodities, with the tax revenues used to subsidize farmers to produce less. This reform measure caused prices to rise. *Additional effects: Roosevelt's reform measures*

Another response to the problems of the Depression was the National Industrial Recovery Act. This act established the National Recovery Administration, an agency that set minimum wages and maximum hours for workers and set limits on production and prices. Other laws passed by Congress between 1935 and 1940 strengthened federal regulation of power, interstate commerce, and air traffic. *Additional effects: NIRA, other laws, and so on*

Roosevelt also changed the federal tax structure to redistribute American income.

Additional effects: Social Security, WPA, and so on

One of the most important results of the Depression was the Social Security Act of 1935, which established unemployment insurance and provided financial aid for the blind and disabled and for dependent children and their mothers. The Works Progress Administration (WPA) gave jobs to over two million workers, who built public buildings, roads, streets, bridges, and sewers. The WPA also employed artists, musicians, actors, and writers. The Public Works Administration (PWA) cleared slums and created public housing. In the National Labor Relations Act (1935), workers received a guarantee of government protection for their unions against unfair labor practices by management.

Conclusion—restatement of thesis

Strong concluding statement

As a result of the economic collapse known as the Great Depression, Americans saw their government take responsibility for providing immediate relief, for helping the economy recover, and for taking steps to ensure that the situation would not be repeated. The economic, political, and social impact of the laws passed during the 1930s is still with us, helping to keep our government and our economy stable.

Notice that in her answer, the student does not include any irrelevant material: she does not, for example, describe the conditions of people's lives in detail, blame anyone in particular, discuss the president's friends and enemies, or consider parallel events in other countries. She covers only what the question asks for. Notice, too, how topic sentences (**"One result of the Depression . . ."; "In response to the problems caused by the Depression . . ."; "One of the most important results of the Depression . . ."**) keep the primary purpose of the discussion in focus and guide her instructor through the essay.

Writing in the Workplace

Employers value good writing skills. In fact, to ensure that job applicants can communicate effectively, some businesses now include a writing assessment as part of the hiring process. Employers know that a good part of each workday is spent reading business communications. They also know that the higher people go in a company, the more they write, and poorly written memos, letters, and reports can cost businesses millions of dollars each year. Because writing is so important on the job, the writing skills you learn in college can give you a definite advantage in the workplace.

10a Writing Letters of Application

A **letter of application** (also called a **cover letter**) summarizes your qualifications for a specific position.

Begin your letter of application by identifying the specific job you are applying for and stating where you heard about it—in a newspaper, in a professional journal, on a website, or from your school's job placement service, for example. Be sure to include the date of the advertisement and the exact title of the position. End your introduction with a statement that expresses your confidence in your ability to do the job.

In the body of your letter, supply the information that will convince your reader that you are qualified—for example, relevant courses you have taken and pertinent employment experience. Be sure to address the specific points mentioned in the advertisement. You want to show the employer how closely your knowledge and skills match those needed by the company. Above all, emphasize your strengths, and explain how they relate to the job for which you are applying.

Conclude by saying that you have enclosed your résumé and that you are available for an interview. (Be sure to include your phone number and your email address.)

Before you send your letter, proofread carefully. At this stage of the application process, errors in spelling or grammar could easily disqualify you.

Note: After you have been interviewed, be sure to send a follow-up email to the person (or persons) who interviewed you. First, thank your interviewer for taking the time to see you. Then, briefly summarize your qualifications and mention your interest in the position. Because many applicants do not write follow-up emails, this kind of message can make a very positive impression.

Sample Letter of Application

Heading

246 Hillside Drive
Urbana, IL 61801
Kr237@metropolis.105.com

March 19, 2015

Inside
address

Mr. Maurice Snyder, Personnel Director
Guilford, Fox, and Morris
22 Hamilton Street
Urbana, IL 61822

Salutation
(followed
by a colon)

Dear Mr. Snyder:

My college advisor, Dr. Raymond Walsh, has told me that you are
interested in hiring a part-time intern. I believe that my academic
background and my work experience qualify me for this position.

Body

I am presently a junior accounting major at the University of Illinois.
During the past year, I have taken courses in taxation, trusts, and
business law. I am also proficient in *Sage 50* and *QuickBooks Pro*.
Last spring, I gained practical accounting experience by working
in our department's tax clinic.

Double-
spaced →

After I graduate, I hope to earn a master's degree in taxation and
then return to the Urbana area. I believe that my experience in
taxation as well as my familiarity with the local business community would enable me to contribute to your firm.

Single-
spaced →

I have enclosed a résumé for your review. I will be available for an
interview any time after March 23. I look forward to hearing from you.

Complimentary
close

Sincerely yours,

Written
signature

Sandra Kraft

Typed
signature

Sandra Kraft

Additional
data

Enc: Résumé

EXERCISE 10.1

Look through current job listings available through your school's placement service. Choose one job, and write a letter of application in which you summarize your achievements and discuss your qualifications for the position.

10b Designing Print Résumés

A **résumé** lists relevant information about your education, your job experience, your goals, and your personal interests.

The majority of résumés are submitted electronically as email attachments although some hiring managers still prefer paper résumés. Either way, the guidelines are the same.

There is no single correct format for a résumé. You will most likely arrange your résumé in **chronological order** (see page 112), listing your education and work experience in sequence (beginning with the most recent). Your résumé should be brief—one page is usually sufficient for an undergraduate—easy to read, clear and emphatic, logically organized, and free of errors. Emphasize important information with italics, bullets, boldface, or different fonts.

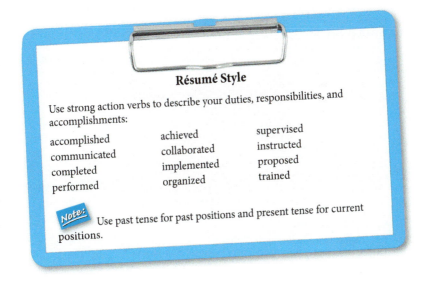

Résumé Style

Use strong action verbs to describe your duties, responsibilities, and accomplishments:

accomplished	achieved	supervised
communicated	collaborated	instructed
completed	implemented	proposed
performed	organized	trained

Note: Use past tense for past positions and present tense for current positions.

Sample Résumé: Chronological Order

KAREN L. OLSON

SCHOOL
3812 Hamilton St. Apt. 18
Philadelphia, PA 19104
215-382-0831
olsont@dunm.ocs.drexel.edu

HOME
110 Ascot Ct.
Harmony, PA 16037
412-452-2944

EDUCATION

DREXEL UNIVERSITY, Philadelphia, PA 19104
Bachelor of Science in Graphic Design
Anticipated Graduation: May 2016
Cumulative Grade Point Average: 3.2 on a 4.0 scale

COMPUTER SKILLS AND COURSEWORK

HARDWARE
Familiar with both Macintosh and PC systems

SOFTWARE
Adobe Creative Cloud, QuarkXPress 2015, CorelDRAW Graphics Suite X7

COURSES
Corporate Identity, Environmental Graphics, Typography, Photography, Painting and Print-making, Sculpture, Computer Imaging, Art History

EMPLOYMENT EXPERIENCE

THE TRIANGLE, Drexel University, Philadelphia, PA 19104
January 2013–present
Graphics Editor. Design all display advertisements submitted to Drexel's student newspaper.

UNISYS CORPORATION, Blue Bell, PA 19124
June–September 2013, Cooperative Education
Graphic Designer. Designed interior pages as well as covers for target marketing brochures. Created various logos and spot art designed for use on interoffice memos and departmental publications.

CHARMING SHOPPES, INC, Bensalem, PA 19020
June–December 2012, Cooperative Education
Graphic Designer/Fashion Illustrator. Created graphics for future placement on garments. Did some textile designing. Drew flat illustrations of garments to scale in computer. Prepared presentation boards.

DESIGN AND IMAGING STUDIO, Drexel University, Philadelphia, PA 19104
October 2011–June 2012
Monitor. Supervised computer activity in studio. Answered telephone. Assisted other graphic design students in using computer programs.

ACTIVITIES AND AWARDS

The Triangle, Graphics Editor: 2013–present
Kappa Omicron Nu Honor Society, vice president: 2012–present
Graphics Group, vice president: 2011–present
Dean's List: spring 2011, fall and winter 2012,

REFERENCES AND PORTFOLIO

Available upon request.

10c Designing Electronic Résumés

Two types of electronic résumés—scannable and web-based—are gaining in popularity.

1 Scannable Résumés

Many employers request scannable résumés that they can store in a database for future reference. If you have to prepare such a résumé, keep in mind that scanners will not pick up columns, bullets, or italics and that shaded or colored paper will make your résumé difficult to scan.

Whereas in a print résumé you use specific action verbs (**edited**) to describe your accomplishments, in a scannable résumé you also use key nouns (**editor**) that can be entered into a company database. These words will help employers find your résumé when they carry out a keyword search for applicants with certain skills. To facilitate a keyword search, applicants often include a Skills section on their résumé. For example, if you wanted to emphasize your computer skills, you would include keywords such as *Microsoft Suite, Adobe Creative Cloud,* and *C++.*

Sample Résumé: Scannable

Deborah Keller
2000 Clover Lane   Phone: (817) 735-9120
Fort Worth, TX 76107   Email: kell5@aol.com

Employment Objective: Entry-level position in an organization that will enable me to use my academic knowledge and the skills that I learned in my work experience.

Education:

University of Texas at Arlington, Bachelor of Science in Civil Engineering, May 2015. Major: Structural Engineering. Graduated Magna Cum Laude. Overall GPA: 3.754 on a 4.0 base.

Scholastic Honors and Awards:

Member of Phi Eta Sigma First-Year Academic Honor Society, Chi Epsilon Civil Engineering Academic Society, Tau Beta Pi Engineering Academic Society, Golden Key National Honor Society.

Jack Woolf Memorial Scholarship for Outstanding Academic Performance.

Grant from the Society of Women Engineers.

Cooperative Employment Experience:

Johnson County Electric Cooperative, Clebume, TX, Jan. 2015 to June 2015. Junior Engineer in Plant Dept. of Maintenance and Construction Division. Inspected and supervised in-plant construction. Devised solutions to construction problems. Estimated costs of materials for small construction projects. Presented historical data relating to the function of the department.

Dallas-Fort Worth International Airport, Tarrant County, TX, Dec. 2013 to June 2014. Assistant Engineer. Supervised and inspected airfield paving, drainage, and utility projects as well as terminal building renovations. Performed on-site and laboratory soil tests. Prepared concrete samples for load testing.

Dallas-Fort Worth International Airport, Tarrant County, TX, Jan. 2013 to June 2013. Draftsperson in Design Office. Prepared contract drawings and updated base plans as well as designed and estimated costs for small construction projects.

Skills:

Organizational and leadership skills. Written and oral communication skills, C++, PC, Macintosh, Windows 10, Mac OS X, Microsoft Suite, Adobe Creative Cloud, and Internet client software. Computer model development. Technical editor.

2 Web-Based Résumés

It is becoming common to post a version of your résumé on a website such as *Monster.com* (Figure 10.1) or *CareerBuilder.com*. Usually, a web-based résumé is an alternative to a print résumé that you have mailed or a scannable version that you have submitted to a database or sent as an email attachment.

FIGURE 10.1 *Monster.com,* a popular website for posting résumés.

EXERCISE 10.2

Prepare two versions of your résumé—one print and the other scannable— that you could include with the letter of application you wrote for Exercise 10.1. How are these two résumés alike? How are they different?

10d Writing Memos

Memos communicate information within an organization. Begin your memo with a purpose statement, followed by a background section. In the body of your memo, support your main point. If your memo is short, use bulleted or numbered lists to emphasize information. If it is more than two or three paragraphs, use headings to designate individual sections. End your memo by stating your conclusions and recommendations.

Sample Memo

Opening component

TO: Ina Ellen, Senior Counselor
FROM: Kim Williams, Student Tutor Supervisor
SUBJECT: Construction of a Tutoring Center
DATE: November 9, 2015

Purpose statement

This memo proposes the establishment of a tutoring center in the Office of Student Affairs.

BACKGROUND
Under the present system, tutors must work with students at a number of facilities scattered across the university campus. As a result, tutors waste a lot of time running from one facility to another and are often late for appointments.

Body

NEW FACILITY
I propose that we establish a tutoring facility adjacent to the Office of Student Affairs. The two empty classrooms next to the office, presently used for storage of office furniture, would be ideal for this use. We could furnish these offices with the desks and file cabinets already stored in these rooms.

BENEFITS
The benefits of this facility would be the centralizing of the tutoring services and the proximity of the facility to the Office of Student Affairs. The tutoring facility could also use the secretarial services of the Office of Student Affairs.

Conclusion

RECOMMENDATIONS
To implement this project we would need to do the following:
1. Clean up and paint rooms 331 and 333
2. Use folding partitions to divide each room into five single-desk offices
3. Use stored office equipment to furnish the center

These changes would do much to improve the tutoring service. I look forward to discussing this matter with you in more detail.

10e Writing Email

In many workplaces, virtually all internal (and some external) communications are transmitted as email. Although personal email tends to be quite informal, business email should observe the conventions of standard written communication.

CHECKLIST
Writing Email

The following guidelines can help you communicate effectively in digital business environments:

❑ Write in complete sentences. Avoid the slang, imprecise diction, and abbreviations that are commonplace in personal email.

❑ Use an appropriate tone. Address readers with respect, just as you would in a standard business letter.

❑ Include a subject line that clearly identifies your content. If your subject line is vague, your email may be deleted without being read.

❑ Make your message as short as possible. Because most emails are read on the screen, long discussions are difficult to follow. If you have additional content that needs to be conveyed, include it in an attachment.

❑ Use short paragraphs, and leave an extra space between paragraphs.

❑ Use lists and internal headings to make your message easier to read and understand. (Keep in mind, however, that your recipient may not be able to view certain formatting elements, such as boldface, italics, and indentation.)

❑ Take the time to edit your email, and delete excess words and phrases.

❑ Proofread carefully before sending your email. Look for errors in grammar, spelling, and punctuation.

❑ Make sure that your list of recipients is accurate and that you do not send your email to unintended recipients.

❑ Do not send your email until you are absolutely certain your message says exactly what you want it to say.

❑ Do not forward an email unless you have the permission of the sender.

❑ Watch what you write. Always remember that email written at work is the property of the employer, who has the legal right to access it, even without your permission.

CHAPTER 11

Designing Effective Documents

Document design refers to a set of guidelines that help you determine how to design a piece of written work—print or digital—so that it communicates your ideas clearly and effectively. Although formatting conventions—for example, how tables and charts are constructed and how information is arranged on a title page—may differ from discipline to discipline, all well-designed documents share the same general characteristics: *an effective format, clear headings, useful lists,* and *helpful visuals.*

11a Creating an Effective Visual Format

An effective document contains visual cues that help readers identify, read, and interpret information on a page. For example, wide margins can give a page a balanced, uncluttered appearance; white space can set off and emphasize information; and a distinctive type size and typeface can make a word or phrase stand out on a page.

❶ Margins

Margins frame a page and keep it from looking overcrowded. Because long lines of text can overwhelm readers and make a document difficult to read, a page should have margins of at least one inch all around. If the material you are writing about is highly technical or unusually difficult, use wider margins (one and a half inches).

In general, you should **justify** (uniformly align, except for paragraph indentations) the left-hand margin.

❷ White Space

White space is the area of a page that is intentionally left blank. Used effectively, white space can isolate material and focus a reader's attention on it. You can use white space around a block of text—a paragraph or a section, for example—or around visuals such as charts, graphs, and photographs. In documents such as flyers and brochures, you might use white space to set off blocks of text for emphasis. Used judiciously, white space can eliminate clutter, break a discussion into manageable components, and help readers process information more easily.

Close-Up BORDERS, HORIZONTAL RULES, AND SHADING

Most word-processing programs enable you to create borders, horizontal rules, and shaded areas of text. Border and shading options are usually found under the Format menu of your word-processing program. With these features, you can select line style, thickness, and color and adjust white space, boxed text, and the degree of shading. Keep in mind that these features should be used only when appropriate, so check with your instructor.

3 Color

Color (when used in moderation) can emphasize and clarify information while making it visually appealing. In addition to using color to emphasize information, you can use a color scheme to set off and identify different types of information—for example, titles can be one color and subheadings can be another, complementary color. You can also use color to differentiate the segments of a chart or the bars on a graph. Remember, however, that too many colors can confuse readers and detract from your visual emphasis.

4 Typeface and Type Size

Your computer gives you a wide variety of typefaces and type sizes (measured in **points**) from which to choose. **Typefaces** are distinctively designed sets of letters, numbers, and punctuation marks. The typeface you choose should be suitable for your purpose and audience. In your academic writing, avoid fancy or elaborate typefaces—*script* or 𝔬𝔩𝔡 𝔈𝔫𝔤𝔩𝔦𝔰𝔥, for example— that call attention to themselves and are difficult to read. Instead, select a typeface that is simple and direct—Courier, Times New Roman, or Arial, for example. In nonacademic documents—such as web pages and flyers—decorative typefaces may be used to emphasize a point or attract a reader's attention.

You also have a wide variety of **type sizes** available to you. For most of your academic essays, you will use 10- or 12-point type (headings will sometimes be larger). Documents such as advertisements, brochures, and web pages, however, may use a variety of type sizes.

5 Line Spacing

Line spacing refers to the amount of space between the lines of a document. If the lines are too far apart, the text will seem to lack cohesion; if the lines are too close together, the text will appear crowded and be difficult to read. The type of writing you do may determine line spacing: the paragraphs of business letters, memos, and some reports are usually single-spaced and separated by a double space, but the paragraphs of academic essays are usually double-spaced.

11b Using Headings

Used effectively, **headings** act as signals that help readers process information, and they also break up a text, making it inviting and easy to read. Headings also add a sense of structure and organization to a document. Because different academic disciplines have different requirements concerning headings, consult the appropriate style manual (or your instructor) before inserting headings in an essay.

1 Number of Headings

The number of headings you use depends on the document. A long, complicated document will need more headings than a shorter, less complicated one. Keep in mind that too few headings may not be of much use, but too many headings will make your document look like an outline.

2 Phrasing

Headings should be brief, informative, and to the point. They can be single words—**Summary** or **Introduction**, for example—or they can be phrases (always stated in **parallel** terms): **Traditional Family Patterns, Alternate Family Patterns, Modern Family Patterns**. Finally, headings can be questions (**How Do You Choose a Major?**) or statements (**Choose Your Major Carefully**).

See
18a

3 Indentation

Indenting is one way of distinguishing one level of heading from another. The more important a heading is, the closer it is to the left-hand margin: first-level headings are justified left, second-level headings are indented one-half inch, and third-level headings are indented further. Headings and subheadings may also be *centered, placed flush left*, or *run into the text*.

4 Typographical Emphasis

You can emphasize important words in headings by using **boldface**, *italics*, or ALL CAPITAL LETTERS. Used in moderation, these distinctive type styles make a text easier to read. Used excessively, however, they slow readers down.

5 Consistency

Headings at the same level should have the same typeface, type size, spacing, and color. Thus, if one first-level heading is boldfaced and centered, all other first-level headings must be boldfaced and centered. Using consistent patterns reinforces the connection between content and ideas and makes a document easier to understand.

Note: Never separate a heading from the text that goes with it: if a heading is at the bottom of one page and the text that goes with it is on the next page, move the heading onto the next page so that readers can see the heading and the text together.

11c Constructing Lists

By breaking a long discussion into a series of key ideas, a list makes information easier to understand. By isolating individual pieces of information this way and by providing visual cues (such as bullets or numbers), a list also directs readers to important information on a page.

CHECKLIST
Constructing Effective Lists
When constructing a list, follow these guidelines:

❏ **Indent each item.** Each item in a list should be indented so that it stands out from the text around it.

❏ **Set off items with numbers or bullets.** Use **bullets** when items are not organized according to any particular sequence or priority (the members of a club, for example). Use **numbers** when you want to indicate that items are organized according to a sequence (the steps in a process, for example).

❏ **Introduce a list with a complete sentence.** Do not simply drop a list into a document; introduce it with a complete sentence (followed by a colon) that tells readers what to look for in the list.

❏ **Use parallel structure.** Lists are easiest to read when all items are parallel and about the same length.

A decrease in several factors can cause high unemployment:
* consumer spending
* factory orders
* factory output

❏ **Punctuate correctly.** If the items in a list are fragments (as in the example above), begin each item with a lowercase letter, and do not end with a period. However, if the items in a list are complete sentences (as in the example below), begin each item with a capital letter and end with a period.

Here are the three steps we must take to reduce our spending:
1. We must cut our workforce by 10 percent.
2. We must use less expensive vendors.
3. We must decrease overtime payments.

❏ **Don't overuse lists.** Too many lists will give readers the impression that you are simply listing points instead of discussing them.

Figure 11.1 shows a page from a student's report that incorporates some of the effective design elements discussed in **11a–c.** Notice that the use of different typefaces and type sizes contributes to the document's overall readability.

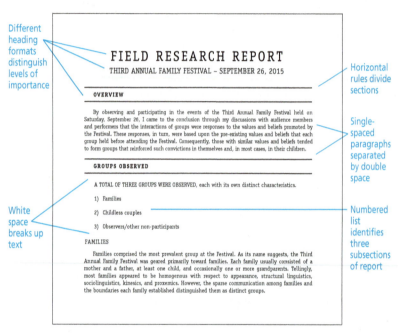

Different heading formats distinguish levels of importance

Horizontal rules divide sections

Single-spaced paragraphs separated by double space

White space breaks up text

Numbered list identifies three subsections of report

FIGURE 11.1 A well-designed page from a student's report.
© Cengage Learning.

EXERCISE 11.1

Select two different documents—for example, a page from a procedure manual and an invitation, or a report and a flyer. Then, make a list of the design elements each document contains. Finally, evaluate the relative effectiveness of the two documents, given their intended audiences.

11d Using Visuals

Visuals, such as tables, graphs, diagrams, and photographs, can help you convey complex ideas that are difficult to communicate with words and can also help you attract readers' attention.

1 Tables

Tables present data in a condensed, visual format—arranged in rows and columns. Tables may contain numerical data, text, or a combination of the two. When you plan a table, make sure you include only the data that you will need; discard information that is too detailed or difficult to understand. Keep in mind that tables can distract readers, so include only those necessary to support your points. (The table in Figure 11.2 reports the student writer's original research and therefore does not require documentation.)

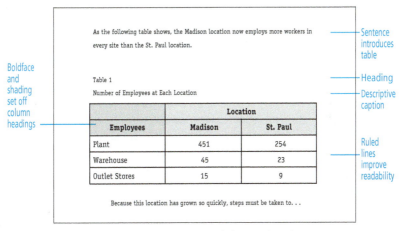

As the following table shows, the Madison location now employs more workers in every site than the St. Paul location. — Sentence introduces table

Boldface and shading set off column headings

Table 1 — Heading
Number of Employees at Each Location — Descriptive caption

Employees	Location	
	Madison	St. Paul
Plant	451	254
Warehouse	45	23
Outlet Stores	15	9

Ruled lines improve readability

Because this location has grown so quickly, steps must be taken to. . .

FIGURE 11.2 Table in a student essay. © Cengage Learning.

2 Graphs

Like tables, **graphs** present data in visual form. Whereas tables may present specific numerical data, graphs convey the general pattern or trend that the data suggest. Because graphs tend to be more general (and therefore less accurate) than tables, they are frequently accompanied by tables. Figure 11.3 on page 124 is an example of a bar graph showing data from a source.

3 Diagrams

A **diagram** calls readers' attention to specific details of a mechanism or object. Diagrams are often used in scientific and technical writing to clarify concepts that are difficult to explain in words. Figure 11.4 on page 124, which illustrates the sections of an orchestra, serves a similar purpose in a music education essay.

4 Photographs

Photographs enable you to show exactly what something or someone looks like—an animal in its natural habitat, a work of fine art, or an actor in

the demographics of college students are changing. According to a 2002 US Department of Education report titled *Nontraditional Undergraduates*, the percentage of students who could be classified as "nontraditional" has increased over the last decade (see fig. 1).

Data —

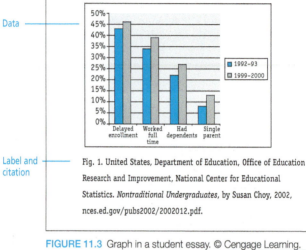

Label and citation —

Fig. 1. United States, Department of Education, Office of Education Research and Improvement, National Center for Educational Statistics. *Nontraditional Undergraduates*, by Susan Choy, 2002, nces.ed.gov/pubs2002/2002012.pdf.

FIGURE 11.3 Graph in a student essay. © Cengage Learning. Data © US Department of Education.

The sections of an orchestra are arranged precisely to allow for a powerful and cohesive performance. Fig. 1 illustrates the placement of individual sections of an orchestra.

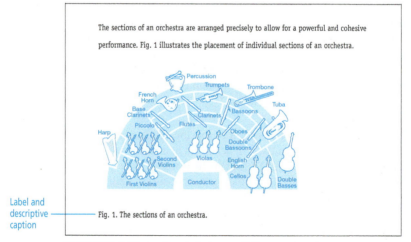

Label and descriptive caption —

Fig. 1. The sections of an orchestra.

FIGURE 11.4 Diagram in a student essay. © Cengage Learning.

costume, for example. Although it is easy to paste photographs directly into a text, you should do so only when they support or illustrate your points. The photograph of a wooded trail in Figure 11.5 illustrates the student writer's description.

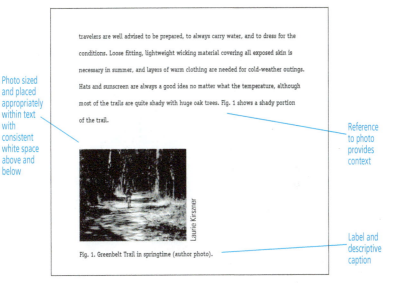

Photo sized and placed appropriately within text with consistent white space above and below

Reference to photo provides context

Label and descriptive caption

travelers are well advised to be prepared, to always carry water, and to dress for the conditions. Loose fitting, lightweight wicking material covering all exposed skin is necessary in summer, and layers of warm clothing are needed for cold-weather outings. Hats and sunscreen are always a good idea no matter what the temperature, although most of the trails are quite shady with huge oak trees. Fig. 1 shows a shady portion of the trail.

Laurie Kirszner

Fig. 1. Greenbelt Trail in springtime (author photo).

FIGURE 11.5 Photograph in a student essay. © Cengage Learning.

CHECKLIST

Using Visuals

When using visuals in your documents, follow these guidelines:

❑ Use a visual only when it contributes something important to the discussion, not for embellishment.

❑ Use the visual only if you plan to discuss it in the text of your document (place the visual in an appendix if you do not).

❑ Introduce each visual with a complete sentence.

❑ Follow each visual with a discussion of its significance.

❑ Leave wide margins around each visual.

❑ Place the visual as close as possible to the section of your document in which it is discussed.

❑ Label each visual appropriately.

❑ Document each visual borrowed from a source.

EXERCISE 11.2

Analyze the chart in Figure 11.6, noting the visual elements that are used to convey the billing costs of material, labor, and equipment on a construction project. Summarize the data in a brief paragraph. Then, list the advantages and disadvantages of presenting the data visually as opposed to verbally.

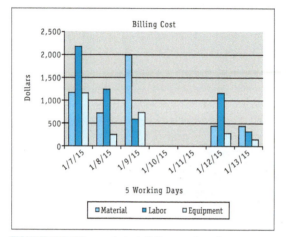

FIGURE 11.6 Billing cost chart. © Cengage Learning.

11e   Using Desktop Publishing

During your college career, you may be required to use your computer for **desktop publishing**—using graphics as well as words to produce documents. For example, you may produce a brochure, flyer, or newsletter for a student organization to which you belong or as a service-learning project for a course you are taking. (Figures 11.7 and 11.8 show a student brochure.) Brochures and flyers are frequently aimed at consumers of a product or service or at members of an organization. These documents may be informative, persuasive, or both.

Most word-processing programs, such as *Microsoft Word*, contain templates that can help you design your flyer, newsletter, or brochure. With these templates, you can select layouts, color schemes, and typefaces, as well as document dimensions and paper sizes.

EXERCISE 11.3

Create a promotional document for an organization on your campus. Before you begin the document design process, interview someone affiliated with the organization to determine the type of information you will need, the format in which the information should be delivered, and the image the organization wishes to project to the campus community.

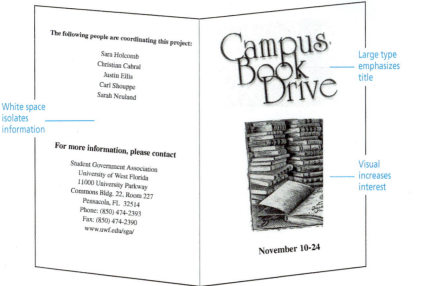

The following people are coordinating this project:

Sara Holcomb
Christian Cabral
Justin Ellis
Carl Shouppe
Sarah Neuland

For more information, please contact

Student Government Association
University of West Florida
11000 University Parkway
Commons Bldg. 22, Room 227
Pensacola, FL 32514
Phone: (850) 474-2393
Fax: (850) 474-2390
www.uwf.edu/sga/

Campus Book Drive

November 10-24

Large type emphasizes title

White space isolates information

Visual increases interest

FIGURE 11.7 Front and back cover of brochure. © University of West Florida Students

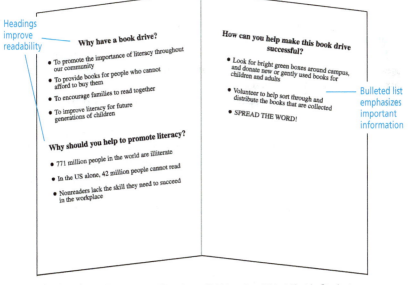

Headings improve readability

Why have a book drive?

- To promote the importance of literacy throughout our community
- To provide books for people who cannot afford to buy them
- To encourage families to read together
- To improve literacy for future generations of children

Why should you help to promote literacy?

- 771 million people in the world are illiterate
- In the US alone, 42 million people cannot read
- Nonreaders lack the skill they need to succeed in the workplace

How can you help make this book drive successful?

- Look for bright green boxes around campus, and donate new or gently used books for children and adults
- Volunteer to help sort through and distribute the books that are collected
- SPREAD THE WORD!

Bulleted list emphasizes important information

FIGURE 11.8 Inside pages of brochure. © University of West Florida Students

CHAPTER 12

Composing in Digital Environments

In email, social networking sites, digital classroom environments, blogs, wikis, and chat rooms, electronic communication occurs daily on a wide variety of topics. Because of the nature of the Internet, online communication is different from print communication, specifically in the ways readers interact with the text.

12a Considering Audience and Purpose

The most obvious difference between digital communication and print communication is the nature of the **audience**. Audiences for print documents are relatively passive: they read a discussion in linear fashion from beginning to end, form their own ideas about it, and then stop. Depending on the writing situation, however, audiences for electronic documents often respond differently. Although in some cases readers may be passive, in other cases they can be quite active, posting and emailing responses and directly communicating with the writer (sometimes in real time) as well as with one another.

The **purpose** of an electronic document may also be different from that of a print document. Unlike print documents, which appear as carefully crafted finished products, electronic documents may be written in immediate response to other people's arguments or ideas. In fact, by including links to a writer's email address or to a blog, some online documents are works in progress, encouraging readers to respond—or, in the case of wikis, to add or edit content. For this reason, in addition to trying to inform or persuade, the purpose of an electronic document may also be to support, refute, react, clarify, expand, or elicit a response.

Increasingly, however, the line between print and electronic documents is blurring. For one thing, all different types of writing now are being published online. For example, scholarly articles are often published in online-only journals, and news stories appear in both electronic and print forms. When a print article is published online, it usually includes some web-specific features, such as links to other articles or streaming video. As online writing becomes the norm, writers need to understand the advantages that this medium offers.

EXERCISE 12.1

Find a document that someone has posted on the web. Identify the elements that make it different from a print document. Then, decide what else the writer could have done to make the document more effective.

12b Writing in a Digital Classroom

Much of the writing you do in a digital classroom involves **collaboration**, a process in which more than one person contributes to the creation, revising, and editing of a document. In some cases, students write a draft of a document and then post it or distribute it electronically to members of a peer-editing group, who then make revision suggestions. Comments can be sent via email or can be inserted into the document with *Microsoft Word*'s Comment tool or with Track Changes. In other cases, students meet in groups (either electronically or face-to-face) and jointly contribute to the prewriting, drafting, revision, and editing of a document.

See 12c

Observing Netiquette

Netiquette refers to the guidelines that responsible users of the Internet should follow when they write in cyberspace. When you communicate via the Internet, keep the following guidelines in mind:

- **Don't shout.** All-uppercase letters indicate that a person is SHOUTING.
- **Watch your tone.** Make sure you send the message you actually intend to send. What might seem humorous or clever to you may seem disrespectful to someone else.
- **Be careful what you write.** Be sure to consider carefully what you have written. Remember that digital files are permanent. Once you hit *Send*, it is often too late to call the message back.
- **Don't flame.** When you flame, you send an insulting electronic message. This tactic is not only immature, but also rude and annoying.
- **Make sure you use the correct electronic address.** Be certain that your message goes to the right person. Nothing is more embarrassing than sending an email to the wrong address.
- **Use your computer ethically and responsibly.** Don't use computer labs for personal communications or for entertainment. Not only is this a misuse of the facility but it also ties up equipment that others may be waiting to use.

Central to this type of instruction is communication between students and between instructors and students. With **synchronous communication**, all parties involved in the communication process are online at the same time and can be involved in a real-time conversation. Chatrooms, instant messaging, and texting are examples of synchronous communication. With **asynchronous communication**, there is a delay between the time a message is sent and the time it is received. Asynchronous exchanges occur with email, blogs, wikis, web forums, and discussion groups.

More and more often, both in online environments and in traditional classrooms, instructors are using the Internet as well as specific web-based technology to teach writing. Some of the most popular tools that students use to create web-based content in an electronic writing environment are discussed in the pages that follow.

1 Using Email

Email enables you to exchange ideas with classmates, ask questions of your instructors, and communicate with the writing center or other campus services. You can insert email links in web documents, and you can transfer files as email attachments from one computer to another. In many classes, you submit writing assignments as email attachments.

Close-Up   SENDING EMAIL TO INSTRUCTORS

When you write email messages to your instructors, keep in mind that your communication should be fairly formal. Use the type of language that you would use to address a supervisor in a work environment. Include clear subject lines, and use appropriate salutations ("Dear Professor Jewett," never "Hi Prof") and complimentary closes.

---

2 Using Blogs

A **blog** (short for web log) is like an online personal journal. Most blogs offer commentary, news, or personal reflections and reactions—usually presented in reverse chronological order, with the most recent entry first. Blogs can also function as online diaries, communicating the personal views of the author.

Blogs are not limited to text; they can contain photographs, videos, music, audio, and personal artwork as well as links to websites. Most course management systems (such as *Blackboard* and *Canvas*) make it easy for instructors or students to create a blog and post comments. In addition, Web 2.0 technologies, such as *Blogger* and *WordPress*, are open-source platforms that students can use to create their own blogs. Although many blogs are open to everyone, some are password protected.

On a class blog, students can post informal responses to readings and class discussions, and they can brainstorm or try out ideas there before they write. Blogs also give students a chance to get comments from other students who read and react to their posts.

3 Using Wikis

Unlike a blog, which is created by an individual and does not allow visitors to edit the posted content, a **wiki** (Hawaiian for *fast* or *quick*) is a website that allows users to add, remove, or change content. The best-known wiki is *Wikipedia*, the online encyclopedia.

In the writing classroom, wikis are used for collaborative writing. They allow students to add (or delete) content while working on collaboratively produced projects. Groups of students use wikis to brainstorm and to compile class notes. Wiki sites also enable students to view the history of a revision and to compare the relative merits of various drafts of an essay. In research projects, wikis allow students to collaborate on developing research questions, to exchange hyperlinks, to share bibliographical information, to collaborate on drafts of their essays, and to get help with documentation.

4 Using Discussion Lists

Discussion lists are electronic mailing lists to which users must subscribe. They enable individuals to communicate with groups of people interested in particular topics. (Many schools, and even individual courses, have discussion lists.) Subscribers to a discussion list send messages to a main email address, and these messages are routed to all members of the group. Discussion lists can be especially useful in composition classes, permitting students to post comments on reading assignments as well as to discuss other subjects with the entire class.

5 Using Podcasts

Originally, the term **podcast** referred to material that could be downloaded to Apple's iPod. Now, however, it refers to any audio broadcast that has been converted to an MP3 or similar format for playback on the Internet. You can access a podcast with a computer, with an iPad or iPhone, or with an MP3 playback device.

Podcasting is becoming increasingly common in college classrooms. On the most basic level, instructors podcast class lectures that students can access at their leisure. Instructors also use podcasts to give feedback on students' projects, to distribute supplementary material such as audio recordings or speeches, to record student presentations, or to communicate class information or news. Students may also be asked to analyze podcasts of political speeches, radio programs, or short stories from radio programs such as National Public Radio's *Selected Shorts*. Some instructors even ask students to make their own podcasts. For example, students can read their own essays and add sound clips or visual files.

6 Using *Twitter* and *Facebook*

Some instructors use *Twitter* as a tool to teach writing. For example, because tweets have a one-hundred-and-forty character limit, they force students to be concise. So, an instructor may ask students to tweet their thesis statements to the class, thereby encouraging them to state the thesis in clear, concise language. In addition, instructors can use *Twitter* as an easy way to get in touch with students (*Don't forget. Class cancelled tomorrow.*) or to reinforce important course concepts (*Your arguments must be supported by evidence. Look out for logical fallacies.*).

Some instructors form *Facebook* groups and post links to websites, documents, and other links on the group pages, where students can ask questions about class assignments and discuss topics that interest them. (Joining these groups is usually optional because some students have concerns about *Facebook*'s privacy policies.)

12c Writing Collaboratively Online

As you already know, **writing collaboratively** means creating works that have more than one author. Every time you post a written passage and get feedback from a member of a class, you are engaging in collaborative writing. (In fact, when your instructors write comments on rough drafts of essays or discuss your work with you in conference, they are collaborating with you.) Digital writing environments present special opportunities for collaboration. For example, if your writing class has an online component, your instructor has most likely set up a virtual space where writing can be posted and commented on. In addition, electronic tools such as email, text messages, wikis, and blogs allow for collaboration at every stage of the writing process.

1 Peer Review

See
5c2

Participating in peer review online has a number of advantages. You can easily exchange projects with members of a group or even with the entire class, and you can get feedback on your work from a number of people. If you are working on a group project, you do not have to arrange meetings or travel to campus. In fact, most of your collaborative activities can take place in front of your computer. In many cases, you can get information from classmates at any time simply by posting a message on an electronic bulletin board or by sending an email. Finally, because most of your communications are archived, you will usually have a record of your drafts and your correspondence.

Although online writing environments present unique opportunities for collaboration, they also present challenges. Because feedback can come from so many different sources—for example, from blogs, chat rooms, and wikis as well as from editorial suggestions made with *Word*'s Comment tool—it is easy to become overwhelmed by your classmates' comments and suggestions. For this reason, it is extremely important to keep track of the various drafts of your essay and to keep your own ideas separate from the comments you get in response to your essay.

One way to avoid confusion is to think carefully before you set up files for any writing project that will be peer reviewed. When you save a draft of your essay (or any other document related to your writing—brainstorming notes, for example), make sure you clearly label and date it—and possibly even number it. In addition, save all emails you receive from members of your peer-review group in files that contain the name of the assignment and the date. Even if your course management program archives and categorizes all discussion board communication into threads, it is a good idea to download and file important messages.

If for some reason you need to compare two drafts of an essay, use the Track Changes "Compare Documents" tool, which highlights all additions, deletions, and edits to a document. Some document management systems—*Writeboard*, for example—allow you to access every version of a piece of writing that you have saved. This feature enables you to revise and edit a document without losing an earlier version that might possibly be better.

2 Group Projects

Sometimes you may be assigned to a group or team to work together on a writing project—for example, a proposal, a **brochure,** a flyer, or even a web page. When you work online as part of a group, you follow many of the same procedures that you do in any online collaboration. In addition, you follow procedures that are specifically tailored to working as a group.

See 11e

CHECKLIST

Working in a Group

As you set up and organize your group, keep the following advice in mind:

❑ **Decide how your group will meet.** Will you exchange comments in a chat room or post comments on a discussion board? (Often, your instructor will make this decision for you, but sometimes you will have to decide for yourself.) Some instant message and chat room technologies allow multiuser discussions and enable you to record and save transcripts of discussions for use later.

❑ **Divide tasks.** Make sure each member of the group knows exactly what to do. For example, one person might be responsible for coordinating the project, another for finding information, another for finding visuals, another for writing, and still another for revising and editing.

continued

Working in a Group *(continued)*

❑ **Determine how you will collaborate.** Will you send drafts to each other as email attachments? Will you work on a wiki site? Or, will you use some other method?

❑ **Keep a list of email and phone numbers.** Set up an email or text message group so that you can easily communicate with everyone at the same time.

❑ **Set up files to store communications.** Make sure you keep a file (or files) of all communications sent and received from members of the group.

❑ **Agree on technology.** Make sure everyone is using compatible technology—for example, the same version of *Word*. In addition, if you are using a tool such as a wiki, make sure that all members of the group understand how it works.

❑ **Decide on editing guidelines in advance.** To avoid confusion, agree on a consistent way to respond to writing—for example, offering suggestions with *Word*'s Comment tool.

❑ **Set up a realistic schedule.** Be sure to set up a schedule that includes deadlines and due dates, and be sure group members understand their assigned responsibilities and are willing (and able) to meet deadlines.

❑ **Agree on specific dates for checking progress.** Check in with one another periodically to make sure you are all on schedule. Don't let a missed deadline take the group by surprise.

❑ **Get your instructor's approval.** Before you begin working on your group project, make sure your instructor approves of your plans.

EXERCISE 12.2

What digital tools does your writing instructor use on a regular basis? What other tools do you think could be used to teach writing?

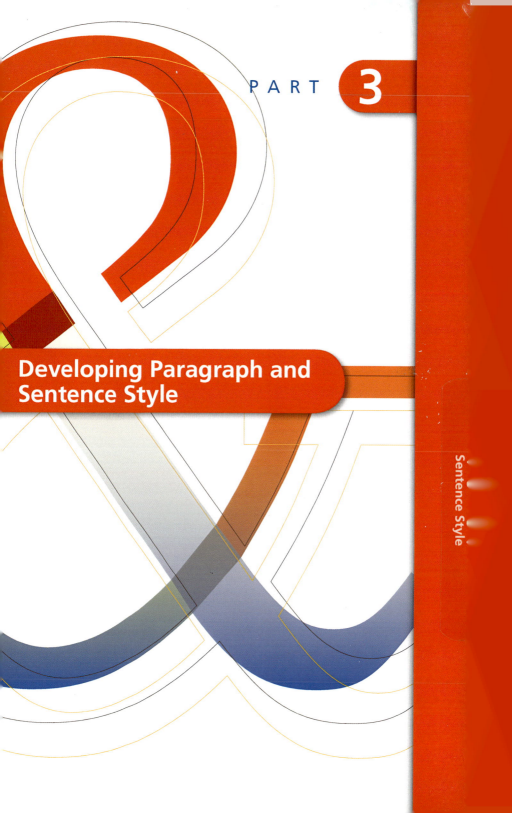

Developing Paragraph and Sentence Style

Developing Paragraph and Sentence Style

CHAPTER **13**

Writing Effective Paragraphs

A **paragraph** is a group of related sentences. A paragraph may be complete in itself or part of a longer piece of writing.

13a Writing Unified Paragraphs

A paragraph is **unified** when it develops a single main idea. The **topic sentence** states the main idea of the paragraph, and the other sentences in the paragraph support that idea.

1 Using Topic Sentences

A topic sentence is often placed at the beginning of a paragraph. Occasionally, however, a topic sentence may occur at the end of a paragraph, particularly if a writer wants to present an unexpected conclusion.

Topic Sentence at the Beginning A topic sentence at the beginning of a paragraph tells readers what to expect and helps them to understand your paragraph's main idea immediately.

> I was a listening child, careful to hear the very different sounds of Spanish and English. Wide-eyed with hearing, I'd listen to sounds more than words. First, there were English (*gringo*) sounds. So many words were still unknown that when the butcher or the lady at the drugstore said something to me, exotic polysyllabic sounds would bloom in the midst of their sentences. Often the speech of people in public seemed to me very loud, booming with confidence. The man behind the counter would literally ask, "What can I do for you?" But by being so firm and so clear, the sound of his voice said that he was a *gringo*; he belonged in public society. (Richard Rodriguez, *Aria: Memoir of a Bilingual Childhood*)

Topic Sentence at the End A topic sentence at the end of a paragraph is useful if you are presenting an unusual or hard-to-accept idea. If you present facts and examples before you state your conclusion, you are more likely to convince readers that your conclusion is reasonable.

> These sprays, dusts and aerosols are now applied almost universally to farms, gardens, forests, and homes—nonselective chemicals that have the power to kill every insect, the "good" and the "bad," to still the song of birds

and the leaping of fish in the streams, to coat the leaves with a deadly film, and to linger on in soil—all this though the intended target may be only a few weeds or insects. Can anyone believe it is possible to lay down such a barrage of poisons on the surface without making it unfit for life? They should not be called "insecticides," but "biocides." (Rachel Carson, "The Obligation to Endure," *Silent Spring*)

2 Testing for Unity

In a unified paragraph, each sentence supports the main idea in the topic sentence. The following paragraph is not unified because it includes sentences that do not support the main idea.

Paragraph Lacking Unity

One of the first problems I had as a college student was learning to use a computer. All students were required to buy a computer before school started. Throughout the first semester, we took a special course to teach us to use a computer. My laptop has a large memory and can do graphics and spreadsheets. It has a large retina display screen and a wireless keyboard and trackpad. My parents were happy that I had a computer, but they were concerned about the price. Tuition was high, and when they added in the price of the computer, it was almost out of reach. To offset expenses, I got a part-time job in the school library.

Sentences do not support main idea

When he revised, the writer deleted the sentences about his parents' financial situation and the computer's characteristics and added details related to his main idea (expressed in his topic sentence).

Revised Paragraph

One of the first problems I had as a college student was learning to use a computer. All first-year students were required to buy a computer before school started. Throughout the first semester, we took a special course to teach us to use the computer. In theory this system sounded fine, but in my case it was a disaster. Most of the students in my computer orientation course already knew how to work with spreadsheets, presentation software, and wikis. They were also familiar with the course management software that my college uses. They could navigate the discussion boards and use the chat function that was part of my composition course. The high school that I attended didn't have this (or any) system, so I felt that I was at a great disadvantage. By the end of the first week, I was convinced that I would never be able to keep up with the rest of the class.

Sentences now support main idea

EXERCISE 13.1

The following paragraph is unified by one main idea, but that idea is not explicitly stated. Identify the main idea, write a topic sentence that expresses it, and decide where in the paragraph to place it.

"Lite" can mean that a product has fewer calories, or less fat, or less sodium, or it can simply mean that the product has a "light" color, texture, or taste. It may also mean none of these. Food can be advertised as 86 percent fat free when it is actually 50 percent fat because the term "fat free" is based on weight, and fat is extremely light. Another misleading term is "no cholesterol," which is found on some products that never had any cholesterol in the first place. Peanut butter, for example, contains no cholesterol—a fact that manufacturers have recently made an issue—but it is very high in fat and so would not be a very good food for most dieters. Sodium labeling presents still another problem. The terms "sodium free," "very low sodium," "low sodium," "reduced sodium," and "no salt added" have very specific meanings, frequently not explained on the packages on which they appear.

13b Writing Coherent Paragraphs

A paragraph is **coherent** when all its sentences clearly relate to one another. You can create coherence by arranging details according to an organizing principle, by using transitional words and phrases, by using parallel structure, and by repeating key words and phrases.

1 Arranging Details

Even if its sentences are all about the same subject, a paragraph lacks coherence if the sentences are not arranged according to a general organizing principle— that is, if they are not arranged *spatially*, *chronologically*, or *logically*.

- **Spatial order** establishes the perspective from which readers will view details. For example, an object or scene can be viewed from top to bottom or from near to far. Spatial order is central to **descriptive paragraphs**. See 13d2
- **Chronological order** presents events in sequence, using transitional words and phrases that establish the time order of events—*at first, yesterday, later, in 1930*, and so on. Chronological order is central to **narrative paragraphs** and **process paragraphs**. See 13d1, 4
- **Logical order** presents details or ideas in terms of their logical relationships to one another. Transitional words and phrases such as *first, second*, and *finally* establish these relationships and lead readers through the paragraphs. For example, a paragraph may move from *general to specific* or from *least important to most important*. Logical order is central to **exemplification paragraphs** and **comparison-and-contrast paragraphs**. See 13d3, 6

2 Using Transitional Words and Phrases

Transitional words and phrases create coherence in paragraphs by emphasizing the spatial, chronological, and logical organizing principles discussed above. The following paragraph, which has no transitional words or phrases, illustrates just how important these words and phrases are.

Paragraph without Transitional Words and Phrases

Napoleon certainly made a change for the worse by leaving his small kingdom of Elba. He went back to Paris, and he abdicated for a second time. He fled to Rochefort in hope of escaping to America. He gave himself up to the English captain of the ship *Bellerophon*. He suggested that the Prince Regent grant him asylum, and he was refused. All he saw of England was the Devon coast and Plymouth Sound as he passed on to the remote island of St. Helena. He died on May 5, 1821, at the age of fifty-two.

In the narrative paragraph above, the topic sentence clearly states the main idea of the paragraph, and the rest of the sentences support this idea. Because of the absence of transitional words and phrases, however, readers cannot tell exactly how one event in the paragraph relates to another in time. Notice how much clearer this passage is once transitional words and phrases (such as *after, finally, once again*, and *in the end*) have been added.

Paragraph with Transitional Words and Phrases

Napoleon certainly made a change for the worse by leaving his small kingdom of Elba. After Waterloo, he went back to Paris, and he abdicated for a second time. A hundred days after his return from Elba, he fled to Rochefort in hope of escaping to America. Finally, he gave himself up to the English captain of the ship *Bellerophon*. Once again, he suggested that the Prince Regent grant him asylum, and once again, he was refused. In the end, all he saw of England was the Devon coast and Plymouth Sound as he passed on to the remote island of St. Helena. After six years of exile, he died on May 5, 1821, at the age of fifty-two. (Norman Mackenzie, *The Escape from Elba*)

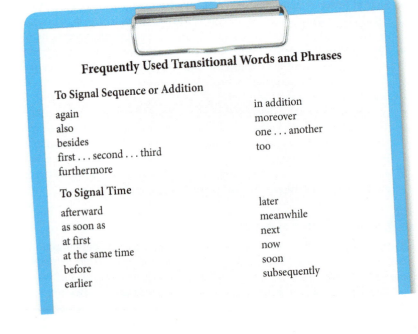

Frequently Used Transitional Words and Phrases

To Signal Sequence or Addition

again
also
besides
first . . . second . . . third
furthermore

in addition
moreover
one . . . another
too

To Signal Time

afterward
as soon as
at first
at the same time
before
earlier

later
meanwhile
next
now
soon
subsequently

finally
in the meantime

then
until

To Signal Comparison

also
by the same token
in comparison

likewise
similarly

To Signal Contrast

although
but
despite
even though
however
in contrast
instead
meanwhile

nevertheless
nonetheless
on the contrary
on the one hand . . . on
   the other hand
still
whereas
yet

To Introduce Examples

for example
for instance
namely

specifically
thus

To Signal Narrowing of Focus

after all
indeed
in fact
in other words

in particular
specifically
that is

To Introduce Conclusions or Summaries

as a result
consequently
in conclusion
in other words

in summary
therefore
thus
to conclude

To Signal Concession

admittedly
certainly
granted

naturally
of course

To Introduce Causes or Effects

accordingly
as a result
because
consequently
hence

since
so
then
therefore

3 Using Parallel Structure

See
16c,
18a

Parallelism—the use of matching words, phrases, clauses, or sentence structures to emphasize similar ideas—can create coherence in a paragraph. Note
in the following paragraph how parallel constructions beginning with "He
was . . ." link (and emphasize) Thomas Jefferson's accomplishments.

> Thomas Jefferson was born in 1743 and died at Monticello,
> Virginia, on July 4, 1826. During his eighty-four years, he
> accomplished a number of things. Although best known for his draft
> of the Declaration of Independence, Jefferson was a man of many
> talents who had a wide intellectual range. He was a patriot who was
> one of the revolutionary founders of the United States. He was a reformer
> who, when he was governor of Virginia, drafted the Statute
> for Religious Freedom. He was an innovator who drafted an ordinance
> for governing the West and devised the first decimal monetary system. He
> was a president who abolished internal taxes, reduced the national debt,
> and made the Louisiana Purchase. And, finally, he was an architect who
> designed Monticello and the University of Virginia. (student writer)

4 Repeating Key Words and Phrases

Repeating **key words and phrases** throughout a paragraph connects the sentences to one another and to the paragraph's main idea. The following paragraph repeats the key word *mercury* to help readers focus on the subject.

> Mercury poisoning is a problem that has long been recognized.
> "Mad as a hatter" refers to the condition prevalent among
> nineteenth-century workers who were exposed to mercury during
> the manufacturing of felt hats. Workers in many other industries,
> such as mining, chemicals, and dentistry, were similarly affected.
> In the 1950s and 1960s, there were cases of mercury poisoning in
> Minamata, Japan. Research showed that there were high levels of
> mercury pollution in streams and lakes surrounding the village. In
> the United States, this problem came to light in 1969, when a New
> Mexico family got sick from eating food tainted with mercury. Since
> then, pesticides containing mercury have been withdrawn from
> the market, and chemical wastes can no longer be dumped into
> the ocean. (student writer)

5 Achieving Coherence between Paragraphs

See
13e1

The same methods you use to establish coherence within paragraphs can also
link the paragraphs in an essay. (You can also use a transitional paragraph
as a bridge between two paragraphs.) The following group of related paragraphs shows how the strategies discussed in **13b1-4** create coherence from
paragraph to paragraph.

A language may borrow a word directly or indirectly. A direct borrowing means that the borrowed item is a native word in the language it is borrowed from. *Festa* was borrowed directly from French and can be traced back to Latin *festa*. On the other hand, the word *algebra* was borrowed from Spanish, which in turn borrowed it from Arabic. Thus *algebra* was indirectly borrowed from Arabic, with Spanish as an intermediary.

Some languages are heavy borrowers. Albanian has borrowed so heavily that few native words are retained. On the other hand, most Native American languages have borrowed little from their neighbors.

English has borrowed extensively. Of the 20,000 or so words in common use, about three-fifths are borrowed. Of the 500 most frequently used words, however, only two-sevenths are borrowed, and because these "common" words are used over and over again in sentences, the actual frequency of appearance of native words is about 80 percent. Morphemes such as *and, be, have, it, of, the, to, will, you, on, that*, and *is* are all native to English. (Victoria Fromkin and Robert Rodman, *An Introduction to Language*)

These paragraphs are arranged in logical order, moving from the general concept of borrowing words to a specific language (English). In addition, each topic sentence repeats a variation of the word group *A language may borrow*. Throughout the three paragraphs, some form of this word group (as well as *word* and the names of various languages) appears in almost every sentence.

EXERCISE 13.2

A. Read the following paragraph, and determine how the author achieves coherence. Underline parallel elements, repeated words, and transitional words and phrases that link sentences.

> Some years ago the old elevated railway in Philadelphia was torn down and replaced by the subway system. This ancient El with its barnlike stations containing nut-vending machines and scattered food scraps had, for generations, been the favorite feeding ground of flocks of pigeons, generally one flock to a station along the route of the El. Hundreds of pigeons were dependent upon the system. They flapped in and out of its stanchions and steel work or gathered in watchful little audiences about the feet of anyone who rattled the peanut-vending machines. They even watched people who jingled change in their hands, and prospected for food under the feet of the crowds who gathered between trains. Probably very few among the waiting people who tossed a crumb to an eager pigeon realized that this El was like a food-bearing river, and that the life which haunted its banks was dependent upon the running of the trains with their human freight. (Loren Eiseley, *The Night Country*)

B. Revise the following student paragraph to make it more coherent.

> The theory of continental drift was first put forward by Alfred Wegener in 1912. The continents fit together like a gigantic jigsaw puzzle.

The opposing Atlantic coasts, especially South America and Africa, seem to have been attached. He believed that at one time, probably 225 million years ago, there was one supercontinent. This continent broke into parts that drifted into their present positions. The theory stirred controversy during the 1920s and eventually was ridiculed by the scientific community. In 1954, the theory was revived. The theory of continental drift is accepted as a reasonable geological explanation of the continental system. (student writer)

13c Writing Well-Developed Paragraphs

A paragraph is **well developed** when it includes all the supporting information—examples, statistics, expert opinion, and so on—that readers need to understand and accept its main idea.

Keep in mind that length alone does not determine whether a paragraph is well developed. To determine the amount and kind of support you need, consider your audience, your purpose, and your paragraph's main idea.

1 Testing for Adequate Development

At first glance, the following paragraph may seem adequately developed.

Underdeveloped Paragraph

> From Thanksgiving until Christmas, children and their parents are bombarded by ads for violent toys and games. Toy manufacturers persist in thinking that only toys that appeal to children's aggressiveness will sell. Despite claims that they (unlike action toys) have educational value, video games have escalated the level of violence. The real question is why parents continue to buy these violent toys and games for their children. (student writer)

Although the paragraph above may seem to be adequately developed, it does not include enough support for its main idea—that children and parents are "bombarded by ads for violent toys and games."

2 Revising Underdeveloped Paragraphs

You can strengthen underdeveloped paragraphs like the preceding one by adding specific examples that illustrate the points made in the paragraph.

Revised Paragraph (Examples Added)

> From Thanksgiving until Christmas, children and their parents are bombarded by ads for violent toys and games. Toy manufacturers persist in thinking that only toys that appeal to children's aggressiveness will
Examples > sell. One television commercial praises the merits of a commando team that attacks and captures a miniature enemy base. Toy soldiers wear

realistic uniforms and carry automatic rifles, pistols, knives, grenades, and ammunition. Another commercial shows laughing children shooting one another with plastic rocket launchers and tanklike vehicles. Despite claims that they (unlike action toys) have educational value, video games have escalated the level of violence. The most popular video games— such as *Grand Theft Auto V* and *Resident Evil 6*—depict graphic violence, criminal behavior, nudity, and other objectionable material. One game allows players to hack up and destroy zombies with a variety of weapons, such as swords, picks, and chainsaws as well as guns and grenades. Other best-selling games graphically simulate hand-to-hand combat on city streets and feature dismembered bodies and the sound of breaking bones. The real question is why parents continue to buy these violent toys and games for their children.

Examples (margin note)

EXERCISE 13.3

Write a paragraph for two of the following topic sentences. Be sure to include all the examples and other support necessary to develop the paragraphs adequately. Assume that you are writing your paragraphs for the students in your composition class.

1. First-year students can take specific steps to make sure that they are successful in college.
2. Setting up a first apartment can be quite a challenge.
3. Whenever I get depressed, I think of _____, and I feel better.
4. The person I admire most is _____.
5. If I won the lottery, I would do three things.

13d Patterns of Paragraph Development

Patterns of paragraph development—*narration, description, exemplification,* and so on—reflect the way a writer arranges material to express ideas most effectively.

1 Narration

A **narrative** paragraph tells a story by presenting events in chronological (time) order. Most narratives move in a logical, orderly sequence from beginning to end, from first event to last. Clear transitional words and phrases (*later, after that*) and time markers (*in 1990, two years earlier, the next day*) establish the chronological sequence.

My academic career almost ended as soon as it began when, three weeks after I arrived at college, I decided to pledge a fraternity. By midterms, I was wearing a pledge cap and saying "Yes, sir" to every fraternity brother I met. When classes were over, I ran errands for the fraternity members, and after dinner I socialized and worked on projects with the other people in my pledge class. In between these activities, I

Topic sentence establishes subject of narrative

Sequence of events (margin notes)

tried to study. Somehow I managed to write essays, take tests, and attend lectures. By the end of the semester, though, my grades had slipped, and I was exhausted. It was then that I began to ask myself some important questions. I realized that I wanted to be popular, but not at the expense of my grades and my future career. At the beginning of my second semester, I dropped out of the fraternity and got a job in the biology lab. Looking back, I realize that it was then that I actually began to grow up. (student writer)

2 Description

A **descriptive** paragraph communicates how something looks, sounds, smells, tastes, or feels. The most natural arrangement of details in a description reflects the way you actually look at a person, scene, or object: near to far, top to bottom, side to side, or front to back. This arrangement of details is made clear by transitions that identify precise spatial relationships: *next to, near, beside, under, above,* and so on.

Sometimes a descriptive paragraph (such as the one below) does not have an explicitly stated topic sentence. Instead, it is unified by a **dominant impression**—the central or unifying mood created by the details in the description.

No topic sentence

Details create dominant impression

When you are inside the jungle, away from the river, the trees vault out of sight. It is hard to remember to look up the long trunks and see the fans, strips, fronds, and sprays of glossy leaves. Inside the jungle you are more likely to notice the snarl of climbers and creepers round the trees' boles, the flowering bromeliads and epiphytes in every bough's crook, and the fantastic silk-cotton tree trunks thirty or forty feet across, trunks buttressed in flanges of wood whose curves can make three high walls of a room—a shady, loamy-aired room where you would gladly live, or die. (Annie Dillard, "In the Jungle")

3 Exemplification

An **exemplification** paragraph supports a topic sentence with a series of specific examples (or, sometimes, with a single extended example). These examples can be drawn from observation, experience, or research.

Topic sentence identifies paragraph's main idea

Series of examples

Illiterates cannot travel freely. When they attempt to do so, they encounter risks that few of us can dream of. They cannot read traffic signs and, while they often learn to recognize and to decipher symbols, they cannot manage street names which they haven't seen before. The same is true for bus and subway stops. While ingenuity can sometimes help a man or woman to discern directions from familiar landmarks, buildings, cemeteries, churches, and the like, most illiterates are virtually immobilized. They seldom wander past the streets and neighborhoods they know. Geographical paralysis becomes a bitter metaphor for their entire existence. They are immobilized in almost every sense we can imagine. They can't move up. They can't move out. They cannot see beyond. Illiterates may take an oral test for drivers' permits in most sections of America. It is a questionable concession. Where will they go? How will they get there? How will they get home? Could it be that some of us might like it better if they stayed where they belong? (Jonathan Kozol, *Illiterate America*)

4 Process

Process paragraphs describe how something works, presenting a series of steps in strict chronological order. The topic sentence identifies the process, and the rest of the paragraph presents the steps. Transitional words such as *first, then, next, after this,* and *finally* link steps in the process.

> Members of the court have disclosed, however, the general way the conference is conducted. It begins at ten A.M. and usually runs on until late afternoon. At the start each justice, when he enters the room, shakes hands with all others there (thirty-six handshakes altogether). The custom, dating back generations, is evidently designed to begin the meeting at a friendly level, no matter how heated the intellectual differences may be. The conference takes up, first, the applications for review—a few appeals, many more petitions for certiorari. Those on the Appellate Docket, the regular paid cases, are considered first, then the pauper's applications on the Miscellaneous Docket. (If any of these are granted, they are then transferred to the Appellate Docket.) After this the justices consider, and vote on, all the cases argued during the preceding Monday through Thursday. These are tentative votes, which may be and quite often are changed as the opinion is written and the problem thought through more deeply. There may be further discussion at later conferences before the opinion is handed down. (Anthony Lewis, *Gideon's Trumpet*)

Topic sentence identifies process

Steps in process

Close-Up INSTRUCTIONS

When a process paragraph presents **instructions** to enable readers to actually perform the process, it is written in the present tense and in the imperative mood—"*Remove* the cover . . . and *check* the valve."

5 Cause and Effect

A **cause-and-effect** paragraph explores causes or predicts or describes results; sometimes a single cause-and-effect paragraph does both. Clear transitional words and phrases such as *one cause, another cause, a more important result, because,* and *as a result* convey the cause-and-effect relationship.

Some paragraphs examine **causes**.

> The main reason that a young baby sucks his thumb seems to be that he hasn't had enough sucking at the breast or bottle to satisfy his sucking needs. Dr. David Levy pointed out that babies who are fed every 3 hours don't suck their thumbs as much as babies fed every 4 hours, and that babies who have cut down on nursing time from 20 minutes to 10 minutes . . . are more likely to suck their thumbs than babies who still have to work for 20 minutes. Dr. Levy fed a litter of puppies with a medicine dropper so that they had no chance

Topic sentence establishes major cause

Cause explored in detail

to suck during their feedings. They acted just the same as babies who don't get enough chance to suck at feeding time. They sucked their own and each other's paws and skin so hard that the fur came off. (Benjamin Spock, *Baby and Child Care*)

Other paragraphs focus on **effects**.

Topic sentence establishes major effect

Discussion of other effects

On December 8, 1941, the day after the Japanese attack on Pearl Harbor in Hawaii, my grandfather barricaded himself with his family—my grandmother, my teenage mother, her two sisters and two brothers—inside of his home in La'ie, a sugar plantation village on Oahu's North Shore. This was my maternal grandfather, a man most villagers called by his last name, Kubota. It could mean either "Wayside Field" or else "Broken Dreams," depending on which ideograms he used. Kubota ran La'ie's general store, and the previous night, after a long day of bad news on the radio, some locals had come by, pounded on the front door, and made threats. One was said to have brandished a machete. They were angry and shocked, as the whole nation was in the aftermath of the surprise attack. Kubota was one of the few Japanese Americans in the village and president of the local Japanese language school. He had become a target for their rage and suspicion. A wise man, he locked all his doors and windows and did not open his store the next day, but stayed closed and waited for news from some official. (Garrett Hongo, "Kubota")

6 Comparison and Contrast

Comparison-and-contrast paragraphs examine the similarities and differences between two subjects. **Comparison** focuses on similarities; **contrast** emphasizes differences. A comparison-and-contrast paragraph can be organized in one of two ways: **point-by-point** or **subject-by-subject**.

Point-by-point comparisons discuss two subjects together, alternating points about one subject with comparable points about the other.

Topic sentence establishes comparison

Alternating points about the two subjects

There are two Americas. One is the America of Lincoln and Adlai Stevenson; the other is the America of Teddy Roosevelt and the modern superpatriots. One is generous and humane, the other narrowly egotistical; one is self-critical, the other self-righteous; one is sensible, the other romantic; one is good-humored, the other solemn; one is inquiring, the other pontificating; one is moderate, the other filled with passionate intensity; one is judicious and the other arrogant in the use of great power. (J. William Fulbright, *The Arrogance of Power*)

Subject-by-subject comparisons treat one subject completely and then move on to the other subject. In the following paragraph, the writer shifts from one subject to the other with the transitional word *however*.

First, it is important to note that men and women regard conversation quite differently. For women it is a passion, a sport, an activity even more important to life than eating because it doesn't involve weight gain. The first sign of closeness among women is when they find themselves engaging in endless, secretless rounds of conversation with one another. And as soon as a woman begins to relax and feel comfortable in a relationship with a man, she tries to have that type of conversation with him as well. However, the first sign that a man is feeling close to a woman is when he admits that he'd rather she please quiet down so he can hear the TV. A man who feels truly intimate with a woman often reserves for her and her alone the precious gift of one-word answers. Everyone knows that the surest way to spot a successful long-term relationship is to look around a restaurant for the table where no one is talking. Ah . . . now that's real love. (Merrill Markoe, "Men, Women, and Conversation")

Topic sentence establishes comparison

First subject discussed

Second subject discussed

7 Division and Classification

Division paragraphs take a single item and break it into its components.

The blood can be divided into four distinct components: plasma, red cells, white cells, and platelets. Plasma is 90 percent water and holds a great number of substances in suspension. It contains proteins, sugars, fat, and inorganic salts. Plasma also contains urea and other by-products from the breaking down of proteins, hormones, enzymes, and dissolved gases. In addition, plasma contains the red blood cells that give it color, the white cells, and the platelets. The red cells are most numerous; they get oxygen from the lungs and release it in the tissues. The less numerous white cells are part of the body's defense against invading organisms. The platelets, which occur in almost the same number as white cells, are responsible for clotting. (student writer)

Topic sentence identifies components

Components discussed

Classification paragraphs take many separate items and group them into categories according to the qualities or characteristics they share.

Charles Babbage, an English mathematician, reflecting in 1830 on what he saw as the decline of science at the time, distinguished among three major kinds of scientific fraud. He called the first "forging," by which he meant complete fabrication—the recording of observations that were never made. The second category he called "trimming"; this consists of manipulating the data to make them look better, or, as Babbage wrote, "in clipping off little bits here and there from those observations which differ most in excess from the mean and in sticking them on to those which are too small." His third category was data selection, which he called "cooking"—the choosing of those data that fitted the researcher's hypothesis and the discarding of those that did not. To this day, the serious discussion of scientific fraud has not improved on Babbage's typology. (Morton Hunt, *New York Times Magazine*)

Topic sentence establishes categories

Categories discussed

8 Definition

Definition paragraphs develop formal definitions by using other patterns—for instance, defining *happiness* by telling a story (narration) or defining a hybrid car by explaining how it works (process).

The following definition paragraph is developed by means of exemplification: it begins with a formal definition of *gadget* and then presents an example.

Topic sentence gives formal definition

Definition expanded with examples

A gadget is a small device that is nearly always novel in design or concept and it often has no proper name. For example, the semaphore which signals the arrival of the mail in our rural mailbox certainly has no proper name. It is a contrivance consisting of a piece of shingle. Call it what you like, it saves us frequent frustrating trips to the mailbox in winter when you have to dress up and wade through snow to get there. That's a gadget! (*Smithsonian*)

EXERCISE 13.4

A. Read each of the following paragraphs, and then answer these questions: In general terms, how could each paragraph be developed further? What pattern of development might be used in each case?

B. Choose one paragraph, and rewrite it to develop it further.

1. Many new words and expressions have entered the English language in the last couple of decades. Some of them come from the world of computers. Others come from popular music. Still others have politics as their source. There are even some expressions that have their origins in films or television shows.

2. Making a good spaghetti sauce is not a particularly challenging task. First, assemble the basic ingredients: garlic, onion, mushrooms, green pepper, and ground beef. Sauté these ingredients in a large saucepan. Then, add canned tomatoes, tomato paste, and water, and stir. At this point, you are ready to add the spices: oregano, parsley, basil, and salt and pepper. Don't forget a bay leaf! Simmer for about two hours, and serve over spaghetti.

3. High school and college are not at all alike. Courses are a lot easier in high school, and the course load is lighter. In college, teachers expect more from students; they expect higher quality work, and they assign more of it. Assignments tend to be more difficult and more comprehensive, and deadlines are usually shorter. Finally, college students tend to be more focused on a particular course of study—even a particular career—than high school students are.

13e Writing Special Kinds of Paragraphs

So far, this chapter has focused on **body paragraphs**, the paragraphs that carry the weight of your essay's discussion. Other kinds of paragraphs—*transitional paragraphs, introductory paragraphs,* and *concluding paragraphs*—have special functions in an essay.

1 Transitional Paragraphs

A **transitional paragraph** connects one section of an essay to another. At their simplest, transitional paragraphs can be single sentences that move readers from one point to the next.

What is true for ants is also true for people.

More often, however, writers use transitional paragraphs to summarize what they have already said before they move on to a new point. The following transitional paragraph uses a series of questions to sum up some of the ideas the writer has been discussing. In the next part of his essay, he goes on to answer these questions.

Can we bleed off the mass of humanity to other worlds? Right now the number of human beings on Earth is increasing by 80 million per year, and each year that number goes up by 1 and a fraction percent. Can we really suppose that we can send 80 million people per year to the Moon, Mars, and elsewhere, and engineer those worlds to support those people? And even so, nearly remain in the same place ourselves? (Isaac Asimov, "The Case against Man")

2 Introductory Paragraphs

An **introductory paragraph** prepares readers for the essay to follow. It typically introduces the subject, narrows it, and then states the essay's thesis.

Christine was just a girl in one of my classes. I never knew much about her except that she was strange. She didn't talk much. Her hair was dyed black and purple, and she wore heavy black boots and a black turtleneck sweater, even in the summer. She was attractive—in spite of the ring she wore through her left eyebrow—but she never seemed to care what the rest of us thought about her. Like the rest of my classmates, I didn't really want to get close to her. It was only when we were assigned to do our chemistry project together that I began to understand why Christine dressed the way she did. (student writer)

To arouse their audience's interest, writers may vary this direct approach by using one of the following introductory strategies.

Strategies for Effective Introductions

Quotation or Series of Quotations

When Mary Cassatt's father was told of her decision to become a painter, he said: "I would rather see you dead." When Edgar Degas saw a show of Cassatt's etchings, his response was: "I am not willing to admit that a woman can draw that well." (Mary Gordon, "Mary Cassatt")

Question or Series of Questions

Of all the disputes agitating the American campus, the one that seems to me especially significant is that over "the canon." What should be taught in the humanities and social sciences, especially in introductory courses? What is the place of the classics? How shall we respond to those professors who attack "Eurocentrism" and advocate "multiculturalism"? This is not the sort of tedious quarrel that now and then flutters through the academy; it involves matters of public urgency. I propose to see this dispute, at first, through a narrow, even sectarian lens, with the hope that you will come to accept my reasons for doing so. (Irving Howe, "The Value of the Canon")

Definition

Moles are collections of cells that can appear on any part of the body. With occasional exceptions, moles are absent at birth. They first appear in the early years of life, between ages two and six. Frequently, moles appear at puberty. New moles, however, can continue to appear throughout life. During pregnancy, new moles may appear and old ones darken. There are three major designations of moles, each with its own unique distinguishing characteristics. (student writer)

Controversial Statement

Many Americans would probably be surprised to learn that Head Start has not been an unqualified success. Founded in 1965, the Head Start program provides early childhood education, social services, and medical check-ups to poor children across the United States. In recent years, it has also focused on the children of migrant workers and on children who are homeless. For the most part, Americans view Head Start not just as a success but also as a model for other social programs. What many people do not know, however, is that although Head Start is a short-term success for many children, the ambitious long-term goals of the program have not been met. For this reason, it may be time to consider making significant changes in the way Head Start is run. (student writer)

Close-Up INTRODUCTORY PARAGRAPHS

An introductory paragraph should make readers want to read further. For this reason, avoid opening statements that simply announce your subject ("In my essay, I will talk about Lady Macbeth") or that undercut your credibility ("I don't know much about alternative energy sources, but I would like to present my opinion about the subject").

3 Concluding Paragraphs

A **concluding paragraph** typically begins by reinforcing the essay's thesis and then moves to more general comments. Whenever possible, it should end with a sentence that readers will remember.

> As an Arab-American, I feel I have the best of two worlds. I'm proud to be part of the melting pot, proud to contribute to the tremendous diversity of cultures, customs and traditions that makes this country unique. But Arab-bashing—public acceptance of hatred and bigotry—is something no American can be proud of. (Ellen Mansoor Collier, "I Am Not a Terrorist")

Writers may also use any of the following concluding strategies to end their essays.

Strategies for Effective Conclusions

Prediction

Looking ahead, [we see that] prospects may not be quite as dismal as they seem. As a matter of fact, we are not doing so badly. It is something of a miracle that creatures who evolved as nomads in an intimate, small-band, wide-open-spaces context manage to get along at all as villagers or surrounded by strangers in cubicle apartments. Considering that our genius as a species is adaptability, we may yet learn to live closer and closer to one another, if not in utter peace, then far more peacefully than we do today. (John Pheiffer, "Seeking Peace, Making War")

Warning

The Internet is the twenty-first century's talking drum, the very kind of grassroots communication tool that has been such a powerful source of education and culture for our people since slavery. But this talking drum we have not yet learned to play. Unless we master the new information

(continued)

Strategies for Effective Conclusions (*continued*)

technology to build and deepen the forms of social connection that a tragic history has eroded, African-Americans will face a form of cyber-segregation in the next century as devastating to our aspirations as Jim Crow segregation was to those of our ancestors. But this time, the fault will be our own. (Henry Louis Gates Jr., "One Internet, Two Nations")

Recommendation for Action

Computers have revolutionized learning in ways that we have barely begun to appreciate. We have experienced enough, however, to recognize the need to change our thinking about our purposes, methods, and outcome of higher education. Rather than resisting or postponing change, we need to anticipate and learn from it. We must harness the technology and use it to educate our students more effectively than we have been doing. Otherwise, we will surrender our authority to those who can. (Peshe Kuriloff, "If John Dewey Were Alive Today, He'd Be a Webhead")

Quotation

Apart from what any critic had to say about my writing. I knew I had succeeded where it counted when my mother finished reading my book and gave me her verdict: "So easy to read." (Amy Tan, "Mother Tongue")

Close-Up   CONCLUDING PARAGRAPHS

Because a dull conclusion can weaken an essay, try to make your conclusion as interesting as you can. Your conclusion is your essay's last word, so don't waste time repeating your introduction in different words or apologizing or undercutting your credibility ("I may not be an expert" or "At least, this is my opinion"). And remember, your conclusion should not introduce new points or go off in new directions.

Building Sentences

A **sentence** is an independent grammatical unit that includes a subject and a predicate and expresses a complete thought.

The quick brown fox jumped over the lazy dog.

It came from outer space.

A **simple subject** is a noun or noun substitute (*fox, it*) that tells who or what the sentence is about. A **simple predicate** is a verb or **verb phrase** (*jumped, came*) that tells or asks something about the subject. The **complete subject** of a sentence includes the simple subject plus all its modifiers (*the quick brown fox*). The **complete predicate** includes the verb or verb phrase as well as all the words associated with it—such as modifiers, objects, and complements (*jumped over the lazy dog, came from outer space*).

See
14b1

> **MULTILINGUAL TIP**
>
> In some languages, such as Spanish, the subject of a sentence can sometimes be omitted. In English, however, every sentence must have a subject.

14a   Constructing Simple Sentences

A **simple sentence** consists of at least one subject and one predicate. Simple sentences conform to one of five basic patterns.

1 Subject + Intransitive Verb (s + v)

The most basic simple sentence consists of just a subject and a verb or **verb phrase** (the **main verb** plus all its **auxiliary verbs**).

See
20c1

s   v

The price of gold rose.

s   v

Stock prices may fall.

Here the verbs *rose* and *may fall* are **intransitive**—that is, they do not need an object to complete their meaning.

2 Subject + Transitive Verb + Direct Object (s + v + do)

Another kind of simple sentence consists of the subject, a verb, and a direct object.

MULTILINGUAL TIP

To determine whether a verb is intransitive or transitive, consult a dictionary. Remember, though, that some verbs, such as *write*, can be intransitive or transitive.

She <u>wrote</u> all night. (intransitive)

She <u>wrote</u> an essay about her semester in Spain. (transitive)

    s   v   do
<u>Van Gogh</u> <u>created</u> *The Starry Night.*

    s v do
<u>Caroline</u> <u>saved</u> Jake.

Here the verbs *created* and *saved* are **transitive**—each requires an object to complete its meaning in the sentence. In each sentence, the **direct object** indicates where the verb's action is directed and who or what is affected by it.

3 Subject + Transitive Verb + Direct Object + Object Complement (s + v + do + oc)

Some simple sentences include an **object complement**, a word or phrase that renames or describes the direct object.

   s v do oc
The <u>class</u> <u>elected</u> Bridget treasurer. (Object complement *treasurer* renames direct object *Bridget.*)

 s v   do oc
I <u>found</u> the exam easy. (Object complement *easy* describes direct object *exam.*)

4 Subject + Linking Verb + Subject Complement (s + v + sc)

See 20c1

Another kind of simple sentence consists of a subject, a **linking verb** (a verb that connects a subject to its complement), and the **subject complement** (the word or phrase that describes or renames the subject).

   s   v sc
The <u>injection</u> <u>was</u> painless.

   s   v sc
The <u>frog</u> <u>became</u> a prince.

Note that the linking verb is like an equal sign, equating the subject with its complement (*frog = prince*).

5 **Subject + Transitive Verb + Indirect Object + Direct Object (s + v + io + do)**

Some simple sentences include an **indirect object**, which indicates to whom or for whom the verb's action was done.

s   v   io   do

Cyrano <u>wrote</u> Roxanne a poem. (Cyrano wrote a poem for Roxanne.)

s   v   io   do

The officer <u>handed</u> Frank a ticket. (The officer handed a ticket to Frank.)

EXERCISE 14.1

In each of the following sentences, underline the subject once and the predicate twice. Then, label direct objects (DO), indirect objects (IO), subject complements (SC), and object complements (OC).

sc

Example: Isaac Asimov <u>was</u> a science fiction writer.

1. Isaac Asimov first saw science fiction stories in his parents' Brooklyn store.
2. He practiced writing by telling his schoolmates stories.
3. Asimov published his first story in *Astounding Science Fiction*.
4. The magazine's editor, John W. Campbell, encouraged Asimov to continue writing.
5. The young writer researched scientific principles to make his stories more accurate.
6. Asimov's "Foundation" series of novels is a "future history."
7. The World Science Fiction Convention gave the series a Hugo Award.
8. Sometimes Asimov used "Paul French" as a pseudonym.
9. *Biochemistry and Human Metabolism* was Asimov's first nonfiction book.
10. Asimov coined the term *robotics*.

14b Identifying Phrases and Clauses

Individual words may be combined into *phrases* and *clauses*.

1 Identifying Phrases

A **phrase** is a group of related words that lacks a subject or predicate or both and functions as a single part of speech. It cannot stand alone as a sentence.

- A **verb phrase** consists of a main verb and all its auxiliary verbs.

  Time <u>is flying</u>.

- A **noun phrase** includes a noun or pronoun plus all related modifiers.

  I'll climb <u>the highest mountain</u>.

- A **prepositional phrase** consists of a preposition, its object, and any modifiers of that object.

They discussed the ethical implications <u>of the animal studies</u>.

He was last seen heading <u>into the orange sunset</u>.

- A **verbal phrase** consists of a **verbal** (participle, gerund, or infinitive) and its related objects, modifiers, or complements. A verbal phrase may be a **participial phrase**, a **gerund phrase**, or an **infinitive phrase**.

<u>Encouraged by the voter turnout</u>, the candidate predicted a victory. (participial phrase)

<u>Taking it easy</u> always makes sense. (gerund phrase)

The jury recessed <u>to evaluate the evidence</u>. (infinitive phrase)

- An **absolute phrase** usually consists of a noun and a participle, accompanied by modifiers. It modifies an entire independent clause rather than a particular word or phrase.

<u>Their toes tapping</u>, they watched the auditions.

2 Identifying Clauses

A **clause** is a group of related words that includes a subject and a predicate. An **independent** (main) **clause** can stand alone as a sentence, but a **dependent** (subordinate) **clause** cannot. It must always be combined with an independent clause to form a **complex sentence**.

See 14d

[Lucretia Mott was an abolitionist.] [She was also a pioneer for women's rights.] (two independent clauses)

[Lucretia Mott was an abolitionist] [who was also a pioneer for women's rights.] (independent clause, dependent clause)

[Although Lucretia Mott is widely known for her support of women's rights,] [she was also a prominent abolitionist.] (dependent clause, independent clause)

Dependent clauses may be *adjective*, *adverb*, or *noun* clauses.

- **Adjective clauses**, sometimes called **relative clauses**, modify nouns or pronouns and always follow the nouns or pronouns they modify. They are introduced by relative pronouns—*that, what, whatever, which, who, whose, whom, whoever,* or *whomever*—or by the adverbs *where* or *when*.

The television series *M*A*S*H*, <u>which depicted life in an army hospital in Korea during the Korean War</u>, ran for eleven years. (Adjective clause modifies the noun *M*A*S*H*.)

William Styron's novel *Sophie's Choice* is set in Brooklyn, <u>where the narrator lives in a house painted pink</u>. (Adjective clause modifies the noun *Brooklyn*.)

- **Adverb clauses** modify single words (verbs, adjectives, or adverbs), entire phrases, or independent clauses. They are always introduced by subordinating conjunctions. Adverb clauses provide information to answer the questions *how? where? when? why?* and *to what extent?*

Exhausted <u>after the match was over</u>, Kim decided to take a long nap. (Adverb clause modifies *exhausted*, telling *when* Kim was exhausted.)

Mark will go <u>wherever there's a party</u>. (Adverb clause modifies *will go*, telling *where* Mark will go.)

<u>Because 75 percent of its exports are fish products</u>, Iceland's economy is heavily dependent on the fishing industry. (Adverb clause modifies independent clause, telling *why* the fishing industry is so important.)

- **Noun clauses** function as subjects, objects, or complements. A noun clause may be introduced by a relative pronoun or by *whether, when, where, why*, or *how*.

<u>What you see</u> is <u>what you get</u>. (Noun clauses serve as subject and subject complement.)

They finally decided <u>which candidate was most qualified</u>. (Noun clause serves as direct object of verb *decided*.)

Note: Some dependent clauses, called **elliptical clauses**, are grammatically incomplete but can still be easily understood from the context of the sentence. Typically, a part of the subject or predicate (or the entire subject or predicate) is missing: *Although [they were] full, they could not resist dessert.*

EXERCISE 14.2

Which of the following groups of words are independent clauses? Which are dependent clauses? Which are phrases? Label each word group *IC, DC,* or *P.*

Example: Coming through the rye. (P)

1. Beauty is truth.
2. When knights were bold.
3. In a galaxy far away.
4. He saw stars.
5. I hear a symphony.
6. Whenever you're near.
7. The clock struck ten.
8. The red planet.
9. Slowly I turned.
10. For the longest time.

14c Building Compound Sentences

A **compound sentence** consists of two or more independent clauses joined with *coordinating conjunctions, transitional words or phrases, correlative conjunctions, semicolons,* or *colons.*

1 Using Coordinating Conjunctions

You can join two independent clauses with a **coordinating conjunction**—*and, or, nor, but, for, so,* or *yet*—preceded by a comma.

She carried a thin, small cane made from an umbrella, and with this she kept tapping the frozen earth in front of her. (Eudora Welty, "A Worn Path")

In the fall the war was always there, but we did not go to it any more. (Ernest Hemingway, "In Another Country")

2 Using Transitional Words and Phrases

You can join two independent clauses with a **transitional word or phrase**, preceded by a semicolon (and followed by a comma).

Aerobic exercise can help lower blood pressure; however, people with high blood pressure should still limit salt intake.

The saxophone does not belong to the brass family; in fact, it is a member of the woodwind family.

See 13b2

Note: Commonly used transitional words and phrases include **conjunctive adverbs** such as *however, therefore, nevertheless, consequently, finally, still,* and *thus* as well as expressions such as *for example, in fact, on the other hand,* and *for instance.*

3 Using Correlative Conjunctions

See 20g

You can use correlative conjunctions to join two independent clauses into a compound sentence.

Either he left his coat in his locker, or he left it on the bus.

4 Using Semicolons

See 31a

A semicolon can join two closely related independent clauses into a compound sentence.

Alaska is the largest state; Rhode Island is the smallest.

Theodore Roosevelt was president after the Spanish-American War; Andrew Johnson was president after the Civil War.

5 Using Colons

A colon can join two independent clauses.

See 34a

He got his orders: he was to leave for Fort Drum on Sunday.

They thought they knew the outcome: Truman would lose to Dewey.

Close-Up USING COMPOUND SENTENCES

Joining independent clauses into compound sentences helps to show readers the relationships between the clauses. Compound sentences can indicate the following relationships:

- Addition (*and, in addition, not only . . . but also*)
- Contrast (*but, however*)
- Causal relationships (*so, therefore, consequently*)
- Alternatives (*or, either . . . or*)

EXERCISE 14.3

Add appropriate coordinating conjunctions, transitional words or phrases, or correlative conjunctions (as indicated) to combine each pair of sentences into one well-constructed compound sentence that retains the meaning of the original pair. Be sure to use correct punctuation.

Example: The American population is aging, so people People seem to be increasingly concerned about what they eat. (coordinating conjunction)

1. The average American consumes more than 150 pounds of sugar each year. Most of us eat much more sugar than any other food additive, including salt. (transitional word or phrase)
2. Many of us are determined to reduce our sugar intake. We have consciously eliminated sweets from our diets. (transitional word or phrase)
3. Unfortunately, sugar is not found only in sweets. It is also found in many processed foods. (correlative conjunction)
4. Processed foods such as puddings and cake contain sugar. Foods such as ketchup and spaghetti sauce do too. (coordinating conjunction)
5. We are trying to cut down on sugar. We find limiting sugar intake extremely difficult. (coordinating conjunction)
6. Processors may use sugar in foods for taste. They may also use it to help prevent foods from spoiling and to improve the texture and appearance of food. (correlative conjunction)

7. Sugar comes in many different forms. It is easy to overlook on a package label. (coordinating conjunction)
8. Sugar may be called sucrose or fructose. It may also be called corn syrup, corn sugar, brown sugar, honey, or molasses. (coordinating conjunction)
9. No sugar is more nourishing than the others. It really does not matter which is consumed. (transitional word or phrase)
10. Sugars contain empty calories. Whenever possible, they should be avoided. (transitional word or phrase)

(Adapted from *Jane Brody's Nutrition Book*)

14d Building Complex Sentences

A **complex sentence** consists of one **independent clause** and at least one **dependent clause**.

A dependent clause cannot stand alone; it must be combined with an independent clause to form a sentence. In a complex sentence, a **subordinating conjunction** or **relative pronoun** links the independent and dependent clauses and indicates the relationship between them.

dependent clause   independent clause
[<u>After</u> the town was evacuated,] [the hurricane began.]

independent clause   dependent clause
[Officials watched the storm,] [<u>which</u> threatened to destroy the town.]

Note: Sometimes a dependent clause may be embedded within an independent clause.

dependent clause
Town officials, [<u>who</u> were very concerned,] watched the storm.

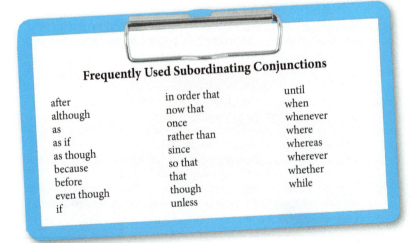

Frequently Used Subordinating Conjunctions

after	in order that	until
although	now that	when
as	once	whenever
as if	rather than	where
as though	since	whereas
because	so that	wherever
before	that	whether
even though	though	while
if	unless	

Relative Pronouns

that	whatever	who (whose, whom)
what	which	whoever (whomever)

Close-Up   USING COMPLEX SENTENCES

When you join clauses to create complex sentences, you help readers to see the relationships between your ideas. Complex sentences can indicate the following relationships:

- Time relationships (*before, after, until, when, since*)
- Contrast (*however, although*)
- Causal relationships (*therefore, because, so that*)
- Conditional relationships (*if, unless*)
- Location (*where, wherever*)
- Identity (*who, which, that*)

EXERCISE 14.4

Use a subordinating conjunction or relative pronoun to combine each of the following pairs of sentences into one well-constructed complex sentence. Be sure to choose a connecting word that indicates the relationship between the two sentences. You may have to change or reorder words.

Example: ~~Some~~ *Because some* colleges are tightening admissions requirements~~.~~ *, their* ~~Their~~ pool of students is growing smaller.

1. Many high school graduates are currently out of work. They need new skills for new careers.
2. Talented high school students are usually encouraged to go to college. Some high school graduates are now starting to see that a college education may not guarantee them a job.
3. A college education can cost a student more than $100,000. Vocational education is becoming an increasingly attractive alternative.
4. Vocational students complete their work in fewer than four years. They can enter the job market more quickly.
5. Nurses' aides, paralegals, travel agents, and computer technicians do not need college degrees. They have little trouble finding work.

6. Some four-year colleges are experiencing growth. Public community colleges and private trade schools are growing much more rapidly.
7. The best vocational schools are responsive to the needs of local businesses. They train students for jobs that actually exist.
8. For instance, a school in Detroit might offer advanced automotive design. A school in New York City might focus on fashion design.
9. Other schools offer courses in horticulture, respiratory therapy, and computer programming. They are able to place their graduates easily.
10. Laid-off workers, recent high school graduates, and even college graduates are reexamining vocational education. They all hope to find rewarding careers.

Close-Up COMPOUND-COMPLEX SENTENCES

A **compound-complex sentence** consists of two or more independent clauses and at least one dependent clause.

dependent clause
[When small foreign imports began dominating the US automobile
           independent clause   independent clause
industry,] [consumers were very responsive,] but [American auto workers

were dismayed.]

CHAPTER **15**

Writing Varied Sentences

Using **varied** sentences can make your writing livelier and more interesting and can also ensure that you emphasize the most important ideas in your sentences.

15a Varying Sentence Length

Strings of short simple sentences can be tedious—and sometimes hard to follow, as the following paragraph illustrates.

John Peter Zenger was a newspaper editor. He waged and won an important battle for freedom of the press in America. He criticized the policies of the British governor. He was charged with criminal libel as a result. Zenger's lawyers were disbarred. Andrew Hamilton defended him. Hamilton convinced the jury that Zenger's criticisms were true. Therefore, the statements were not libelous.

You can revise choppy sentences like the ones in the paragraph above by using *coordination, subordination,* or *embedding* to combine them with adjacent sentences.

❶ Using Coordination

Coordination pairs similar elements—words, phrases, or clauses—giving equal weight to each. The following revision links two of the choppy simple sentences in the paragraph above with *and* to create a **compound sentence**.

See 14c

John Peter Zenger was a newspaper editor. He waged and won an important battle for freedom of the press in America. He criticized the policies of the British governor, and as a result, he was charged with criminal libel. Zenger's lawyers were disbarred. Andrew Hamilton defended him. Hamilton convinced the jury that Zenger's criticisms were true. Therefore, the statements were not libelous.

❷ Using Subordination

Subordination places the more important idea in the independent clause and the less important idea in the dependent clause. The following revision of the preceding paragraph uses subordination to change two simple sentences into dependent clauses, creating two **complex sentences**.

See 14d

John Peter Zenger was a newspaper editor who waged and won an important battle for freedom of the press in America. He criticized the policies of the British governor, and as a result, he was charged with criminal libel. When Zenger's lawyers were disbarred, Andrew Hamilton defended him. Hamilton convinced the jury that Zenger's criticisms were true. Therefore, the statements were not libelous.

❸ Using Embedding

Embedding is the working of additional words and phrases into a sentence. In the following revision, the sentence *Hamilton convinced the jury . . .* has been reworded to create a phrase (*convincing the jury*) that is embedded into another sentence, where it now modifies the independent clause *Andrew Hamilton defended him.*

MULTILINGUAL TIP

Some multilingual students rely on simple sentences and coordination in their writing because they are afraid of making sentence structure errors. The result is a monotonous style. To add variety, try using **subordination** and **embedding** (explained in **15a2** and **15a3**) in your sentences.

John Peter Zenger was a newspaper editor who waged and won an important battle for freedom of the press in America. He criticized the policies of the British governor, and as a result, he was charged with criminal libel. When Zenger's lawyers were disbarred, Andrew Hamilton defended him, convincing the jury that Zenger's criticisms were true. Therefore, the statements were not libelous.

This final revision of the original string of choppy sentences is interesting and readable because its sentences are varied and logically linked. The short simple sentence at the end has been retained for emphasis.

EXERCISE 15.1

Using coordination, subordination, and embedding, revise this string of choppy simple sentences into a more varied and interesting paragraph.

▶The first modern miniature golf course was built in New York in 1925. ▶It was an indoor course with 18 holes. ▶Entrepreneurs Drake Delanoy and John Ledbetter built 150 more indoor and outdoor courses. ▶Garnet Carter made miniature golf a worldwide fad. ▶Carter built an elaborate miniature golf course. ▶He later joined with Delanoy and Ledbetter. ▶Together they built more miniature golf courses. They abbreviated playing distances. They highlighted the game's hazards at the expense of skill. This made the game much more popular. By 1930, there were 25,000 miniature golf courses in the United States. Courses grew more elaborate. Hazards grew more bizarre. The craze spread to London and Hong Kong. The expansion of miniature golf grew out of control. Then, interest in the game declined. By 1931, most miniature golf courses were out of business. The game was revived in the early 1950s. Today, there are between eight and ten thousand miniature golf courses. The architecture of miniature golf remains an enduring form of American folk art. (Adapted from *Games*)

15b Varying Sentence Openings

Rather than beginning every sentence with the subject (*I* or *It*, for example), add interest and variety by beginning with a modifying *word*, *phrase*, or *clause*.

Beginning with Modifying Words

Proud and relieved, they watched their daughter receive her diploma. (adjectives)

Hungrily, he devoured his lunch. (adverb)

Beginning with Modifying Phrases

For better or worse, credit cards are now widely available to college students. (prepositional phrase)

Located on the west coast of Great Britain, Wales is part of the United Kingdom. (participial phrase)

His artistic interests expanding, Picasso designed ballet sets and illustrated books. (absolute phrase)

Beginning with Modifying Clauses

<u>After President Woodrow Wilson was incapacitated by a stroke,</u> his wife unofficially performed many presidential duties. (adverb clause)

EXERCISE 15.2

Each of these sentences begins with the subject. Revise each so that it has a different opening; then, identify your opening strategy.

In The Names,

Example: N. Scott Momaday, the prominent Native American writer, tells the story of his first fourteen years ⌃ in *The Names.* (prepositional phrase)

1. Momaday was taken as a very young child to Devil's Tower, the geological formation in Wyoming that is called Tsoai (Bear Tree) in Kiowa, and there he was given the name Tsoai-talee (Bear Tree Boy).
2. The Kiowa myth of the origin of Tsoai is about a boy who playfully chases his seven sisters up a tree, which rises into the air as the boy is transformed into a bear.
3. The boy-bear becomes increasingly ferocious and claws the bark of the tree, which becomes a great rock with a flat top and deeply scored sides.
4. The sisters climb higher and higher to escape their brother's wrath, and eventually they become the seven stars of the Big Dipper.
5. This story, from which Momaday received one of his names, appears in his works *The Way to Rainy Mountain, House Made of Dawn,* and *The Ancient Child.*

CHAPTER **16**

Writing Emphatic Sentences

In speaking, we emphasize certain ideas and deemphasize others with intonation and gesture; in writing, we convey **emphasis**—the relative importance of ideas—through the selection and arrangement of words.

16a Conveying Emphasis through Word Order

Because readers tend to focus on the beginning and end of a sentence, you should place the most important information there.

1 Begin with Important Ideas

Placing key ideas at the beginning of a sentence stresses their importance. The unedited version of the following sentence places emphasis on the study, not on those who conducted it. Editing can shift this focus to place the emphasis on the researcher, not the study.

> ~~In a landmark study of alcoholism,~~ Dr. George Vaillant
> *, in a landmark study of alcoholism,*
> ˄followed two hundred Harvard graduates and four hundred
>
> inner-city, working-class men from the Boston area.

Straightforward writing tasks—laboratory reports, technical papers, business correspondence, and the like—call for sentences that present vital information first and qualifiers later.

> New targeted therapies for treating cancer have been the subject of a good deal of research. (emphasizes the treatment, not the research)

> Dividends will be paid if the stockholders agree. (emphasizes the dividends, not the stockholders)

Close-Up USING *THERE IS* AND *THERE ARE*

Using an empty phrase such as *there is* or *there are* at the beginning of a sentence generally weakens the sentence.

> *MIT places*
> ˄~~There is~~ heavy emphasis on the development of computational skills˄ ~~at MIT.~~

2 End with Important Ideas

Placing key elements at the end of a sentence is another way to convey their importance.

Use a Colon or a Dash A colon or a dash can emphasize an important word or phrase by isolating it at the end of a sentence.

> Beth had always dreamed of owning one special car: a 1953 Corvette.

> The elderly need a good deal of special attention—and they deserve that attention.

Close-Up PLACING TRANSITIONAL WORDS AND PHRASES

When placed at the end of a sentence, conjunctive adverbs and other transitional words or expressions lose their power to indicate the relationship between ideas. Placed earlier in the sentence, transitional words and phrases can link ideas and add emphasis.

See 13b2

however,
Smokers do have rights; ‸they should not try to impose their habit on

others,‸ ~~however.~~

Use Climactic Word Order **Climactic word order**, the arrangement of a series of items from the least to the most important, places emphasis on the most important idea at the end of the sentence.

Binge drinking can lead to sexual abuse, traffic accidents, and even death. (Death is the most serious consequence.)

EXERCISE 16.1

Underline the most important idea in each sentence of the following paragraph. Then, identify the strategy that the writer uses to emphasize each idea. Is the key idea placed at the beginning or the end of a sentence? Does the writer use climactic order?

▶Listening to diatribes by angry callers or ranting about today's news, the talk radio host spreads ideas over the air waves. ▶Every day at the same time, the political talk show host discusses national events and policies, the failures of the opposing views, and the foibles of the individuals who espouse those opposing views. ▶Listening for hours a day, some callers become recognizable contributors to many different talk radio programs. ▶Other listeners are less devoted, tuning in only when they are in the car and never calling to voice their opinions. Political radio hosts usually structure their programs around a specific agenda, espousing the party line and ridiculing the opponent's position. With a style of presentation aimed both at entertainment and information, the host's ideas become caricatures of party positions. Sometimes, in order to keep the information lively and interesting, a host may either state the issues too simply or deliberately mislead the audience. A host can excuse these errors by insisting that the show is harmless: it's for entertainment, not information. Many are concerned about how the political process is affected by this misinformation.

ml 49f

3 Experiment with Word Order

In English sentences, the most common word order is subject-verb-object (or subject-verb-complement). By intentionally departing from this expected word order, you can emphasize the word, phrase, or clause that you have relocated.

> More modest and less inventive than Turner's paintings are John Constable's landscapes.

Here the writer calls attention to the modifying phrase *more modest and less inventive than Turner's paintings* by inverting word order, placing the complement and the verb before the subject.

EXERCISE 16.2

Revise the following sentences to make them more emphatic. For each, decide which ideas should be highlighted, and place these key ideas at sentence beginnings or endings. Use climactic order or depart from conventional word order where appropriate.

1. Some police departments want to upgrade their firepower because criminals are better armed than ever before.
2. Previously, felons used so-called Saturday night specials, small-caliber six-shot revolvers.
3. Now, semiautomatic pistols capable of firing fifteen to twenty rounds, along with paramilitary weapons such as the AK-47, have replaced these weapons.
4. Police are adopting weapons such as new fast-firing shotguns and 9mm automatic pistols in order to gain an equal footing with their adversaries.
5. Faster reloading and a hair trigger are two of the numerous advantages that automatic pistols, the weapons of choice among law-enforcement officers, have over the traditional .38-caliber police revolver.

16b Conveying Emphasis through Sentence Structure

As you construct sentences, try to emphasize more important ideas and de-emphasize less important ones.

1 Use Cumulative Sentences

A **cumulative sentence** begins with an independent clause, followed by additional words, phrases, or clauses that expand or develop it.

> She holds me in strong arms, arms that have chopped cotton, dismembered trees, scattered corn for chickens, cradled infants, shaken the daylights out of half-grown upstart teenagers. (Rebecca Hill, *Blue Rise*)

Because a cumulative sentence presents its main idea first, it tends to be clear and straightforward. (Most English sentences are cumulative.)

2 Use Periodic Sentences

A **periodic sentence** moves from supporting details, expressed in modifying phrases and dependent clauses, to the key idea, which is placed in the independent clause at the end of the sentence.

Unlike World War II, which ended decisively with an unconditional surrender, the war in Vietnam did not end when American troops withdrew.

Note: In some periodic sentences, the modifying phrase or dependent clause comes between subject and predicate: *Columbus, after several discouraging and unsuccessful voyages, finally reached America.*

EXERCISE 16.3

A. Bracket the independent clause(s) in each sentence, and underline each modifying phrase and dependent clause. Label each sentence cumulative or periodic.

B. Relocate the supporting details to make cumulative sentences periodic and periodic sentences cumulative, adding words or rephrasing to make your meaning clear.

C. Discuss with a classmate how your revision changes the emphasis of the original sentence.

Example: Feeling isolated, sad, and frightened, [the small child sat alone in the train depot.] (periodic)

Revised: The small child sat alone in the train depot, feeling isolated, sad, and frightened. (cumulative)

1. However different in their educational opportunities, both Jefferson and Lincoln as young men became known to their contemporaries as "hard students." (Douglas L. Wilson, "What Jefferson and Lincoln Read," *Atlantic Monthly*)

2. The road came into being slowly, league by league, river crossing by river crossing. (Stephen Harrigan, "Highway 1," *Texas Monthly*)

3. Without willing it, I had gone from being ignorant of being ignorant to being aware of being aware. (Maya Angelou, *I Know Why the Caged Bird Sings*)

16c Conveying Emphasis through Parallelism and Balance

By reinforcing the similarity between grammatical elements, parallelism can help you emphasize information.

See 18a

We seek an individual who is a self-starter, who owns a late-model automobile, and who is willing to work evenings.

Do not pass Go; do not collect $200.

The Faust legend is central in Benét's *The Devil and Daniel Webster*, in Goethe's *Faust*, and in Marlowe's *Dr. Faustus*.

A **balanced sentence** is neatly divided between two parallel structures—for example, two independent clauses in a compound sentence. The symmetrical structure of a balanced sentence adds emphasis by highlighting similarities or differences between the ideas in the two clauses.

In the 1950s, the electronic miracle was the television; in the 1980s, the electronic miracle was the computer.

Alive, the elephant was worth at least a hundred pounds; dead, he would only be worth the value of his tusks, five pounds, possibly. (George Orwell, "Shooting an Elephant")

16d　Conveying Emphasis through Repetition

See 17b

Unnecessary repetition makes sentences dull and monotonous as well as wordy.

He had a good pitching arm and also could field well and was also a fast runner.

Effective repetition, however, can emphasize key words or ideas.

They decided to begin again: to begin hoping, to begin trying to change, to begin working toward a goal.

During those years when I was just learning to speak, my mother and father addressed me only in Spanish; in Spanish I learned to reply. (Richard Rodriguez, *Aria: Memoir of a Bilingual Childhood*)

EXERCISE 16.4

Revise the sentences in this paragraph, using parallelism and balance to highlight corresponding elements and using repetition of key words and phrases to add emphasis. You may combine sentences and add, delete, or reorder words.

▶Many readers distrust newspapers and news sites. ▶They also distrust what they read in magazines. ▶They do not trust what they hear on the radio and what television shows them, either. ▶Of these media, newspapers have been the most responsive to audience criticism. ▶Some newspapers even have ombudsmen. ▶They are supposed to listen to readers' complaints. ▶They are also charged with acting on these grievances. One complaint that many people have is that newspapers are inaccurate. Newspapers' disregard for people's privacy is another of many readers' criticisms. Reporters are seen as arrogant, and readers feel that journalists can be unfair. They feel that reporters tend to glorify criminals, and they believe there is a tendency to place too much emphasis on bizarre or offbeat stories. Finally, readers complain about poor writing and editing. Polls show that despite its efforts to respond to reader criticism, the press continues to face hostility. (Adapted from *Newsweek*)

16e Conveying Emphasis through Active Voice

See
22d

ml
49a6

The <u>active voice</u> is generally more emphatic than the <u>passive voice</u>.

Passive: The prediction that oil prices will rise is being made by economists.

Active: Economists are predicting that oil prices will rise.

Notice that the passive voice sentence above does not specify who is performing the action. In a passive voice sentence, the subject is the recipient of the action, so the actor fades into the background (*by economists*)—or may even be omitted entirely (*the prediction . . . is being made*). In contrast, active voice places the emphasis where it belongs: on the actor or actors (*Economists*).

Sometimes, of course, you *want* to stress the action rather than the actor; when this is the case, use the passive voice.

Passive: The West was explored by Lewis and Clark. (stresses the exploration of the West, not who explored it)

Active: Lewis and Clark explored the West. (stresses the contribution of the explorers)

Note: Passive voice is also used when the identity of the person performing the action is irrelevant or unknown (*The course was canceled*). For this reason, the passive voice is frequently used in scientific and technical writing: *The beaker was filled with a saline solution.*

EXERCISE 16.5

Revise this paragraph to eliminate awkward or excessive use of passive constructions.

▶Jack Dempsey, the heavyweight champion between 1919 and 1926, had an interesting but uneven career. ▶He was considered one of the greatest boxers of all time. ▶Dempsey began fighting as "Kid Blackie," but his career did not take off until 1919, when Jack "Doc" Kearns became his manager. ▶Dempsey won the championship when Jess Willard was defeated by him in Toledo, Ohio, in 1919. ▶Dempsey immediately became a popular sports figure; President Franklin D. Roosevelt was one of his biggest fans. Influential friends were made by Jack Dempsey. Boxing lessons were given by him to the actor Rudolph Valentino. He made friends with Douglas Fairbanks Sr., Damon Runyon, and J. Paul Getty. Hollywood serials were made by Dempsey, but the title was lost by him to Gene Tunney, and Dempsey failed to regain it the following year. After his boxing career declined, a restaurant was opened by Dempsey, and many major sporting events were attended by him. This exposure kept him in the public eye until he lost his restaurant. Jack Dempsey died in 1983.

Writing Concise Sentences

A sentence is not concise simply because it is short; a **concise** sentence contains only the words necessary to make its point.

Close-Up TEXT MESSAGES

If you send texts, which are limited to 160 characters, you already use certain strategies to make your writing concise: you omit articles and other nonessential words, and you use nonstandard spellings *(nite)*, abbreviations, and shorthand *(RU home?)*. However, this kind of language is not acceptable in college writing, where you need to use other strategies (such as those discussed in this chapter) to make your writing concise.

17a Eliminating Wordiness

Whenever possible, delete nonessential words—*deadwood, utility words*, and *circumlocution*—from your writing.

1 Eliminating Deadwood

The term **deadwood** refers to unnecessary phrases that take up space and add nothing to meaning.

Many
~~There were many~~ factors ~~that~~ influenced his decision to become a priest.

The two plots are ~~both~~ similar in ~~the way~~ that they trace the characters' increasing rage.

This
~~In this~~ article ~~it~~ discusses lead poisoning.

is
The most tragic character in *Hamlet* ~~would have to be~~ Ophelia.

Deadwood also includes unnecessary statements of opinion, such as *I believe, I feel, it seems to me, as far as I'm concerned*, and *in my opinion*.

2 Eliminating Utility Words

Utility words function as filler and have no real meaning in a sentence. Utility words include nouns with imprecise meanings (*factor, situation, type, aspect,* and so on); adjectives so general that they are almost meaningless (*good, bad, important*); and common adverbs denoting degree (*basically, actually, quite, very, definitely*). Often, you can just delete the utility word; if you cannot, replace it with a more precise word.

Registration
~~The registration situation~~ ᵥwas disorganized.

an
The scholarship ~~basically~~ offered Fran ᵥ~~a good~~ opportunity to study Spanish in Spain.

It was ~~actually~~ a worthwhile book, but I did not ~~completely~~ finish it.

3 Avoiding Circumlocution

Circumlocution is taking a roundabout way to say something (using ten words when five will do). Instead of complicated constructions, use specific words and concise phrases that come right to the point.

The   *probably*
~~It is not unlikely that the~~ ᵥtrend will ᵥcontinue.

The curriculum was ~~of a~~ unique ~~nature~~.

while
Joe was in the army ᵥ~~during the same time that~~ I was in college.

Close-Up   REVISING WORDY PHRASES

A wordy phrase can almost always be replaced by a more concise, more direct term.

Wordy	Concise
at the present time	now
at this point in time	now
for the purpose of	for
due to the fact that	because
on account of	because
until such time as	until
in the event that	if
by means of	by
in the vicinity of	near
have the ability to	can

EXERCISE 17.1

Revise the following paragraph to eliminate deadwood, utility words, and circumlocution. Whenever possible, delete wordy phrases or replace them with more concise expressions.

►For all intents and purposes, the shopping mall is no longer an important factor in the American cultural scene. ►In the '80s, shopping malls became gathering places where teenagers met, walkers came to get in a few miles, and shoppers who were looking for a wide selection and were not concerned about value went to shop. ►There are several factors that have worked to undermine the mall's popularity. ►First, due to the fact that today's shoppers are more likely to be interested in value, many of them have headed to the discount stores. ►Today's shopper is now more likely to shop in discount stores or bulk-buying warehouse stores than in the small, expensive specialty shops in the large shopping malls. Add to this a resurgence of the values of community, and we can see how mall shopping would have to be less attractive than shopping at local stores. Many malls actually have up to 20 percent empty storefronts, and some have had to close down altogether. Others have met the challenge by expanding their roles from shopping centers into community centers. They have added playgrounds for the children and more amusements and restaurants for the adults. They have also appealed to the growing sense of value shopping by giving gift certificates and discounts to shoppers who spend money in their stores. For a while, it seemed as if the huge shopping malls that had become familiar cultural icons were dying out, replaced by online shopping. Now, however, it looks as if some of those icons just might make it and survive by reinventing themselves as more than just places to shop.

17b   Eliminating Unnecessary Repetition

See
16d

Although **repetition** can make your sentences more emphatic, unnecessary repetition and **redundant** word groups (repeated words or phrases that say the same thing, such as *true facts, free gift, armed gunman,* and *unanticipated surprise*) can lessen the impact of your writing.

You can correct unnecessary repetition by using any of the following strategies.

1 Deleting Redundancy

People's clothing ~~attire~~ can reveal a good deal about their personalities.

The two candidates share several positions ~~in common.~~

2 Creating an Appositive

Red Barber ~~was~~ a sportscaster. ~~He was~~ known for his colorful expressions.

3 Creating a Compound Sentence

John F. Kennedy was the youngest man ever elected president./
and
,He was the first Catholic to hold this office.

4 Creating a Complex Sentence

, which
Americans value freedom of speech,/Freedom of speech is guaranteed by the First Amendment.

EXERCISE 17.2

Eliminate any unnecessary repetition of words or ideas in this paragraph. Also revise to eliminate deadwood, utility words, and circumlocution.

▶For a wide variety of different reasons, more and more people today are choosing a vegetarian diet. ▶There are three kinds of vegetarians: strict vegetarians eat no animal foods at all; lactovegetarians eat dairy products, but they do not eat meat, fish, poultry, or eggs; and ovolactovegetarians eat eggs and dairy products, but they do not eat meat, fish, or poultry. ▶Famous vegetarians include such well-known people as George Bernard Shaw, Leonardo da Vinci, Ralph Waldo Emerson, Henry David Thoreau, and Mahatma Gandhi. ▶Like these well-known vegetarians, the vegetarians of today have good reasons for becoming vegetarians. For instance, some religions recommend a vegetarian diet. Some of these religions are Buddhism, Brahmanism, and Hinduism. Other people turn to vegetarianism for reasons of health or for reasons of hygiene. These people believe that meat is a source of potentially harmful chemicals, and they believe meat contains infectious organisms. Some people feel meat may cause digestive problems and may lead to other difficulties as well. Other vegetarians adhere to a vegetarian diet because they feel it is ecologically wasteful to kill animals after we feed plants to them. These vegetarians believe we should eat the plants. Finally, there are facts and evidence to suggest that a vegetarian diet may possibly help people live longer lives. A vegetarian diet may do this by reducing the incidence of heart disease and lessening the incidence of some cancers. (Adapted from *Jane Brody's Nutrition Book*)

17c Tightening Rambling Sentences

The combination of nonessential words, unnecessary repetition, and complicated syntax creates **rambling sentences**. Revising rambling sentences frequently requires extensive editing.

1 Eliminating Excessive Coordination

When you string a series of independent clauses together with coordinating conjunctions, you create a rambling, unfocused <u>compound sentence</u> that

See 14c

presents your ideas as if they all have equal weight. To revise such sentences, identify the main idea or ideas, and then subordinate the supporting details.

Wordy: Puerto Rico is a large island, and it is mountainous, and it has steep slopes, and they fall to gentle plains along the coast.

Concise: A large island, Puerto Rico is mountainous, with steep slopes falling to gentle plains along the coast. (Puerto Rico's mountainous terrain is the sentence's main idea.)

2 Eliminating Adjective Clauses

See
14b2

A series of **adjective clauses** is also likely to produce a rambling sentence. To revise, substitute more concise modifying words or phrases for the adjective clauses.

Wordy: *Moby-Dick*, which is a novel about a white whale, was written by Herman Melville, who was friendly with Nathaniel Hawthorne, who urged him to revise the first draft.

Concise: *Moby-Dick*, a novel about a white whale, was written by Herman Melville, who revised the first draft at the urging of his friend Nathaniel Hawthorne.

3 Eliminating Passive Constructions

See
22d1

Excessive use of the **passive voice** can create rambling sentences. Correct this problem by changing passive to active voice.

ml
49a6

~~Water rights are being fought for in court by~~ Indian tribes such as
                                    are fighting in court for water rights.
the Papago in Arizona and the Pyramid Lake Paiute in Nevada/˄

4 Eliminating Wordy Prepositional Phrases

See
14b1

When you revise, substitute adjectives or adverbs for wordy **prepositional phrases**.

           dangerous   *exciting*
The trip was˄~~one of danger~~ but also˄~~one of excitement~~.

           confidently   *authoritatively*
He spoke˄~~in a confident manner~~ and˄~~with a lot of authority~~.

5 Eliminating Wordy Noun Constructions

See
14b1

Substitute strong verbs for wordy **noun phrases**.

           decided
We have˄~~made the decision~~ to postpone the meeting until ~~the~~
                          appear
~~appearance of~~ all the board members˄.

                          accumulates
Sometimes ~~there is an accumulation of~~ water˄on the roof.

EXERCISE 17.3

Revise the rambling sentences in these paragraphs by eliminating excessive coordination; unnecessary use of the passive voice; and overuse of adjective clauses, prepositional phrases, and noun constructions. As you revise, make your sentences more concise by deleting nonessential words and unnecessary repetition.

▶Some colleges that have been in support of fraternities for a number of years are at this time in the process of conducting a reevaluation of the position of those fraternities on campus. ▶In opposition to the fraternities are a fair number of students, faculty members, and administrators who claim fraternities are inherently sexist, which they say makes it impossible for the groups to exist in a coeducational institution, which is supposed to offer equal opportunities for members of both sexes. ▶More and more members of the college community also see fraternities as elitist as well as sexist and favor their abolition. ▶In addition, many point out that fraternities are associated with dangerous practices, such as hazing and alcohol abuse.

However, some students, faculty, and administrators remain wholeheartedly in support of traditional fraternities, which they believe are responsible for helping students make the acquaintance of people and learn the leadership skills that they believe will be of assistance to them in their future lives as adults. Supporters of fraternities believe that students should retain the right to make their own social decisions and that joining a fraternity is one of those decisions, and they also believe fraternities are responsible for providing valuable services. Some of these are tutoring, raising money for charity, and running campus safe-ride services. Therefore, these individuals are not of the opinion that the abolition of traditional fraternities makes sense.

CHAPTER **18**

Using Parallelism

Parallelism—the use of matching words, phrases, or clauses to express equivalent ideas—adds unity, balance, and coherence to your writing. Effective parallelism makes sentences easier to follow and emphasizes relationships between equivalent ideas, but **faulty parallelism** can create awkward sentences that obscure your meaning and confuse readers.

See
18b

18a Using Parallelism Effectively

Parallelism highlights the correspondence between *items in a series, paired items*, and elements in *lists and outlines*.

1 With Items in a Series

Items in a series should be presented in parallel terms.

Eat, drink, and be merry.

I came; I saw; I conquered.

Baby food consumption, toy production, and school construction are likely to decline as the US population grows older.

Three factors influenced his decision to seek new employment: his desire to relocate, his need for greater responsibility, and his dissatisfaction with his current job.

Note: For information on punctuating elements in a series, **see 30b** and **31c**.

2 With Paired Items

Paired words, phrases, or clauses should be presented in parallel terms.

The thank-you note was short but sweet.

Roosevelt represented the United States, and Churchill represented Great Britain.

The research focused on muscle tissue and nerve cells.

Ask not what your country can do for you; ask what you can do for your country. (John F. Kennedy, inaugural address)

Paired elements linked by **correlative conjunctions** (such as *not only/but also, both/and, either/or, neither/nor,* and *whether/or*) should always be parallel.

The design team paid close attention not only to color but also to texture.

Parallelism is also used with paired elements linked by *than* or *as.*

Richard Wright and James Baldwin chose to live in Paris rather than to remain in the United States.

Success is as much a matter of hard work as a matter of luck.

3 In Lists and Outlines

Items in a list should be parallel.

The Irish potato famine had four major causes:

1. The establishment of the landlord-tenant system
2. The failure of the potato crop
3. The reluctance of England to offer adequate financial assistance
4. The passage of the Corn Laws

Elements in a **formal outline** should also be parallel.

See 4c4

EXERCISE 18.1

Identify the parallel elements in these sentences by bracketing parallel phrases and clauses.

Example: Manek spent six years in America [going to school] and [working for a computer company].

1. After he completed his engineering degree, Manek returned to India to visit his large extended family and to find a wife.
2. Unfamiliar with marriage practices in India and accustomed to the American notion of marriage for love, Manek's American friends disapproved of his plans.
3. Not only Manek but also his parents wanted an arranged marriage.
4. He didn't believe that either you married for love or you had a loveless marriage.
5. His parents' marriage, an arranged one, continues happily; his aunt's marriage, also arranged, has lasted thirty years.

18b Revising Faulty Parallelism

Faulty parallelism occurs when elements in a sentence that express equivalent ideas are not presented in parallel terms.

Many residents of developing countries lack adequate housing,

adequate

adequate food, and ~~their~~ health-care facilities ~~are also~~

~~inadequate.~~

To correct faulty parallelism, match nouns with nouns, verbs with verbs, and phrases or clauses with similarly constructed phrases or clauses.

weight training,

Popular exercises for men and women include spinning, ~~weights~~, and jogging.

having

I look forward to hearing from you and to ~~have~~ an opportunity to tell you more about myself.

Close-Up REPEATING KEY WORDS

Although the use of similar grammatical structures may be enough to convey parallelism, sometimes sentences are even clearer if certain key words (for example, articles, prepositions, and the *to* in infinitives) are also repeated in each element of a pair or a series. In the following sentence, repeating the preposition *by* makes it clear that *not* applies only to the first phrase.

Computerization has helped industry by not allowing labor costs to
skyrocket,ₐ*by* increasing the speed of production, andₐ*by* improving efficiency.

EXERCISE 18.2

Identify and correct faulty parallelism in these sentences. Then, underline the parallel elements—words, phrases, and clauses—in your corrected sentences. If a sentence is already correct, mark it with a *C*, and underline the parallel elements.

Example: Alfred Hitchcock's films include *North by Northwest, Vertigo,*

Psycho, and he also directed *Notorious,* and *Saboteur.*

1. The world is divided between those with boots on and those who discover continents.
2. World leaders, members of Congress, and religious groups are all concerned about global climate change.
3. A national task force on education recommended improving public education by making the school day longer, higher teachers' salaries, and integrating more technology into the curriculum.
4. The fast food industry has expanded to include many kinds of restaurants: those that serve pizza, fried chicken chains, some offering Mexican-style menus, and hamburger franchises.
5. The consumption of Scotch in the United States is declining because of high prices, tastes are changing, and increased health awareness has led many whiskey drinkers to switch to wine or beer.

CHAPTER 19

Choosing Words

19a Choosing an Appropriate Level of Diction

Diction, which comes from the Latin word for *say*, refers to the choice and use of words. Different audiences and situations call for different levels of diction.

1 Formal Diction

Formal diction is grammatically correct and uses words familiar to an educated audience. A writer who uses formal diction often maintains emotional distance from the audience by avoiding *I* and *you*. In addition, the tone of the writing—as determined by word choice, sentence structure, and choice of subject—is dignified and objective.

2 Informal Diction

Informal diction is the language that people use in conversation and in informal emails. You should use informal diction in your college writing only to reproduce speech or dialect or to give an essay a conversational tone.

Colloquial Diction **Colloquial diction** is the language of everyday speech. Contractions—*isn't, I'm*—are typical, as are **clipped forms**— *phone* for *telephone*, *TV* for *television*, *dorm* for *dormitory*. Other colloquialisms include placeholders such as *kind of* and utility words such as *nice* for *acceptable*, *funny* for *odd*, and *great* for almost anything. Colloquial English also includes expressions such as *get across* for *communicate*, *come up with* for *find*, and *check out* for *investigate*.

Slang **Slang**, language that calls attention to itself, is used to establish or reinforce identity within a group—urban teenagers, rock musicians, or computer users, for example. One characteristic of slang is that it is usually short-lived, coming into existence and fading out much more quickly than other words do. Because slang terms can emerge and disappear so quickly, no dictionary—not even a dictionary of slang—can list all or even most of the slang terms currently in use.

Note: In personal email and instant messages, writers commonly use **emoticons** and **emojis** that indicate emotions or feelings—and **text shorthand**, such as *BTW* or *2 day*. This kind of shorthand is inappropriate in academic essays or emails to professors or supervisors.

Regionalisms　**Regionalisms** are words, expressions, and idiomatic forms that are used in particular geographical areas but may not be understood by a general audience. In eastern Tennessee, for example, a paper bag is a *poke*, and empty soda bottles are *dope bottles*. And New Yorkers stand *on line* for a movie, whereas people in most other parts of the country stand *in line*.

Nonstandard Diction　**Nonstandard diction** refers to words and expressions not generally considered a part of standard English—words such as *ain't, nohow, anywheres, nowheres, hisself,* and *theirselves.*

No absolute rules distinguish standard from nonstandard usage. In fact, some linguists reject the idea of nonstandard usage altogether, arguing that this designation relegates both the language and those who use it to second-class status.

Note: Keep in mind that colloquial expressions, slang, regionalisms, and nonstandard diction are almost always inappropriate in your college writing.

3　College Writing

The level of diction appropriate for college writing depends on your assignment and your audience. A personal-experience essay calls for a somewhat informal style, but a research paper, an exam, or a report requires a more formal level of diction. In general, most college writing falls somewhere between formal and informal English, using a conversational tone but maintaining grammatical correctness and using a specialized vocabulary when the situation requires it. (This is the level of diction that is used in this book.)

MULTILINGUAL TIP

Some of the spoken expressions you learn from other students or from television are not appropriate for use in college writing. When you hear new expressions, pay attention to the contexts in which they are used.

Close-Up　EMAILS TO INSTRUCTORS

Instructors have varying opinions about how students should address them. Unless you are told otherwise, however, think of emails to your instructors as business communications. Avoid highly informal salutations, such as "Hi prof"; instead, use a more formal salutation, such as "Dr. Sweeny."

EXERCISE 19.1

After reading the following paragraph, underline the words and phrases that identify it as formal diction. Then, rewrite the paragraph, using the level of diction that you would use in your college writing. Consult a dictionary if necessary.

In looking at many small points of difference between species, which, as far as our ignorance permits us to judge, seem quite unimportant, we must not forget that climate, food, etc., have no doubt produced some direct effect. It is also necessary to bear in mind that owing to the law of correlation, when one part varies and the variations are accumulated through natural selection, other modifications, often of the most unexpected nature, will ensue. (Charles Darwin, *The Origin of Species*)

19b Choosing the Right Word

Choosing the right word to use in a particular context is very important. If you use the wrong word—or even *almost* the right one—you run the risk of misrepresenting your ideas.

1 Denotation and Connotation

A word's **denotation** is its basic dictionary meaning, what it stands for without any emotional associations. A word's **connotations** are the emotional, social, and political associations it has in addition to its denotative meaning.

Word	Denotation	Connotation
politician	someone who holds a political office	opportunist; wheeler-dealer

Selecting a word with the appropriate connotation can be challenging. For example, the word *skinny* has negative connotations, whereas *thin* is neutral, and *slender* is positive. And words and expressions such as *mentally ill, insane, neurotic, crazy, psychopathic,* and *emotionally disturbed,* although similar in meaning, have different emotional, social, and political connotations. If you use terms without considering their connotations, you run the risk of undercutting your credibility, to say nothing of confusing and possibly angering readers.

Close-Up USING A THESAURUS

Unlike a dictionary, which lists the definitions of words, a **thesaurus** lists **synonyms** (words that have the same meaning—for example, *well* and *healthy*) and **antonyms** (words that have opposite meanings—for example, *courage* and *cowardice*). Most online dictionaries, as well as *Microsoft Word*, enable you to access a thesaurus.

When you consult a thesaurus, remember that no two words have exactly the same meaning. Use synonyms carefully, checking a dictionary to make sure the connotation of the synonym is very close to that of the original word.

EXERCISE 19.2

The following words have negative connotations. For each, list one word with a similar meaning whose connotation is neutral and another whose connotation is positive.

Example: *Negative*   skinny
             Neutral   thin
             Positive   slender

1. deceive
2. antiquated
3. pushy
4. pathetic
5. cheap
6. blunder
7. weird
8. rhetoric
9. shack
10. stench

2 Euphemisms

A **euphemism** is a mild or polite term used in place of a blunt or harsh term that describes something unpleasant or embarrassing. College writing is no place for euphemisms. Say what you mean—*pregnant*, not *expecting*; *died*, not *passed away*; and *strike*, not *work stoppage*.

3 Specific and General Words

Specific words refer to particular persons, items, or events; **general** words denote entire classes or groups. *Queen Elizabeth II*, for example, is more specific than *monarch*; *jeans* is more specific than *clothing*; and *SUV* is more specific than *vehicle*. Although you can use general words to describe entire classes of items, you should use specific words to clarify such generalizations.

Close-Up   USING SPECIFIC WORDS

Take particular care to avoid general words such as *nice*, *great*, and *terrific* that say nothing and could be used in almost any sentence. These utility words convey only enthusiasm, not precise meanings. Replace them with more specific words.

See
17a2

4 Abstract and Concrete Words

Abstract words—*beauty, truth, justice,* and so on—refer to ideas, qualities, or conditions that cannot be perceived by the senses. **Concrete** words name things that readers can see, hear, taste, smell, or touch. The more concrete your words and phrases, the more vivid the image you evoke in the reader's mind.

EXERCISE 19.3

Revise the following paragraph from a job application letter by substituting specific, concrete language for general or abstract words and phrases. Exchange your revision with a classmate.

►I have had several part-time jobs lately. ►Some of them would qualify me for the position you advertised. ►In my most recent job, I sold products in a store. My supervisor said I was a good worker who had a number of valuable qualities. I am used to dealing with different types of people in different settings. I feel that my qualifications would make me a good candidate for your job opening.

19c Using Figures of Speech

Writers often use **figures of speech** (such as *similes* and *metaphors*) to go beyond the literal meanings of words. By doing so, they make their writing more vivid or emphatic.

Close-Up COMMONLY USED FIGURES OF SPEECH

- A **simile** is a comparison between two unlike things on the basis of a shared quality. A simile is introduced by *like* or *as*.

  Like travelers with exotic destinations on their minds, the graduates were remarkably forgetful. (Maya Angelou, *I Know Why the Caged Bird Sings*)

- A **metaphor** also compares two dissimilar things, but instead of saying that one thing is *like* another, it *equates* them.

  All the world's a stage,
  And all the men and women merely players; . . . (William Shakespeare, *As You Like It*)

- An **analogy** explains an unfamiliar item or concept by comparing it to a more familiar one.

  According to Robert Frost, writing free verse is like playing tennis without a net.

- **Personification** gives an idea or inanimate object human attributes, feelings, or powers.

  Truth strikes us from behind, and in the dark, as well as from before in broad daylight. (Henry David Thoreau, *Journals*)

- A **hyperbole** (or overstatement) is an intentional exaggeration for emphasis. For example, Jonathan Swift uses hyperbole in his essay "A Modest Proposal" when he suggests that eating Irish babies would help the English solve their food shortage.

- **Understatement** intentionally makes something seem less important than it actually is.

  According to Mao Tse-tung, a revolution is not a tea party.

19d Avoiding Inappropriate Language

1 Jargon

Jargon is the specialized or technical vocabulary of a trade, profession, or academic discipline. Although it is useful for communicating in the field for which it was developed, outside that field it is often imprecise and confusing. For example, business executives may want departments to *interface* effectively, and sociologists may identify the need for *perspectivistic thinking* to achieve organizational goals. If they are addressing other professionals in their respective fields, using these terms can facilitate communication. If, however, they are addressing a general audience, these terms are often confusing.

2 Neologisms

Neologisms are newly coined words that are not part of standard English. New situations call for new words, however, and frequently a neologism will become an accepted part of the language—*app, locavore, phishing, blog*, and *outsource*, for example. Other coined words are never fully accepted—for example, the neologisms created when the suffix *-wise* is added to existing words, creating nonstandard words such as *weatherwise, sportswise, timewise*, and *productwise*.

3 Pretentious Diction

Good writing is clear and direct, not pompous or flowery. Revise to eliminate **pretentious diction**, inappropriately elevated and wordy language.

<p>   <i>asleep</i>   <i>thought</i>   <i>hiking</i></p>

As I fell ~~into slumber~~, I ~~cogitated~~ about my day ~~ambling~~ through ~~the splendor of~~ the Appalachian Mountains.

Frequently, pretentious diction is formal diction used in a relatively informal situation. In such a context, it is out of place. For every pretentious word, there is a clear and direct alternative.

Pretentious	Clear	Pretentious	Clear
ascertain	discover	reside	live
commence	start	terminate	end
implement	carry out	utilize	use
minuscule	small	individual	person

4 Clichés

Clichés are tired expressions that have lost their impact because they have been used so often. At one time, expressions such as the following might have called up vivid images in a reader's mind, but because of overuse, they have become clichés—pat, meaningless phrases.

back in the day
the bottom line
it is what it is
face the music
game plan
give 110 percent
smoking gun
a level playing field
a perfect storm
wake up and smell the coffee
old school
what goes around comes around

Writers sometimes resort to clichés when they run out of ideas. To capture your readers' attention, take the time to think of original expressions.

MULTILINGUAL TIP

Many multilingual students have learned a long list of English idioms. Some of these, however, have become clichés. Although becoming familiar with these idioms can help you understand them when you encounter them, university instructors discourage students from using clichés in their writing, preferring language that is more original and more precise.

EXERCISE 19.4

Go through a news website or magazine, and list the examples of jargon, neologisms, pretentious diction, or clichés that you find. Then, substitute more appropriate words for the ones you identified. Discuss with a classmate your interpretation of each word and of the word you chose to put in its place. **&**

19e Avoiding Offensive Language

Most of us want to live in a society where all people—regardless of background, gender, race, sexual orientation, age, or physical condition—are able to realize their full potential. Language that undercuts this goal has no place in civil discourse and should be avoided—in the workplace, in the classroom, and in our daily lives. Although people certainly have the right to express themselves, they should be aware of the potentially negative consequences—moral, ethical, and practical—of their words. Because the language we use not only expresses our ideas but also shapes our thinking, it is in everyone's best interest to avoid using words that could insult, degrade, or otherwise harm others.

Writers should use language free of bias to ensure fair treatment of groups and individuals. In addition to avoiding the use of any language that demeans or discriminates, strive to use accurate, inclusive language at all times. To do this, describe people and groups with an appropriate level of specificity and be sensitive to labels.

1 Stereotypes

Racial and Ethnic Identity Use terms that indicate national or regional origins rather than generalized ones. Be clear about whether you are referring to a racial or ethnic group. These groups are proper nouns and should be capitalized.

Possible bias: A group consisting of *Asian* students volunteered for the study.

Bias-free: A group consisting of *Japanese, Vietnamese, and South Korean* students volunteered for the study..

Age Favor terms such as "older adults" and "older people" over terms that have negative connotations such as "seniors," "the elderly," and "the aged." The latter tend to stereotype and marginalize older age groups.

Possible bias: All of the tenants in this apartment building are *seniors*.

Bias-free: All of the tenants in this apartment building are *65 years and older*.

Socioeconomic Status Socioeconomic status includes more than income. Be sensitive in using appropriate descriptors for income, education, occupational prestige, and perceptions of social class.

Possible bias: The community center serves free meals to *the homeless*.

Bias-free: The community center serves free meals to *people experiencing homelessness*.

Sexual Orientation Use specific terms for orientation rather than generalized ones. Avoid inaccurate or pejorative terms for sexual orientation.

Possible bias: Frankie is a *homosexual*.

Bias-free: Frankie is a *gay man*.

Disability Disability is a broad term that includes physical, psychological, intellectual, and socioemotional impairments. Provide specific names of conditions rather than categories.

Possible bias: The *drug addict* checked into a residential treatment facility.

Bias-free: The *person with substance use disorder* checked into a residential treatment facility.

2 Sexist Language

Avoid **sexist language**—language that reinforces and promotes gender stereotypes. Extending beyond the use of derogatory words, sexist language assumes that some professions are exclusive to one gender—for instance, that *nurse* denotes only women and that *engineer* denotes only men. The use of outdated job titles, such as *postman* for *letter carrier, fireman* for *firefighter*, and *stewardess* for *flight attendant* is also considered sexist.

Sexist language also occurs when a writer fails to apply the same terminology to both men and women. For example, refer to two scientists with PhDs not as Dr. Sagan and Mrs. Yallow, but as Dr. Sagan and Dr. Yallow. Refer to two writers as James and Wharton, or Henry James and Edith Wharton, not James and Mrs. Wharton.

In your writing, always use *women* when referring to adult females. Use *Ms.* as the form of address when a woman's marital status is unknown or irrelevant (for example, in business correspondence). Finally, avoid using the generic *he* or *him* when your subject could be either male or female. Use the singular or plural *they* instead.

Sexist: Before boarding, each passenger should make certain that he has his ticket.

Revised with the singular they: Before boarding, each passenger should make certain that they have their ticket.

Revised with the plural they: Before boarding, passengers should make certain that they have their tickets.

Note: *They*—rather than *he or she*—is now the preferred gender-neutral term. Be aware that the use of the singular *they* has long been viewed as grammatically incorrect, so its adoption has met some resistance.

Close-Up ELIMINATING SEXIST LANGUAGE

For every sexist usage, there is usually a nonsexist alternative.

Sexist Usage	Possible Revisions
Mankind	People, human beings
Man's accomplishments	Human accomplishments
Man-made	Synthetic
Female engineer/lawyer/accountant, and so on; male model	Engineer/lawyer/accountant, and so on; model
Policeman/woman	Police officer
Salesman/woman/girl	Salesperson, sales representative
Businessman/woman	Businessperson, executive
Everyone should complete his application by Tuesday.	Everyone should complete their application by Tuesday.
	All students should complete their applications by Tuesday.

EXERCISE 19.5

Suggest at least one alternative form for each of the following words or phrases. In each case, comment on the advantages and disadvantages of the alternative you recommend. If you feel that a particular term is not sexist, explain why.

- forefathers
- man-eating shark
- manpower
- workman's compensation
- men at work
- waitress
- first baseman
- congressman
- manhunt
- longshoreman
- committeeman
- (to) man the battle stations

- the common man
- point man
- draftsman
- man overboard
- fisherman
- foreman
- manned space program
- gentleman's agreement
- no man's land
- spinster
- old maid
- old wives' tale

EXERCISE 19.6

Each of the following pairs of terms includes a feminine form that was at one time in wide use; some are still used to some extent. Which do you think are likely to remain in our language for some time, and which do you think will disappear? Explain your reasoning.

heir/heiress
benefactor/benefactress
murderer/murderess
actor/actress
hero/heroine
host/hostess
aviator/aviatrix
executor/executrix

author/authoress
poet/poetess
tailor/seamstress
comedian/comedienne
villain/villainess
prince/princess
widow/widower

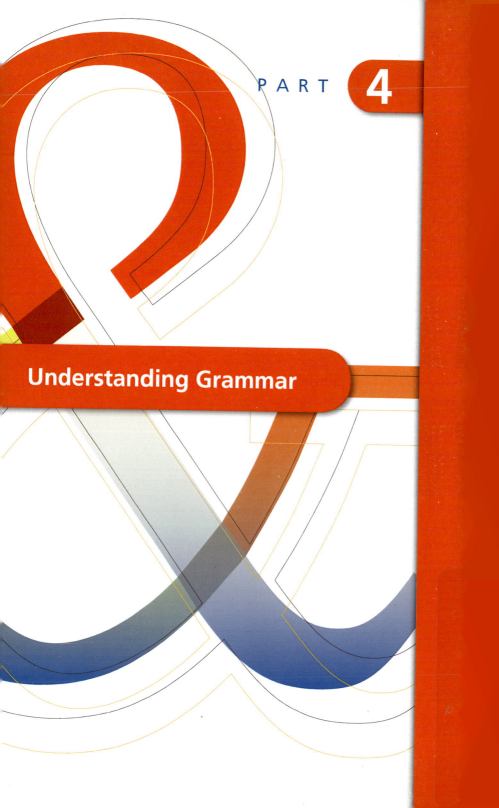

PART 4

Understanding Grammar

Understanding Grammar

CHAPTER 20

Using the Parts of Speech

The eight basic **parts of speech**—the building blocks for all English sentences—are *nouns, pronouns, verbs, adjectives, adverbs, prepositions, conjunctions,* and *interjections.* How a word is classified depends on its function in a sentence.

20a Using Nouns

Nouns name people, animals, places, things, ideas, actions, or qualities.

ml 49b

A **common noun** names any one of a class of people, places, or things: *artist, judge, building, event, city.*

A **proper noun,** always capitalized, designates a particular person, place, or thing: *Mary Cassatt, World Trade Center, Crimean War.*

A **count noun** names something that can be counted: five *dogs,* two dozen *grapes.*

A **noncount noun** names a quantity that is not countable: *time, dust, work, gold.* Noncount nouns generally have only a singular form.

A **collective noun** designates a group thought of as a unit: *committee, class, navy, band, family.* Collective nouns are generally singular unless the members of the group are referred to as individuals.

See 26a5

An **abstract noun** designates an intangible idea or quality: *love, hate, justice, anger, fear, prejudice.*

20b Using Pronouns

Pronouns are words used in place of nouns. The word for which a pronoun stands is called its **antecedent**.

ml 49c

If you use a quotation in your essay, you must document it. (Pronoun *it* refers to antecedent *quotation.*)

A **personal pronoun** stands for a person or thing. Personal pronouns include *I, me, we, us, my, mine, our, ours, you, your, yours, he, she, it, its, him, his, her, hers, they, them, their,* and *theirs.*

The firm made Debbie an offer, and she couldn't refuse it.

See
26b3

An indefinite pronoun does not refer to any particular person or thing, so it does not require an antecedent. Indefinite pronouns include *another, any, each, few, many, some, nothing, one, anyone, everyone, everybody, everything, someone, something, either,* and *neither*.

Many are called, but few are chosen.

A **reflexive pronoun** ends with *-self* and refers to a recipient of an action that is the same as the initiator of the action. The reflexive pronouns are *myself, yourself, himself, herself, itself, oneself, themselves, ourselves,* and *yourselves*.

They found themselves in downtown Pittsburgh.

An **intensive pronoun** emphasizes a noun or pronoun that directly precedes it. (Intensive pronouns have the same form as reflexive pronouns.)

Darrow himself was sure his client was innocent.

A **relative pronoun** introduces an adjective clause or a noun clause in a sentence. Relative pronouns include *which, who, whom, that, what, whose, whatever, whoever, whomever,* and *whichever*.

Gandhi was the charismatic man who helped lead India to independence. (introduces adjective clause)

Whatever happens will be a surprise. (introduces noun clause)

An **interrogative pronoun** introduces a question. Interrogative pronouns include *who, which, what, whom, whose, whoever, whatever,* and *whichever*.

Who is at the door?

A **demonstrative pronoun** points to a particular thing or group of things. *This, that, these,* and *those* are demonstrative pronouns.

This is one of Shakespeare's early plays.

A **reciprocal pronoun** denotes a mutual relationship. The reciprocal pronouns are *each other* and *one another. Each other* indicates a relationship between two individuals; *one another* denotes a relationship among more than two.

Romeo and Juliet declared their love for each other.

Concertgoers jostled one another in the ticket line.

Note: Although different types of pronouns may have the same form, they are distinguished from one another by their function in a sentence.

20c Using Verbs

1 Recognizing Verbs

A <u>verb</u> may express an action or a state of being.

ml
49a

He <u>ran</u> for the train. (physical action)

He <u>worried</u> about being late. (emotional action)

Elizabeth II <u>became</u> queen after the death of her father, George VI. (state of being)

Verbs can be classified into two groups: *main verbs* and *auxiliary verbs*.

Main Verbs **Main verbs** carry most of the meaning in a sentence. Some main verbs are **action verbs.**

Emily Dickinson <u>wrote</u> poetry.

Other main verbs function as linking verbs. A **linking verb** does not show any physical or emotional action. Its function is to link the sentence's subject to a **subject complement**, a word or phrase that renames or describes the subject.

Carbon disulfide <u>smells</u> bad.

Frequently Used Linking Verbs

appear	believe	look	seem	taste
be	feel	prove	smell	turn
become	grow	remain	sound	

Auxiliary Verbs Auxiliary verbs (also called **helping verbs**), such as *be* and *have*, combine with main verbs to form **verb phrases.** Auxiliary verbs indicate tense, voice, or mood.

[auxiliary] [main verb] [auxiliary] [main verb]

The train <u>has started</u>. We <u>are leaving</u> soon.

[verb phrase]   [verb phrase]

Certain auxiliary verbs, known as **modal auxiliaries**, indicate necessity, possibility, willingness, obligation, or ability.

In the future, farmers <u>might</u> cultivate seaweed as a food crop.

Coal mining <u>would</u> be safer if dust were controlled in the mines.

Modal Auxiliaries

can	might	ought [to]	will
could	must	shall	would
may	need [to]	should	

2 Recognizing Verbals

Verbals, such as *known* or *swimming* or *to go*, are verb forms that act as adjectives, adverbs, or nouns. A verbal can never serve as a sentence's main verb unless it is used with one or more auxiliary verbs (*has known*, *should be swimming*). Verbals include *participles, infinitives*, and *gerunds*.

Participles Virtually every verb has a **present participle**, which ends in *-ing* (*loving, learning, going, writing*), and a **past participle**, which usually ends in *-d* or *-ed* (*agreed, learned*). Some verbs have <u>irregular</u> past participles (*gone, begun, written*). Participles may function in a sentence as adjectives or as nouns.

See 22a2

Twenty brands of <u>running</u> shoes were displayed at the exhibition. (Present participle *running* serves as adjective modifying noun *shoes*.)

The <u>crowded</u> bus went past those waiting at the corner. (Past participle *crowded* serves as adjective modifying noun *bus*.)

The <u>wounded</u> were given emergency first aid. (Past participle *wounded* serves as a noun, the sentence's subject.)

Note: Participles also combine with helping verbs to form the perfect tense and the <u>progressive tense</u>.

See 22b2–3

Infinitives An **infinitive** is made up of *to* and the base form of the verb: *to defeat*. (The **base form** is the form of the verb used with *I, you, we*, and *they* in the present tense.) An infinitive may function as an adjective, an adverb, or a noun.

Ann Arbor was clearly the place <u>to be</u>. (Infinitive serves as adjective modifying noun *place*.)

They say that breaking up is hard <u>to do</u>. (Infinitive serves as adverb modifying adjective *hard*.)

Carla went outside <u>to think</u>. (Infinitive serves as adverb modifying verb *went*.)

<u>To win</u> was everything. (Infinitive serves as noun, the sentence's subject.)

Gerunds **Gerunds** (which, like present participles, end in *-ing*) always function as nouns.

<u>Seeing</u> is <u>believing</u>. (Gerund *seeing* serves as sentence's subject; gerund *believing* serves as subject complement.)

He worried about <u>interrupting</u>. (Gerund *interrupting* is object of preposition *about*.)

Andrew loves <u>skiing</u>. (Gerund *skiing* is direct object of verb *loves*.)

Note: When the *-ing* form of a verb is used as a noun, it is a *gerund*; when it is used as an adjective, it is a *present participle*.

20d Using Adjectives

<u>Adjectives</u> describe, limit, qualify, or in some other way modify nouns or pronouns.

ml
49d

1 Descriptive Adjectives

Descriptive adjectives name a quality of the noun or pronoun they modify.

After the game, they were <u>exhausted</u>.

They ordered a <u>chocolate</u> soda and a <u>butterscotch</u> sundae.

Some descriptive adjectives are formed from common nouns or from verbs (*friend/friendly, agree/agreeable*). Others, called **proper adjectives**, are formed from proper nouns.

A <u>Shakespearean</u> sonnet consists of an octave and a sestet.

Two or more words may be joined (hyphenated before a noun, without a hyphen after a noun) to form a <u>compound adjective</u>: *His parents are very <u>well-read</u> people; most people are not so <u>well read</u>.*

See
38b1

ml
49b2–3

2 Determiners

When articles, pronouns, numbers, and the like function as adjectives, limiting or qualifying nouns or pronouns, they are referred to as **determiners**.

- **Articles** (*a, an, the*)

  The boy found a four-leaf clover.

- **Possessive nouns**

  Lesley's mother lives in New Jersey.

- **Possessive pronouns** (the personal pronouns *my, your, his, her, its, our, their*)

  Their lives depended on my skill.

- **Demonstrative pronouns** (*this, these, that, those*)

  This song reminds me of that song we heard yesterday.

- **Interrogative pronouns** (*what, which, whose*)

  Whose book is this?

- **Indefinite pronouns** (*another, each, both, many, any, some*, and so on)

  Both candidates agreed to return another day.

- **Relative pronouns** (*what, whatever, which, whichever, whose, whoever*)

  I forgot whatever reasons I had for leaving.

- **Numbers** (*one, two, first, second*, and so on)

  The first time I played baseball, I got only one hit.

20e Using Adverbs

ml
49d1

Adverbs describe the action of verbs or modify adjectives, other adverbs, or complete phrases, clauses, or sentences. They answer the questions "How?" "Why?" "Where?" "When?" "Under what conditions?" and "To what extent?"

He walked rather hesitantly toward the front of the room. (walked *how*?)

Let's meet tomorrow for coffee. (meet *when*?)

Adverbs that modify other adverbs or adjectives limit or qualify the words they modify.

He pitched an almost perfect game.

Interrogative adverbs—*how, when, why*, and *where*—introduce questions.

Why did the compound darken?

Conjunctive adverbs act as <u>transitional words</u>, joining and relating independent clauses. Conjunctive adverbs may appear in various positions in a sentence.

See
13b2

> Jason forgot to register for chemistry. <u>However</u>, he managed to sign up during the drop/add period.
>
> Jason forgot to register for chemistry; <u>however</u>, he managed to sign up during the drop/add period.
>
> Jason forgot to register for chemistry. He managed, <u>however</u>, to sign up during the drop/add period.
>
> Jason forgot to register for chemistry. He managed to sign up during the drop/add period, <u>however</u>.

Frequently Used Conjunctive Adverbs

accordingly	furthermore	meanwhile	similarly
also	hence	moreover	still
anyway	however	nevertheless	then
besides	incidentally	next	thereafter
certainly	indeed	nonetheless	therefore
consequently	instead	now	thus
finally	likewise	otherwise	undoubtedly

20f Using Prepositions

A <u>preposition</u> introduces a noun or pronoun (or a phrase or clause) that functions in the sentence as a noun, linking it to other words in the sentence. The word or word group the preposition introduces is called its **object**.

ml
49e

       prep   obj   prep   obj

They received a postcard <u>from</u> Bobby telling <u>about</u> his trip.

Frequently Used Prepositions

about	beneath	inside	since
above	beside	into	through

(continued)

Frequently Used Prepositions (*continued*)

across	between	like	throughout
after	beyond	near	to
against	by	of	toward
along	concerning	off	under
among	despite	on	underneath
around	down	onto	until
as	during	out	up
at	except	outside	upon
before	for	over	with
behind	from	past	within
below	in	regarding	without

20g Using Conjunctions

Conjunctions connect words, phrases, clauses, or sentences.

- **Coordinating conjunctions** (*and, or, but, nor, for, so, yet*) connect words, phrases, or clauses of equal weight.

  The choice was simple: chicken or fish. (*Or* links two nouns.)

  The United States is a government "of the people, by the people, and for the people." (*And* links three prepositional phrases.)

  Thoreau wrote *Walden* in 1854, and he died in 1862. (*And* links two independent clauses.)

- **Correlative conjunctions,** always used in pairs, also link grammatically equivalent items.

Correlative Conjunctions

both . . . and
either . . . or
just as . . . so

neither . . . nor
not only . . . but also
whether . . . or

Both Hancock <u>and</u> Jefferson signed the Declaration of Independence. (Correlative conjunctions link two nouns.)

<u>Either</u> I will renew my lease, <u>or</u> I will move. (Correlative conjunctions link two independent clauses.)

- **Subordinating conjunctions** include *since, because, although, if, after, when, while, before, unless,* and so on. A subordinating conjunction introduces a dependent (subordinate) clause, connecting it to an independent (main) clause to form a **complex sentence**.

See 14d

<u>Although</u> drug use is a serious concern for parents, many parents are afraid to discuss it with their children.

It is best to diagram your garden <u>before</u> you start to plant it.

20h Using Interjections

Interjections are exclamations used to express emotion: *Oh! Ouch! Wow! Alas! Hey!* These words are grammatically independent; that is, they do not have a grammatical function in a sentence.

An interjection may be set off in a sentence by commas.

The message, <u>alas</u>, arrived too late.

For greater emphasis, an interjection can be punctuated as an independent unit, set off with an exclamation point.

<u>Alas!</u> The message arrived too late.

Note: Other kinds of words may also be used in isolation. They include *yes, no, hello, good-bye, please,* and *thank you.* All such words, including interjections, are collectively referred to as **isolates**.

CHAPTER 21

Using Pronouns

21a Understanding Pronoun Case

Case is the form a noun or pronoun takes to indicate its function in a sentence. **Nouns** change form only in the possessive case: the *cat's* eyes, *Molly's* book. **Pronouns**, however, have three cases: *subjective, objective,* and *possessive*.

Pronoun Case Forms

Subjective						
I	he, she	it	we	you	they	who whoever

Objective						
me	him, her	it	us	you	them	whom whomever

Possessive						
my mine	his, her hers	its	our ours	your yours	their theirs	whose

1 Subjective Case

A pronoun takes the **subjective case** in the following situations.

> **Subject of a Verb:** <u>I</u> bought a new mountain bike.
>
> **Subject Complement:** It was <u>he</u> who volunteered to drive.

2 Objective Case

A pronoun takes the **objective case** in the following situations.

> **Direct Object:** Our supervisor asked Adam and <u>me</u> to work on the project.

Indirect Object: The plumber's bill gave <u>him</u> quite a shock.

Object of a Preposition: We own ten shares of stock between <u>us</u>.

3 Possessive Case

A pronoun takes the **possessive case** when it indicates ownership. The possessive case is also used before a <u>gerund</u>.

See 20c2

> Napoleon gave <u>his</u> approval to <u>their</u> ruling Naples. (*His* indicates ownership; *ruling* is a gerund.)

Close-Up *I* AND *ME*

I is not necessarily more appropriate than *me*. In the following situation, *me* is correct.

> Just between you and <u>me</u> [not *I*], I think the data are inconclusive. (*Me* is the object of the preposition *between*.)

EXERCISE 21.1

Underline the correct form of the pronoun within the parentheses. Compare your choices with those of a classmate.

Example: Toni Morrison, Alice Walker, and (<u>she</u>, her) are perhaps the most widely recognized African American women writing today.

1. Both Walt Whitman and (he, him) wrote a great deal of poetry about nature.
2. Our instructor gave Matthew and (me, I) an excellent idea for our project.
3. The sales clerk objected to (me, my) returning the sweater.
4. I understand (you, your) being unavailable to work tonight.
5. The waiter asked Michael and (me, I) to move to another table.

21b Determining Pronoun Case in Special Situations

1 Comparisons with *Than* or *As*

When a comparison ends with a pronoun, the pronoun's function in the sentence determines your choice of pronoun case. If the pronoun functions as a subject, use the subjective case; if it functions as an object, use the objective case. You can determine the function of the pronoun by completing the comparison.

> Darcy likes John more than <u>I</u>. (*. . . more than I like John: I* is the subject.)
>
> Darcy likes John more than <u>me</u>. (*. . . more than she likes me: me* is the object.)

2 *Who* and *Whom*

The case of the pronouns *who* and *whom* depends on their function *within their own clause.* When a pronoun serves as the subject of its clause, use *who* or *whoever*; when it functions as an object, use *whom* or *whomever.*

> The Salvation Army gives food and shelter to <u>whoever</u> is in need. (*Whoever* is the subject of the dependent clause *whoever is in need.*)
>
> I wonder <u>whom</u> jazz musician Miles Davis influenced. (*Whom* is the object of *influenced* in the dependent clause *whom jazz musician Miles Davis influenced.*)

Close-Up   PRONOUN CASE IN QUESTIONS

To determine whether to use subjective case (*who*) or objective case (*whom*) in a question, use a personal pronoun to answer the question. If the pronoun in your answer is the subject, use *who*; if the pronoun is the object, use *whom*.

> <u>Who</u> wrote *The Age of Innocence*? <u>She</u> wrote it. (subject)
>
> <u>Whom</u> do you support for mayor? I support <u>him</u>. (object)

---

3 Appositives

ml
49c4

An **appositive** is a noun or noun phrase that identifies or renames an adjacent noun or pronoun. The case of a pronoun in an appositive depends on the function of the word the appositive identifies or renames.

> Two recording artists, <u>he</u> and Smokey Robinson, had contracts with Motown Records. (*Artists* is the subject of the sentence, so the pronoun in the appositive *he and Smokey Robinson* takes the subjective case.)
>
> We heard two Motown recording artists, Smokey Robinson and <u>him</u>. (*Artists* is the object of the verb *heard,* so the pronoun in the appositive *Smokey Robinson and him* takes the objective case.)

4 *We* and *Us* before a Noun

When a first-person plural pronoun directly precedes a noun, the case of the pronoun depends on the way the noun functions in the sentence.

> <u>We</u> women must stick together. (*Women* is the subject of the sentence, so the pronoun *we* takes the subjective case.)

> Teachers make learning easy for <u>us</u> students. (*Students* is the object of the preposition *for*, so the pronoun *us* takes the objective case.)

EXERCISE 21.2

Using the word in parentheses, combine each pair of sentences into a single sentence. You may change word order and add or delete words.

Example: After he left the band The Police, bass player Sting continued as a solo artist. He once taught middle-school English. (who)

Revised: After he left the band The Police, bass player Sting, who once taught middle-school English, continued as a solo artist.

▶ 1. Herb Ritts has photographed world leaders, leading artistic figures in dance and drama, and a vanishing African tribe. He got his start by taking photographs of Hollywood stars. (who)
▶ 2. Tim Green has written several novels about a fictional football team. He played for the Atlanta Hawks and has a degree in law. (who)
  3. Some say Carl Sagan did more to further science education in America than any other person. He wrote many books on science and narrated many popular television shows. (who)
  4. Jodie Foster has won two Academy Awards for her acting. She was a child star. (who)
  5. Sylvia Plath met the poet Ted Hughes at Cambridge University in England. She later married him. (whom)

21c Revising Pronoun Reference Errors

An **antecedent** is the word or word group to which a pronoun refers. The connection between a pronoun and its antecedent should always be clear. If the **pronoun reference** is not clear, you will need to revise the sentence.

ml
49c1

Alicia forgot her cell phone.

The students missed their train.

1 Ambiguous Antecedent

Sometimes it is not clear to which antecedent a pronoun—for example, *this, that, which,* or *it*—refers. In such cases, eliminate the ambiguity by substituting a noun for the pronoun.

When you make a promise to give someone a gift, you should
keep ~~it.~~ *that promise.* (The pronoun *it* can refer either to *promise* or to *gift*.)

2 Remote Antecedent

The farther a pronoun is from its antecedent, the more difficult it is for readers to make a connection between them. If a pronoun and its antecedent are far apart, replace the pronoun with a noun.

During the mid-1800s, many Czechs began to immigrate to America.

By 1860, about 23,000 Czechs had left their country; by 1900, 13,000
Czech immigrants were coming to ~~its~~ *America's* shores each year.

3 Nonexistent Antecedent

Sometimes a pronoun—for example, *this*—refers to an antecedent that does not appear in the sentence. In such cases, add the missing antecedent.

Some one-celled organisms contain chlorophyll yet are considered
animals. This *paradox* illustrates the difficulty of classifying single-celled

organisms. (What does *this* refer to?)

Note: Colloquial expressions such as "*It* says online" and "*They* said on the news," which refer to unidentified antecedents, are not acceptable in college writing. Substitute the appropriate noun for the unclear pronoun: "*The online article says . . .*"; "*In his commentary, Chuck Todd said . . .*"

4 *Who, Which,* and *That*

In general, *who* refers to people or to animals that have names. *Which* and *that* refer to things or to unnamed animals. When referring to an antecedent, be sure to choose the appropriate pronoun (*who, which,* or *that*).

David Henry Hwang, who wrote the Tony Award-winning play *M. Butterfly*, also wrote *Chinglish*.

The spotted owl, which lives in old growth forests, is in danger of extinction.

Houses that are built today are usually more energy efficient than those built twenty years ago.

Never use *that* to refer to a person.

The man *who* ~~that~~ won the hot-dog-eating contest is my neighbor.

Note: Use *which* to introduce **nonrestrictive clauses**, which are always set off with commas. Use *that* to introduce **restrictive clauses**, which are not set off with commas. (*Who* can introduce either restrictive or nonrestrictive clauses.)

See 30d1

EXERCISE 21.3

Analyze the pronoun reference errors in each of the following sentences. After doing so, revise each sentence by substituting an appropriate noun or noun phrase for the underlined pronoun.

Example: Jefferson asked Lewis to head the expedition, and Lewis selected
Clark
₍him as his associate. (*Him* refers to a nonexistent antecedent.)

1. The purpose of the expedition was to search out a land route to the Pacific and to gather information about the West. The Louisiana Purchase increased the need for it.
2. The expedition was going to be difficult. They trained the men in Illinois, the starting point.
3. Clark and most of the men who descended the Yellowstone River camped on the bank. It was beautiful and wild.
4. Both Jefferson and Lewis had faith that he would be successful in this transcontinental journey.
5. The expedition was efficient, and only one man was lost. This was extraordinary.

CHAPTER **22**

Using Verbs

22a **Understanding Verb Forms**

Every verb has four **principal parts**: a **base form** (the present tense form of the verb used with *I*), a **present participle** (the *-ing* form of the verb), a **past tense form**, and a **past participle**.

Note: The verb *be* is the one exception to this definition; its base form is *be*.

1 Regular Verbs

A **regular verb** forms both its past tense and its past participle by adding *-d* or *-ed* to the base form of the verb.

Principal Parts of Regular Verbs

Base Form	Past Tense Form	Past Participle
smile	smiled	smiled
talk	talked	talked
jump	jumped	jumped

2 Irregular Verbs

Irregular verbs do not follow the pattern discussed above. The chart that follows lists the principal parts of the most frequently used irregular verbs.

Frequently Used Irregular Verbs

Base Form	Past Tense Form	Past Participle
arise	arose	arisen
awake	awoke, awaked	awoken, awaked
be	was/were	been
beat	beat	beaten
begin	began	begun
bend	bent	bent
bet	bet, betted	bet
bite	bit	bitten
blow	blew	blown
break	broke	broken
bring	brought	brought
build	built	built
burst	burst	burst
buy	bought	bought

Base Form	Past Tense Form	Past Participle
catch	caught	caught
choose	chose	chosen
cling	clung	clung
come	came	come
cost	cost	cost
deal	dealt	dealt
dig	dug	dug
dive	dived, dove	dived
do	did	done
drag	dragged	dragged
draw	drew	drawn
drink	drank	drunk
drive	drove	driven
eat	ate	eaten
fall	fell	fallen
fight	fought	fought
find	found	found
fly	flew	flown
forget	forgot	forgotten, forgot
freeze	froze	frozen
get	got	gotten
give	gave	given
go	went	gone
grow	grew	grown
hang (execute)	hanged	hanged
hang (suspend)	hung	hung
have	had	had
hear	heard	heard
keep	kept	kept
know	knew	known
lay	laid	laid
lead	led	led
lend	lent	lent
let	let	let
lie (recline)	lay	lain
lie (tell an untruth)	lied	lied
make	made	made
prove	proved	proved, proven
read	read	read
ride	rode	ridden
ring	rang	rung
rise	rose	risen
run	ran	run
say	said	said

(continued)

Frequently Used Irregular Verbs (continued)

Base Form	Past Tense Form	Past Participle
see	saw	seen
set (place)	set	set
shake	shook	shaken
shrink	shrank, shrunk	shrunk, shrunken
sing	sang	sung
sink	sank	sunk
sit	sat	sat
sneak	sneaked, snuck	sneaked, snuck
speak	spoke	spoken
speed	sped, speeded	sped, speeded
spin	spun	spun
spring	sprang	sprung
stand	stood	stood
steal	stole	stolen
strike	struck	struck, stricken
swear	swore	sworn
swim	swam	swum
swing	swung	swung
take	took	taken
teach	taught	taught
throw	threw	thrown
wake	woke, waked	waked, woken
wear	wore	worn
wring	wrung	wrung
write	wrote	written

Close-Up *LIE/LAY AND SIT/SET*

Lie means "to recline" and does not take an object ("He likes to *lie* on the floor"); *lay* means "to place" or "to put" and does take an object ("He wants to *lay* a rug on the floor").

Base Form	Past Tense Form	Past Participle
lie	lay	lain
lay	laid	laid

Sit means "to assume a seated position" and does not take an object ("She wants to *sit* on the table"); *set* means "to place" or "to put" and usually takes an object ("She wants to *set* a vase on the table").

Base Form	Past Tense Form	Past Participle
sit	sat	sat
set	set	set

EXERCISE 22.1

Complete the sentences in the following paragraph with an appropriate form of the verbs in parentheses.

Example: An air of mystery surrounds many of those who have ____*sung*____ (sing) and played the blues.

▶The legendary blues musician Robert Johnson supposedly _____ (sell) his soul to the devil in order to become a guitar virtuoso. ▶Myth has it that the young Johnson could barely chord his instrument and annoyed other musicians by trying to sit in at clubs, where he _____ (sneak) onto the bandstand to play every chance he got. He disappeared for a short time, the story goes, and when he returned he was a phenomenal guitarist, having _____ (swear) a Faustian oath to Satan. Johnson's song "Crossroads Blues"—rearranged and recorded by the sixties band Cream as simply "Crossroads"—supposedly recounts this exchange, telling how Johnson _____ (deal) with the devil. Some of his other songs, such as "Hellhound on My Trail," are allegedly about the torment he suffered as he _____ (fight) for his soul.

EXERCISE 22.2

Complete the following sentences with appropriate forms of the verbs in parentheses.

Example: Mary Cassatt ____*laid*____ down her paintbrush. (lie, lay)

▶ 1. Impressionist artists of the nineteenth century preferred everyday subjects and used to _____ fruit on a table to paint. (sit, set)
▶ 2. They were known for their technique of _____ dabs of paint quickly on canvas, giving an "impression" of a scene, not extensive detail. (lying, laying)
3. Claude Monet's *Women in the Garden* features one woman in the foreground who _____ on the grass in a garden. (sit, set)

4. In Pierre Auguste Renoir's *Nymphs*, two nude figures talk while _____ on flowers in a garden. (lying, laying)

5. Paul Cézanne liked to _____ in front of his subject as he painted and often completed paintings out of doors rather than in a studio. (sit, set)

22b Understanding Tense

ml
49a2

Tense is the form a verb takes to indicate when an action occurred or when a condition existed.

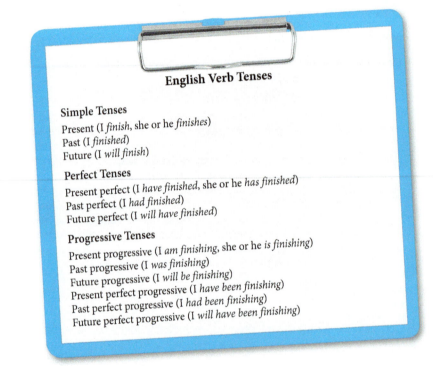

English Verb Tenses

Simple Tenses
Present (I *finish*, she or he *finishes*)
Past (I *finished*)
Future (I *will finish*)

Perfect Tenses
Present perfect (I *have finished*, she or he *has finished*)
Past perfect (I *had finished*)
Future perfect (I *will have finished*)

Progressive Tenses
Present progressive (I *am finishing*, she or he *is finishing*)
Past progressive (I *was finishing*)
Future progressive (I *will be finishing*)
Present perfect progressive (I *have been finishing*)
Past perfect progressive (I *had been finishing*)
Future perfect progressive (I *will have been finishing*)

① Using the Simple Tenses

The **simple tenses** include *present, past,* and *future.*

- The **present tense** usually indicates an action that is taking place at the time it is expressed in speech or writing. It can also indicate an action that occurs regularly.

I <u>see</u> your point. (an action taking place when it is expressed)

We <u>wear</u> wool in the winter. (an action that occurs regularly)

Close-Up SPECIAL USES OF THE PRESENT TENSE

The present tense has four special uses:

1. **To indicate future time:** The grades arrive next Thursday.
2. **To state a generally held belief:** Studying pays off.
3. **To state a scientific truth:** An object at rest tends to stay at rest.
4. **To discuss a literary work:** *Family Installments* tells the story of a Puerto Rican family.

• The **past tense** indicates that an action has already taken place.

John Glenn orbited the earth three times on February 20, 1962. (an action completed in the past)

As a young man, Mark Twain traveled through the Southwest. (an action that occurred once or many times in the past but did not extend into the present)

• The **future tense** indicates that an action will or is likely to take place.

Halley's Comet will reappear in 2061. (a future action that will definitely occur)

The growth of community colleges will probably continue. (a future action that is likely to occur)

2 Using the Perfect Tenses

The **perfect tenses** indicate actions that were or will be completed before other actions or conditions. The perfect tenses are formed with the appropriate tense form of the auxiliary verb *have* plus the past participle.

• The **present perfect** tense can indicate two types of continuing action beginning in the past.

Dr. Kim has finished studying the effects of BHA on rats. (an action that began in the past and is finished at the present time)

My mother has invested her money wisely. (an action that began in the past and extends into the present)

• The **past perfect** tense indicates an action occurring before a certain time in the past.

By 1946, engineers had built the first electronic digital computer.

- The **future perfect** tense indicates that an action will be finished by a certain future time.

By Tuesday, the transit authority <u>will have run</u> out of money.

Close-Up COULD HAVE, SHOULD HAVE, AND WOULD HAVE

Do not use the preposition *of* after *would*, *should*, *could*, and *might*. Use the auxiliary verb *have* after these words.

have
I should ˄of left for class earlier.

---

❸ Using the Progressive Tenses

The **progressive tenses** indicate continuing action. They are formed with the appropriate tense of the verb *be* plus the present participle.

- The **present progressive** tense indicates that something is happening at the time it is expressed in speech or writing.

The volcano <u>is erupting</u>, and lava <u>is flowing</u> toward the town.

- The **past progressive** tense indicates two kinds of past action.

Roderick Usher's actions <u>were becoming</u> increasingly bizarre. (a continuing action in the past)

The French revolutionary Marat was stabbed to death while he <u>was bathing</u>. (an action occurring at the same time in the past as another action)

- The **future progressive** tense indicates a continuing action in the future.

The treasury secretary <u>will be monitoring</u> the money supply regularly.

- The **present perfect progressive** tense indicates action continuing from the past into the present and possibly into the future.

Rescuers <u>have been working</u> around the clock.

- The **past perfect progressive** tense indicates that a past action went on until another one occurred.

Before President Kennedy was assassinated, he <u>had been working</u> on civil rights legislation.

- The **future perfect progressive** tense indicates that an action will continue until a certain future time.

  By eleven o'clock we <u>will have been driving</u> for seven hours.

4 Using Verb Tenses in a Sentence

You use different tenses in a sentence to indicate that actions are taking place at different times. By choosing tenses that accurately express these times, you enable readers to follow the sequence of actions.

- *When a **verb** appears in a dependent clause, its tense depends on the tense of the main verb in the independent clause.* When the main verb in the independent clause is in the past tense, the verb in the dependent clause is usually in the past or past perfect tense. When the main verb in the independent clause is in the past perfect tense, the verb in the dependent clause is usually in the past tense. (When the main verb in the independent clause is in any tense except the past or past perfect, the verb in the dependent clause may be in any tense needed for meaning.)

Main Verb	Verb in Dependent Clause
George Hepplewhite <u>was</u> (past) an English cabinetmaker	who <u>designed</u> (past) distinctive chair backs.
The battle <u>had ended</u> (past perfect)	by the time reinforcements <u>arrived</u>. (past)

- *When an **infinitive** appears in a verbal phrase, the tense it expresses depends on the tense of the sentence's main verb.* The *present infinitive* (the *to* form of the verb) indicates an action happening at the same time as or later than the main verb. The *perfect infinitive* (*to have* plus the past participle) indicates action happening earlier than the main verb.

Main Verb	Infinitive
I <u>went</u>	<u>to see</u> the Eagles play last week. (The going and seeing occurred at the same time.)
I <u>want</u>	<u>to see</u> the Eagles play tomorrow. (Wanting occurs in the present, and seeing will occur in the future.)
I would <u>like</u>	<u>to have seen</u> the Eagles play. (Liking occurs in the present, and seeing would have occurred in the past.)

- *When a **participle** appears in a verbal phrase, its tense depends on the tense of the sentence's main verb.* The *present participle* indicates action happening at the same time as the action of the main verb. The *past participle* or the *present perfect participle* indicates action occurring before the action of the main verb.

Participle	Main Verb
<u>Addressing</u> the 1896 Democratic Convention,	William Jennings Bryan <u>delivered</u> his Cross of Gold speech. (The addressing and the delivery occurred at the same time.)
<u>Having written</u> her research paper,	Sophia <u>studied</u> for her history final. (The writing occurred before the studying.)

EXERCISE 22.3

A verb is missing from each of the following sentences. Fill in the form of the verb indicated in parentheses.

Example: The Outer Banks __*stretch*__ (stretch: present) along the North Carolina coast for more than 175 miles.

1. Many portions of the Outer Banks of North Carolina _____ (give: present) the visitor a sense of history and timelessness.
2. Many students of history _____ (read: present perfect) about the Outer Banks and its mysteries.
3. It was on Roanoke Island in the 1580s that English colonists _____ (establish: past) the first settlement in the New World.
4. That colony vanished soon after it was settled, _____ (become: present participle) known as the famous "lost colony."
5. By 1718, the pirate Blackbeard _____ (made: past perfect) the Outer Banks a hiding place for his treasures.
6. It was at Ocracoke, in fact, that Blackbeard _____ (meet: past) his death.
7. Even today, fortune hunters _____ (search: present progressive) the Outer Banks for Blackbeard's hidden treasures.
8. The Outer Banks are also famous for Kitty Hawk and Kill Devil Hills; even as technology has advanced into the space age, the number of tourists flocking to the site of the Wright brothers' epic flight _____. (grow: present perfect progressive)
9. Long before that famous flight occurred, however, the Outer Banks _____ (claim: past perfect) countless ships along its ever-shifting shores, resulting in its nickname—the "Graveyard of the Atlantic."
10. If the Outer Banks continue to be protected from the ravages of overdevelopment and commercialization, visitors _____ (enjoy: future progressive) the mysteries of this tiny finger of land for years to come.

22c Understanding Mood

Mood is the form a verb takes to indicate whether a writer is making a statement, asking a question, giving a command, or expressing a wish or a contrary-to-fact statement. There are three moods in English:

- The **indicative** mood expresses an opinion, states a fact, or asks a question: *Jackie Robinson had a great impact on professional baseball.* The indicative is the mood used in most English sentences.
- The **imperative** mood is used in commands and direct requests. Usually, the imperative includes only the base form of the verb without a subject: *Use a dictionary.*
- The **subjunctive** mood is not as common as it once was, but it is still used to express wishes, contrary-to-fact statements, and requests or recommendations.

1 Forming the Subjunctive Mood

The **present subjunctive** uses the base form of the verb, regardless of the subject. The **past subjunctive** has the same form as the past tense of the verb. (However, when *be* is used as an auxiliary verb, it takes the form *were* regardless of the number or person of the subject.)

Dr. Gorman suggested that I study the Cambrian Period. (present subjunctive)

I wish I were going to Europe. (past subjunctive)

2 Using the Subjunctive Mood

The **present subjunctive** may be used in *that* clauses after words such as *ask, suggest, require, recommend,* and *demand.*

The report recommended that juveniles be given mandatory counseling.

Captain Ahab insisted that his crew hunt the white whale.

The **past subjunctive** may be used in **conditional statements** (statements beginning with *if* that are contrary to fact, including statements that express a wish).

If John were here, he could see Marsha. (John is not here.)

The father acted as if he were having the baby. (The father couldn't be having the baby.)

I wish I were more organized. (expresses a wish)

Note: In many situations, the subjunctive mood can sound stiff or formal. To eliminate the need for a subjunctive construction, rephrase the sentence.

to
The group asked ~~that~~ the city council ban smoking in public places.

EXERCISE 22.4

Complete each sentence in the following paragraph by inserting the appropriate form (indicative, imperative, or subjunctive) of the verb in parentheses. Compare your choices with those of a classmate.

Harry Houdini was a famous escape artist. ▶He _____ (perform) escapes from every type of bond imaginable: handcuffs, locks, straitjackets, ropes, sacks, and sealed chests underwater. ▶In Germany, workers _____ (challenge) Houdini to escape from a packing box. ▶If he _____ (be) to escape, they would admit that he _____ (be) the best escape artist in the world. Houdini accepted. Before getting into the box, he asked that the observers _____ (give) it a thorough examination. He then asked that a worker _____ (nail) him into the box. "_____ (place) a screen around the box," he ordered after he had been sealed inside. In a few minutes, Houdini _____ (step) from behind the screen. When the workers demanded that they _____ (see) the box, Houdini pulled down the screen. To their surprise, they saw the box with the lid still nailed tightly in place.

22d Understanding Voice

Voice is the form a verb takes to indicate whether the subject of the verb acts or is acted upon. When the subject of a verb does something—that is, acts—the verb is in the **active voice**. When the subject of a verb receives the action—that is, is acted upon—the verb is in the **passive voice**.

Active Voice: Hart Crane <u>wrote</u> *The Bridge*.

Passive Voice: *The Bridge* <u>was written</u> by Hart Crane.

Close-Up   ACTIVE VERSUS PASSIVE VOICE

Because the active voice emphasizes the person or thing performing an action, it is usually briefer, clearer, and more emphatic than the passive voice. For this reason, you should usually use the active voice in your college writing.

Some scientific disciplines, however, encourage the use of the passive voice. The purpose is to convey objectivity—to shift the focus away from the scientists and to emphasize the experimental results.

DDT <u>was found</u> in soil samples. (Passive voice emphasizes the discovery of DDT; who found it is not important.)

Grits <u>are eaten</u> throughout the South. (Passive voice emphasizes the fact that grits are eaten, not who eats them.)

① Changing Verbs from Passive to Active Voice

You can change a verb from passive to active voice by making the subject of the passive verb the object of the active verb. The person or thing performing the action then becomes the subject of the new sentence.

Passive: The novel *Frankenstein* <u>was written</u> by Mary Shelley.

Active: Mary Shelley <u>wrote</u> the novel *Frankenstein*.

2 Changing Verbs from Active to Passive Voice

You can change a verb from active to passive voice by making the object of the active verb the subject of the passive verb. The person or thing performing the action then becomes the object of the passive verb.

Active: Sir James Murray <u>compiled</u> *The Oxford English Dictionary*.

Passive: *The Oxford English Dictionary* <u>was compiled</u> by Sir James Murray.

EXERCISE 22.5

Decide which passive voice sentences in the following paragraph should be in the active voice, and rewrite those sentences.

▶Rockets were invented by the Chinese about AD 1000. ▶Gunpowder was packed into bamboo tubes and ignited by means of a fuse. ▶These rockets were fired by soldiers at enemy armies and usually caused panic. ▶In thirteenth-century England, an improved form of gunpowder was introduced by Roger Bacon. ▶As a result, rockets were used in battles and were a common—although unreliable—weapon. In the early eighteenth century, a twenty-pound rocket that traveled almost two miles was constructed by William Congreve, an English artillery expert. By the late nineteenth century, thought was given to supersonic speeds by the physicist Ernst Mach, and the sonic boom was predicted by him. The first liquid-fuel rocket was launched by the American Robert Goddard in 1926. A pamphlet written by him anticipated almost all future rocket developments. As a result of his pioneering work, he is called the father of modern rocketry.

EXERCISE 22.6

Decide which active voice sentences in the following paragraph should be in the passive voice, and rewrite those sentences.

▶The Regent Diamond is one of the world's most famous and coveted jewels. ▶A slave discovered the 410-carat diamond in 1701 in an Indian mine. ▶Over the years, people stole and sold the diamond several times. In 1717, the regent of France bought the diamond for an enormous sum, but during the French Revolution, it disappeared again. Someone later found it in a ditch in Paris. Eventually, Napoleon had the diamond set into his ceremonial sword. At last, when the French monarch fell, the government placed the Regent Diamond in the Louvre, where it remains today.

Using Adjectives and Adverbs

23a Understanding Adjectives and Adverbs

Adjectives modify nouns and pronouns. **Adverbs** modify verbs, adjectives, or other adverbs—or entire phrases, clauses, or sentences. Both adjectives and adverbs describe, limit, or qualify other words, phrases, or clauses.

The *function* of a word in a sentence, not its *form*, determines whether it is an adjective or an adverb. Although many adverbs (such as *immediately* and *hopelessly*) end in *-ly*, others (such as *almost* and *very*) do not. Moreover, some words that end in *-ly* (such as *lively*) are adjectives.

> **MULTILINGUAL TIP**
> For information on correct placement of adjectives and adverbs in a sentence, **see 49d1**. For information on correct order of adjectives in a series, **see 49d2**.

23b Using Adjectives

See 20c1

Use an **adjective**, not an adverb, to modify a noun or a pronoun. Also use an adjective as a subject complement. A **subject complement** is a word that follows a linking verb and modifies the sentence's subject, not its verb. A linking verb does not show physical or emotional action. *Seem, appear, believe, become, grow, turn, remain, prove, look, sound, smell, taste, feel*, and the forms of the verb *be* are (or can be used as) linking verbs.

> Michelle seemed <u>brave</u>. (*Seemed* shows no action, so it is a linking verb. Because *brave* is a subject complement that modifies the subject *Michelle*, it takes the adjective form.)

> Michelle smiled <u>bravely</u>. (*Smiled* shows action, so it is not a linking verb. Because *bravely* modifies *smiled*, it takes the adverb form.)

Note: Sometimes the same verb can function as either a linking verb or an action verb: *He remained <u>stubborn</u>.* (He was still stubborn.) *He remained <u>stubbornly</u>.* (He remained, in a stubborn manner.)

Use an adjective—not an adverb—as an **object complement**, a word that follows a sentence's direct object and modifies that object and not the verb. Objects are nouns or pronouns, so their modifiers must be adjectives.

Most people called him <u>timid</u>. (People consider him to be timid; here *timid* is an object complement that modifies *him*, the sentence's direct object, so the adjective form is correct.)

Most people called him <u>timidly</u>. (People were timid when they called him; here *timidly* modifies the verb *called*—not the object—so the adverb form is correct.)

23c Using Adverbs

Use an **adverb**, not an adjective, to modify a verb, an adjective, or another adverb—or an entire phrase, clause, or sentence.

       very well
Most students did ~~great~~ on the midterm. (*Very* modifies *well*; *well* modifies *did*.)

       conservatively
My parents dress a lot more ~~conservative~~ than my friends do. (*More* modifies *conservatively*; *conservatively* modifies *dress*.)

Close-Up USING ADJECTIVES AND ADVERBS

In informal speech, adjective forms such as *good, bad, sure, real, slow, quick,* and *loud* are often used to modify verbs, adjectives, and adverbs. Avoid these informal modifiers in college writing.

    really well
The program ran ~~real good~~ the first time we tried it, but the new system
    badly
performed ~~bad~~.

EXERCISE 23.1

Revise each of the incorrect sentences in the following paragraph so that only adjectives modify nouns and pronouns and only adverbs modify verbs, adjectives, or other adverbs.

▶A popular self-help trend in the United States today is motivational podcasts. ▶These podcasts, with titles like *How to Attract Love, Freedom from Acne,* and *I Am a Genius,* are intended to address every problem known to modern society—and to solve these problems quick and easy. ▶The podcasts are said to work because they contain "hidden messages" that bypass conscious defense mechanisms. ▶The listener hears only music or relaxing sounds, like waves rolling slow and steady. At decibel levels perceived only subconsciously, positive words and phrases are embedded, usually by someone who speaks deep and rhythmic. The top-selling podcasts are those that help listeners lose weight or quit smoking real fast. The popularity of such material is not hard to understand. They promise easy solutions to complex problems.

EXERCISE 23.2

Being careful to use adjectives—not adverbs—as subject complements and object complements, write five sentences in imitation of each of the following sentences. Consult the list of linking verbs in **20c1**, and use a different linking verb in each of your sentences.

▶ 1. Julie looked worried.
2. Dan considers his collection valuable.

23d Using Comparative and Superlative Forms

Most adjectives and adverbs have **comparative** and **superlative** forms.

Comparative and Superlative Forms

Form	Function	Example
Positive	Describes a quality; does not indicate a comparison	big, easily
Comparative	Indicates a comparison between *two* qualities (greater or lesser)	bigger, more easily
Superlative	Indicates a comparison among *more than two* qualities (greatest or least)	biggest, most easily

Note: Some adverbs, particularly those indicating time, place, and degree (*almost, very, here*, and *immediately*), do not have comparative or superlative forms.

1 Regular Comparative Forms

To form the comparative, all one-syllable adjectives and many two-syllable adjectives (particularly those that end in *-y, -ly, -le, -er,* and *-ow*) add *-er*: *slower, funnier.* (Note that a final *y* becomes *i* before *-er* is added.)

Other two-syllable adjectives and all long adjectives form the comparative with *more: more famous, more incredible.*

Adverbs ending in *-ly* also form the comparative with *more: more slowly.* Other adverbs use the *-er* ending to form the comparative: *sooner.*

All adjectives and adverbs indicate a lesser degree with *less: less lovely, less slowly.*

2 Regular Superlative Forms

Adjectives that form the comparative with *-er* add *-est* to form the superlative: *nicest, funniest.* Adjectives that indicate the comparative with *more* use *most* to indicate the superlative: *most famous, most challenging.*

The majority of adverbs use *most* to indicate the superlative: *most quickly.* Others use the *-est* ending: *soonest.*

All adjectives and adverbs use *least* to indicate the least degree: *least interesting, least willingly.*

Close-Up USING COMPARATIVES AND SUPERLATIVES

- Never use both *more* and *-er* to form the comparative or both *most* and *-est* to form the superlative.

  Nothing could have been ~~more~~ easier.

  Jack is the ~~most~~ meanest person in town.

- Never use the superlative when comparing only two things.

  taller
  Stacy is the ~~tallest~~ of the two sisters.

- Never use the comparative when comparing more than two things.

  earliest
  We chose the ~~earlier~~ of the four appointments.

---

3 Irregular Comparative and Superlative Forms

Some adjectives and adverbs have irregular comparative and superlative forms.

Irregular Comparative and Superlative Forms

	Positive	Comparative	Superlative
Adjectives:	good	better	best
	bad	worse	worst
	a little	less	least
	many, some, much	more	most
Adverbs:	well	better	best
	badly	worse	worst

Close-Up   ILLOGICAL COMPARATIVE AND SUPERLATIVE FORMS

Many adjectives—for example, *perfect, unique, excellent, impossible, parallel, empty*, and *dead*—are **absolutes** and therefore can have no comparative or superlative forms.

　　　　　　　　　better
"The Cask of Amontillado" is a ~~more excellent~~ story than "The Tell-Tale Heart."

　　　a
I saw ~~the most~~ unique vase in the museum.

These adjectives can, however, be modified by words that suggest approaching the absolute state—*nearly* or *almost*, for example.

He revised until his draft was almost perfect.

Note: Some adverbs, particularly those indicating time, place, and degree (*almost, very, here, immediately*), do not have comparative or superlative forms.

EXERCISE 23.3

Supply the correct comparative and superlative forms for each of the following adjectives or adverbs. Then, use each form in a sentence.

Example: strange   stranger   strangest

The story had a *strange* ending.
The explanation sounded *stranger* each time I heard it.
This is the *strangest* gadget I have ever seen.

1.	difficult	6.	softly
2.	eccentric	7.	embarrassing
3.	confusing	8.	well
4.	bad	9.	often
5.	mysterious	10.	tiny

CHAPTER **24**

Revising Fragments

24a Recognizing Fragments

A **fragment** is an incomplete sentence—a phrase or clause that is punctuated as if it were a complete sentence. A sentence may be incomplete for any of the following reasons:

● **It has no subject.**

Many astrophysicists now believe that galaxies are distributed in clusters. And even form supercluster complexes.

● **It has no verb.**

Every generation has its defining moments. Usually the events with the most news coverage.

● **It has neither a subject nor a verb.**

Researchers are engaged in a variety of studies. Suggesting a link between alcoholism and heredity. (*Suggesting* is a **verbal,** which cannot serve as a sentence's main verb.)

● **It is a dependent clause.**

Bishop Desmond Tutu was awarded the Nobel Peace Prize. Because he fought to end apartheid.

The pH meter and the spectrophotometer are two scientific instruments. <u>That changed the chemistry laboratory dramatically.</u>

Note: A sentence cannot consist of a single clause that begins with a subordinating conjunction (such as *because*) or a relative pronoun (such as *that*); moreover, unless it is a question, a sentence cannot consist of a single clause beginning with *when, where, who, which, what, why*, or *how*.

Close-Up   IDENTIFYING FRAGMENTS

A fragment is especially confusing when it comes between two independent clauses and readers cannot tell which of the two clauses completes the fragment's thought. For instance, it is impossible to tell to which independent clause the underlined fragment in each of the following sequences belongs.

The course requirements were changed last year. <u>Because a new professor was hired at the very end of the spring semester.</u> I was unable to find out about this change until after preregistration.

In *The Ox-Bow Incident*, the crowd is convinced that the men are guilty. <u>Even though the men insist they are innocent and Davies pleads for their lives.</u> They are hanged.

EXERCISE 24.1

Identify each of the following word groups as either a fragment (F) or a complete sentence (CS). Be prepared to explain why each fragment is not a complete sentence.

1. Consisting of shortness of breath, a high fever, and a racing pulse.
2. Held in contempt of court by the presiding judge.
3. Walking to the end of the road and back is good exercise.
4. On her own at last, after many years of struggle for independence.
5. Because he felt torn between two cultures.
6. With boundaries extending from the ocean to the bay.
7. Although language study can be challenging.
8. In addition, a new point guard will be a valuable addition to the team.
9. Defeated by his own greed but not in the least regretful.
10. Moreover, the continued presence of troops in the Middle East.

Close-Up REVISING FRAGMENTS

If you identify a fragment in your writing, use one of the following two strategies to revise it:

1. Attach the fragment to an adjacent independent clause.

   and
   According to German legend, Lohengrin is the son of Parzival./ ~~And~~ a knight of the Holy Grail.

   because
   Pioneers traveled west./ ~~Because~~ they hoped to find a better life.

2. Turn the fragment into a sentence.

   Lancaster County, Pennsylvania, is home to many Pennsylvania Dutch.
   They are descended
   ~~Descended~~ from German immigrants. (missing subject and verb added)

   City
   Property taxes rose sharply. ~~Although city~~ services declined. (subordinating conjunction *although* deleted)

24b Revising Dependent Clause Fragments

A **dependent clause** contains both a subject and a verb, but it cannot stand alone as a sentence. Because it needs an independent clause to complete its meaning, a **dependent clause** (also called a *subordinate clause*) must always be attached to at least one independent clause to form a complete sentence. You can recognize a dependent clause because it is always introduced by a **subordinating conjunction** (*although, because,* and so on) or a **relative pronoun** (*that, which, who,* and so on).

See 14d

In most cases, the best way to correct a dependent clause fragment is to join the dependent clause to an adjacent independent clause, creating a complex sentence.

because
The United States declared war./ ~~Because~~ the Japanese bombed Pearl Harbor. (Dependent clause has been attached to an independent clause, creating a complex sentence.)

, which
The battery is dead./ ~~Which~~ means the car won't start. (Dependent clause has been attached to an independent clause, creating a complex sentence.)

Another way to correct a dependent clause fragment is to delete the subordinating conjunction or relative pronoun, turning the fragment into a complete sentence.

The
The United States declared war. ~~Because the~~ Japanese bombed Pearl Harbor. (Subordinating conjunction *because* has been deleted; the result is a new sentence.)

This
The battery is dead. ~~Which~~ means the car won't start. (Relative pronoun *which* has been replaced by *this;* the result is a new sentence.)

Note: Simply deleting or replacing the subordinating conjunction or relative pronoun, as in the two examples above, is usually the least desirable way to revise a dependent clause fragment because it is likely to create two choppy sentences and because it does not clearly indicate the logical relationship between the two clauses.

EXERCISE 24.2

Identify the fragments in the following paragraph. Then, correct each fragment either by attaching the fragment to an independent clause or by deleting or replacing the subordinating conjunction or relative pronoun to create a sentence that can stand alone. (In some cases, you will have to replace a relative pronoun with another word that can serve as the subject.)

▶The drive-in movie came into being just after World War II. ▶When both movies and cars were central to the lives of many Americans. ▶Drive-ins were especially popular with teenagers and young families during the 1950s. ▶When cars and gas were relatively inexpensive. ▶Theaters charged by the carload. ▶Which meant that a group of teenagers or a family with several children could spend an evening at the movies for a few dollars. ▶In 1958, when the fad peaked, there were over four thousand drive-ins in the United States. ▶While today there are just a few hundred. Many of these are in the Sunbelt, especially in California. Although many Sunbelt drive-ins continue to thrive because of the year-round warm weather. Many northern drive-ins are in financial trouble. Because land is so expensive. Some drive-in owners break even only by operating flea markets or swap meets in daylight hours. While others, unable to attract customers, are selling their theaters to land developers. Soon, drive-ins may be a part of our nostalgic past. Which will be a great loss for many who enjoy them.

24c Revising Phrase Fragments

A **phrase** provides information—description, examples, and so on—about other words or word groups in a sentence. However, because it lacks a subject, a verb, or both, a phrase cannot stand alone as a sentence.

Close-Up FRAGMENTS INTRODUCED BY TRANSITIONS

See 13b2

Many phrase fragments are word groups that are introduced by transitional words and phrases, such as *also, finally, in addition*, and *now*, but are missing subjects and verbs. To correct such a fragment, you need to add the missing subject and verb.

It was also
˄Also a step in the right direction.

he found
Finally,˄a new home for the family.

we need
In addition,˄three new keyboards for the computer lab.

1 Prepositional Phrase Fragments

See 20f

ml 49e

A **prepositional phrase** consists of a preposition, its object, and any modifiers of the object.

To correct a prepositional phrase fragment, attach it to the independent clause that contains the word or word group modified by the prepositional phrase.

for
President Lyndon Johnson did not seek a second term/˄For a number of reasons. (Prepositional phrase has been attached to an independent clause, creating a complete sentence.)

in
He ran sixty yards for a touchdown/˄In the final minutes of the game. (Prepositional phrase has been attached to an independent clause, creating a complete sentence.)

EXERCISE 24.3

Read the following passage and identify the sentence fragments. Then, correct each one by attaching it to the independent clause that contains the word or word group it modifies.

▶Most college athletes are caught in a conflict. ▶Between their athletic and academic careers. ▶Sometimes college athletes' responsibilities on the playing field make it hard for them to be good students. ▶Often, athletes must make a choice. ▶Between sports and a degree. ▶Some athletes would not be able to afford college. ▶Without athletic scholarships. ▶Ironically, however, their commitments (training, exercise, practice, and travel to out-of-town games, for example) deprive athletes. ▶Of valuable classroom time. ▶The role of college athletes is constantly being questioned. Critics suggest that athletes exist only to participate in and promote college athletics. Because of the importance of this role to academic institutions, scandals occasionally develop. With coaches and even faculty members arranging to inflate athletes' grades to help them remain eligible. For participation in sports. Some universities even lower admissions standards. To help remedy this and other inequities. The controversial Proposition 48, passed at the NCAA convention in 1982, established minimum College Board scores and grade standards for student athletes. But many people feel that the NCAA remains overly concerned. With profits rather than with education. As a result, college athletic competition is increasingly coming to resemble pro sports. From the coaches' pressure on the players to win to the network television exposure to the wagers on the games' outcomes.

2 Verbal Phrase Fragments

A verbal phrase consists of a **verbal**—a present participle (*walking*), past participle (*walked*), infinitive (*to walk*), or gerund (*walking*)—plus related objects and modifiers (*walking along the lonely beach*). Because a verbal cannot serve as a sentence's main verb, a verbal phrase is not a complete sentence and should not be punctuated as one.

To correct a verbal phrase fragment, you can attach the verbal phrase to an adjacent independent clause that contains the words (a subject or verb or both) that are needed to make the fragment a sentence.

In 1948, India became an independent country./ ~~Divided~~ *divided* into the nations of India and Pakistan. (Verbal phrase has been attached to a related independent clause, creating a complete sentence.)

A familiar trademark can increase a product's sales./ *, reminding* ~~Reminding~~ shoppers that the product has a long-standing reputation. (Verbal phrase has been attached to a related independent clause, creating a complete sentence.)

Or, you can change the verbal to a verb and add a subject.

In 1948, India became an independent country. *It was divided* ~~Divided~~ into the nations of India and Pakistan. (Verb *was divided* has replaced verbal *divided*, and subject *it* has been added; the result is a complete sentence.)

A familiar trademark can increase a product's sales. *It reminds* ~~Reminding~~ shoppers that the product has a long-standing reputation. (Verb *reminds* has replaced verbal *reminding*, and subject *it* has been added; the result is a complete sentence.)

EXERCISE 24.4

Identify the sentence fragments in the following paragraph and correct each one. Either attach the fragment to a related independent clause, or add a subject and a verb to create a complete sentence.

►Many food products have well-known trademarks. ►Identified by familiar faces on product labels. ►Some of these symbols have remained the same, while others have changed considerably. ►Products such as Sun-Maid Raisins, Betty Crocker potato mixes, Quaker Oats, and Uncle Ben's Rice use faces. ►To create a sense of quality and tradition and to encourage shopper recognition of the products. ►Many of the portraits have been updated several times. ►To reflect changes in society. Betty Crocker's portrait, for instance, has changed many times since its creation in 1936. Symbolizing women's changing roles. The original Chef Boy-ar-dee has also changed. Turning from the young Italian chef Hector Boiardi into a white-haired senior citizen. Miss Sunbeam, trademark of Sunbeam Bread, has had her hairdo modified several times since her first appearance in 1942; the Blue Bonnet girl, also created in 1942, now has a more modern look, and Aunt Jemima has also been changed. Slimmed down a bit in 1965. Similarly, the Campbell's Soup kids are less chubby now than in the 1920s when they first appeared. Still, manufacturers are very careful about selecting a trademark or modifying an existing one. Typically spending a good deal of time and money on research before a change is made.

3 Appositive Fragments

An **appositive**—a noun or noun phrase that identifies or renames an adjacent noun or pronoun—cannot stand alone as a sentence.

To correct an appositive fragment, attach the appositive to the independent clause that contains the word the appositive renames.

Brian was the star forward of the Blue Devils/. ~~The~~ *, the* team with the best record. (Appositive has been attached to an independent clause, creating a complete sentence.)

Piero della Francesca was a leader of the Umbrian school of

painting/. ~~A~~ *, a* school that remained close to the traditions of Gothic

art. (Appositive has been attached to an independent clause, creating a complete sentence.)

Sometimes an appositive consists of a word or phrase such as *that is, for example, for instance, namely*, or *such as*, followed by an example.

To correct this kind of appositive fragment, attach the appositive to the preceding independent clause.

Fairy tales are full of damsels in distress./~~Such~~ *, such* as Cinderella and Rapunzel.

Note: Sometimes you can correct an appositive fragment by embedding the appositive within an independent clause.

Some popular novelists ^*—for example, Charles Dickens and Mark Twain—* are highly respected in later generations. ~~For example, Charles Dickens and Mark Twain.~~

See 34a1

Close-Up LISTS

When an appositive fragment takes the form of a list, add a colon to connect the list to the independent clause that introduces it.

Tourists often outnumber residents in four European cities./ Venice, Florence, Canterbury, and Bath.

EXERCISE 24.5

Identify the fragments in this paragraph, and correct them by attaching each one to the independent clause containing the word the appositive identifies or renames.

▶Until the early 1900s, communities in West Virginia, Tennessee, and Kentucky were isolated by the mountains that surrounded them. ▶The great chain of the Appalachian Mountains. ▶Set apart from the emerging culture of a growing America and American language, these communities retained a language rich with the dialect of Elizabethan English and sprinkled with hints of a Scotch-Irish influence. ▶In the 1910s and '20s, the communities in these mountains began to long for a better future for their children. ▶The key to that future, as they saw it, was education. In some communities, that education took the form of Settlement Schools. Schools led by idealistic young graduates of eastern women's colleges. These teachers taught the basic academic subjects. Such as reading, writing, and mathematics. They also schooled their students in the culture of the mountains. For example, the crafts, music, and folklore of the Appalachians. In addition, they taught them skills that would help them survive when the coal market began to decline. The Settlement Schools attracted artisans from around the world. Quilters, weavers, basketmakers, and carpenters. The schools also opened the mountains to the world, leading to the decline of the Elizabethan dialect.

24d Revising Detached Compounds

The last part of a **compound predicate**, **compound object,** or **compound complement** cannot stand alone as a sentence.

To correct this type of fragment, connect the detached part of the compound to the sentence to which it belongs.

People with dyslexia have trouble reading*/* ~~And~~ *and* may also find it difficult to write. (Detached part of the compound predicate has been connected to the sentence to which it belongs.)

They took only a compass and a canteen*./* ~~And~~ *and* some trail mix. (Detached part of the compound object has been connected to the sentence to which it belongs.)

When their supplies ran out they were surprised*/* ~~And~~ *and* hungry. (Detached part of the compound complement has been connected to the sentence to which it belongs.)

EXERCISE 24.6

Identify the fragments in this passage, and correct them by connecting each detached compound to the sentence to which it belongs.

▶As more and more Americans discover the pleasures of the wilderness, our national parks are feeling the stress. ▶Wanting to get away for a weekend or a week, hikers and backpackers stream from the cities into nearby state and national parks. ▶They bring with them a hunger for the wilderness. ▶But very little knowledge about how to behave ethically in the wild. ▶They also do not know how to keep themselves safe. ▶Some of them think of the national parks as inexpensive amusement parks. ▶Without proper camping supplies and lacking enough food and water for their trip, they are putting at risk their lives and the lives of those who will be called on to save them. ▶One family went for a hike up a desert canyon with an eight-month-old infant. ▶And their seventy-eight-year-old grandmother. Although the terrain was difficult, they were not wearing the proper shoes. Or good socks. They did not even carry a first aid kit. Or a map or compass. They were on an unmarked trail in a little-used section of Bureau of Land Management lands. And following vague directions from a friend. Soon, they were lost. They had not brought water or food. Or even rain gear or warm clothes. Luckily for them, they had brought a cell phone. By the time they called for help, however, it was getting dark and a storm was building. A rescue plane eventually located the family. And brought them to safety. Still, a little planning before they hiked in an inhospitable area, and a little awareness and preparedness for the terrain they were traveling in, would have saved this family much worry. And the taxpayers a lot of money.

24e Using Fragments Intentionally

Fragments are often used in speech as well as in personal email, text messages, and other informal writing—as well as in journalism, political slogans, creative writing, bumper stickers, and advertising.

In professional and academic writing, however, sentence fragments are generally not acceptable.

CHECKLIST

Using Fragments Intentionally

In college writing, it is acceptable to use fragments in the following special situations:

❏ In lists

❏ In captions that accompany visuals

❏ In topic outlines

❏ In quoted dialogue

❏ In *PowerPoint* presentations

❏ In titles and subtitles of essays and reports

CHAPTER **25**

Revising Run-Ons

25a Recognizing Comma Splices and Fused Sentences

See 14b2

A **run-on** is an error that occurs when two **independent clauses** are joined incorrectly. There are two kinds of run-ons: *comma splices* and *fused sentences*.

A **comma splice** is a run-on that occurs when two independent clauses are joined with just a comma. A **fused sentence** is a run-on that occurs when two independent clauses are joined with no punctuation.

Comma Splice: Charles Dickens created the character of Mr. Micawber, he also created Uriah Heep.

Fused Sentence: Charles Dickens created the character of Mr. Micawber he also created Uriah Heep.

25b Correcting Comma Splices and Fused Sentences

To correct a comma splice or fused sentence, use one of the following four strategies:

1. Add a period between the clauses, creating two separate sentences.
2. Add a semicolon between the clauses, creating a compound sentence.
3. Add a coordinating conjunction between the clauses, creating a compound sentence.
4. Subordinate one clause to the other, creating a complex sentence.

1 Add a Period

You can add a period between the independent clauses, creating two separate sentences. This is a good strategy to use when the clauses are long or when they are not closely related.

In 1894, Frenchman Alfred Dreyfus was falsely convicted of

treason. /, His struggle for justice made his case famous.

Close-Up COMMA SPLICES AND FUSED SENTENCES

Using a comma to punctuate an interrupted quotation that consists of two complete sentences creates a comma splice. Instead, use a period.

"This is a good course," Eric said /, "in fact, I wish I'd taken it sooner."

---

2 Add a Semicolon

You can add a **semicolon** between two closely related clauses that convey parallel or contrasting information. The result will be a **compound sentence**.

See 31a

In pre–World War II western Europe, only a small elite had access to

a university education /; however, this situation changed dramatically

after the war.

See
13b2

Note: When you use a <u>transitional word or phrase</u> (such as *however, there-fore*, or *for example*) to connect two independent clauses, the transitional element must be preceded by a semicolon and followed by a comma. If you link the two clauses with just a comma, you create a comma splice; if you omit punctuation entirely, you create a fused sentence.

3 Add a Coordinating Conjunction

You can use a coordinating conjunction (*and, or, but, nor, for, so, yet*) to join two closely related clauses of equal importance into one **compound sentence**. The coordinating conjunction you choose indicates the relationship between the clauses: addition (*and*), contrast (*but, yet*), causality (*for, so*), or a choice of alternatives (*or, nor*). Be sure to include a comma before the coordinating conjunction.

Elias Howe invented the sewing machine,⌃*and* Julia Ward Howe was a poet and social reformer.

4 Create a Complex Sentence

When the ideas in two independent clauses are not of equal importance, you can use a subordinating conjunction or relative pronoun to join the clauses into one **complex sentence**, placing the less important idea in the dependent clause. The subordinating conjunction or relative pronoun you choose indicates how the clauses are related.

Stravinsky's 1913 ballet *The Rite of Spring* shocked Parisians/⌃*because* the dancing seemed erotic.

Lady Mary Wortley Montagu⌃*, who* had suffered from smallpox herself, ~~she~~ helped spread the practice of inoculation in the eighteenth century.

Close-Up ACCEPTABLE COMMA SPLICES

In a few special cases, comma splices are acceptable. For instance, a comma is conventionally used in dialogue between a statement and a tag question, even though each is a separate independent clause.

This is Ron's house, isn't it?

I'm not late, am I?

In addition, commas may be used to connect two short, balanced independent clauses or two or more short parallel independent clauses, especially when one clause contradicts the other.

Commencement isn't the end, it's the beginning.

EXERCISE 25.1

Identify the comma splices and fused sentences in the following paragraph. Correct each in two of the four possible ways discussed in **25b**. If a sentence is correct, leave it alone.

Example: The fans rose in their seats, the game was almost over.

Revised: The fans rose in their seats; the game was almost over.
The fans rose in their seats because the game was almost over.

▶Entrepreneurship is the study of small businesses, college students are embracing it enthusiastically. ▶Many schools offer one or more courses in entrepreneurship these courses teach the theory and practice of starting a small business. ▶Students are signing up for courses, moreover, they are starting their own businesses. ▶One student started with a car-waxing business, now he sells condominiums. Other students are setting up catering services they supply everything from waiters to bartenders. One student has a thriving cake-decorating business, in fact, she employs fifteen students to deliver the cakes. All over the country, student businesses are selling everything from tennis balls to bagels, the student owners are making impressive profits. Formal courses at the graduate as well as undergraduate level are attracting more business students than ever, several schools (such as Baylor University, the University of Southern California, and Babson College) even offer degree programs in entrepreneurship. Many business school students are no longer planning to be corporate executives instead, they plan to become entrepreneurs.

EXERCISE 25.2

Combine each of the following sentence pairs into one sentence without creating comma splices or fused sentences. In each case, either connect the clauses into a compound sentence (with a semicolon or with a comma and a coordinating conjunction) or subordinate one clause to the other to create a complex sentence. You may have to add, delete, reorder, or change words or punctuation.

▶ 1. Several recent studies indicate that many American high school students have little knowledge of history. This is affecting our future as a democratic nation and as individuals.

▶ 2. Many American seventeen-year-olds cannot identify the countries the United States fought against in World War II. One-third think Columbus reached the New World after 1750.

▶ 3. Several reasons have been given for this decline in historical literacy. The main reason is the way history is taught.

▶ 4. This problem is bad news. The good news is that there is increasing agreement among educators about what is wrong with current methods of teaching history.

5. History can be exciting and engaging. Too often, it is presented in a boring manner.
6. Students are typically expected to memorize dates, facts, and names. History as adventure—as a "good story"—is frequently neglected.
7. One way to avoid this problem is to use good textbooks. Textbooks should be accurate, lively, and focused.
8. Another way to create student interest in historical events is to use primary sources instead of so-called comprehensive textbooks. Autobiographies, journals, and diaries can give students insight into larger issues.
9. Students can also be challenged to think about history by taking sides in a debate. They can learn more about connections among historical events by writing essays than by taking multiple-choice tests.
10. Finally, history teachers should be less concerned about specific historical details. They should be more concerned about conveying the wonder of history.

CHAPTER **26**

Revising Agreement Errors

ml
49a1

Agreement is the correspondence between words in number, gender, or person. Subjects and verbs <u>agree</u> in **number** (singular or plural) and **person** (first, second, or third); pronouns and their antecedents agree in number, person, and **gender** (masculine, feminine, or neuter).

26a Making Subjects and Verbs Agree

Singular subjects take singular verbs, and plural subjects take plural verbs.

> **Singular:** <u>Hydrogen peroxide</u> <u>is</u> an unstable compound.

> **Plural:** <u>Characters</u> <u>are</u> not well developed in O. Henry's short stories.

ml
49a2

See
26a4

<u>Present tense</u> verbs, except *be* and *have*, add *-s* or *-es* when the subject is third-person singular. Third-person singular subjects include nouns; the personal pronouns *he, she, it,* and *one*; and many <u>indefinite pronouns</u>.

> The <u>president</u> <u>has</u> the power to veto congressional legislation.

> <u>She</u> frequently <u>cites</u> statistics to support her assertions.

> In every group, <u>somebody</u> <u>emerges</u> as a natural leader.

Present tense verbs do not add *-s* or *-es* when the subject is a plural noun, a first-person or second-person pronoun (*I, we, you*), or a third-person plural pronoun (*they*).

Experts <u>recommend</u> that dieters avoid salty processed meat.

In our Bill of Rights, <u>we</u> <u>guarantee</u> all defendants the right to a speedy trial.

At this stratum, <u>you</u> <u>see</u> rocks dating back fifteen million years.

<u>They</u> <u>say</u> that even some wealthy people default on their student loans.

In the following special situations, subject-verb agreement can cause problems for writers.

1 When Words Come between Subject and Verb

If a modifying phrase comes between subject and verb, the verb should agree with the subject, not with a word in the modifying phrase.

The <u>sound</u> of the drumbeats <u>builds</u> in intensity in Eugene O'Neill's play *The Emperor Jones*.

The <u>games</u> won by the intramural team <u>are</u> usually few and far between.

This rule also applies to phrases introduced by *along with, as well as, in addition to, including*, and *together with*: Heavy <u>rain</u>, *together with high winds*, <u>causes</u> hazardous driving conditions.

2 When Compound Subjects Are Joined by *And*

Compound subjects joined by *and* usually take plural verbs.

<u>Navigation systems</u> and <u>antilock brakes</u> <u>are</u> standard on many new cars.

There are, however, two exceptions to this rule. First, compound subjects joined by *and* that stand for a single idea or person are treated as a unit and take singular verbs.

<u>Rhythm and blues</u> <u>is</u> a forerunner of rock and roll.

Second, when *each* or *every* precedes a compound subject joined by *and*, the subject takes a singular verb.

Every <u>desk</u> and <u>file cabinet</u> <u>was</u> searched before the letter was found.

3 When Compound Subjects Are Joined by *Or*

Compound subjects joined by *or* (or by *either . . . or* or *neither . . . nor*) may take either a singular or a plural verb.

If both subjects are singular, use a singular verb; if both subjects are plural, use a plural verb. If one subject is singular and the other is plural, the verb agrees with the subject that is nearer to it.

Either radiation treatments or chemotherapy is combined with surgery for the most effective results. (Singular verb agrees with *chemotherapy*.)

Either chemotherapy or radiation treatments are combined with surgery for effective results. (Plural verb agrees with *treatments*.)

4 With Indefinite Pronoun Subjects

ml
49c3

Most indefinite pronouns—*another, anyone, everyone, one, each, either, neither, anything, everything, something, nothing, nobody,* and *somebody*—are singular and take singular verbs.

Anyone is welcome to apply for this grant.

Some indefinite pronouns—*both, many, few, several, others*—are plural and take plural verbs.

Several of the articles are useful.

A few indefinite pronouns—*some, all, any, more, most,* and *none*—can be singular or plural, depending on the noun they refer to.

Of course, some of this trouble is to be expected. (*Some* refers to *trouble*.)

Some of the spectators are getting restless. (*Some* refers to *spectators*.)

5 With Collective Noun Subjects

A **collective noun** names a group of persons or things—for instance, *navy, union, association, band.* When a collective noun refers to a group as a unit (as it usually does), it takes a singular verb; when it refers to the individuals or items that make up the group, it takes a plural verb.

To many people, the royal family symbolizes Great Britain. (The family, as a unit, is the symbol.)

The family all eat at different times. (Each member eats separately.)

Note: If a plural verb sounds awkward with a collective noun, reword the sentence: *Family members all eat at different times.*

Phrases that name fixed amounts—*three-quarters, twenty dollars, the majority*—are treated like collective nouns. When the amount denotes a unit, it takes a singular verb; when it denotes part of the whole, it takes a plural verb.

Three-quarters of his usual salary is not enough to live on.
(*Three-quarters* denotes a unit.)

Three-quarters of workshop participants improve dramatically. (*Three-quarters* denotes part of the group.)

Note: The number is always singular, and *a number* is always plural: *The number* of voters has declined; *A number* of students have missed the opportunity to preregister.

6 When Singular Subjects Have Plural Forms

A singular subject takes a singular verb even if the form of the subject is plural.

Politics makes strange bedfellows.

Statistics deals with the collection, classification, analysis, and interpretation of data.

When such a word has a plural meaning, however, use a plural verb.

Her politics are too radical for her parents. (*Politics* refers not to the science of political government but, rather, to political principles or opinions.)

The statistics prove him wrong. (*Statistics* denotes not a body of knowledge but the numerical facts or data themselves.)

Note: Some words retain their Latin plural forms, which do not look like English plural forms. Be particularly careful to use the correct verbs with such words: *criterion is, criteria are; medium is, media are; bacterium is, bacteria are; datum is, data are.*

7 When Subject-Verb Order Is Inverted

Even when **word order** is inverted so that the verb comes before the subject (as it does in questions and in sentences beginning with *there is* or *there are*), the subject and verb must agree.

ml 49f

Is either answer correct?

There is a monument to Emiliano Zapata in Mexico City.

There are currently thirteen US courts of appeals.

8 With Linking Verbs

A **linking verb** should agree with its subject, not with the subject complement.

See 20c1

The problem was termites.

Here, the verb *was* correctly agrees with the subject *problem*, not with the subject complement *termites*. If *termites* were the subject, the verb would be plural: *Termites were the problem.*

See
20b

9 With Relative Pronouns

When you use a **relative pronoun** (*who, which, that*, and so on) to introduce a dependent clause, the verb in that clause should agree in number with the pronoun's **antecedent** (the word to which the pronoun refers).

The farmer is among the ones who suffer during a grain embargo.
(Verb *suffer* agrees with plural antecedent *ones*.)

The farmer is the only one who suffers during a grain embargo.
(Verb *suffers* agrees with singular antecedent *one*.)

EXERCISE 26.1

Some of the following sentences are correct, but others contain common errors in subject-verb agreement. If a sentence is correct, mark it with a *C*; if it has an error, correct it.

1. *I Love Lucy* is one of those television shows that almost all Americans have seen at least once.
2. The committee presented its findings to the president.
3. Neither Western novels nor science fiction appeal to me.
4. Stage presence and musical ability makes a rock performer successful today.
5. *It's a Wonderful Life*, like many old Christmas movies, seems to be shown on television every year.
6. Hearts are my grandmother's favorite card game.
7. The best part of B. B. King's songs are the guitar solos.
8. Time and tide waits for no man.
9. Sports are my main pastime.
10. *Vincent and Theo* is Robert Altman's movie about the French Impressionist painter Vincent van Gogh and his brother.

26b   Making Pronouns and Antecedents Agree

See
20b

ml
49c

A **pronoun** must agree with its **antecedent**—the word or word group to which the pronoun refers.

Singular pronouns—such as *he, him, she, her, it, me, myself*, and *oneself*—should refer to singular antecedents. (*They* can also be used as a singular pronoun.) Plural pronouns—such as *we, us, they, them*, and *their*—should refer to plural antecedents.

In the following special situations, pronoun-antecedent agreement can present challenges for writers.

1 With Compound Antecedents

In most cases, use a plural pronoun to refer to a **compound antecedent** (two or more antecedents connected by *and*).

Mormonism and Christian Science were influenced in their beginnings by Shaker doctrines.

However, this rule has several exceptions:

- If a compound antecedent denotes a single unit—one person, thing, or idea—use a singular pronoun to refer to the compound antecedent.

  In 1904, the husband and father brought his family from Russia to the United States.

- Use a singular pronoun when a compound antecedent is preceded by *each* or *every*.

  Every programming language and software application has its limitations.

- Use a singular pronoun to refer to two or more singular antecedents linked by *or* or *nor*.

  Neither Thoreau nor Whitman lived to see his work read widely.

- When one part of a compound antecedent is singular and one part is plural, the pronoun agrees in person and number with the closer antecedent.

  Neither the child nor her parents had fastened their seatbelts.

2 With Collective Noun Antecedents

If the meaning of the collective noun antecedent is singular (as it will be in most cases), use a singular pronoun. If the meaning is plural, use a plural pronoun.

The nurses' union announced its plan to strike. (All the members acted as one.)

The team ran onto the court and took their positions. (Each member acted individually.)

3 With Indefinite Pronoun Antecedents

See
26a4

Most **indefinite pronouns**—*each, either, neither, one, anyone,* and the like—are singular and take singular pronouns.

ml
49c3

Neither of the men had his proposal ready by the deadline.

Each of these neighborhoods has its own traditions and values.

A few indefinite pronouns are plural; some others can be singular or plural.

Close-Up THE SINGULAR THEY

They is not always a plural pronoun—it can also be a singular pronoun. Always use *they* if it is someone's preferred pronoun.

Julien can present their own viewpoint.

Avoid using *he or she, him or her,* or *his or her* with indefinite pronoun antecedents or otherwise to refer to people in general. Instead, use the singular *they, them,* and *their.*

Everyone can present their own viewpoint.

Or, you can make the sentence's subject plural.

All participants can present their own viewpoints.

See 19e2

The use of *his* alone to refer to a singular indefinite pronoun (*Everyone can present his own viewpoint*) is considered sexist language.

EXERCISE 26.2

In the following sentences, find and correct any errors in subject-verb or pronoun-antecedent agreement.

▶ 1. The core of a computer is a collection of electronic circuits that are called the central processing unit.

▶ 2. Computers, because of advanced technology that allows the central processing unit to be placed on a chip, a thin square of semiconducting material, has been greatly reduced in size.

▶ 3. Before broadband technologies, computers could "talk" to each other over phone lines through a modem, an acronym for *modulator-demodulator*.

▶ 4. Pressing keys on keyboards resembling typewriter keyboards generate electronic signals that are input for the computer.

▶ 5. Computers have built-in memory storage, and equipment such as flash drives or portable hard drives provide external memory.

6. RAM (random-access memory), the erasable and reusable computer memory, hold the computer program, the computations executed by the program, and the results.

7. After computer programs are "read" from a drive, the computer uses the instructions as needed to execute the program.

8. ROM (read-only memory), the permanent memory that is "read" by the computer but cannot be changed, are used to store programs that are needed frequently.
9. A number of video games with impressive graphics, sound, and color is available for home computers.
10. Although some computer users write their own programs, most buy ready-made software programs such as the ones that allows a computer to be used as a video game console.

CHAPTER **27**

Revising Misplaced and Dangling Modifiers

A **modifier** is a word, phrase, or clause that describes, limits, or qualifies another word in a sentence. A modifier should be placed close to the word it modifies.

Wendy watched the storm, fierce and threatening. (*Fierce and threatening* modifies *storm*.)

Faulty modification is the awkward or confusing placement of modifiers or the modification of nonexistent words.

27a Revising Misplaced Modifiers

A **misplaced modifier** is a word or word group whose placement suggests that it modifies one thing when it is intended to modify another.

Wendy watched the storm, fierce

~~Fierce~~ and threatening/ ~~Wendy watched the storm.~~/ (The storm, not Wendy, was fierce and threatening.)

The lawyer argued that the defendant, with

~~With~~ an IQ of just 52, ~~the lawyer argued that the defendant~~ should not get the death penalty. (The defendant, not the lawyer, had an IQ of 52.)

1 Place Modifying Words Precisely

Limiting modifiers—such as *almost, only, even, hardly, merely, nearly, exactly, scarcely, simply*, and *just*—should always immediately precede the words they modify. A different placement will change the meaning of the sentence.

Nick *just* set up camp at the edge of town. (He did it just now.)

Just Nick set up camp at the edge of town. (He did it alone.)

Nick set up camp *just* at the edge of town. (His camp was precisely at the edge.)

When a limiting modifier is placed so that it is not clear whether it modifies a word before it or one after it, it is called a **squinting modifier**.

The life that everyone thought would fulfill her <u>totally</u> bored her.

To correct a squinting modifier, place the modifier so that it is clear which word it modifies.

The life that everyone thought would <u>totally</u> fulfill her bored her.
(Everyone expected her to be totally fulfilled.)

The life that everyone thought would fulfill her bored her <u>totally</u>.
(She was totally bored.)

EXERCISE 27.1

In the following sentence pairs, the modifier in each sentence points to a different word. Underline the modifier and draw an arrow to the word it modifies. Then, explain the meaning of each sentence.

Example: She <u>just</u> came in wearing a hat. (She just now entered.)

   She came in wearing <u>just</u> a hat. (She wore only a hat.)

1. He wore his almost new jeans.
   He almost wore his new jeans.
2. He had only three dollars in his pocket.
   Only he had three dollars in his pocket.
3. I don't even like freshwater fish.
   I don't like even freshwater fish.
4. I go only to the beach on Saturdays.
   I go to the beach only on Saturdays.
5. He simply hated driving.
   He hated simply driving.

2 Relocate Misplaced Phrases

Placing a modifying phrase incorrectly can change the meaning of a sentence or create an unclear or confusing (or even unintentionally humorous) construction.

To avoid ambiguity, place phrases as close as possible to the words they modify.

- Place **verbal phrase** modifiers directly before or directly after the words they modify.

Roller-skating along the shore,
Jane watched the boats, ~~roller skating along the shore.~~

- Place **prepositional phrase** modifiers immediately after the words they modify.

with no arms
Venus de Milo is a statue created by a famous artist, ~~with no arms.~~

EXERCISE 27.2

Underline the modifying verbal phrases or prepositional phrases in each sentence, and draw arrows to the words they modify.

Example: Calvin is the Democrat running for town council.

1. The bridge across the river swayed in the wind.
2. The spectators on the shore were involved in the action.
3. Mesmerized by the spectacle, they watched the drama unfold.
4. The spectators were afraid of a disaster.
5. Within the hour, the state police arrived.
6. They closed off the area with roadblocks.
7. Drivers approaching the bridge were asked to stop.
8. Meanwhile, on the bridge, the scene was chaos.
9. Drivers in their cars were paralyzed with fear.
10. Struggling against the weather, the police managed to rescue everyone.

EXERCISE 27.3

Use the phrase that follows each sentence as a modifier in that sentence. Then, underline the modifier, and draw an arrow to indicate the word it modifies.

Example: He approached the lion. (with fear in his heart)

With fear in his heart, he approached the lion.

1. The lion paced up and down in his cage, ignoring the crowd. (watching Jack)
2. Jack stared back at the lion. (in terror)
3. The crowd around them grew. (anxious to see what would happen)
4. Suddenly, Jack heard a terrifying growl. (from deep in the lion's throat)
5. Jack ran from the zoo, leaving the lion behind. (scared to death)

③ Relocate Misplaced Dependent Clauses

A dependent clause that serves as a modifier must be clearly related to the word it modifies.

● An **adjective clause** appears immediately *after* the word it modifies.

During the Civil War, Lincoln was the president <u>who governed the United States.</u>

● An **adverb clause** can appear in various positions, as long as its relationship to the word it modifies is clear.

<u>When Lincoln was president,</u> the Civil War raged.

The Civil War raged <u>when Lincoln was president.</u>

EXERCISE 27.4

Relocate the misplaced verbal phrases, prepositional phrases, or dependent clauses so that they clearly point to the words or word groups they modify.

Example: *Silent Running* is a film ^*with Bruce Dern* about a scientist left alone in space ^. ~~with Bruce Dern.~~

1. She realized that she had married the wrong man after the wedding.
2. *The Prince and the Pauper* is a novel about an exchange of identities by Mark Twain.
3. The energy was used up in the ten-kilometer race that he was saving for the marathon.
4. He loaded the bottles and cans into his new car, which he planned to leave at the recycling center.
5. The manager explained the sales figures to the board members using a graph.

27b Revising Intrusive Modifiers

An **intrusive modifier** awkwardly interrupts a sentence, making it difficult to understand.

● Revise when a long modifying phrase comes between an auxiliary verb and a main verb.

Without
^She had, ~~without~~ giving it a second thought or considering the conse-
she had
quences, ^planned to reenlist.

- Revise when an adverb phrase or clause comes between a subject and a verb (or between a verb and its object or complement).

was contested

The election ‸ because officials discovered that some people had voted

more than once /‸ ~~was contested.~~

- Revise when a modifier creates an awkward **split infinitive**—that is, when a modifier comes between the word *to* and the base form of the verb.

defeat his opponent

He hoped to ‸ quickly and easily ‸ ~~defeat his opponent.~~

Note: A split infinitive is acceptable when the intervening modifier is short, especially if the alternative would be awkward or ambiguous: *She expected to almost beat her previous record.*

EXERCISE 27.5

Revise these sentences so that the modifying phrases or clauses do not interrupt an infinitive, separate an auxiliary verb from a main verb, or separate a subject from a verb or a verb from its object or complement.

Despite the playwright's best efforts, a

Example: ‸A play can sometimes be /~~ despite the playwright's best efforts,~~/ mystifying to the audience.

1. The people in the audience, when they saw the play was about to begin and realized the orchestra had finished tuning up and had begun the overture, finally quieted down.
2. They settled into their seats, expecting to very much enjoy the first act.
3. However, most people were, even after watching and listening for twenty minutes and paying close attention to the drama, completely baffled.
4. In fact, the play, because it had nameless characters, no scenery, and a rambling plot that did not seem to be heading anywhere, puzzled even the drama critics.
5. Finally, one of the three major characters explained, speaking directly to the audience, what the play was really about.

27c Revising Dangling Modifiers

A **dangling modifier** is a word or phrase that cannot logically modify any word in the sentence.

Dangling: Using this drug, many undesirable side effects are experienced. (Who is using this drug?)

- One way to correct a dangling modifier is to **create a new subject** by adding a word that the modifier (*using this drug*) can logically modify.

Revised: Using this drug, patients experience many undesirable side effects.

- Another way to correct a dangling modifier is to **create a dependent clause**.

Revised: When they use this drug, patients experience many undesirable side effects.

These two options for correcting dangling modifiers are further illustrated below.

1 Creating a New Subject

the technician lifted

Using a pair of forceps, the skin of the rat's abdomen was lifted. (Modifier cannot logically modify *skin*.)

Meg found

With fifty more pages to read, War and Peace was absorbing. (Modifier cannot logically modify *War and Peace*.)

2 Creating a Dependent Clause

Before   was implemented,

To implement a plus/minus grading system, all students were polled. (Modifier cannot logically modify *students*.)

Because the magazine had been on

On the newsstands only an hour, its sales surprised everyone. (Modifier cannot logically modify *sales*.)

See
22d

ml
49a6

Close-Up   DANGLING MODIFIERS AND THE PASSIVE VOICE

Most sentences that include dangling modifiers are in the passive voice. Changing the passive voice to active voice often corrects the dangling modifier.

EXERCISE 27.6

Eliminate the dangling modifier from each of the following sentences. Either supply a word that the dangling modifier can logically modify, or change the dangling modifier into a dependent clause.

Example: Skiing down the mountain, my hat flew off. (dangling modifier)

Revised: Skiing down the mountain, I lost my hat. (new subject added)
             As I skied down the mountain, my hat flew off. (dependent clause)

1. Writing for eight hours every day, her lengthy books are published every year or so.
2. As an out-of-state student without a car, it was difficult to get to off-campus cultural events.
3. To build a campfire, kindling is necessary.
4. With every step upward, the trees became sparser.
5. Being an amateur tennis player, my backhand is weaker than my forehand.
6. When exiting the train, the station will be on your right.
7. Driving through the Mojave, the bleak landscape was oppressive.
8. By requiring auto manufacturers to further improve emission-control devices, the air quality will get better.
9. Using a piece of filter paper, the ball of sodium is dried as much as possible and placed in a test tube.
10. Surrounded by acres of farmland, our nearest neighbor is far away.

C H A P T E R   **28**

Revising Awkward or Confusing Sentences

The most common causes of awkward or confusing sentences are *unnecessary shifts, mixed constructions, faulty predication,* and *illogical comparisons.*

28a   Revising Unnecessary Shifts

1   Shifts in Tense

Verb **tense** in a sentence (or in a related group of sentences) should only shift for a good reason—to indicate changes of time, for example. Unnecessary shifts in tense can be confusing.

See
22b

ml
49a2

I registered for the advanced philosophy seminar because I wanted a

challenge. However, after the first week I ~~start~~ *started* having trouble

understanding the reading. (unnecessary shift from past to present)

Jack Kerouac's novel *On the Road* follows a group of friends who

~~drove~~ *drive* across the United States. (unnecessary shift from present to past)

See
8b

Note: Discussions of literary works generally use the present tense.

See
22d

ml
49a6

2 Shifts in Voice

Unnecessary shifts from active to passive **voice** (or from passive to active) can be confusing.

F. Scott Fitzgerald wrote *This Side of Paradise*, and later *The*

Great Gatsby ~~was written.~~ *wrote* (unnecessary shift from active to passive)

3 Shifts in Mood

See
22c

Unnecessary shifts in **mood** also create awkward sentences.

Next, heat the mixture in a test tube, and ~~you should make~~ *be* sure it does not boil. (unnecessary shift from imperative to indicative)

4 Shifts in Person and Number

ml
49a1

Person indicates who is speaking (first person—*I, we*), who is spoken to (second person—*you*), and who is spoken about (third person—*he, she, it,* or *they*). Most often, unnecessary shifts between the second and third person are responsible for awkward sentences.

When ~~someone~~ *you* looks for a car loan, you should compare the interest rates of several banks. (unnecessary shift from third to second person)

See
26b1

Number indicates one (singular—*novel, it*) or more than one (plural—*novels, they, them*). Singular pronouns should refer to singular **antecedents** and plural pronouns to plural antecedents.

ml
49a1

~~A skyscraper is a building~~ *Skyscrapers are buildings* with more than 60 floors; they are found mainly in big cities. (unnecessary shift from singular to plural)

5 Shifts from Direct to Indirect Discourse

Direct discourse reports the exact words of a speaker or writer. It is always enclosed in quotation marks and is often accompanied by an **identifying tag** (*he says, she said*).

Indirect discourse summarizes the words of a speaker or writer. No quotation marks are used, and the reported words are often introduced with the word *that* or, in the case of questions, with *who, what, why, whether, how,* or *if.*

Direct Discourse: My instructor said, "I want your project by this Friday."

Indirect Discourse: My instructor said that he wanted my project by this Friday.

Unnecessary shifts between indirect and direct discourse are often confusing.

During the trial, John Brown repeatedly defended his actions and

said that_∧ *he was* ~~I am~~ not guilty. (unnecessary shift from indirect to direct discourse)

My mother asked, _∧*"Are you* ~~was I~~ ever going to get a job*?"* ./_∧ (unnecessary shift from direct to indirect discourse)

EXERCISE 28.1

Read the following sentences, and eliminate any shifts in tense, voice, mood, person, or number. Some sentences are correct, and some can be revised in more than one way.

Example: When_∧ ~~one~~ *you* examines the history of the women's movement, you see that it had many different beginnings.

▶ 1. Some historians see World War II and women's work in the factories as the beginning of the push toward equal rights for women.

▶ 2. Women went to work in the textile mills of Lowell, Massachusetts, in the late 1800s, and her efforts at reforming the workplace are seen by many as the beginning of the equal rights movement.

▶ 3. Farm girls from New Hampshire, Vermont, and western Massachusetts came to Lowell to make money, and they wanted to experience life in the city.

▶ 4. The factories promised the girls decent wages, and parents were promised by them that their daughters would live in a safe, wholesome environment.

▶ 5. Dormitories were built by the factory owners; they are supposed to ensure a safe environment for the girls.

6. First, visit the loom rooms at the Boott Mills Factory, and then you should tour a replica of a dormitory.

7. When one visits the working loom room at the factory, you are overcome with a sense of the risks and dangers the girls faced in the mills.

8. For a mill girl, moving to the city meant freedom and an escape from the drudgery of farm life; it also meant they had to face many new social situations for which they were not always prepared.

9. Harriet Robinson wrote *Loom and Spindle*, the story of her life as a mill girl, and then a book of poems was published.
10. When you look at the lives of the loom girls, one can see that their work laid part of the foundation for women's later demands for equal rights.

28b Revising Mixed Constructions

A **mixed construction** is created when an introductory dependent clause, prepositional phrase, or independent clause is incorrectly used as the subject of a sentence.

Because she studies every day, ~~explains why~~ she gets good grades. (dependent clause incorrectly used as subject)

, you can
By calling for information, ~~is the way to~~ learn more about the benefits of ROTC. (prepositional phrase incorrectly used as subject)

Being
~~He was~~ late made him miss the first act of the play. (independent clause incorrectly used as subject)

EXERCISE 28.2

Revise the following mixed constructions so their parts fit together both grammatically and logically.

Investing
Example: ~~By investing~~ in commodities made her rich.

1. In implementing the "motor voter" bill has made it easier for people to register to vote.
2. She sank the basket was the reason they won the game.
3. Just because situations change, does not change the characters' hopes and dreams.
4. By dropping the course would be his only chance to avoid a low GPA.
5. Because she works for a tobacco company explains why she is against laws prohibiting smoking in restaurants.

28c Revising Faulty Predication

Faulty predication occurs when a sentence's subject and predicate do not logically go together.

1 Incorrect Use of *Be*

See
20c1
Faulty predication is especially common in sentences that contain a <u>linking verb</u>—a form of the verb *be*, for example—and a subject complement.

caused
Mounting costs and decreasing revenues ~~were~~ the downfall of the hospital.

This sentence incorrectly states that mounting costs and decreasing revenues *were* the downfall of the hospital when, in fact, they were the *reasons* for its downfall.

2 *Is When* or *Is Where*

Faulty predication occurs when a one-sentence definition includes the construction *is where* or *is when*. (In a definition, *is* must be preceded and followed by a noun or a noun phrase.)

the construction of
Taxidermy is ~~where you construct~~ a lifelike representation of an animal from its preserved skin.

3 *The Reason . . . Is Because*

Faulty predication occurs when the phrase *the reason is* precedes *because*. In this situation, *because* (which means "for the reason that") is redundant and should be deleted.

that
The reason we drive is ~~because~~ we are afraid to fly.

EXERCISE 28.3

Revise the following sentences to eliminate faulty predication. Keep in mind that each sentence may be revised in more than one way.

Traffic
Example: ~~The reason traffic~~ jams occur at 8 a.m. and 5:30 p.m. ~~is~~ because too many people work traditional rather than staggered hours.

1. Inflation is when the purchasing power of currency declines.
2. Hypertension is where blood pressure is elevated.
3. Television and the Internet were the decline in students' reading scores.
4. Some people say the reason for the increasing violence in American cities is because guns are too easily available.
5. The reason for all the congestion in American cities is because too many people live too close together.

28d Revising Incomplete or Illogical Comparisons

A comparison tells how two things are alike or unlike. When you make a comparison, be sure that it is *complete* (that it identifies the two items being compared) and *logical* (that it equates two items that can logically be compared).

than Nina's.
My chemistry course is harder./˄ (What two things are being compared?)

dog's
A pig's intelligence is greater than a ˄ ~~dog~~. (illogically compares *intelligence* to *a dog*)

EXERCISE 28.4

Revise the following sentences to correct any incomplete or illogical comparisons.

Example: Technology-based industries are concerned about inflation as much

are.
as service industries./˄

1. Opportunities in technical writing are more promising than business writing.
2. Technical writing is more challenging.
3. In some ways, technical writing requires more attention to detail and is, therefore, more difficult.
4. Business writers are concerned about clarity as much as technical writers.
5. Technology-based industries may one day create more writing opportunities than any other industry.

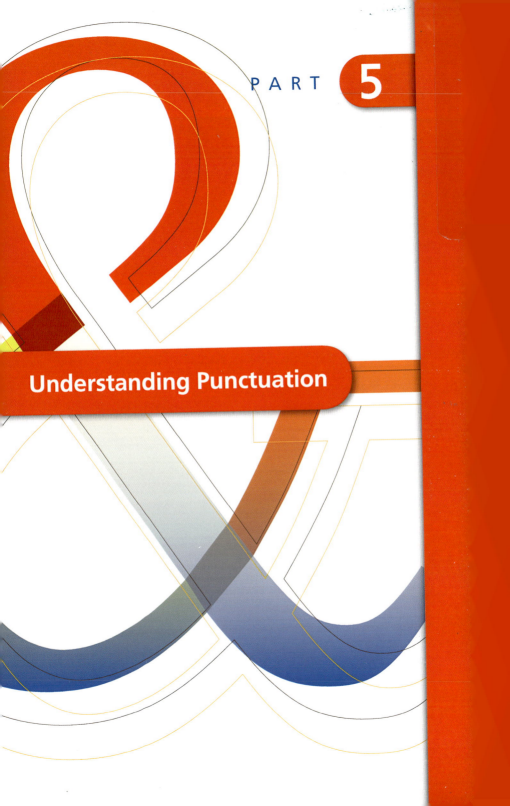

PART 5

Understanding Punctuation

Understanding Punctuation

OVERVIEW OF SENTENCE PUNCTUATION: COMMAS, SEMICOLONS, COLONS, DASHES, PARENTHESES

(Further explanations and examples are located in the sections listed in parentheses after each example.)

SEPARATING INDEPENDENT CLAUSES

With a Comma and a Coordinating Conjunction

The House approved the bill, but the Senate rejected it. (**30a**)

With a Semicolon

Paul Revere's *The Boston Massacre* is traditional American protest art; Edward Hicks's paintings are socially conscious art with a religious strain. (**31a**)

With a Semicolon and a Transitional Word or Phrase

Thomas Jefferson brought two hundred vanilla beans and a recipe for vanilla ice cream back from France; thus, he gave America its all-time favorite ice-cream flavor. (**31b**)

With a Colon

A *U.S. News & World Report* survey has revealed a surprising fact: Americans spend more time at malls than anywhere else except at home and at work. (**34a2**)

SEPARATING ITEMS IN A SERIES

With Commas

Chipmunk, raccoon, and *Mugwump* are Native American words. (**30b1**)

With Semicolons

Laramie, Wyoming; Wyoming, Delaware; and Delaware, Ohio were three of the places they visited. (**31c**)

SETTING OFF EXAMPLES, EXPLANATIONS, OR SUMMARIES

With a Colon

She had one dream: to play professional basketball. (**34a2**)

With a Dash

"Study hard," "Respect your elders," "Don't talk with your mouth full" — Sharon had often heard her parents say these things. (**34b2**)

SETTING OFF NONESSENTIAL MATERIAL

With a Pair of Commas

Jonas Salk, not Albert Sabin, developed the first polio vaccine. (**30d3**)

With a Single Comma

His fear increasing, he waited to enter the haunted house. (**30d4**)

With Dashes

Neither of the boys—both nine-year-olds—had any history of violence. (**34b1**)

With Parentheses

In some European countries (notably Sweden and Denmark), high-quality day care is offered at little or no cost to parents. (**34c1**)

CHAPTER 29

Using End Punctuation

29a Using Periods

1 Ending a Sentence

Use a period to signal the end of a statement, a mild command or polite request, or an indirect question.

Something is rotten in Denmark. (statement)

Be sure to have the oil checked before you start out. (mild command)

When the bell rings, please exit in an orderly fashion. (polite request)

They wondered whether the water was safe to drink. (indirect question)

2 Marking an Abbreviation

Use a period in most abbreviations.

Mr. Spock   1600 Pennsylvania Ave.   9 p. m.

Dr. Who   Aug.   etc.

If an abbreviation ends the sentence, do not add another period.

He promised to be there at 6 a.m./

However, do add a question mark if the sentence is a question.

Did he arrive at 6 p.m.?

If the abbreviation falls *within* a sentence, use normal punctuation after the period.

He promised to be there at 6 p.m., but he forgot.

3 Marking Divisions in Dramatic, Poetic, and Biblical References

Use periods to separate act, scene, and line numbers in plays; book and line numbers in long poems; and chapter and verse numbers in biblical references. (Do not space between the periods and the elements they separate.)

Dramatic Reference: *Hamlet* 2.2.1–5

Poetic Reference: *Paradise Lost* 7.163–67

Biblical Reference: Judges 4.14

Note: In **MLA parenthetical references,** titles of classic literary works and books of the Bible are often abbreviated: **(*Ham.* 2.2.1-5); (Judg. 4.14).**

See 47a1

4 Marking Divisions in Electronic Addresses

Periods, along with other punctuation marks (such as slashes and colons), are frequently used in electronic addresses (URLs).

http://cengage.com/english/kirsznermandell

Note: When you type a URL, do not end it with a period, and do not add spaces after periods within the address.

Close-Up   ABBREVIATIONS WITHOUT PERIODS

Abbreviations composed of all capital letters do not usually require periods unless they are the initials of people's names (E. B. White). Familiar abbreviations of the names of corporations or government agencies and abbreviations of scientific and technical terms do not require periods.

EPA	DNA	PTSD	ADHD
TMZ	NYPD	NFL	

Acronyms—new words formed from the initial letters or first few letters of a series of words—do not include periods.

modem	op-ed	scuba
OSHA	AIDS	NAFTA

Clipped forms (commonly accepted shortened forms of words, such as *flu, dorm, math,* and *fax*) do not include periods.

Postal abbreviations do not include periods.

NY	CA	MS	FL	TX

EXERCISE 29.1

Correct these sentences by adding missing periods and deleting unnecessary ones. If a sentence is correct, mark it with a *C*.

Example: Their mission changed the war.

► 1. Julius Caesar was killed in 44 B.C.
► 2. Dr. McLaughlin worked hard to earn his Ph.D..
3. Carmen was supposed to be at A.F.L.-C.I.O. headquarters by 2 p.m.; however, she didn't get there until 10 p.m.
4. After she studied the fall lineup proposed by N.B.C., she decided to work for C.B.S.
5. Representatives from the U.M.W. began collective bargaining after an unsuccessful meeting with Mr. Pritchard, the coal company's representative.

29b Using Question Marks

1 Marking the End of a Direct Question

Use a question mark to signal the end of a direct question.

Who was at the door?

2 Marking Questionable Dates or Numbers

Use a question mark in parentheses to indicate uncertainty about a date or number.

Aristophanes, the Greek playwright, was born in 448 (**?**) BC and died in 380 (**?**) BC.

3 Editing Misused Question Marks

Do not use question marks in the following situations.

After an Indirect Question Use a period, not a question mark, with an **indirect question** (a question that is not quoted directly).

The personnel officer asked whether he knew how to type?

With Other Punctuation Do not use other punctuation along with question marks along with other punctuation (except for closing quotation marks).

"Can it be true?," he asked.

With Another Question Mark Do not use more than one question mark to end a sentence.

You did what?? Are you crazy??

To Convey Sarcasm Do not use question marks to convey sarcasm. Instead, suggest your attitude through word choice.

                    not very
I refused his generous (?) offer.

In an Exclamation Do not use a question mark after an exclamation that is phrased as a question.

!
Will you please stop that at once?
                                  ^

29c Using Exclamation Points

An exclamation point is used to signal the end of an emotional or emphatic statement, an emphatic interjection, or a forceful command.

Remember the *Maine*!

"No! Don't leave!"

Finish this job at once!

Note: Except for recording dialogue, exclamation points are almost never appropriate in college writing. Even in informal writing, use exclamation points sparingly—and never use two or more in a row.

EXERCISE 29.2

Correct the use of question marks and other punctuation in the following sentences.

Example: She asked whether Freud's theories were accepted during his lifetime?.

1. He wondered whether he should take a nine o'clock class?
2. The instructor asked, "Was the Spanish-American War a victory for America."
3. Are they really going to China??!!
4. He took a modest (?) portion of dessert—half a pie!
5. "Is *data* the plural of *datum*?," he inquired.

CHAPTER 30

Using Commas

30a Setting Off Independent Clauses

See
20g

Use a comma when you form a compound sentence by linking two independent clauses with a **coordinating conjunction** (*and, but, or, nor, for, yet, so*)
or with a pair of <u>correlative conjunctions</u>.

The House approved the bill **,** but the Senate rejected it.

<u>Either</u> the hard drive is full **,** <u>or</u> the network is too slow.

Note: You may omit the comma if two clauses connected by a coordinating
conjunction are very short: *Seek and ye shall find; Love it or leave it.*

EXERCISE 30.1

Combine each of the following sentence pairs into one compound sentence,
adding commas where necessary.

Example: Emergency medicine became an approved medical specialty in

, and now

1979. Now, pediatric emergency medicine is becoming

increasingly important. (and)

1. Pope Benedict did not hesitate to visit Cuba. He did not hesitate to
   meet with former president Fidel Castro. (nor)
2. Advertisers place brand-name products in prominent positions in
   films. The products are seen and recognized by large audiences.
   (and)
3. Unisex insurance rates may have some drawbacks for women. These
   rates may be very beneficial. (or)
4. Cigarette advertising no longer appears on television. It does appear
   in print media. (but)
5. Dorothy Day founded the Catholic Worker movement in the 1930s.
   Her followers still dispense free food, medical care, and legal advice
   to the needy. (and)

30b Setting Off Items in a Series

1 Coordinate Elements

Use commas between items in a series of three or more **coordinate elements** (words, phrases, or clauses joined by a coordinating conjunction).

Chipmunk, *raccoon*, and *Mugwump* are Native American words.

You may pay by check, with a credit or debit card, or in cash.

Brazilians speak Portuguese, Colombians speak Spanish, and Haitians speak French and Creole.

To avoid ambiguity, always use a comma before the *and* (or other coordinating conjunction) that separates the last two items in a series: *He was inspired by his parents, the Dalai Lama, and Mother Teresa.*

Note: If phrases or clauses in a series already contain commas, use semicolons to separate the items.

See 31c

2 Coordinate Adjectives

Use a comma between items in a series of two or more **coordinate adjectives**—adjectives that modify the same word or word group—unless they are joined by a conjunction.

MULTILINGUAL TIP

If you have difficulty determining the order of adjectives in a series, see 49d2.

She brushed her long, shining hair.

The baby was tired and cranky and wet. (no commas required)

CHECKLIST

Punctuating Adjectives in a Series

❏ If you can reverse the order of the adjectives or insert *and* between the adjectives without changing the meaning, the adjectives are coordinate, and you should use a comma.

She brushed her long, shining hair.
She brushed her shining, long hair.
She brushed her long [and] shining hair.

❏ If you cannot reverse the order of the adjectives or insert *and*, the adjectives are not coordinate, and you should not use a comma.

Ten red balloons fell from the ceiling.
Red ten balloons fell from the ceiling.
Ten [and] red balloons fell from the ceiling.

Note: Numbers—such as *ten*—are not coordinate with other adjectives.

EXERCISE 30.2

Correct the use of commas in the following sentences, adding or deleting commas and words where necessary. If a sentence is punctuated correctly, mark it with a *C*.

Example: Neither dogs, snakes, bees, nor dragons frighten her.

1. Seals, whales, dogs, lions and horses all are mammals.
2. Mammals are warm-blooded vertebrates that bear live young, nurse them, and usually have fur.
3. Seals are mammals, but lizards, and snakes, and iguanas are reptiles, and salamanders are amphibians.
4. Amphibians also include frogs, and toads and newts.
5. Eagles geese ostriches turkeys chickens and ducks are classified as birds.

30c Setting Off Introductory Elements

1 Dependent Clauses

A **dependent clause** that begins a sentence is generally set off from the rest of the sentence by a comma.

> *When war came to Baghdad* , many victims were children.

If an introductory dependent clause is short and designates time, you may omit the comma— provided the sentence will be clear without it.

> When I exercise I drink plenty of water.

2 Verbal and Prepositional Phrases

An introductory verbal phrase is usually set off by a comma.

> Thinking that this might be his last chance , Peary struggled toward the North Pole. (participial phrase)

> To write well , one must read a lot. (infinitive phrase)

Close-Up USING COMMAS WITH VERBAL PHRASES

See
14b1

A verbal phrase that serves as a subject of a sentence is not set off by a comma.

Laughing out loud/can release tension. (gerund phrase)

To know him/ is to love him. (infinitive phrase)

An introductory **prepositional phrase** is also usually set off by a comma.

> During the Depression , movie attendance rose. (prepositional phrase)

However, if an introductory prepositional phrase is short and no ambiguity is possible, you may omit the comma.

> After lunch I took a four-hour nap.

3 Transitional Words and Phrases

When a <u>transitional word or phrase</u> begins a sentence, it is usually set off from the rest of the sentence with a comma.

See 13b2

> However , any plan that is enacted must be fair.
>
> In other words , we cannot act hastily.

EXERCISE 30.3

Add commas in the following paragraph where necessary to set off an introductory element from the rest of a sentence.

> ▶While childhood is shrinking adolescence is expanding. ▶Whatever the reason girls are maturing earlier, beginning puberty at increasingly younger ages. ▶What's more both boys and girls are staying in the nest longer. ▶At present, it is not unusual for children to stay in their parents' home through their twenties or early thirties, delaying adulthood and extending adolescence. To some who study the culture this increase in adolescence portends dire consequences. With teenage hormones running amuck for longer the problems of teenage pregnancy and sexually transmitted diseases loom large. Young boys' spending long periods of their lives without responsibilities is also a recipe for disaster. However others see this "youthing" of American culture in a more positive light. Without a doubt adolescents are creative, lively, and more willing to take risks. If we channel their energies carefully they can contribute, even in their extended adolescence, to American culture and technology.

30d Setting Off Nonessential Material

Sometimes words, phrases, or clauses *contribute* to the meaning of a sentence but are not *essential* for conveying the sentence's main point. Use commas to set off such **nonessential material** whether it appears at the beginning, in the middle, or at the end of a sentence.

1 Nonrestrictive Modifiers

Use commas to set off **nonrestrictive modifiers**, which supply information that is not essential to the meaning of the words they modify. (Do *not* use commas to set off **restrictive modifiers**, which supply information that is essential to the meaning of the words they modify.)

> **Nonrestrictive (commas required):** Actors , who have inflated egos , are often insecure. (*All* actors—not just those with inflated egos—are insecure.)

> **Restrictive (no commas):** Actors who have inflated egos are often insecure. (Only those actors with inflated egos—not all actors—are insecure.)

In the following examples, commas set off only nonrestrictive modifiers—those that supply nonessential information. Commas do not set off restrictive modifiers, which supply essential information.

Adjective Clauses

> **Nonrestrictive:** He ran for the bus , which was late as usual.

> **Restrictive:** Speaking in public is something that most people fear.

Prepositional Phrases

> **Nonrestrictive:** The clerk , with a nod , dismissed me.

> **Restrictive:** The man with the gun demanded their money.

Verbal Phrases

> **Nonrestrictive:** The marathoner , running her fastest , beat her previous record.

> **Restrictive:** The candidates running for mayor have agreed to a debate.

Appositives

> **Nonrestrictive:** *Citizen Kane* , Orson Welles's first film , made him famous.

> **Restrictive:** The film *Citizen Kane* made Orson Welles famous.

CHECKLIST

Restrictive and Nonrestrictive Modifiers

To determine whether a modifier is restrictive or nonrestrictive, ask yourself these questions:

❑ Is the modifier essential to the meaning of the noun it modifies (*The man with the gun*, not just any man)? If so, it is restrictive and does not take commas.

❑ Is the modifier introduced by *that* (*something that most people fear*)? If so, it is restrictive. *That* cannot introduce a nonrestrictive clause.

❑ Can you delete the relative pronoun without causing ambiguity or confusion (*something [that] most people fear*)? If so, the clause is restrictive.

❑ Is the appositive more specific than the noun that precedes it (*the film* Citizen Kane)? If so, it is restrictive.

Close-Up USING COMMAS WITH *THAT* AND *WHICH*

- *That* introduces only restrictive clauses, which are not set off by commas.

  I bought a used car that cost $2,000.

- *Which* introduces only nonrestrictive clauses, which are set off by commas.

  The used car I bought, which cost $2,000, broke down after a week.

EXERCISE 30.4

Insert commas where necessary to set off nonrestrictive modifiers.

►The Statue of Liberty which was dedicated in 1886 has undergone extensive renovation. ►Its supporting structure whose designer was the French engineer Alexandre Gustave Eiffel is made of iron. The Statue of Liberty created over a period of nine years by sculptor Frédéric-Auguste Bartholdi stands 151 feet tall. The people of France who were grateful for American help in the French Revolution raised the money to pay the sculptor who created the statue. The people of the United States contributing over $100,000 raised the money for the pedestal on which the statue stands.

2 Transitional Words and Phrases

Transitional words and phrases—which include conjunctive adverbs such as *however, therefore, thus,* and *nevertheless* as well as expressions such as *for example* and *on the other hand*—qualify, clarify, and make connections. However, they are not essential to the sentence's meaning. For this reason, they are always set off by commas when they interrupt a clause or when they begin or end a sentence.

See 13b2

The Outward Bound program , for example , is considered safe.

In fact , Outward Bound has an excellent reputation.

Other programs are not so safe , however.

Note: When a transitional word or phrase joins two independent clauses, it must be preceded by a semicolon and followed by a comma: *Laughter is the best medicine ; of course , penicillin also comes in handy sometimes.*

3 Contradictory Phrases

A phrase that expresses contradiction is usually set off by commas.

This medicine is taken after meals , never on an empty stomach.

Jonas Salk , not Albert Sabin , developed the first polio vaccine.

4 Absolute Phrases

An **absolute phrase**, which includes a noun or pronoun and a participle and modifies an entire independent clause, is always set off by a comma from the independent clause it modifies.

His fear increasing , he waited to enter the haunted house.

Many soldiers were lost in Southeast Asia , their bodies never recovered.

5 Miscellaneous Nonessential Material

Other nonessential material usually set off by commas includes tag questions, names in direct address, mild interjections, and *yes* and *no*.

This is your first day on the job , isn't it?

I wonder , Mr. Honeywell , whether Mr. Albright deserves a raise.

Well , it's about time.

Yes , that's what I thought.

EXERCISE 30.5

Set off the nonessential elements in these sentences with commas. If a sentence is correct, mark it with a *C*.

Example: Piranhas like sharks will attack and eat almost anything if the opportunity arises.

1. Kermit the Frog is a Muppet a cross between a marionette and a puppet.
2. The common cold a virus is frequently spread by hand contact not by mouth.
3. The account in the Bible of Noah's Ark and the forty-day flood may be based on an actual deluge.
4. Many US welfare recipients, such as children, the aged, and the severely disabled, are unable to work.
5. The submarine *Nautilus* was the first to cross under the North Pole wasn't it?
6. The 1958 Ford Edsel was advertised with the slogan "Once you've seen it, you'll never forget it."
7. Superman was called Kal-El on the planet Krypton; on earth however he was known as Clark Kent not Kal-El.
8. Its sales topping any of his previous singles "Heartbreak Hotel" was Elvis Presley's first million-seller.
9. Two companies Nash and Hudson joined in 1954 to form American Motors.
10. A firefly is a beetle not a fly and a prairie dog is a rodent not a dog.

Using Commas in Other Conventional Contexts

1 With Direct Quotations

In most cases, use commas to set off a direct quotation from the **identifying tag**—the phrase that identifies the speaker (*he said, she answered*, and so on).

> Emerson said to Whitman **,** "I greet you at the beginning of a great career."

> "I greet you at the beginning of a great career **,**" Emerson said to Whitman.

> "I greet you **,**" Emerson said to Whitman **,** "at the beginning of a great career."

When the identifying tag comes between two complete sentences, however, the tag is introduced by a comma but followed by a period.

> "Winning isn't everything **,**" Coach Vince Lombardi once said **.** "It's the only thing."

If the first sentence of an interrupted quotation ends with a question mark or exclamation point, do not use commas.

> "Should we hold the front page **?**" she asked. "It's a slow news day."

> "Hold the front page **!**" he cried. "There's breaking news **!**"

2 With Titles or Degrees Following a Name

> Hamlet **,** prince of Denmark **,** is Shakespeare's most famous character.

> Michael Crichton **,** MD **,** wrote *Jurassic Park*.

3 In Addresses and Dates

When a date or an address falls within a sentence, use a comma after the last element.

> On January 28 **,** 1986 **,** the space shuttle *Challenger* exploded.

> Her address is 600 West End Avenue **,** New York **,** NY 10024.

Note: When only the month and year are given, do not use a comma to separate the month from the year: *August 1983*. Do not use a comma to separate the street number from the street or the state name from the ZIP code.

4 In Salutations and Closings

In informal correspondence, use commas following salutations and closings. Also use commas in both informal and business correspondence following the complimentary close.

Dear John ,	Love ,
Dear Aunt Sophie ,	Sincerely ,

See 10a **Note:** In business letters, always use a colon, not a comma, after the salutation.

5 In Long Numbers

For a number of four digits or more, place a comma before every third digit, counting from the right.

1 , 200	120 , 000
12 , 000	1 , 200 , 000

Note: Commas are not used in long page and line numbers, address numbers, telephone numbers, or ZIP codes (or in four-digit year numbers).

EXERCISE 30.6

Add commas where necessary to set off quotations, names, dates, addresses, and numbers.

1. India became independent on August 15 1947.
2. The UAW has more than 1500000 dues-paying members.
3. Nikita Khrushchev, former Soviet premier, once said "We will bury you!"
4. Mount St. Helens, northeast of Portland Oregon, began erupting on March 27 1980 and eventually killed at least thirty people.
5. Located at 1600 Pennsylvania Avenue Washington DC, the White House is a popular tourist attraction.
6. In 1956, playing before a crowd of 64519 fans in Yankee Stadium in New York New York, Don Larsen pitched the first perfect game in World Series history.
7. Lewis Thomas MD was born in Flushing New York and attended Harvard Medical School in Cambridge Massachusetts.
8. In 1967 2000000 people worldwide died of smallpox, but in 1977 only about twenty people died.
9. "The reports of my death" Mark Twain remarked "have been greatly exaggerated."
10. The French explorer Jean Nicolet landed at Green Bay Wisconsin in 1634, and in 1848 Wisconsin became the thirtieth state; it has 10355 lakes and a population of more than 5700000.

30f   Using Commas to Prevent Misreading

In some cases, you need to use a comma to avoid ambiguity. For example, consider the following sentence:

Those who can **,** sprint the final lap.

Without the comma, *can* appears to be an auxiliary verb ("Those who can sprint . . ."), and the sentence seems incomplete. Because the comma tells readers to pause, it eliminates confusion.

Also use a comma to acknowledge the omission of a repeated word, usually a verb, and to separate words or phrases repeated consecutively.

Pam carried the box; Tim **,** the suitcase.

Everything bad that could have happened **,** happened.

EXERCISE 30.7

Add commas where necessary to prevent misreading.

Example: Whatever will be **,** will be.

1. According to Maria Frank's computer is obsolete.
2. Da Gama explored Florida; Pizarro Peru.
3. By Monday evening students must begin preregistration for fall classes.
4. Whatever they built they built with care.
5. When batting practice carefully.
6. Brunch includes warm muffins topped with whipped butter and freshly brewed coffee.
7. Students go to school to learn not to play sports.
8. Technology has made what once seemed not possible possible.

30g   Editing Misused Commas

Do not use commas in the following situations.

1 To Join Two Independent Clauses

A comma alone cannot join two independent clauses; it must be followed by a coordinating conjunction. Using just a comma to connect two independent clauses creates a **comma splice**.

See Ch. 25

The season was unusually cool, *but* the orange crop was not seriously harmed.

2 To Set Off Restrictive Modifiers

Commas are not used to set off **restrictive modifiers**.

See 30d1

"Women, who seek to be equal to men, lack ambition" (attributed to Timothy Leary).

The film, *Malcolm X*, was directed by Spike Lee.

3 Before or After a Series

Do not use a comma to introduce or to close a series.

Three important criteria are, fat content, salt content, and taste.

Quebec, Ontario, and Alberta, are Canadian provinces.

4 Between Inseparable Grammatical Constructions

Do not place a comma between grammatical elements that cannot be logically separated: a subject and its predicate, a verb and its complement or direct object, a preposition and its object, or an adjective and the word or phrase it modifies.

A woman with dark red hair, opened the door. (comma incorrectly placed between subject and predicate)

Louis Braille developed, an alphabet of raised dots for the blind. (comma incorrectly placed between verb and object)

They relaxed somewhat during, the last part of the obstacle course. (comma incorrectly placed between preposition and object)

Wind-dispersed weeds include the well-known and plentiful, dandelions, milkweed, and thistle. (comma incorrectly placed between adjective and words it modifies)

5 Between a Verb and an Indirect Quotation or Indirect Question

Do not use a comma between a verb and an indirect quotation or between a verb and an indirect question.

General Douglas MacArthur vowed, that he would return. (comma incorrectly placed between verb and indirect quotation)

The landlord asked, if we would sign a two-year lease. (comma incorrectly placed between verb and indirect question)

6 Between Phrases Linked by Correlative Conjunctions

See 20g Do not use a comma to separate two phrases linked by **correlative conjunctions**.

Forty years ago, most college students had access to neither photocopiers, nor pocket calculators.

Both typewriters, and tape recorders were generally available, however.

7 In Compounds That Are Not Composed of Independent Clauses

Do not use a comma before a coordinating conjunction (such as *and* or *but*) when it joins two elements of a compound subject, predicate, object, complement, or auxiliary verb.

Plagues,/ and pestilence were common during the Middle Ages. (compound subject)

Many nontraditional students are returning to college,/ and tend to do well there. (compound predicate)

Mattel has marketed a doctor's lab coat,/ and an astronaut suit for its Barbie doll. (compound object)

People buy bottled water because it is convenient,/ and fashionable. (compound complement)

She can,/ and will be ready to run in the primary. (compound auxiliary verb)

8 Before a Dependent Clause at the End of a Sentence

Do not use a comma before a dependent clause that falls at the end of a sentence.

Jane Addams founded Hull House in 1889,/ because she wanted to help Chicago's poor.

EXERCISE 30.8

Unnecessary commas have been intentionally added to some of the sentences that follow. Delete any unnecessary commas. If a sentence is correct, mark it with a *C*.

Example: Spring fever,/ is a common ailment.

▶ 1. A book is like a garden, carried in the pocket. (Arab proverb)
▶ 2. Like the iodine content of kelp, air freight, is something most Americans have never pondered. (*Time*)
   3. Charles Rolls, and Frederick Royce manufactured the first Rolls-Royce Silver Ghost, in 1907.
   4. The hills ahead of him were rounded domes of grey granite, smooth as a bald man's pate, and completely free of vegetation. (Wilbur Smith, *Flight of the Falcon*)
   5. Food here is scarce, and cafeteria food is vile, but the great advantage to Russian raw materials, when one can get hold of them, is that they are always fresh and untampered with. (Andrea Lee, *Russian Journal*)

Using Semicolons

A **semicolon** is used only between items of equal grammatical rank: two independent clauses, two phrases, and so on.

31a Separating Independent Clauses

Use a semicolon between closely related independent clauses that convey parallel or contrasting information but are not joined by a coordinating conjunction.

> Paul Revere's *The Boston Massacre* is an early example of American protest art; Edward Hicks's later "primitive" paintings are socially conscious art with a religious strain.

 Note: Using only a comma or no punctuation at all between independent clauses creates a **run-on**.

See Ch. 25

EXERCISE 31.1

Add semicolons to separate independent clauses, adding or deleting other punctuation where necessary. Then, reread the paragraph to make certain no run-ons remain.

Example: *Birth of a Nation* was one of the earliest epic movies ; it was based on the book *The Klansman*.

▶During the 1950s movie attendance declined because of the increasing popularity of television. ▶As a result, numerous gimmicks were introduced to draw audiences into theaters. ▶One of the first of these was Cinerama, in this technique three pictures were shot side by side and projected onto a curved screen. ▶Next came 3-D, complete with special glasses, *Bwana Devil* and *The Creature from the Black Lagoon* were two early 3-D ventures. ▶*The Robe* was the first picture filmed in Cinemascope in this technique a shrunken image was projected on a screen twice as wide as it was tall. Smell-O-Vision (or Aroma-rama) enabled audiences to smell the scenes, it was a challenge to get one odor out of the theater in time for the next smell to be introduced. William Castle's *Thirteen Ghosts* introduced special glasses for cowardly viewers, the red part of the glasses was the "ghost viewer" and the green part was the "ghost remover." Perhaps the ultimate in movie gimmicks accompanied the film *The Tingler* seats in the theater were wired to generate mild electric shocks. Unfortunately, the shocks set off a chain reaction, leading to hysteria in the theater. During the 1960s, such gimmicks all but disappeared, viewers were able once again to simply sit back and enjoy a movie. In 1997, *Mr. Payback*, a short interactive film, introduced a new gimmick, it allowed viewers to vote on how they wanted the plot to unfold.

31b Separating Independent Clauses Introduced by Transitional Words and Phrases

Use a semicolon before a **transitional word or phrase** that joins two independent clauses. (The transitional element is followed by a comma.)

See 13b2

> Thomas Jefferson brought two hundred vanilla beans and a recipe for vanilla ice cream back from France**;** **thus,** he gave America its all-time favorite ice-cream flavor.

EXERCISE 31.2

Combine each of the following sentence groups into one sentence that contains only two independent clauses. Use a semicolon and the transitional word or phrase in parentheses to join the two clauses, adding commas within clauses where necessary. You will need to add, delete, relocate, or change some words. There is no one correct version; keep experimenting until you find the arrangement you feel is most effective.

Example: The Aleutian Islands are located off the west coast of Alaska. They
; in fact, they
are an extremely remote chain of islands. They are sometimes

called America's Siberia. (in fact)

▶ 1. The Aleutians lie between the North Pacific Ocean and the Bering Sea. The weather there is harsh. Dense fog, 100-mph winds, and even tidal waves and earthquakes are not uncommon. (for example)
▶ 2. These islands constitute North America's largest network of active volcanoes. The Aleutians boast some beautiful scenery. The islands are relatively unexplored. (still)
3. The Aleutians are home to a wide variety of birds. Numerous animals, such as fur seals and whales, are found there. These islands may house the largest concentration of marine animals in the world. (in fact)
4. During World War II, thousands of American soldiers were stationed on Attu Island. They were stationed on Adak Island. The Japanese eventually occupied both islands. (however)
5. The islands' original population of native Aleuts was drastically reduced in the eighteenth century by Russian fur traders. Today, the total population is just over 8,000. US military employees comprise more than half of this. (consequently)

(Adapted from *National Geographic*)

31c Separating Items in a Series

Use semicolons between items in a series when one or more of the items already include commas.

I have visited Laramie, Wyoming; Wyoming, Delaware; and Delaware, Ohio.

EXERCISE 31.3

Replace commas with semicolons where necessary to separate internally punctuated items in a series. (For information on the use of semicolons with quotation marks, see **33e2**.)

Example: Luxury automobiles have some strong selling points: they are status

symbols/ some, such as the Corvette, appreciate in value/ and

they are usually comfortable and well appointed.

1. The history of modern art seems at times to be a collection of "isms": Impressionism, a term that applies to painters who attempted to depict contemporary life by reproducing an "impression" of what the eye sees, Abstract Expressionism, which applies to artists who stress emotion and the unconscious in their nonrepresentational works, and, more recently, Minimalism, which applies to painters and sculptors whose work reasserts the physical reality of the object.
2. Although the term *Internet* is widely used to refer only to the web and email, the Internet consists of a variety of discrete elements, including social media sites, which allow users to share images and videos on an unbelievably broad range of topics, interactive communication forums, such as blogs, discussion forums, and chat rooms, and FTP, which allows users to download material from remote computers.
3. Three of rock and roll's best-known guitar heroes played with the "British Invasion" group The Yardbirds: Eric Clapton, the group's first lead guitarist, went on to play with John Mayall's Bluesbreakers, Cream, and Blind Faith, and then became a popular solo act, Jeff Beck, the group's second guitarist, though not as visible as Clapton, made rock history with the Jeff Beck Group and inventive solo albums, and Jimmy Page, the group's third and final guitarist, transformed the remnants of the original group into the premier heavy metal band, Led Zeppelin.
4. Some of the most commonly confused words in English are *aggravate*, which means "to worsen," and *irritate*, which means "to annoy," *continual*, which means "recurring at intervals," and *continuous*, which means "an action occurring without interruption," *imply*, which means

"to hint, suggest," and *infer*, which means "to conclude from," and
compliment, which means "to praise," and *complement*, which means
"to complete or add to."

5. Tennessee Williams wrote *The Glass Menagerie*, which is about
Laura Wingfield, a disabled young woman, and her family, *A Streetcar
Named Desire*, which starred Marlon Brando, and *Cat on a Hot Tin
Roof*, which won a Pulitzer Prize.

31d   Editing Misused Semicolons

Do not use semicolons in the following situations.

1 Between a Dependent and an Independent Clause

Use a comma, not a semicolon, between a dependent and an independent
clause.

> Because new drugs can now suppress the body's immune reaction;
> fewer organ transplants are rejected by the body.

2 Between a Phrase and a Clause

Use a comma, not a semicolon, between a phrase and a clause.

> Increasing rapidly; computer crime poses a challenge for government,
> financial, and military agencies.

3 To Introduce a List

Use a colon, not a semicolon, to introduce a <u>list</u>.

> Millions of people spend time every day on four of the most popular
>
> social networking sites; *Twitter, Facebook, LinkedIn*, and *Pinterest*.

See 34a1

 Always use a complete sentence followed by a colon to introduce a list.

4 To Introduce a Quotation

Do not use a semicolon to introduce <u>quoted speech or writing</u>.

See 33a

> Marie Antoinette may not have said; "Let them eat cake."

EXERCISE 31.4

Read the paragraph on page 282 carefully. Then, add semicolons where
necessary, and delete incorrectly used ones, substituting other punctuation
where necessary.

▶Barnstormers were aviators; who toured the country after World War I, giving people short airplane rides and exhibitions of stunt flying, in fact, the name *barnstormer* was derived from the use of barns as airplane hangars. ▶Americans' interest in airplanes had all but disappeared after the war. ▶The barnstormers helped popularize flying; especially in rural areas. ▶Some were pilots who had flown in the war; others were just young men with a thirst for adventure. They gave people rides in airplanes; sometimes charging a dollar a minute. For most passengers, this was their first ride in an airplane, in fact, sometimes it was their first sight of one. After Lindbergh's 1927 flight across the Atlantic; Americans suddenly needed no encouragement to embrace aviation. The barnstormers had outlived their usefulness; and an era ended. (Adapted from William Goldman, *Adventures in the Screen Trade*)

CHAPTER 32

Using Apostrophes

Use an apostrophe to form the possessive case, to indicate omissions in contractions, and to form certain plurals.

32a Forming the Possessive Case

The possessive case indicates ownership. In English, the possessive case of nouns and indefinite pronouns is indicated either with a phrase that includes the word *of* (the hands *of* the clock) or with an apostrophe and, in most cases, an *s* (the clock's hands).

1 Singular Nouns and Indefinite Pronouns

To form the possessive case of singular nouns and **indefinite pronouns**, add -'s.

"The Monk's Tale" is one of Chaucer's *Canterbury Tales*.

When we would arrive was anyone's guess.

2 Singular Nouns Ending in -s

To form the possessive case of **singular nouns that end in** -s, add -'s in most cases.

Chris's goal was to become a surgeon.

Reading Henry James's *The Ambassadors* was not Maris's idea of fun.

The class's time was changed to 8 a.m.

Note: With some singular nouns that end in *-s*, pronouncing the possessive ending as a separate syllable can sound awkward. In such cases, it is acceptable to use just an apostrophe: *Crispus Attucks' death, Aristophanes' Lysistrata, Achilles' left heel.*

Do not use an apostrophe to form the possessive case of a title that already contains an *-'s* ending; use a phrase instead.

The staging of
A Midsummer Night's Dream's ~~staging~~ presents a challenge.

3 Regular Plural Nouns

To form the possessive case of **regular plural nouns** (those that end in *-s* or *-es*), add only an apostrophe.

The Readers' Guide to Periodical Literature is available online.

Laid-off employees received two weeks' severance pay and three months' medical benefits.

The Lopezes' three children are triplets.

4 Irregular Plural Nouns

To form the possessive case of **nouns that have irregular plurals**, add *-'s*.

Long after they were gone, the geese's honking could still be heard.

The Children's Hour is a play by Lillian Hellman; *The Women's Room* is a novel by Marilyn French.

The two oxen's yokes were securely attached to the cart.

5 Compound Nouns or Groups of Words

To form the possessive case of **compound nouns** or of word groups, add *-'s* to the last word.

The editor-in-chief's position is open.

He accepted the Secretary of State's resignation under protest.

This is someone else's responsibility.

6 Two or More Items

To indicate **individual ownership** of two or more items, add *-'s* to each item.

Ernest Hemingway's and Gertrude Stein's writing styles have some similarities. (Hemingway and Stein have two separate writing styles.)

To indicate **joint ownership**, add -'s only to the last item.

Gilbert and Sullivan's operettas include *The Pirates of Penzance* and *The Mikado.* (Gilbert and Sullivan collaborated on both operettas.)

EXERCISE 32.1

Change each word or phrase in parentheses to its possessive form. In some cases, you may have to use a phrase to indicate the possessive.

Example: The (children) toys were scattered all over their (parents) bedroom.

The children's toys were scattered all over their parents' bedroom.

1. Jane (Addams) settlement house was called Hull House.
2. (*A Room of One's Own*) popularity increased with the rise of feminism.
3. The (chief petty officer) responsibilities are varied.
4. Vietnamese (restaurants) numbers have grown dramatically in ten (years) time.
5. (Charles Dickens) and (Mark Twain) works have sold millions of copies.

32b Indicating Omissions in Contractions

1 Omitted Letters

Apostrophes replace omitted letters in contractions that combine a pronoun and a verb (*he* + *will* = *he'll*) or the elements of a verb phrase (*do* + *not* = *don't*).

Frequently Used Contractions

it's (it is, it has)
he's (he is, he has)
she's (she is, she has)
who's (who is, who has)
isn't (is not)
wouldn't (would not)
couldn't (could not)
don't (do not)
won't (will not)

let's (let us)
we've (we have)
they're (they are)
we'll (we will)
I'm (I am)
we're (we are)
you'd (you would)
we'd (we would)
they'd (they had)

Note: Contractions are very informal. Do not use contractions in college writing unless you are quoting a source that uses them.

Close-Up   USING APOSTROPHES

Be careful not to confuse contractions (which always include apostrophes) with the possessive forms of personal pronouns (which never include apostrophes).

Contractions	**Possessive Forms**
Who's on first?	Whose book is this?
They're playing our song.	Their team is winning.
It's raining.	Its paws were muddy.
You're a real pal.	Your résumé is impressive.

EXERCISE 32.2

In the following sentences, correct any errors in the use of apostrophes. (Remember, apostrophes are used in contractions but not in possessive pronouns.) If a sentence is correct, mark it with a *C*.

Whose
Example: ~~Who's~~ troops were sent to Afghanistan?

1. Its never easy to choose a major; whatever you decide, your bound to have second thoughts.
2. Olive Oyl asked, "Whose that knocking at my door?"
3. Their watching too much television; in fact, they're eyes are glazed.
4. Whose coming along on the backpacking trip?
5. The horse had been badly treated; it's spirit was broken.
6. Your correct in assuming its a challenging course.
7. Sometimes even you're best friends won't tell you your boring.
8. They're training had not prepared them for the hardships they faced.
9. It's too early to make a positive diagnosis.
10. Robert Frost wrote the poem that begins, "Who's woods these are I think I know."

2 Omitted Numbers

In informal writing, an apostrophe may be used to replace the century in a year.

Crash of '29   class of '10   '57 Chevy

In college writing, however, write out the year in full: *the Crash of 1929, the class of 2010, a 1957 Chevrolet.*

32c Forming Plurals

In a few special situations, add -'s to form plurals.

Plurals of Letters

The Italian language has no *j*'s, *k*'s, or *w*'s.

Plurals of Words Referred to as Words

The supervisor would accept no *if*'s, *and*'s, or *but*'s.

See
37c

Note: **Elements spoken of as themselves** (letters, numerals, or words) are set in italic type; the plural ending, however, is not.

Apostrophes are not used in plurals of abbreviations (including acronyms) or numbers.

DVDs   WACs   1960s

EXERCISE 32.3

In the following sentences, form correct plurals for the letters and words in parentheses. Underline to indicate italics where necessary.

Example: The word *bubbles* contains three (b).
             The word *bubbles* contains three *b*'s.

1. She closed her letter with a row of (x) and (o) to indicate kisses and hugs.
2. The three (R) are reading, writing, and 'rithmetic.
3. The report included far too many (maybe) and too few (definitely).
4. The word bookkeeper contains two (o), two (k), and three (e).
5. His email included many (please) and (thank you).

32d Editing Misused Apostrophes

Do not use apostrophes with plural nouns that are not possessive.

The Thompson's are not at home.

Down vest's are very warm.

The Philadelphia 76er's have had good years and bad.

Do not use apostrophes to form the possessive case of personal pronouns.

This ticket must be your's or her's.

The next turn is their's.

Her doll had lost it's right eye.

The next great moment in history is our's.

EXERCISE 32.4

In the following sentences, correct all errors in the use of apostrophes to form noun plurals or the possessive case of personal pronouns.

Example: Dr. Sampson's lecture's were more interesting than her's.

1. The Schaefer's seats are right next to our's.
2. Most of the college's in the area offer courses open to outsider's as well as to their own students.
3. The network completely revamped it's daytime programming.
4. Is the responsibility for the hot dog concession Cynthia's or your's?
5. Romantic poets are his favorite's.
6. Debbie returned the books to the library, forgetting they were her's.
7. Cultural revolution's do not occur very often, but when they do they bring sweeping change's.
8. Roll-top desk's are eagerly sought by antique dealer's.
9. A flexible schedule is one of their priorities, but it isn't one of our's.
10. Is your's the red house or the brown one?

CHAPTER 33

Using Quotation Marks

Use quotation marks to set off brief passages of quoted speech or writing, to set off certain titles, and to set off words used in special ways. Do not use quotation marks when quoting long passages of prose or poetry.

33a Setting Off Quoted Speech or Writing

When you quote a word, phrase, or brief passage of someone else's speech or writing, enclose the quoted material in a pair of quotation marks.

Gloria Steinem said, "We are becoming the men we once hoped to marry."

Galsworthy writes that Aunt Juley is "prostrated by the blow" (329). (Note that in this example from a student essay, the end punctuation follows the parenthetical documentation.)

> ## Close-Up　USING QUOTATION MARKS WITH DIALOGUE
>
> When you record **dialogue** (conversation between two or more people), enclose the quoted words in quotation marks. Begin a new paragraph each time a new speaker is introduced.
>
> When you are quoting several paragraphs of dialogue by one speaker, begin each new paragraph with quotation marks. However, use closing quotation marks only at the end of the *entire quoted passage*, not at the end of each paragraph.

Special rules govern the punctuation of a quotation when it is used with an **identifying tag**, a phrase (such as *he said*) that identifies the speaker or writer.

1 Identifying Tag in the Middle of a Quoted Passage

Use a pair of commas to set off an identifying tag that interrupts a quoted passage.

"In the future," pop artist Andy Warhol once said , "everyone will be world famous for fifteen minutes."

If the identifying tag follows a complete sentence but the quoted passage continues, use a period after the tag. Begin the new sentence with a capital letter, and enclose it in quotation marks.

"Be careful," Erin warned. "Reptiles can be tricky."

2 Identifying Tag at the Beginning of a Quoted Passage

Use a comma after an identifying tag that introduces quoted speech or writing.

The Raven repeated , "Nevermore."

See
34a3
Use a **colon** instead of a comma before a quotation if the identifying tag is a complete sentence.

She gave her final answer : "No."

3 Identifying Tag at the End of a Quoted Passage

Use a comma to set off a quotation from an identifying tag that follows it.

"Be careful out there ," the sergeant warned.

If the quotation ends with a question mark or an exclamation point, use that punctuation mark instead of the comma. In this situation, the tag begins with a lowercase letter even though it follows end punctuation.

"Is Ankara the capital of Turkey?" she asked.

"Oh boy!" he cried.

Note: For information on using quotation marks with other punctuation, see **33e**.

EXERCISE 33.1

Add quotation marks and other punctuation to these sentences where necessary to set off quotations from identifying tags.

Example: Wordsworth's phrase "splendour in the grass" was used as the title of a movie about young lovers.

1. Few people can explain what Descartes's words I think, therefore I am actually mean.
2. Gertrude Stein said, You are all a lost generation.
3. Freedom of speech does not guarantee anyone the right to yell fire in a crowded theater, she explained.
4. There's no place like home, Dorothy insisted.
5. If everyone will sit down the teacher announced the exam will begin.

33b Setting Off Long Prose Passages and Poetry

1 Long Prose Passages

Do not enclose a **long prose passage** (a passage of more than four lines) in quotation marks. Instead, set it off by indenting the entire passage one-half inch from the left-hand margin. Double-space above and below the quoted passage, and double-space between lines within it. Introduce the passage with a colon, and place parenthetical documentation one space after the end punctuation.

> The following portrait of Aunt Juley illustrates several of the devices Galsworthy uses throughout *The Forsyte Saga*, such as a journalistic detachment that is almost cruel in its scrutiny, a subtle sense of the grotesque, and an ironic stance:
>
>> Aunt Juley stayed in her room, prostrated by the blow. Her face, discoloured by tears, was divided into compartments by the little ridges of pouting flesh which had swollen with emotion. . . . At fixed intervals she went to her drawer, and took from beneath the lavender bags a fresh

pocket-handkerchief. Her warm heart could not bear the thought that Ann was lying there so cold. (329)

Many similar portraits of characters appear throughout the novel.

Close-Up QUOTING LONG PROSE PASSAGES

When you quote a long prose passage that is a single paragraph, do not indent the first line. When quoting two or more paragraphs, however, indent the first line of each paragraph (including the first) an additional one-quarter inch. If the first sentence of the quoted passage does not begin a paragraph in the source, do not indent—but do indent the first line of each subsequent paragraph. If the long passage you are quoting includes material set in a pair of quotation marks, keep those quotation marks.

---

2 Poetry

Treat one line of poetry like a short prose passage: enclose it in quotation marks, and run it into the text.

> One of John Donne's best-known poems begins with the line, "Go and catch a falling star."

See 34e2 If you quote two or three lines of poetry, separate the lines with **slashes** (/), and run the quotation into the text. (Leave one space before and one space after the slash.)

> Alexander Pope writes, "True Ease in Writing comes from Art, not Chance, / As those move easiest who have learned to dance."

See 33b1 If you quote more than three lines of poetry, set them off like a **long prose passage**. (For special emphasis, you may set off fewer lines in this manner.) Do not use quotation marks, and be sure to reproduce punctuation, spelling, capitalization, and indentation *exactly* as they appear in the poem.

> Wilfred Owen, a poet who was killed in action in World War I, expressed the horrors of war with vivid imagery:
>
> Bent double, like old beggars under sacks.
> Knock-kneed, coughing like hags, we cursed through sludge.
> Till on the haunting flares we turned our backs
> And towards our distant rest began to trudge. (lines 1-4)

33c Setting Off Titles

Titles of short works and titles of parts of long works are enclosed in quotation marks. Other titles are <u>italicized</u>.

See 37a

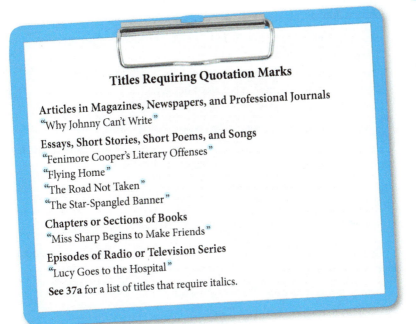

Titles Requiring Quotation Marks

Articles in Magazines, Newspapers, and Professional Journals
"Why Johnny Can't Write"

Essays, Short Stories, Short Poems, and Songs
"Fenimore Cooper's Literary Offenses"
"Flying Home"
"The Road Not Taken"
"The Star-Spangled Banner"

Chapters or Sections of Books
"Miss Sharp Begins to Make Friends"

Episodes of Radio or Television Series
"Lucy Goes to the Hospital"

See 37a for a list of titles that require italics.

33d Setting Off Words Used in Special Ways

Enclose a word used in a special or unusual way in quotation marks. (If you use the phrase *so-called* before the word, do not also use quotation marks.)

> It was clear that adults approved of children who were "readers," but it was not at all clear why this was so. (Annie Dillard)

33e Using Quotation Marks with Other Punctuation

At the end of a quotation, punctuation is sometimes placed before the quotation marks and sometimes placed after the quotation marks.

1 With Final Commas or Periods

At the end of a quotation, place a comma or period *before* the closing quotation marks.

Many, like the poet Robert Frost, think about "the road not taken," but not many have taken "the one less traveled by."

2 With Final Semicolons or Colons

At the end of a quotation, place a semicolon or colon *after* the closing quotation marks.

Students who do not pass the test receive "certificates of completion"; those who pass are awarded diplomas.

Taxpayers were pleased with the first of the candidate's promised "sweeping new reforms": a balanced budget.

3 With Question Marks, Exclamation Points, and Dashes

If a question mark, exclamation point, or dash is part of the quotation, place the punctuation mark *before* the closing quotation marks.

"Who's there?" she demanded.

"Stop!" he cried.

"Should we leave now, or —" Vicki paused, unable to continue.

If a question mark, exclamation point, or dash is *not* part of the quotation, place the punctuation mark *after* the closing quotation marks.

Did you finish reading "The Black Cat"?

Whatever you do, don't yell "Uncle"!

The first story—Updike's "A&P"— provoked discussion.

Close-Up   QUOTATIONS WITHIN QUOTATIONS

Use *single* quotation marks to enclose a quotation within a quotation.

Claire noted, "Liberace always said, 'I cried all the way to the bank.' "

Also use single quotation marks within a quotation to indicate a title that would normally be enclosed in double quotation marks.

I think what she said was, "Play it, Sam. Play 'As Time Goes By.' "

Use *double* quotation marks around quotations or titles within a long prose passage.

See
33b1

If both the quotation and the sentence are questions or exclamations, place the punctuation mark *after* the closing quotation marks.

Who asked, "Is Paris burning"?

33f Editing Misused Quotation Marks

Quotation marks should not be used in the following situations.

1 To Convey Emphasis

Do not use quotation marks to convey emphasis.

William Randolph Hearst's "fabulous" home is a castle called San Simeon.

2 To Set Off Slang or Technical Terms

Do not use quotation marks to set off slang or technical terms. (Note that slang is almost always inappropriate in college writing.)

Dawn is "into" running.
very involved in

"Biofeedback" is sometimes used to treat migraine headaches.

3 To Enclose Titles of Long Works

Titles of long works are italicized, not set in quotation marks.

See 37a

The classic novel "War and Peace" is even longer than the epic poem "Paradise Lost."

Note: Do not use quotation marks (or italics) to set off titles of your own essays.

4 To Set Off Terms Being Defined

Terms being defined are italicized.

The word "tintinnabulation," meaning the ringing sound of bells, is used by Poe in his poem "The Bells."

5 To Set Off Indirect Quotations

Quotation marks should not be used to set off **indirect quotations** (someone else's written or spoken words that are not quoted exactly).

Freud wondered "what a woman wanted."

EXERCISE 33.2

Correct the use of quotation marks in the following sentences. If a sentence is correct, mark it with a *C*.

Example: The "Watergate" incident brought many new expressions into the English language.

► 1. Kilroy was here and Women and children first are two expressions *Bartlett's Familiar Quotations* attributes to "Anon."

► 2. Neil Armstrong said he was making a small step for man but a giant leap for mankind.

► 3. "The answer, my friend", Bob Dylan sang, "is blowin' in the wind".

► 4. The novel was a real "thriller," complete with spies and counterspies, mysterious women, and exotic international chases.

► 5. The sign said, Road liable to subsidence; it meant that we should look out for potholes.

6. One of William Blake's best-known lines—To see a world in a grain of sand—opens his poem Auguries of Innocence.

7. In James Thurber's short story The Catbird Seat, Mrs. Barrows annoys Mr. Martin by asking him silly questions such as Are you tearing up the pea patch? Are you scraping around the bottom of the pickle barrel? and Are you lifting the oxcart out of the ditch?

8. I'll make him an offer he can't refuse, promised "the godfather" in Mario Puzo's novel.

9. What did Timothy Leary mean by "Turn on, tune in, drop out?"

10. George, the protagonist of Bernard Malamud's short story, A Summer's Reading, is something of an "underachiever."

Using Other Punctuation Marks

34a Using Colons

The **colon** is a strong punctuation mark that points readers ahead. When a colon introduces a list or series, explanatory material, or a quotation, it must be preceded by a complete sentence.

1 Introducing Lists or Series

Use colons to set off lists or series, including those introduced by phrases such as *the following* or *as follows*.

Waiting tables requires three skills: memory, speed, and balance.

2 Introducing Explanatory Material

Use colons to introduce material that explains, exemplifies, or summarizes. Frequently, this material is presented as an **appositive**, a word group that identifies or renames an adjacent noun or pronoun.

Diego Rivera is known for a controversial mural: the one commissioned for Rockefeller Center in the 1930s.

She had one dream: to play professional basketball.

Sometimes a colon separates two independent clauses, the second illustrating or explaining the first.

A *U.S. News & World Report* survey revealed a surprising fact: Americans spend more time at malls than anywhere else except at home and at work.

Note: When a complete sentence follows a colon, it may begin with either a capital or a lowercase letter. However, if the sentence is a quotation, the first word is always capitalized (unless it was not capitalized in the source).

3 Introducing Quotations

See
33b1

When you quote a <u>long prose passage</u>, always introduce it with a colon. Also use a colon before a short quotation when it is introduced by a complete sentence.

> With dignity, Bartleby repeated the familiar words: "I prefer not to."

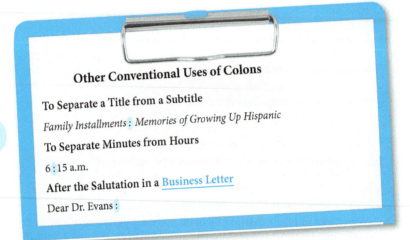

Other Conventional Uses of Colons

To Separate a Title from a Subtitle

See
10a

Family Installments : *Memories of Growing Up Hispanic*

To Separate Minutes from Hours

6 : 15 a.m.

After the Salutation in a <u>Business Letter</u>

Dear Dr. Evans :

4 Editing Misused Colons

Do not use colons in the following situations.

After Expressions Such As For Example Do not use colons after the expressions *for example, such as, namely,* and *that is.* (Remember that when a colon introduces a list or series, a complete sentence must precede the colon.)

> The Eye Institute treats patients with a wide variety of conditions, such as⟋ myopia, glaucoma, and cataracts.

In Verb and Prepositional Constructions Do not place colons between verbs and their objects or complements or between prepositions and their objects.

> James A. Michener wrote⟋ *Hawaii, Centennial, Space,* and *Poland.*

> Hitler's armies marched through⟋ the Netherlands, Belgium, and France.

EXERCISE 34.1

Add colons where appropriate in the following sentences, and delete any mis-used colons.

Example: There was one thing he really hated getting up at 7:00 every morning.

▶ 1. Books about the late John F. Kennedy include the following *A Hero for Our Time*; *Johnny, We Hardly Knew Ye*; *One Brief Shining Moment*; and *JFK: Reckless Youth*.

▶ 2. Only one task remained to tell his boss he was quitting.

3. The story closed with a familiar phrase "And they all lived happily ever after."

4. The sergeant requested: reinforcements, medical supplies, and more ammunition.

5. She kept only four souvenirs a photograph, a matchbook, a theater pro-gram, and a daisy pressed between the pages of *William Shakespeare The Complete Works*.

34b   Using Dashes

1 Setting Off Nonessential Material

Like commas, **dashes** can set off nonessential material, but unlike commas, dashes call attention to the material they set off. Indicate a dash with two un-spaced hyphens (which your word-processing program will automatically convert to a dash).

See 30d

For emphasis, you may use dashes to set off explanations, qualifications, examples, definitions, and appositives.

Neither of the boys — both nine-year-olds — had any history of violence.

Too many parents learn the dangers of swimming pools the hard way — after their toddler has drowned.

2 Introducing a Summary

Use a dash to introduce a statement that summarizes a list or series before it.

"Study hard," "Respect your elders," "Don't talk with your mouth full" — Sharon had often heard her parents say these things.

3 Indicating an Interruption

In dialogue, a dash can mark a hesitation or an unfinished thought.

"I think — no, I know — that this is the worst day of my life," Julie sighed.

Close-Up   EDITING OVERUSED DASHES

Too many dashes can make your writing seem disorganized and out of control, so you should be careful not to overuse them.

Registration was a nightmare—most of the courses I wanted to

take—geology and conversational Spanish, for instance—met at

inconvenient times—or were closed by the time I tried to sign up

for them—it was really depressing—even for registration.

EXERCISE 34.2

Add dashes and other punctuation where needed in the following sentences. If a sentence is correct, mark it with a *C*.

Example: World War I called "the war to end all wars" was, unfortunately, no such thing.

1. Tulips, daffodils, hyacinths, lilies all these flowers grow from bulbs.
2. India a country with a rich cultural history gained independence after two hundred years of British rule.
3. "But it's not" She paused and thought about her next words.
4. He considered several different majors history, English, political science, and business before deciding on journalism.
5. The two words added to the Pledge of Allegiance in the 1950s "under God" remain part of the Pledge today.

34c   Using Parentheses

1 Setting Off Nonessential Material

Use **parentheses** to enclose material that expands, clarifies, illustrates, or supplements. (Note that unlike dashes, parentheses tend to deemphasize the words they enclose.)

In some European countries (notably Sweden and France), high-quality day care is offered at little or no cost to parents.

When a complete sentence set off by parentheses falls within another sentence, it should not begin with a capital letter or end with a period.

The region is so cold (temperatures average in the low twenties) that it is virtually uninhabitable.

When the parenthetical sentence does *not* fall within another sentence, it must begin with a capital letter and end with appropriate punctuation.

The region is very cold. (Temperatures average in the low twenties.)

Close-Up USING PARENTHESES WITH OTHER PUNCTUATION

When parentheses fall within a sentence, punctuation never immediately precedes the opening parenthesis. Punctuation may follow the closing parenthesis, however.

George Orwell's *1984* / (1949), which focuses on the dangers of a totalitarian society, is required reading.

---

2 Using Parentheses in Other Situations

Parentheses are used around letters and numbers that identify points on a list, dates, cross-references, and documentation.

All reports must include the following components: (1) an opening summary, (2) a background statement, and (3) a list of conclusions.

Russia defeated Sweden in the Great Northern War (1700–1721).

Other scholars also make this point (see p. 54).

One critic has called the novel "puerile" (Arvin 72).

EXERCISE 34.3

Add parentheses where appropriate in the following sentences. If a sentence is correct, mark it with a *C*.

Example: The greatest battle of the War of 1812 (the Battle of New Orleans) was fought after the war was declared over.

1. During the Great War 1914–1918, Britain censored letters written from the front lines.

2. Those who lived in towns on the coast such as Dover could often hear the mortar shells across the channel in France.

3. Wilfred Owen wrote his most famous poem "Dulce et Decorum Est" in the trenches in France.

4. The British uniforms with bright red tabs right at the neck were responsible for many British deaths.

5. It was difficult for the War Poets as they are now called to return to writing about subjects other than the horrors of war.

34d Using Brackets

1 Setting Off Comments within Quotations

Brackets within quotations tell readers that the enclosed words are yours and not those of your source. You can bracket an explanation, a clarification, a correction, or an opinion.

> "Even at Princeton he [F. Scott Fitzgerald] felt like an outsider."

If a quotation contains an error, indicate that the error is not yours by following the error with the Latin word *sic* ("thus") in brackets.

> As the website notes, "The octopuss [sic] is a cephalopod mollusk with eight arms."

See 44d1

Note: Use brackets to indicate changes that you make in order to fit a quotation smoothly into your sentence.

2 Replacing Parentheses within Parentheses

When one set of parentheses falls within another, use brackets in place of the inner set.

> In her classic study of American education between 1945 and 1960 (*The Trouble Crusade* [New York: Basic, 1963]), Diane Ravitch addresses issues such as progressive education, race, educational reforms, and campus unrest.

34e Using Slashes

1 Separating One Option from Another

When separating one option from another with a **slash**, do not leave a space before or after the slash.

The either/or fallacy is a common error in logic.

Writer/director Spike Lee will speak at the film festival.

2 Separating Lines of Poetry Run into the Text

When separating lines of poetry run into the text, leave one space before and one space after the slash.

> The poet James Schevill writes, "I study my defects / And learn how to perfect them."

34f Using Ellipses

1 Indicating an Omission in Quoted Prose

Use an **ellipsis**—three *spaced* periods—to indicate that you have omitted words from a prose quotation. Note that an ellipsis in the middle of a quoted passage can indicate the omission of a word, a sentence or two, or even a whole paragraph or more. When deleting material from a quotation, be careful not to change the meaning of the original passage.

> **Original:** "When I was a young man, being anxious to distinguish myself, I was perpetually starting new propositions." (Samuel Johnson)

> **With Omission:** "When I was a young man, . . . I was perpetually starting new propositions."

Note that when you delete words immediately after a punctuation mark (such as the comma in the example above), you retain the punctuation before the ellipsis.

When you delete material at the end of a sentence, place the ellipsis *after* the sentence's period or other end punctuation.

> According to humorist Dave Barry, "from outer space Europe appears to be shaped like a large ketchup stain. . . . " (period followed by ellipsis)

Note: Never begin a quoted passage with an ellipsis.

When you delete material between sentences, place the ellipsis *after* any punctuation that appears in the original passage.

> **Deletion from Middle of One Sentence to End of Another:** According to Donald Hall, "Everywhere one meets the idea that reading is an activity desirable in itself. . . . People surround the idea of reading with piety and do not take into account the purpose of reading." (period followed by ellipsis)

> **Deletion from Middle of One Sentence to Middle of Another:** "When I was a young man, . . . I found that generally what was new was false." (Samuel Johnson) (comma followed by ellipsis)

Note: If a quoted passage already contains ellipses, MLA recommends that you enclose any ellipses of your own in brackets to distinguish them from those that appear in the original quotation.

Close-Up   USING ELLIPSES

If a quotation ending with an ellipsis is followed by parenthetical documen-tation, the final punctuation comes *after* the documentation.

As Jarman argues, "Compromise was impossible . . ." (161) .

2 Indicating an Omission in Quoted Poetry

Use an ellipsis when you omit a word or phrase from a line of poetry. When you omit one or more lines of poetry, use a line of spaced periods. (The length may be equal either to the line above it or to the missing line—but it should not be longer than the longest line of the poem.)

Original:

> Stitch! Stitch! Stitch!
> In poverty, hunger, and dirt,
> And still with a voice of dolorous pitch,
> Would that its tone could reach the Rich,
> She sang this "Song of the Shirt!"
>
> (Thomas Hood)

With Omission:

> Stitch! Stitch! Stitch!
> In poverty, hunger, and dirt,
> . . . .
> She sang this "Song of the Shirt!"

EXERCISE 34.4

Read the following paragraph, and follow the instructions after it, taking care in each case not to delete essential information.

> The most important thing about research is to know when to stop. How does one recognize the moment? When I was eighteen or thereabouts, my mother told me that when out with a young man I should always leave a half-hour before I wanted to. Although I was not sure how this might be accomplished, I recognized the advice as sound, and exactly the same rule applies to research. One must stop *before* one has finished; otherwise, one will never stop and never finish. (Barbara Tuchman, *Practicing History*)

1. Delete words from the middle of one sentence, marking the omission with an ellipsis.

2. Delete words from the middle of one sentence to the middle of another, marking the omission with an ellipsis.
3. Delete words at the end of any sentence, marking the omission with an ellipsis.
4. Delete one complete sentence from the middle of the passage, marking the omission with an ellipsis.

EXERCISE 34.5

Add appropriate punctuation—colons, dashes, parentheses, brackets, or slashes—to the following sentences. If a sentence is correct, mark it with a C.

Example: There was one thing she was sure of‚if she did well at the interview, the job would be hers.

1. Mark Twain Samuel L. Clemens made the following statement "I can live for two months on a good compliment."
2. Liza Minnelli, the actress singer who starred in several films, is the daughter of legendary singer Judy Garland.
3. Saudi Arabia, Oman, Yemen, Qatar, and the United Arab Emirates all these are located on the Arabian Peninsula.
4. John Adams 1735–1826 was the second president of the United States; John Quincy Adams 1767–1848 was the sixth.
5. The sign said, "No tresspassing sic."
6. *Checkmate* a term derived from the Persian phrase meaning "the king is dead" announces victory in chess.
7. The following people were present at the meeting the president of the board of trustees, three trustees, and twenty reporters.
8. Before the introduction of the potato in Europe, the parsnip was a major source of carbohydrates in fact, it was a dietary staple.
9. In the well-researched book *Crime Movies* (New York Norton, 1980), Carlos Clarens studies the gangster genre in film.
10. I remember reading though I can't remember where that Upton Sinclair sold plots to Jack London.

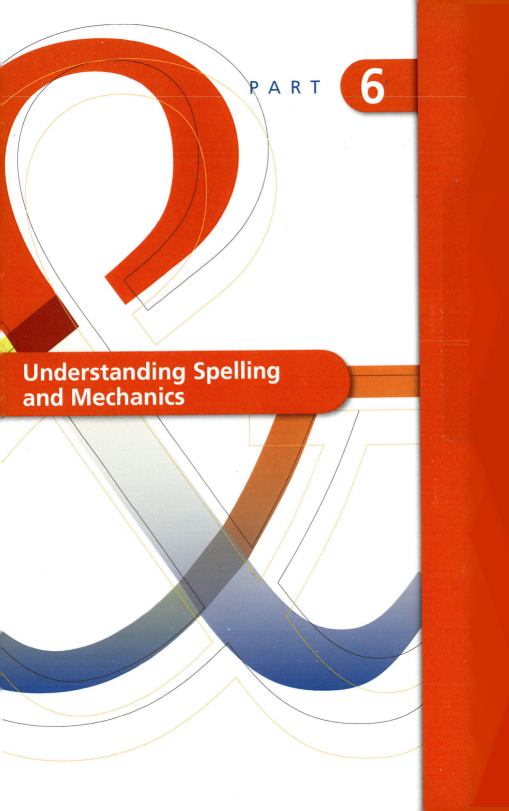

PART 6

Understanding Spelling
and Mechanics

PART 6

Understanding Spelling and Mechanics

Improving Spelling

Most people can spell even difficult words "almost correctly"; usually only one or two letters are wrong. In many cases, memorizing a few rules and their exceptions and learning the correct spelling of the most commonly misspelled words can help you become a better speller.

35a Understanding Spelling and Pronunciation

Because pronunciation often provides few clues to English spelling, you need to pay particular attention to the three problem areas that cause the most misspellings.

1 Words That Are Often Pronounced Carelessly

Most of us pronounce words rather carelessly in everyday speech. Consequently, when spelling, we may leave out, add, or transpose letters.

candidate	library	recognize
environment	lightning	specific
February	nuclear	supposed to
government	perform	surprise
hundred	quantity	used to

2 American and British Spellings

Some words are spelled one way in the United States and another way in Great Britain and the Commonwealth nations.

American	British
color	colour
defense	defence
honor	honour
judgment	judgement
theater	theatre
toward	towards
traveled	travelled

3 Homophones

Homophones are words—such as *accept* and *except*—that are pronounced alike but spelled differently.

accept	to receive
except	other than
affect	to have an influence on (*verb*)
effect	result (*noun*); to cause (*verb*)
its	possessive of *it*
it's	contraction of *it is*
principal	most important (*adjective*); head of a school (*noun*)
principle	a basic truth; rule of conduct

For a full list of these and other homophones, along with their meanings and sentences illustrating their use, **see the Glossary of Usage**.

Close-Up   RUNNING A SPELL CHECK

Even if you run a spell check, you still have to proofread your essays. Remember that a spell checker will not recognize the following kinds of errors:

- A homophone—*accept* for *except* or *there* for *their*, for example.
- A typo that creates a new word—*form* for *from* or *then* for *than*, for example.
- Many capitalization errors—*president Lincoln* instead of *President Lincoln*, for example.

35b   Learning Spelling Rules

Memorizing a few simple rules (and their exceptions) can help you identify and correct words that you have misspelled.

1 The *ie/ei* Combinations

The old rule still stands: use *i* before *e* except after *c* (or when pronounced *ay*, as in *neighbor*).

i **before** *e*	*ei* **after** *c*	*ei* **pronounced** *ay*
belief	ceiling	weigh
chief	deceit	freight
niece	receive	eight

Exceptions: *either, neither, foreign, leisure, weird,* and *seize.* In addition, if the *ie* combination is not pronounced as a unit, the rule does not apply: *atheist, science.*

EXERCISE 35.1

Fill in the blanks with the proper *ie* or *ei* combination. After completing the exercise, use a dictionary or spell checker to check your answers.

Example: conc ___*ei*___ ve

► 1. rec_____pt
► 2. var_____ty
► 3. caff_____ne
► 4. ach_____ve
► 5. kal_____doscope

6. misch_____f
7. effic_____nt
8. v_____n
9. spec_____s
10. suffic_____nt

② Doubling Final Consonants

The only words that double their consonants before a suffix that begins with a vowel (*-ed, -ing*) are those that pass the following three tests:

1. They have one syllable or are stressed on the last syllable.
2. They have only one vowel in the last syllable.
3. They end in a single consonant.

The word *tap* satisfies all three conditions: it has only one syllable, it has only one vowel (*a*), and it ends in a single consonant (*p*). Therefore, its final consonant is doubled before a suffix beginning with a vowel (*tapped, tapping*).

The word *relent,* however, meets only two of the three conditions: it is stressed on the last syllable, and it has one vowel in the last syllable, but it does not end in a single consonant. Therefore, its final consonant is not doubled (*relented, relenting*).

③ Prefixes

The addition of a prefix never affects the spelling of the root (*mis + spell = misspell*). Some prefixes can cause spelling problems, however, because they are pronounced alike although they are not spelled alike: *ante-/anti-, en-/in-, per-/pre-,* and *de-/di-.*

antebellum	antiaircraft
encircle	integrate
perceive	prescribe
deduct	direct

4 Silent e before a Suffix

When a suffix that begins with a consonant is added to a word ending in silent *e*, the *e* is generally kept: *hope/hopeful; lame/lamely; bore/boredom.* **Exceptions:** *argument, truly, ninth, judgment,* and *acknowledgment.*

When a suffix that starts with a vowel is added to a word that ends in a silent *e*, the *e* is generally dropped: *hope/hoping; trace/traced; grieve/grievance; love/lovable.* **Exceptions:** *changeable, noticeable,* and *courageous.*

EXERCISE 35.2

& Combine the following words with the suffixes in parentheses. Keep or drop the silent *e* as you see fit. Then, compare your choices with those of a classmate.

Example: fate (al)
            fatal

▶ 1. surprise (ing)
▶ 2. sure (ly)
▶ 3. force (ible)
▶ 4. manage (able)
▶ 5. due (ly)
  6. outrage (ous)

  7. service (able)
  8. awe (ful)
  9. shame (ing)
 10. shame (less)

5 y before a Suffix

When a word ends in a consonant plus *y*, the *y* generally changes to an *i* when a suffix is added (*beauty + ful = beautiful*). The *y* is kept, however, when the suffix *-ing* is added (*tally + ing = tallying*) and in some one-syllable words (*dry + ness = dryness*).

When a word ends in a vowel plus *y*, the *y* is retained (*joy + ful = joyful; employ + er = employer*). **Exception:** *day + ly = daily.*

EXERCISE 35.3

& Add the endings in parentheses to the following words. Change or keep the final *y* as you see fit. Then, compare your choices with those of a classmate.

Example: party (ing)
            partying

▶ 1. journey (ing)
▶ 2. study (ed)
▶ 3. carry (ing)
▶ 4. shy (ly)
▶ 5. study (ing)
  6. sturdy (ness)

  7. merry (ment)
  8. likely (hood)
  9. plenty (ful)
 10. supply (er)

6 *seed* Endings

Endings with the sound *seed* are nearly always spelled *cede*, as in *precede, intercede, concede,* and so on. **Exceptions:** *supersede, exceed, proceed,* and *succeed.*

7 *-able, -ible*

If the root of a word is itself an independent word, the suffix *-able* is most often used. If the root of a word is not an independent word, the suffix *-ible* is most often used.

*comfort*able   *compat*ible
*agree*able   *incred*ible
*dry*able   *plaus*ible

8 Plurals

Most nouns form plurals by adding *-s: savage/savages, tortilla/tortillas, boat/boats.* There are, however, a number of exceptions.

Words Ending in **-f** *or* **-fe**   Some words ending in *-f* or *-fe* form plurals by changing the *f* to *v* and adding *-es* or *-s: life/lives, self/selves.* Others add just *-s: belief/beliefs, safe/safes.* Words ending in *-ff* take *-s* to form plurals: *tariff/tariffs.*

Words Ending in **-y**   Most words that end in a consonant followed by *y* form plurals by changing the *y* to *i* and adding *-es: baby/babies.* **Exceptions:** proper nouns, such as the *Kennedys* (never the *Kennedies*).

Words that end in a vowel followed by a *y* form plurals by adding *-s: day/days, monkey/monkeys.*

Words Ending in **-o**   Words that end in a vowel followed by *o* form the plural by adding *-s: radio/radios, stereo/stereos, zoo/zoos.* Most words that end in a consonant followed by *o* add *-es* to form the plural: *tomato/tomatoes, hero/heroes.* **Exceptions:** *silo/silos, piano/pianos, memo/memos,* and *soprano/sopranos.*

Words Ending in **-s, -ss, -sh, -ch, -x,** *and* **-z**   These words form plurals by adding *-es: Jones/Joneses, mass/masses, rash/rashes, lunch/lunches, box/boxes, buzz/buzzes.* **Exceptions:** Some one-syllable words that end in *-s* or *-z* double their final consonants when forming plurals: *quiz/quizzes.*

Compound Nouns   **Compound nouns**—nouns formed from two or more words—usually form the plural with the last word in the compound construction: *welfare state/welfare states; snowball/snowballs.* However, where the first word of the compound noun is more important than the others, form the plural with the first word: *sister-in-law/sisters-in-law, attorney general/attorneys general, hole in one/holes in one.*

Foreign Plurals Some words, especially those borrowed from Latin or Greek, keep their foreign plurals. Look up a foreign word's plural form in a dictionary if you do not know it.

Singular	Plural
basis	bases
criterion	criteria
curriculum	curricula
datum	data
larva	larvae
medium	media
memorandum	memoranda
stimulus	stimuli
syllabus	syllabi

Note: Some linguists find Latin and Greek plural endings pretentious and encourage the use of English plural forms—for example, *condominiums* rather than *condominia, stadiums* rather than *stadia,* and *octopuses* rather than *octopi.*

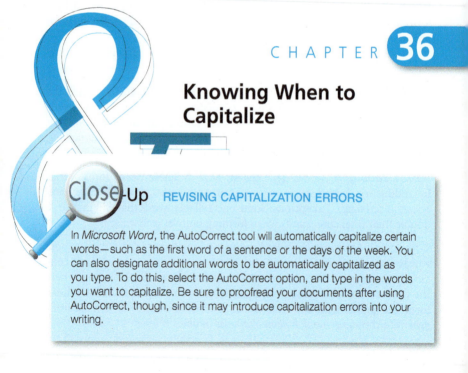

Knowing When to Capitalize

Close-Up REVISING CAPITALIZATION ERRORS

In *Microsoft Word*, the AutoCorrect tool will automatically capitalize certain words—such as the first word of a sentence or the days of the week. You can also designate additional words to be automatically capitalized as you type. To do this, select the AutoCorrect option, and type in the words you want to capitalize. Be sure to proofread your documents after using AutoCorrect, though, since it may introduce capitalization errors into your writing.

36a Capitalizing the First Word of a Sentence

Capitalize the first word of a sentence, including a sentence of quoted speech or writing.

As Shakespeare wrote, "Who steals my purse steals trash."

Do not capitalize a sentence set off within another sentence by dashes or parentheses.

Finding the store closed—it was a holiday—they went home.

The candidates are Frank Lester and Jane Lester (they are not related).

Capitalization is optional when a complete sentence is introduced by a colon.

See
34a

Close-Up USING CAPITAL LETTERS IN POETRY

The first word of a line of poetry is generally capitalized. If the poet uses a lowercase letter to begin a line, however, you should follow that style when you quote the line.

36b Capitalizing Proper Nouns

Proper nouns—the names of specific persons, places, or things—are capitalized, and so are adjectives formed from proper nouns.

1 Specific People's Names

Always capitalize people's names: Kirsten Gillibrand, Barack Obama.

Capitalize a title when it precedes a person's name (Senator Kirsten Gillibrand) or is used instead of the name (Dad). Do not capitalize titles that *follow* names (Kirsten Gillibrand, the senator from New York) or those that refer to the general position, not the particular person who holds it (a stay-at-home dad).

MULTILINGUAL TIP

If you are not sure whether a noun should be capitalized, look it up in a dictionary. Do not capitalize a word simply because you want to emphasize its importance.

You may, however, capitalize titles that indicate very high-ranking positions even when they are used alone or when they follow a name: the Pope; Barack Obama, President of the United States. Never capitalize a title denoting a family relationship when it follows an article or a possessive pronoun (an u̲ncle, his m̲om).

Capitalize titles that represent academic degrees or abbreviations of those degrees even when they follow a name: D̲r. Sanjay Gupta; Sanjay Gupta, M̲D̲.

2 Names of Particular Structures, Special Events, Monuments, and So On

the Brooklyn Bridge   the Taj Mahal
the Great Wall   Mount Rushmore
the World Series   the *Titanic*

Note: Capitalize a common noun, such as *bridge, river, county,* or *lake,* when it is part of a proper noun (L̲ake Erie, Kings C̲ounty).

3 Places and Geographical Regions

Saturn   the Straits of Magellan
Budapest   the Fiji Islands
Walden Pond   the Western Hemisphere

Capitalize *north, south, east,* and *west* when they denote particular geographical regions but not when they designate directions.

There are more tornadoes in Kansas than in the E̲ast. (*East* refers to a specific region.)

Turn w̲est at Broad Street and continue n̲orth to Market. (*West* and *north* refer to directions, not specific regions.)

4 Days of the Week, Months, and Holidays

Saturday   Cinco de Mayo
January   Diwali

5 Historical Periods, Events, Documents, and Names of Legal Cases

the Industrial Revolution   the Treaty of Versailles
the Reformation   the Voting Rights Act
the Battle of Gettysburg   *Brown v. Board of Education*

Note: Names of court cases are italicized in the text of essays, but not in works-cited entries.

6 Philosophic, Literary, and Artistic Movements

Naturalism   Dadaism
Neoclassicism   Expressionism

7 Races, Ethnic Groups, Nationalities, and Languages

African American	Korean
Latino/Latina	Farsi

> **Note:** When the word *black* denotes a race, it is capitalized (*Black*).

8 Religions and Their Followers; Sacred Books and Figures

Islam	the Qur'an	Buddha
the Talmud	Jews	God

> **Note:** It is not necessary to capitalize pronouns that refer to God (although some people do so).

9 Specific Groups and Organizations

the Democratic Party
the International Brotherhood of Electrical Workers
the New York Yankees
the American Civil Liberties Union
the National Rifle Association
the Rolling Stones

> **Note:** When the name of a group or organization is abbreviated, the <u>abbreviation</u> uses capital letters in place of the capitalized words.
>
> See 39b

IBEW	ACLU	NRA

10 Businesses, Government Agencies, and Other Institutions

General Electric	the Environmental Protection Agency
Lincoln High School	the University of Maryland

11 Brand Names and Words Formed from Them

Velcro	Coke	Post-it	Rollerblades	Astroturf

> **Note:** Brand names that over long use have become synonymous with the product—for example, *nylon* and *aspirin*—are no longer capitalized. (Consult a dictionary to determine whether or not to capitalize a familiar brand name.)

Close-Up   USING BRAND NAMES

In general, use generic references, not brand names, in college writing—*photocopy*, not *Xerox*, for example. These generic names are not capitalized.

12 Specific Academic Courses

Sociology 201   English 101

Note: Do not capitalize a general subject area (sociology, zoology) unless it is the name of a language (English, Spanish).

13 Adjectives Formed from Proper Nouns

Freudian slip   Elizabethan era
Platonic ideal   Shakespearean sonnet
Aristotelian logic   Marxist ideology

When words derived from proper nouns have lost their original associations, do not capitalize them: *china* bowl, *french* fries.

36c   Capitalizing Important Words in Titles

In general, capitalize all words in titles with the exception of articles (*a, an,* and *the*), prepositions, coordinating conjunctions, and the *to* in infinitives (unless they are the first or last word in the title or subtitle).

"Dover Beach"   *On the Waterfront*
The Declaration of Independence   *Madame Curie: A Biography*
Across the River and into the Trees "What Friends Are For"

36d   Capitalizing the Pronoun *I*, the Interjection *O*, and Other Single Letters in Special Constructions

Always capitalize the pronoun *I* even if it is part of a contraction (*I'm, I'll, I've*).

Sam and <u>I</u> finally went to Mexico, and <u>I'm</u> glad we did.

Always capitalize the interjection *O*.

Give us peace in our time, O Lord.

However, capitalize the interjection *oh* only when it begins a sentence.

Note: Many other single letters are capitalized in certain usages: an A in history, vitamin B, C major. Check your dictionary to determine whether or not to use a capital letter.

36e Capitalizing Salutations and Closings of Letters

Always capitalize the first word of the salutation of a personal or business letter.

See 10a

Dear Fred,   Dear Mr. Reynolds:

Always capitalize the first word of the complimentary close.

Sincerely,   Very truly yours,

36f Editing Misused Capitals

Do not capitalize words for emphasis or as an attention-getting strategy. If you are uncertain about whether or not a word should be capitalized, consult a dictionary.

1 Seasons

Do not capitalize the names of the seasons—summer, fall, winter, spring—unless they are personified, as in *Old Man Winter*.

2 Centuries and Loosely Defined Historical Periods

Do not capitalize the names of centuries or general historical periods.

seventeenth-century poetry   the automobile age

Do, however, capitalize names of specific historical, anthropological, and geological periods: *Iron Age; Renaissance; Paleozoic Era*.

3 Diseases and Other Medical Terms

Do not capitalize names of diseases or medical tests or conditions unless a proper noun is part of the name or unless the name of the disease is an acronym.

See 29a2

| smallpox | Apgar test | AIDS |
| Lyme disease | autism | Ebola |

EXERCISE 36.1

Capitalize words where necessary in these sentences.

Example: John F. Kennedy won the *p̲ulitzer p̲rize* for his book *p̲rofiles in c̲ourage.*

1. Two of the brontë sisters wrote *jane eyre* and *wuthering heights*, nineteenth-century novels that are required reading in many english classes that focus on victorian literature.

2. It was a beautiful day in the spring—it was april 15, to be exact—but all Ted could think about was the check he had to write to the internal revenue service and the bills he had to pay by friday.

3. Traveling north, they hiked through british columbia, planning a leisurely return on the cruise ship *canadian princess*.

4. Alice liked her mom's apple pie better than aunt nellie's rhubarb pie, but she liked grandpa's punch best of all.

5. A new elective, political science 30, covers the vietnam war from the gulf of tonkin to the fall of saigon, including the roles of ho chi minh, the viet cong, and the buddhist monks; the positions of presidents johnson and nixon; and the influence of groups such as the student mobilization committee and vietnam veterans against the war.

6. When the central high school drama club put on a production of shaw's *pygmalion*, the director xeroxed extra copies of the parts for eliza doolittle and professor henry higgins so he could give them to the understudies.

7. Shaking all over, Bill admitted, "driving on the los angeles freeway is a frightening experience for a kid from brooklyn, even in a bmw."

8. The new united federation of teachers contract guarantees teachers many paid holidays, including columbus day, veterans day, and presidents' day; a week each at christmas and easter; and two full months (july and august) in the summer.

9. The sociology syllabus included the books *beyond the best interests of the child*, *regulating the poor: the functions of public welfare*, and *a welfare mother*; in anthropology, we were to begin by studying the stone age; and in geology, we were to focus on the Mesozoic era.

10. Winners of the nobel peace prize include lech walesa, former leader of the polish trade union solidarity; the reverend dr. martin luther king jr., founder of the southern christian leadership conference; and archbishop desmond tutu of south africa.

CHAPTER 37

Using Italics

37a Setting Off Titles and Names

Use italics for the titles and names listed in the following box. Most other titles are set off with **quotation marks**.

See
33c

Titles and Names Set in Italics

Books: *Twilight, Harry Potter and the Deathly Hallows*

Newspapers: *The Washington Post, The Philadelphia Inquirer*

Magazines and Journals: *Rolling Stone, Scientific American*

Online Magazines and Journals: *salon.com, theonion.com*

Websites or Home Pages: *urbanlegends.com, movie-mistakes.com*

Pamphlets: *Common Sense*

Films: *Citizen Kane, The Hunger Games*

Television Programs: *60 Minutes, The Bachelorette, Fear Factor*

Radio Programs: *All Things Considered, A Prairie Home Companion*

Long Poems: *John Brown's Body, The Faerie Queen*

Plays: *Macbeth, A Raisin in the Sun*

Long Musical Works: *Rigoletto, Eroica*

Software Programs: *Microsoft Word, PowerPoint*

Search Engines and Web Browsers: *Google Chrome, Safari, Internet Explorer*

Databases: *Academic Search Premier, Expanded Academic ASAP Plus*

Paintings and Sculpture: *Guernica, Pietà*

Ships: *Lusitania, U.S.S. Saratoga* (S.S. and U.S.S. are not italicized.)

Trains: *City of New Orleans, The Orient Express*

Aircraft: *The Hindenburg, Enola Gay* (Only particular aircraft, not makes or types such as Piper Cub or Airbus, are italicized.)

Spacecraft: *Challenger, Enterprise*

Video Games: *Halo: Combat Evolved, Grand Theft Auto V*

Names of sacred books, such as the Bible and the Qur'an, and well-known documents, such as the Constitution and the Declaration of Independence, are neither italicized nor placed within quotation marks.

37b Setting Off Foreign Words and Phrases

Italics are often used to set off foreign words and phrases that have not become part of the English language.

> "*C'est la vie*," Madeline said when she saw the long line for the concert.
>
> *Spirochaeta plicatilis* is a corkscrewlike bacterium.

If you are not sure whether a foreign word has been assimilated into English, consult a dictionary.

37c Setting Off Elements Spoken of as Themselves and Terms Being Defined

Use italics to set off letters, numerals, and words that refer to the letters, numerals, and words themselves.

> Is that a *p* or a *g*?
>
> I forget the exact address, but I know it has a *3* in it.
>
> Why doesn't *though* rhyme with *cough*?

Also use italics to set off words and phrases that you go on to define.

> A *closet drama* is a play meant to be read, not performed.

Note: When you quote a dictionary definition, put the word you are defining in italics and the definition itself in quotation marks.

> *Infer* means "to draw a conclusion"; *imply* means "to suggest."

37d Using Italics for Emphasis

Italics may occasionally be used for emphasis.

> Initially, poetry might be defined as a kind of language that says *more* and says it *more intensely* than does ordinary language. (Lawrence Perrine, *Sound and Sense*)

However, overuse of italics is distracting. Instead of italicizing, try to indicate emphasis with word choice and sentence structure.

EXERCISE 37.1

Underline to indicate italics where necessary, and delete any italics that are incorrectly used. If a sentence is correct, mark it with a *C*.

Example: <u>However</u> is a conjunctive adverb, not a coordinating conjunction.

▸ 1. I said Carol, not Darryl.
▸ 2. A *deus ex machina*, an improbable device used to resolve the plot of a fictional work, is used in Charles Dickens's novel Oliver Twist.
▸ 3. He dotted every i and crossed every t.
▸ 4. The Metropolitan Opera's production of Carmen was a tour de force for the principal performers.
▸ 5. *Laissez-faire* is a doctrine holding that government should not interfere with trade.
6. Antidote and anecdote are often confused because their pronunciations are similar.
7. Hawthorne's novels include Fanshawe, The House of the Seven Gables, The Blithedale Romance, and The Scarlet Letter.
8. Words such as mailman, policeman, and fireman have been replaced by nonsexist terms such as letter carrier, police officer, and firefighter.
9. A classic black tuxedo was considered de rigueur at the charity ball, but Jason preferred to wear his *dashiki*.
10. Thomas Mann's novel Buddenbrooks is a bildungsroman.

CHAPTER **38**

Using Hyphens

Hyphens have two conventional uses: to break a word at the end of a line and to link words in certain compounds.

38a Breaking a Word at the End of a Line

Sometimes, you will want to break a word with a hyphen—for example, to fill in excessive space at the end of a line when you want to enhance a document's visual appeal. When you break a word at the end of a line, divide it only between syllables, consulting a dictionary if necessary. Never divide a word at the end of a page, and never hyphenate a one-syllable word. In addition, never leave a single letter at the end of a line or carry only one or two letters to the next line.

See
38b

If you divide a **compound word** at the end of a line, place the hyphen between the elements of the compound (*snow-mobile*, not *snowmo-bile*).

Close-Up DIVIDING ELECTRONIC ADDRESSES (URLS)

MLA style recommends that you break the URL after a mark of punctuation (such as a slash, period, or hyphen). In addition, omit *http://* or *https://* when noting the URL.

38b Dividing Compound Words

A **compound word** consists of two or more words. Some familiar compound words are always hyphenated: *no-hitter, helter-skelter*. Other compounds are always written as one word: *fireplace, peacetime*. Finally, some compounds are always written as two separate words: *labor relations, bunk bed*. A dictionary can tell you whether a particular compound requires a hyphen.

1 Hyphenating with Compound Adjectives

A **compound adjective** is a series of two or more words that function together as an adjective. When a compound adjective *precedes* the noun it modifies, use hyphens to join its elements.

The research team tried to use nineteenth-century technology to design a space-age project.

When a compound adjective *follows* the noun it modifies, do not use hyphens to join its elements.

The three government-operated programs were run smoothly, but the one that was not government operated was short of funds.

Note: A compound adjective formed with an adverb ending in *-ly* is not hyphenated, even when it precedes the noun: *Many upwardly mobile families are on tight budgets.*

Use **suspended hyphens**—hyphens followed by a space or by appropriate punctuation and a space—in a pair or series of compounds that have the same principal elements.

Graduates of two- and four-year colleges were eligible for the grants.

The exam called for sentence-, paragraph-, and essay-length answers.

2 Hyphenating with Certain Prefixes and Suffixes

Use a hyphen between a prefix and a proper noun or proper adjective.

mid-July   pre-Columbian

Use a hyphen to connect the prefixes *all-*, *ex-*, *half-*, *quarter-*, *quasi-*, and *self-* and the suffix *-elect* to a noun.

ex-senator   self-centered   president-elect
quasi-legal   all-inclusive

Note: The words *selfhood, selfish,* and *selfless* do not include hyphens. In these words, *self* is the root, not a prefix.

3 Hyphenating in Compound Numerals and Fractions

Hyphenate compounds that represent numbers below one hundred (even if they are part of a larger number).

the twenty-first century   three hundred sixty-five days

Also hyphenate the written form of a fraction when it modifies a noun.

a two-thirds share of the business

4 Hyphenating for Clarity

Hyphenate to prevent readers from misreading one word for another.

Before we can reform criminals, we must re-form our ideas about prisons.

Hyphenate to avoid certain hard-to-read combinations, such as two *i*'s (*semi-illiterate*) or more than two of the same consonant (*shell-less*).

In most cases, hyphenate between a capital initial and a word when the two combine to form a compound: *A-frame, T-shirt, D-day*.

5 Hyphenating in Coined Compounds

A **coined compound**, one that uses a new combination of words as a unit, requires hyphens.

He looked up with a who-do-you-think-you-are expression.

EXERCISE 38.1

Add hyphens to the compounds in these sentences wherever they are required. Consult a dictionary if necessary.

Example: Alaska was the forty͜ninth state to join the United States.

1. One of the restaurant's blue plate specials is chicken fried steak.
2. Virginia and Texas are both right to work states.
3. He stood on tiptoe to see the near perfect statue, which was well hidden by the security fence.
4. The five and ten cent store had a self service makeup counter and stocked many up to the minute gadgets.
5. The so called Saturday night special is opposed by pro gun control groups.
6. He ordered two all beef patties with special sauce, lettuce, cheese, pickles, and onions on a sesame seed bun.
7. The material was extremely thought provoking, but it hardly presented any earth shattering conclusions.
8. The Red Sox Orioles game was rained out, so the long suffering fans left for home.
9. Bone marrow transplants carry the risk of what is known as a graft versus host reaction.
10. The state funded child care program was considered a highly desirable alternative to family day care.

CHAPTER **39**

Using Abbreviations

Generally speaking, **abbreviations** are not appropriate in college writing except in tables, charts, and works-cited lists. Some abbreviations are acceptable only in scientific, technical, or business writing, or only in a particular discipline. If you have any questions about the appropriateness of a particular abbreviation, consult a style manual for the appropriate field.

Close-Up ABBREVIATIONS IN ELECTRONIC COMMUNICATIONS

Like emoticons and acronyms, which are popular in email and instant messages, shorthand abbreviations and symbols—such as *GR8* and *2NITE*—are common in text messages. Although they are acceptable in informal electronic communications, such abbreviations are not appropriate in college writing or in business communications.

39a Abbreviating Titles

Titles before and after proper names are usually abbreviated.

Mr. Homer Simpson   Rep. Nydia Velázquez
Henry Kissinger, PhD   Prof. Elie Weisel

Do not, however, use an abbreviated title without a name.

doctor
The ~~Dr.~~ diagnosed tuberculosis.

39b Abbreviating Organization Names and Technical Terms

Well-known businesses and government, social, and civic organizations are frequently referred to by capitalized initials. These abbreviations fall into two categories: those in which the initials are pronounced as separate units (MTV) and **acronyms**, in which the initials are pronounced as a word (FEMA).

See 29a2

To save space, you may use accepted abbreviations for complex technical terms that are not well known, but be sure to spell out the full term the first time you mention it, followed by the abbreviation in parentheses.

Citrus farmers have been using ethylene dibromide (EDB), a chemical pesticide, for more than twenty years. Now, however, EDB has contaminated water supplies.

Close-Up ABBREVIATIONS IN MLA DOCUMENTATION

MLA documentation style requires abbreviations of publishers' company names—for example, **Columbia UP** for *Columbia University Press*—in the works-cited list. Do not, however, use such abbreviations in the body of an essay.

See 47a

(continued)

> **ABBREVIATIONS IN MLA DOCUMENTATION** *(continued)*
>
> MLA style also permits the use of abbreviations that designate parts of written works (**ch. 3, sec. 7**)—but only in the works-cited list and parenthetical documentation.
>
> Finally, MLA recommends abbreviating classic literary works and books of the Bible in parenthetical citations: (***Oth.***) for *Othello*, (**Exod.**) for Exodus. These words should not be abbreviated in the text of an essay or in the works-cited list.

39c Abbreviating Dates, Times of Day, and Temperatures

Dates, times of day, and temperatures are often abbreviated.

50 BC (*BC* follows the date)	AD 432 (*AD* precedes the date)
6 a.m.	3:03 p.m.
20°C (Centigrade or Celsius)	180°F (Fahrenheit)

Always capitalize *BC* and *AD*. (The alternatives *BCE*, for "before the common era," and *CE*, for "common era," are also capitalized.) Use lowercase letters for *a.m.* and *p.m.*, but use these abbreviations only when they are accompanied by numbers.

We will see you in the ˄a.m. *morning.*

Note: Avoid the abbreviation *no.* (written either *no.* or *No.*), except in technical writing, and then use it only before a specific number: *The unidentified substance was labeled no. 52.*

39d Editing Misused Abbreviations

In college writing, abbreviations are not used in the following cases.

1 Names of Days, Months, or Holidays

Do not abbreviate days of the week, months, or holidays.

On ˄Sat., Dec. 23, I started my ˄Xmas shopping. *Saturday, December   Christmas*

2 Names of Streets and Places

In general, do not abbreviate names of streets and places.

He lives on Riverside ˄Dr. in ˄NYC. *Drive   New York City.*

Exceptions: The abbreviation *US* is often acceptable (*US Coast Guard*), as is *DC* in *Washington, DC*. Also permissible are *Mt.* before the name of a mountain (*Mt. Etna*) and *St.* in a place name (*St. Albans*).

3 Names of Academic Subjects

Do not abbreviate names of academic subjects.

Psychology   *literature*
~~Psych.~~ and English ~~lit.~~ are required courses.

4 Names of Businesses

Write company names exactly as the firms themselves write them, including the distinction between the ampersand (&) and the word *and*: *AT&T, Charles Schwab & Co., Inc.* Abbreviations for *company, corporation*, and the like are used only along with a company name.

          corporation   *company*
The ~~corp.~~ merged with a ~~co.~~ in Ohio.

5 Latin Expressions

Abbreviations of common Latin phrases such as *i.e.* ("that is"), *e.g.* ("for example"), and *etc.* ("and so forth") are not appropriate in college writing except in notes and bibliographic citations.

                    for example,
Other musicians (~~e.g.,~~ Bruce Springsteen) have also been influenced by Bob Dylan.

                              and other poems.
Poe wrote "The Raven," "Annabel Lee," ~~etc.~~

6 Units of Measurement

In technical and business writing, some units of measurement are abbreviated when they are preceded by a numeral.

The hurricane had winds of 35 mph.

One new hybrid car gets over 50 mpg.

However, MLA style requires that you write out units of measurement and spell out words such as *inches, feet, years, miles, pints, quarts*, and *gallons.*

7 Symbols

The symbols =, +, and # are acceptable in technical and scientific writing but not in nontechnical college writing. The symbols % and $ are acceptable only when used with **numerals** (15%, $15,000), not with spelled-out numbers.

See
40b4, 7

EXERCISE 39.1

Correct any incorrectly used abbreviations in the following sentences, assuming that all are intended for a college audience. If a sentence is correct, mark it with a *C*.

Example: Romeo *&* Juliet is a play by Shakespeare.
                and

▶ 1. The committee meeting, attended by representatives from Action for Children's Television (ACT) and NOW, Sen. Putnam, & the pres. of ABC, convened at 8 A.M. on Mon. Feb. 24 at the YWCA on Germantown Ave.

▶ 2. An econ. prof. was suspended after he encouraged his students to speculate on securities issued by a corp. under investigation by the SEC.

▶ 3. Benjamin Spock, who wrote *Baby and Child Care*, was a respected dr. known throughout the USA.

▶ 4. The FDA banned the use of Red Dye no. 2 in food in 1976, but other food additives are still in use.

▶ 5. The Rev. Dr. Martin Luther King Jr., leader of the SCLC, led the famous Selma, Ala., march.

  6. William Golding, a novelist from the U.K., won the Nobel Prize in lit.

  7. The adult education center, financed by a major technology corp., offers courses in basic subjects such as introductory bio. and tech. writing as well as teaching HTML and XML.

  8. All the brothers in the fraternity agreed to write to Pres. Dexter appealing their disciplinary probation under Ch. 4, Sec. 3, of the IFC constitution.

  9. A 4 qt. (i.e., 1 gal.) container is needed to hold the salt solution.

10. According to Prof. Morrison, all those taking the exam should bring two sharpened no. 2 pencils to the St. Joseph's University auditorium on Sat.

CHAPTER 40

Using Numbers

Convention determines when to use a **numeral** (22) and when to spell out a number (twenty-two). Numerals are commonly used in scientific and technical writing and in journalism, but they are used less often in academic or literary writing.

Note: The guidelines in this chapter are based on the *MLA Handbook,* 8th ed. (2016). APA style, however, requires that all numbers below ten be spelled out if they do not represent specific measurements and that numbers ten and above be expressed in numerals.

See Ch. 48

40a Spelled-Out Numbers versus Numerals

Unless a number falls into one of the categories listed in **40b**, spell it out *if you can do so in one or two words.*

The Hawaiian alphabet has only twelve letters.

Class size stabilized at twenty-eight students.

The subsidies are expected to total about two million dollars.

Numbers *more than two words* long are expressed in figures.

The dietitian prepared 125 sample menus.

The developer of the community purchased 300,000 doorknobs and 153,000 faucets.

Never begin a sentence with a numeral. If necessary, reword the sentence.

Faulty: 250 students are currently enrolled in World History 106.

Revised: Current enrollment in World History 106 is 250 students.

Note: When one number immediately precedes another in a sentence, spell out the first, and use a numeral for the second: *five 3-quart containers.*

40b Conventional Uses of Numerals

1 Addresses

1920 Walnut Street, Philadelphia, PA 19103

2 Dates

January 15, 1929   1914–1919

3 Exact Times

9:16   10 a.m. (or 10:00 a.m.)

Exceptions: Spell out times of day when they are used with *o'clock*: *eleven o'clock*, not *11 o'clock*. Also spell out times expressed in quarter and half hours: *half-past eight, a quarter to ten*.

4 Exact Sums of Money

$25.11 $6,752.00

Note: Always use a numeral (not a spelled-out number) with a $ symbol. You may spell out a round sum of money if you use sums infrequently in an essay, provided you can do so in two or three words: *five dollars; two thousand dollars*.

5 Divisions of Written Works

Use arabic (not roman) numerals for page, chapter, and volume numbers; acts, scenes, and lines of plays; chapters and verses of the Bible; and line numbers of long poems.

6 Measurements before an Abbreviation or Symbol

12″   55 mph
32°   15 cc

7 Percentages and Decimals

80%   3.14

Note: You may spell out a percentage (*eighty percent*) if you use percentages infrequently in an essay, provided the percentage can be expressed in two or three words. Always use a numeral (not a spelled-out number) with a % symbol.

8 Ratios, Scores, and Statistics

In an essay that follows **APA** style, use numerals for numbers presented as a comparison.

See Ch. 48

> Children preferred Fun Flakes over Graino by a ratio of 20 to 1.
>
> The Orioles defeated the Phillies 6 to 0.
>
> The median age of the patients was 42; the mean age was 40.

9 Identification Numbers

> Route 66   Track 8   Channel 12

Note: When writing out large numbers, insert a comma every three digits from the right, beginning after the third digit.

> 3,000   25,000   6,751,098

Do not, however, use commas in four-digit page and line numbers, addresses, or year numbers.

> page 1202   3741 Laurel Ave.   1968

EXERCISE 40.1

Following MLA guidelines, revise the use of numbers in these sentences, making sure usage is correct and consistent. If a sentence uses numbers correctly, mark it with a *C*.

Example: The Empire State Building is ~102~ one hundred and two stories high.

▶ 1. *1984*, a novel by George Orwell, is set in a totalitarian society.
▶ 2. The English placement examination included a 30-minute personal-experience essay, a 45-minute expository essay, and a 150-item objective test of grammar and usage.
▶ 3. In a control group of two hundred forty-seven patients, almost three out of four suffered serious adverse reactions to the new drug.
▶ 4. Before the Thirteenth Amendment to the Constitution, slaves were counted as 3/5 of a person.
▶ 5. The intensive membership drive netted 2,608 new members and additional dues of over 5 thousand dollars.
6. They had only 2 choices: either they could take the yacht at Pier Fourteen, or they could return home to the penthouse at Twenty-seven Harbor View Drive.
7. The atomic number of lithium is three.

8. Approximately 3 hundred thousand schoolchildren in District 6 were given hearing and vision examinations between May third and June 26.

9. The United States was drawn into the war by the Japanese attack on Pearl Harbor on December seventh, 1941.

10. An upper-middle-class family can spend over 450,000 dollars to raise each child up to age 18.

PART 7

Conducting Research and Documenting Sources

CHAPTER 41

Developing a Research Project

Research is the systematic investigation of a topic outside your own knowledge and experience. However, doing research means more than just reading other people's ideas. When you undertake a research project, you become involved in a process that requires you to **think critically**: to evaluate and interpret the ideas explored in your sources and to develop ideas of your own. Whether you are working with print sources (journals, magazines, books) or electronic sources (online catalogs or discovery services, databases, the Internet), in the library or on your own computer, your research will be most efficient if you follow a systematic process. (As an added benefit, such a process will help you avoid unintentional **plagiarism**.)

See
Ch. 6

See
Ch. 46

The Research Process

Activity	Date Due	Date Completed
Move from an Assignment to a Topic, **41a**		
Do Exploratory Research and Formulate a Research Question, **41b**		
Assemble a Working Bibliography, **41c**		
Develop a Tentative Thesis, **41d**		
Do Focused Research, **41e**		
Manage Photocopies, Scans, and Downloaded Material, **41f**		
Take Notes, **41g**		
Fine-Tune Your Thesis, **41h**		
Construct an Outline, **41i**		
Write a Rough Draft, **41j**		
Revise Your Work, **41k**		
Prepare Your Final Draft, **41l**		

41a   Moving from Assignment to Topic

1   Understanding Your Assignment

Every research project begins with an assignment. Before you can find a direction for your research, you must be sure you understand the exact requirements of the specific assignment.

CHECKLIST

Understanding Your Assignment

Asking yourself the following questions will help you focus on your research project:

❑ Has your instructor provided a list of possible topics, or are you expected to select a topic on your own?

❑ Is your purpose to explain? To persuade? Something else?

❑ Is your audience your instructor? Your fellow students? Both? Someone else?

❑ Can you assume that your audience knows a lot (or just a little) about your topic?

❑ When is the completed research project due?

❑ About how long should it be?

❑ Will you be given a specific schedule to follow, or are you expected to set your own schedule?

❑ Is peer review permitted? Is it encouraged? If so, at what stages of the writing process?

❑ Does your instructor expect you to prepare a formal outline?

❑ Are instructor–student conferences required? Are they encouraged?

❑ Will your instructor review notes, outlines, or drafts with you at regular intervals?

❑ Does your instructor require you to keep a research notebook?

❑ What manuscript guidelines and documentation style are you to follow?

❑ What help is available to you—from your instructor, from other students, from experts on your topic, from community resources, from your library staff?

In **Chapters 3–5** of this text, you followed the writing process of Rebecca James as she planned, drafted, and revised a short essay for her first-semester composition course. In her second-semester composition class, Rebecca was given the following assignment prompt:

> Develop a ten- to fifteen-page research project that takes a position on any issue related to the Internet. Keep a research notebook that traces your progress.

Throughout this chapter, you will see examples of the work Rebecca did in response to this assignment.

2 Finding a Topic

Once you understand the requirements and scope of your assignment, you need to decide on a topic. In many cases, your instructor will help you choose a topic, either by providing a list of suitable topics or by suggesting a general subject area—for example, a famous trial, an event that happened on the day you were born, a problem on college campuses, or an issue related to the Internet. Even in these cases, you will still need to choose one of these topics or narrow the subject area to a topic that you can write about: one trial, one event, one problem, or one issue.

If your instructor requires you to select a topic on your own, you should consider several possible topics and weigh both their suitability for research and your interest in them. You decide on a topic for your research paper in much the same way you decide on a topic for a short essay: you read, brainstorm, talk to people, and ask questions. Specifically, you talk to friends and family, coworkers, and perhaps your instructor; attend a library orientation session with your class; read online magazines and news sources, blogs, and *Wikipedia* entries (*Wikipedia* can be a great resource for brainstorming although it would not typically be referenced as a scholarly source in an academic research project); browse the library's online databases (especially those relevant to the discipline); think about your interests; and consider possible topics suggested by your other courses (historical events, scientific developments, and so on).

CHECKLIST

Choosing a Research Topic

As you look for a suitable research topic, keep the following guidelines in mind:

❑ **Are you genuinely interested in your research topic?** Remember that you will be deeply involved with the topic you select for weeks—perhaps even for an entire semester. If you lose interest in your topic, you are likely to see your research as a tedious chore rather than as an opportunity to discover new information, new associations, and new insights.

❑ **Is your topic suitable for research?** Topics limited to your personal experience and those based on value judgments are not suitable for research. For example, "Why Freud's work is better than Jung's" might sound promising, but no amount of research can establish that one person's work is "better" than another's.

❑ **Are the boundaries of your research topic appropriate?** A research topic should be neither too broad nor too narrow. For example, "O.J. Simpson: Murderer or Scapegoat?" is far too broad a topic for a ten-page—or even a hundred-page—treatment, and "One piece of evidence that played a decisive role in the O.J. Simpson murder trial" would probably be too narrow for a ten-page research paper. But how one newspaper reported the trial or how a particular group of people (law-enforcement professionals or college students, for example) reacted to the verdict at the time would work well.

3 Starting a Research Notebook

Keeping a **research notebook**, a combination journal of your reactions and log of your progress, is an important part of the research process. A research notebook maps out your direction and keeps you on track; throughout the research process, it helps you define and redefine the boundaries of your assignment.

In your research notebook (which can be an actual notebook or a digital file), you can record lists of things to do, sources to check, leads to follow up on, appointments, possible community contacts, questions to which you would like to find answers, stray ideas, possible thesis statements or titles, and so on. (Be sure to date your entries and to check off and date work you have completed.)

If you choose to use a digital file, you might consider one of the following options, each with distinct advantages:

1. *Microsoft Word* file plus electronic copies of documents in a folder on your hard drive or flash drive. Most users are very familiar with *Word*, so ease-of-use is a plus.

2. *Google* Drive document with electronic folder in which documents are stored. *Google* Drive has the distinct advantage of being "in the cloud" and so it follows you whereever you go. Also, there is no danger of losing documents if your hard drive crashes.

3. *Zotero* notes plus documents. *Zotero* is free citation software that easily and efficiently stores documents along with all notes and citation information. Also, *Zotero* is synced with your computer, smartphone, and the Internet, so you can work from any device. Consult the *Zotero* website and *Zotero* tutorials on *YouTube* for more information.

As she began her research, Rebecca James created a folder in *Google* Drive in which she planned to keep all the electronic documents for her paper. In a *Google* document that she labeled "Research Notebook," she outlined her schedule and explored some preliminary ideas.

Here is an entry from Rebecca's research notebook in which she discusses how she chose a topic for her research paper.

Excerpt from Research Notebook

Last semester, I wrote an essay for Professor Burks about using *Wikipedia* for college-level research. In class, we'd read *Wikipedia*'s policy statement, "Researching with *Wikipedia*," which helped me to understand *Wikipedia*'s specific limitations for college research. I used a sample *Wikipedia* entry related to my accounting class to support my points about the site's strengths and weaknesses. For my research project, which has to be about the Internet, I want to expand the essay I wrote for my first-semester comp course. This time, I want to talk more about the academic debate surrounding *Wikipedia*. (I asked Professor Burks if it would be OK for me to use this topic for her class this semester, and she said it would be fine. In fact, she really liked the idea.)

EXERCISE 41.1

Enter information about your assignment and your schedule in your research notebook. Next, using your instructor's guidelines for selecting a research topic, begin thinking of possible topics for your paper. Then, explore some preliminary ideas about these topics in your research notebook, and decide which one you want to write about.

41b Doing Exploratory Research and Formulating a Research Question

During **exploratory research**, you develop an overview of your topic, searching the Internet and perhaps looking through the library's online reference collections, such as *Credo Reference* and the *Gale Virtual Reference Library*. Your goal at this stage is to formulate a **research question** that you want your research paper to answer. A research question helps you to decide which sources to seek out, which to examine first, which to examine in depth, and which to skip entirely. (The answer to your research question will be your paper's <u>thesis statement</u>.)

See
41d

When developing a list of keywords to help you focus your online searches, it is often helpful to see how others have framed questions about the same topic. You can gather a list of keywords and phrases (paying particular attention to specific words that appear together) from almost any information resource.

Rebecca began her exploratory research with a preliminary search on *Google* (see Figure 41.1). When she entered the keywords *Wikipedia and academia*, they generated millions of hits, but she wasn't overwhelmed. She had learned in her library orientation that the first ten to twenty items would be most useful to her because the results of a *Google* search are listed in order of relevance to the topic, with the most relevant sites listed first. After a quick review of these items, she did a keyword search in the *Gale* databases to which her library subscribed (see Figure 41.2) and which offers two significant benefits over Google searches:

1. publication date, subject, and document filters to further refine her search results and

2. access to what scholars wrote about her topic and the thesis statements they formulated in response to their own research questions—ones that could help her articulate her own research question.

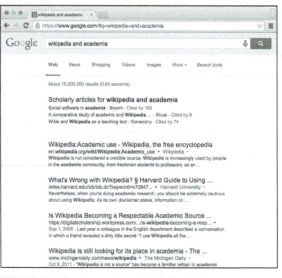

FIGURE 41.1 *Google* search results. © Google, Inc.

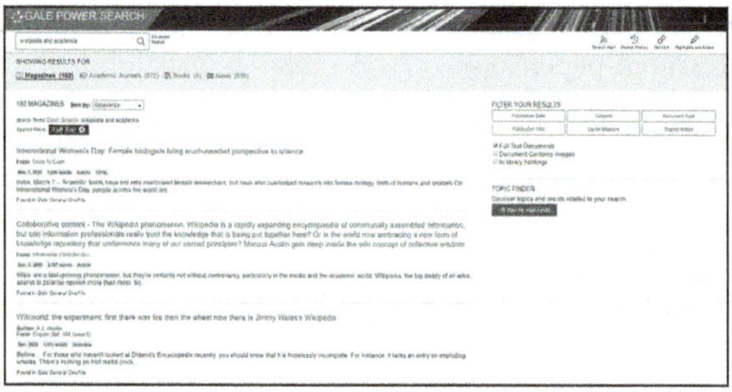

FIGURE 41.2 *Gale* search results. © *Gale*

When she finished her exploratory research, Rebecca was able to decide on a preliminary research question for her project.

Research Question: What effect has *Wikipedia* had on academic research?

She knew she would revise and clarify this question as she continued her research, but for now, it could help her focus.

41c Assembling a Working Bibliography

During your exploratory research, you begin to assemble a **working bibliography** of the sources you consult. This working bibliography will be the basis for your works-cited list, which will include all the sources you cite in your paper.

See 47a2

As you consider each potential source, record full and accurate bibliographic information in your research notebook. Keep records of interviews (including telephone and email interviews), meetings, lectures, films, blogs, and websites as well as print and electronic articles and books. For each source, include basic identifying details—such as the date of an interview, the call number of a hard-copy library book, and the URL of an Internet source. (Make sure the URL is not unique to the search session. Some databases provide what is called a permalink. Such a durable or permanent URL is always preferable to the URL provided by a browser. One way to test the durability of a browser URL is to copy and paste the URL into a different browser and see if it still works.) Also, record the date you downloaded the source (and perhaps the search engine you used to find it as well), or the author of an article accessed from a database. Write up a brief evaluation that includes your comments about the kind of information the source contains, the amount of information offered, its relevance to your topic, and its limitations.

Figures 41.3a and b show two of the sources Rebecca found as she put together her working bibliography.

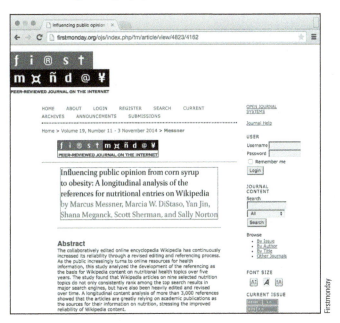

FIGURE 41.3a Internet source for working bibliography.

Proceed With Extreme Caution: Citation to Wikipedia in Light of Contributor Demographics and Content Policies

*Jodi L. Wilson**

Caution is the eldest child of wisdom.
*—Victor Hugo***

ABSTRACT

Courts and advocates have shown an increasing willingness to cite to Wikipedia. This trend has piqued the attention of scholars, who have considered the permanency concerns raised by citations to Wikipedia and critiqued how courts and advocates have used Wikipedia. This Article adds to the growing scholarship on the Wikipedia citation trend by examining the contours of the Wikipedia contributor crowd and the principles underlying Wikipedia's content in order to better inform the evaluation of Wikipedia as a potential authoritative source. Part I provides an overview of the Wikipedia citation trend in cases and federal appellate briefs. Part II describes the ongoing judicial and scholarly debate about citation to Wikipedia. Part III first examines the size and demographics of the Wikipedia contributor crowd by using systems data and published surveys. Part III then examines Wikipedia's editorial and content policies, which guide the Wikipedia contributor crowd in creating content. Finally, Part IV considers the Wikipedia contributor crowd and the editorial and content policies discussed in Part III in the

* Assistant Professor of Law and Director of Legal Methods, The University of Memphis, Cecil C. Humphreys School of Law. I am grateful to Spencer Bell, James Duckworth, Nicholas Margello, Caroline Sapp, and Lacy Ward for their valuable research assistance. I am also grateful to Professor Mason Lowe, Professor Boris Mamlyuk, and Jeff Sheehan for their thoughtful suggestions on earlier drafts. This Article was supported by research funding from The University of Memphis, Cecil C. Humphreys School of Law.

** FORTY THOUSAND QUOTATIONS: PROSE AND POETICAL 23 (Charles Noel Douglas ed., 5d. ed. 1926).

857

FIGURE 41.3b An article accessed from a database for working bibliography.

Following is an example of the source information Rebecca recorded for her working bibliography.

Information for Working Bibliography (in Research Notebook)

Author —	Bauerlein, Mark
Title —	*The Dumbest Generation: How the Digital Age Stupefies Young Americans and Jeopardizes Our Future (or, Don't Trust Anyone Under 30)*
Publication information —	Penguin, 2008.
Evaluation —	Book is several years old, so information may be dated. Chapter 4, "Online Learning and Non-Learning," includes useful discussion of poor writing in *Wikipedia* articles.

As you go about collecting sources and building your working bibliography, be careful to evaluate the quality and relevance of all the materials you examine. Making informed choices early in the research process will save you a lot of time in the long run. (For guidelines on evaluating sources, **see Chapter 43**.)

Do some exploratory research to find a research question for your project, carefully evaluating the relevance and usefulness of each source. Then, compile a working bibliography. When you have finished, reevaluate the usefulness of your sources and plan additional research if necessary.

41d Developing a Tentative Thesis

Your **tentative thesis** is a preliminary statement of the main point you think your research will support. This statement, which you will eventually refine into your paper's **thesis statement**, should answer your research question.

See 41h

As Rebecca James did exploratory research, she learned that some academics see *Wikipedia* as a challenge to their traditional notion of how to conduct research. She thought this would be a good angle to explore further, and she worded her tentative thesis to reflect this idea.

Rebecca's progress from assignment to tentative thesis appears below.

Tentative Thesis

Assignment	Topic	Research Question
Issue related to the Internet	Using *Wikipedia* for college-level research	What effect has *Wikipedia* had on academic research?

Tentative Thesis: The debate surrounding *Wikipedia* has challenged those in the academic community, forcing them to confront the fact that college-level research has changed in recent years.

Because your tentative thesis suggests the specific direction your research will take as well as the scope and emphasis of your paper, it can help you generate a list of the key points you plan to develop in your paper. This list can help you to zero in on the specific areas to explore as you read and take notes.

Rebecca used her tentative thesis to help her generate the following list of points to explore further.

Points to Explore

Tentative thesis: The debate surrounding *Wikipedia* has challenged those in the academic community, forcing them to confront the fact that college-level research has changed in recent years.

- Give background about *Wikipedia*; explain its benefits and drawbacks.
- Talk about who uses *Wikipedia* and for what purposes.
- Explain possible future enhancements to the site.

- Explain college instructors' resistance to *Wikipedia*.
- Talk about efforts made by librarians and others to incorporate *Wikipedia* into academic research.

EXERCISE 41.3

Following your instructor's guidelines, develop a tentative thesis for your research paper, and list the points you plan to develop.

41e Doing Focused Research

During exploratory research, you look at reference works to get an overview of your topic. During **focused research**, however, you dig deeper into your topic: you consult periodical articles, books, and other sources (in print and online) to find the specific information—facts, examples, statistics, definitions, quotations—you need to support your points. Once you have decided on a tentative thesis and made a list of the points you plan to explore, you are ready to begin your focused research.

1 Reading Sources

As you look for information, try to explore as many sources as possible. It makes sense to examine more sources than you actually intend to use so that you can proceed even if some of your sources turn out to be biased, outdated, unreliable, superficial, or irrelevant—in other words, not suitable.

As you explore various sources, quickly evaluate their potential usefulness. For example, if your source is a journal article, read the abstract; if your source is a book, skim the table of contents and the index. Then, if an article or a section of a book seems useful, photocopy it for future reference. As you explore sources online, you may find that you have multiple windows open at once. If this is the case, be especially careful not to paste material you see onscreen directly into your paper. (This practice can lead to plagiarism.) Instead, send yourself the link (or print the pages you need) so you can evaluate the material further later on. (For information on evaluating electronic and print sources, **see Chapter 43**.)

See
Ch. 46

2 Balancing Primary and Secondary Sources

During your focused research, you will encounter both **primary sources** (original documents and observations) and **secondary sources** (interpretations of original documents and observations).

Close-Up DEFINING PRIMARY AND SECONDARY SOURCES

Academic research projects often combine primary and secondary sources. Before you begin any research project, it makes sense to consult with your instructor to clarify the distinction between *primary* and *secondary* for your specific assignment. For Rebecca's project, for example, journal articles that report on studies in which people were interviewed or surveyed might be considered primary sources, as would Rebecca's own experiences with *Wikipedia* or with online research. A book on her subject or a literature review of several studies would be considered a secondary source.

For some research projects, primary sources are essential; however, most research projects in the humanities rely heavily on secondary sources, which provide scholars' insights and interpretations. Remember, though, that the further you get from the primary source, the more chances exist for inaccuracies caused by misinterpretations or distortions.

Primary and Secondary Sources

Primary Source in the Humanities	Secondary Source in the Humanities
Novel, poem, play, film	Scholarly analysis and criticism
Diary, autobiography	Biography
Letter, historical document, speech, oral history	Review
Newspaper or magazine article from the time period being discussed	
Interview	

Primary Source in the Social Sciences and Sciences	Secondary Source in the Social Sciences and Sciences
Raw data from questionnaires or interviews	Literature review
Observation/experiment	
Scientific (empirical) article containing original research	
Case study	

41f Managing Photocopies, Scans, and Downloaded Material

Much of the information you gather will be in the form of photocopies or scanned pages saved as PDFs (of articles, book pages, and so on) and material downloaded from the Internet or from a library database. Learning to manage this source information efficiently will save you a lot of time.

First, do not use the ease of copying and downloading as an excuse to postpone decisions about the usefulness of your sources. After all, you can easily accumulate so many pages that it will be almost impossible for you to keep track of all your information.

Also keep in mind that the sources you find are just raw material, not information that you have already interpreted and evaluated. Making copies of sources is only the first step in the process of taking thorough, careful notes. You still have to evaluate, paraphrase, and summarize your sources' ideas and make connections among them.

Moreover, photocopies, scans, and downloaded material do not give you much flexibility. For example, a single page of text may include information that should be earmarked for several different sections of your paper. This lack of flexibility makes it almost impossible for you to arrange source material into any meaningful order. Just as you would with any source, you will have to take notes on the information you read. These notes will give you the flexibility you need to write your paper.

Close-Up AVOIDING PLAGIARISM

To avoid the possibility of accidental plagiarism, be sure to keep all downloaded material in a separate file—not in your Notes file. After you read this material and decide how to use it, you can move the information you use into your Notes file (along with full source information).

See Ch. 46

41g Taking Notes

As you locate information, take notes to create a record of what you found and where you found it. These notes will help you to fine-tune your thesis and decide how to develop your discussion.

CHECKLIST

Working with Photocopies, Scans, and Downloaded Material

To get the most out of photocopies, scans, and material downloaded from the Internet, follow these guidelines:

❑ Record full and accurate source information, including the inclusive page numbers, electronic address (URL), and any other relevant information, on the first page of each copy.

❑ Do not photocopy or scan a source without reminding yourself—*in writing*—why you are doing so. In pencil or on removable self-stick notes, record your initial responses to the source's ideas, jot down cross-references to other sources or to your notes, and highlight important sections.

❑ Photocopying can be time-consuming and expensive, so try to avoid copying material that is only marginally relevant to your paper.

❑ Keep photocopies in a separate file so you will be able to find them when you need them. Keep all electronic copies of source material together in one clearly labeled folder.

Each piece of information you record in your notes (whether **summarized**, **paraphrased**, or **quoted** from your sources) should be accompanied by a short descriptive heading that indicates its relevance to one of the points you will develop in your paper. Because you will use these headings to guide you as you organize your notes, you should make them as specific as possible. For example, labeling every note for a paper on *Wikipedia* **Wikipedia** or **Internet** will not be very helpful later on. More focused headings—for example, **Wikipedia's popularity** or **college instructors' objections**—will be much more useful.

See Ch. 44

Also include brief comments that make clear your reasons for recording the information. These comments (enclosed in brackets so you will know they are your own ideas, not those of your source) should establish the purpose of your note—what you think it can explain, support, clarify, describe, or contradict—and perhaps suggest its relationship to other notes or to other sources. Any questions you have about the information or its source can also be included in your comment.

MULTILINGUAL TIP

Taking notes in English (rather than in your native language) will make it easier for you to transfer the notes into a draft of your paper. However, you may find it faster and more effective to use your native language when writing your own comments about each note.

Finally, each note should fully and accurately identify the source of the information you are recording. You do not have to write out the complete citation, but you do have to include enough information to identify your source. For example, **Wilson** would be enough to send you back to your working bibliography, where you would be able to find the complete documentation for the author's article.

Following is an example of the notes that Rebecca took.

Notes (in Research Notebook)

Note: Various note-taking programs, such as *Evernote* or *Note.ly* can help you to keep track of your notes.

Close-Up TAKING NOTES

When you take notes, your goal is flexibility: you want to be able to arrange and rearrange information easily and efficiently as your paper takes shape.

Type each individual note (accompanied by source information) under a specific heading rather than listing all information from a single source under the same heading, and be sure to divide notes from one another with extra space or horizontal lines. (As you revise, you can move notes around so notes on the same topic are grouped together.)

CHECKLIST

Taking Notes

❑ **Identify the source of each piece of information,** including the page numbers for quotations from paginated sources.

❑ **Include everything now that you will need later** to understand your note—names, dates, places, connections with other notes—and to remember why you recorded it.

❑ **Distinguish quotations from paraphrases and summaries and your own ideas from those of your sources.** If you copy a source's words, place them in quotation marks (and boldface the quotation marks). If you record your own ideas, enclose them in brackets and boldface them as well. These techniques will help you avoid accidental plagiarism in your paper.

See Ch. 46

❑ **Put an author's ideas into your own words whenever possible,** summarizing and paraphrasing material as well as adding your own observations and analyses.

❑ **Copy quoted material accurately,** using the exact words, spelling, punctuation marks, and capitalization of the original.

❑ **Never paste information from a source directly into your paper.** This practice can lead to plagiarism.

EXERCISE 41.4

Begin focused research for your paper, reading sources carefully and taking notes as you read. Your notes should include paraphrase, summary, and your own observations and analysis as well as quotations.

41h Fine-Tuning Your Thesis

After you have finished your focused research and note-taking, you are ready to refine your tentative thesis into a carefully worded statement that expresses a conclusion your research can support. This **thesis statement** should accurately convey the direction, emphasis, and scope of your paper.

See 4a–c

Keep in mind that your revised thesis statement isn't just a reworded or more polished version of your tentative thesis. In many cases, it has a different focus or emphasis. Remember: if you change the scope or emphasis of your essay, you will need to revise your thesis statement so that it is consistent with the rest of your paper.

As Rebecca did her focused research and took notes, she began to see *Wikipedia* as an important influence on college research—not just an unwelcome upheaval but a challenge with a potentially positive outcome.

Compare Rebecca's tentative thesis with her final thesis statement.

Thesis Statement

Tentative Thesis

The debate surrounding *Wikipedia* has challenged those in the academic community, forcing them to confront the fact that college-level research has changed in recent years.

Thesis Statement

All in all, the debate over *Wikipedia* has been a positive development because it has led the academic community to confront the challenges of open, collaborative software on the web.

EXERCISE 41.5

Review the tentative thesis you developed for Exercise 41.3. Carefully read all the notes you have collected during your focused research, and develop a thesis statement for your paper.

41i Constructing an Outline

See
4d
Once you have a thesis statement, you are ready to construct an outline to guide you as you draft your essay.

See
5c4
A formal outline is different from a scratch outline, which is a list of the key points you tentatively plan to develop. A formal outline—which may be either a **topic outline** or a **sentence outline**—includes all the ideas you will develop, indicating not only the exact order in which you will present these ideas but also the relationship between main points and supporting details. It may also be helpful to list sources by author name or by a brief description of where you plan to use them in your paper.

Note: The outline you construct at this stage is only a guide for you to follow as you write your rough draft. During the revision process, you may want to construct another outline to check the logic of your organization.

Rebecca James made the following topic outline to guide her as she wrote her rough draft.

Formal (Topic) Outline

Thesis statement: All in all, the debate over *Wikipedia* has been a positive development because it has led the academic community to confront the challenges of open, collaborative software on the web.

I. Definition of wiki and explanation of *Wikipedia*

    A. Fast and easy

    B. Range of topics

II. Introduction to *Wikipedia*'s drawbacks

    A. Warnings on "Researching with *Wikipedia*" page

    B. Criticisms in "Reliability of *Wikipedia*" article

    C. Criticisms by academics

        1. Villanova University

        2. Middlebury College history department

III. *Wikipedia*'s unreliability

    A. Lack of citations

B. Factual inaccuracy and bias

C. Vandalism

IV. *Wikipedia*'s poor writing

A. *Wikipedia*'s coding system

B. *Wikipedia*'s influence on students' writing (Bauerlein)

V. *Wikipedia*'s popularity and benefits

A. Wilson's findings (charts)

B. Comprehensive abstracts, links to other sources, and current and comprehensive bibliographies

VI. *Wikipedia*'s advantages over other online encyclopedias

A. Very current information

B. More coverage of popular culture topics

C. "Stub" articles

VII. *Wikipedia*'s ongoing improvements

A. Control measures

B. Users as editors

C. "Talk" page

VIII. *Wikipedia*'s content

A. View of Messner et al.

B. Chart showing increased quality of *Wikipedia* articles over time

IX. Academic community's reservations about *Wikipedia*

A. Academics' failure to keep up with technology

B. Academics' qualifications to improve *Wikipedia*

X. Instructors' and librarians' efforts to use and improve *Wikipedia*

A. Snyder's and Power's support for *Wikipedia*

B. Responsibility of academic community

XI. *Wikipedia* in the classroom

A. *Wikipedia*'s education program

B. Collaborative and critical thinking assignments

XII. Academics' changing view of *Wikipedia*

A. Academics' increasing acceptance

B. Academics' increasing involvement

C. *Wikipedia*'s best practices

EXERCISE 41.6

Carefully review your notes. Then, sort and group them into categories and construct a topic outline for your paper.

Close-Up OUTLINING

Before you begin writing, create a separate file for each major section of your outline. Then, copy your notes into these files in the order in which you intend to use them.

Be sure to label the files clearly for later reference. Each file name should include a reference to the class and assignment for which it was written. For instance, Rebecca's file for the section of her English 102 essay on *Wikipedia*'s ongoing improvements is called "102 Wikipedia Ongoing Improvements." The individual files relating to this project are all collected in a folder titled "Eng 102 Wikipedia." By organizing your files in this way, you can use each file as a guide as you write.

41j Writing a Rough Draft

See 5a

When you are ready to write your **rough draft**, check to be sure you have arranged your notes in the order in which you intend to use them. Follow your outline as you write, using your notes as needed. As you draft, write notes to yourself in brackets, jotting down questions and identifying points that need further clarification and areas that need more development. You can also use *Word*'s Comment tool to add notes.

As you move along, leave space for material you plan to add, and identify phrases or whole sections that you think you may later decide to move or delete. In other words, lay the groundwork for revision.

As your draft takes shape, be sure to supply transitions between sentences and paragraphs to indicate how your points are related. Also be careful to copy source information fully and accurately in this and every subsequent draft, placing documentation as close as possible to the material it identifies.

Like any other essay, a research paper has an introduction, a body, and a conclusion. In your rough draft, as in your outline, you focus on the body of your paper. Don't spend too much time planning your introduction or conclusion at this stage; your ideas will change as you write, and you will need to revise and expand your opening and closing paragraphs later to reflect those changes.

PLANNING GUIDE

RESEARCH PROJECT

Your **assignment** will be to read a variety of sources to help you explore a subject that you want to learn more about.

Your **purpose** will be to interpret and evaluate your sources' ideas and to develop an original idea about your topic.

Your **audience** will usually be your instructor.

INTRODUCTION

- Begin by introducing readers to your subject and suggesting how you will approach it.
- Provide background to help readers understand the context for your discussion, perhaps briefly summarizing research already done on your topic.
- State your thesis, the position your research will support.

> **Thesis statement templates:**
> - Despite . . ., the evidence suggests that . . .
> - Although many people believe . . ., it seems more likely that . . . is actually the case.

BODY PARAGRAPHS

- Begin each paragraph with a topic sentence that corresponds to a section of your outline.
- In each body paragraph, provide support for your thesis, synthesizing source information with ideas of your own.
- Use summary, paraphrase, and quoted material from your sources to support your statements.
- Use different patterns of development to shape the individual paragraphs of your essay.
- Connect sentences and paragraphs with clear transitions, including transitional paragraphs where necessary.
- Be careful to keep track of your sources and to avoid plagiarism.
- Consider including visuals where appropriate.
- Include parenthetical documentation where necessary.

> **Topic sentence templates:**
> - The first (second, final) point/ example is . . .
> - Another point that supports this position is . . .

See 13d

See 13e1

> **Templates for introducing support:**
> - As many scholars observe, . . .
> - Several sources make the case that . . .
> - Another study demonstrates that . . .
> - According to . . ., . . .

CONCLUSION

- Restate your thesis (in different words).
- Summarize your key points.
- End with a strong concluding statement.

> **Concluding statement templates:**
> - As the ongoing debate around this issue suggests, . . .
> - For all the reasons summarized above, . . .
> - Given the supporting evidence outlined here, it seems likely that . . .

Close-Up USING TOPIC SENTENCES AND HEADINGS

Clear, specific topic sentences will help readers follow your discussion.

Without a professional editorial board to oversee its development, *Wikipedia* has several shortcomings that limit its trustworthiness.

See 11b

You can also use headings if they are a convention of the discipline in which you are writing.

Wikipedia's Advantages

Wikipedia has advantages over other online encyclopedias.

1 Working Source Material into Your Paper

In the body of your paper, you evaluate and interpret your sources, comparing different ideas and assessing various points of view. As a writer, your job is to draw your own conclusions, synthesizing information from various sources into a paper that coherently and forcefully presents your own original viewpoint.

See Ch. 45

To turn your notes into well-developed paragraphs, begin with a topic sentence that states the point you want the source to support. Next, introduce the source with an **identifying tag**, followed by the supporting information in the form of summary, paraphrase, or quotation. Then, in a sentence or two, interpret the source material for your readers, explaining its significance to the point you want to make. (Don't forget to include parenthetical documentation.)

See Ch. 44

See 47a1

Be sure to integrate source material smoothly into your paper, clearly and accurately identifying the relationships among various sources (and between those sources' ideas and your own). Your goal here is to interpret your source's ideas for readers—and to give these ideas the emphasis needed to support your own points. If two sources present conflicting interpretations, you should be especially careful to use precise language and accurate transitions to make the contrast apparent (for instance, **Although some academics believe that *Wikipedia* should not be a part of college-level research, Snyder argues . . .**). When two sources agree, you should make this clear (for example, **Like Snyder, Power claims . . .** or **The findings of Messner et al. support Snyder's point**). Such phrasing will provide a context for your own comments and conclusions. If different sources present complementary information about a subject, blend details from the sources carefully, keeping track of which details come from which source.

See 44d

2 Integrating Visuals

See 5b2, 11d

Photographs, diagrams, graphs, and other visuals can enrich your discussion by providing additional support for the points you make. You can create a visual on your own (for example, by taking a photograph or creating a bar graph). You can also scan an appropriate visual from a book or magazine or access an image database. When you add a visual, be sure to provide a caption that identifies the name of the person who created it. This will enable readers to find full source information in your works-cited list.

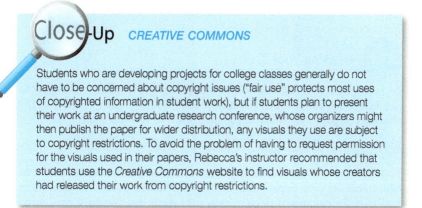

Close-Up *CREATIVE COMMONS*

Students who are developing projects for college classes generally do not have to be concerned about copyright issues ("fair use" protects most uses of copyrighted information in student work), but if students plan to present their work at an undergraduate research conference, whose organizers might then publish the paper for wider distribution, any visuals they use are subject to copyright restrictions. To avoid the problem of having to request permission for the visuals used in their papers, Rebecca's instructor recommended that students use the *Creative Commons* website to find visuals whose creators had released their work from copyright restrictions.

When Rebecca searched *Google*'s image database via the *Creative Commons* website, she found a visual to include in her paper.

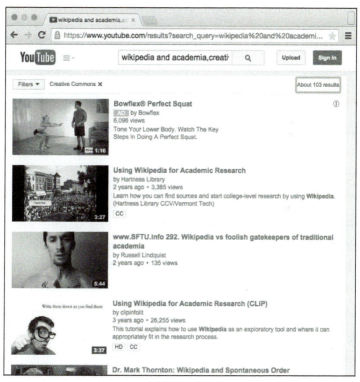

FIGURE 41.4 *Creative Commons* image search results.

EXERCISE 41.7

Write a rough draft of your paper, being careful to incorporate source material and visuals smoothly and to record source information accurately. Begin by drafting the section for which you have the most material.

41k Revising Your Drafts

As you review your drafts, you follow the revision procedures that apply to any essay (**see 5b–c**). In addition, you should review the questions in the checklist on page 358, which apply specifically to research papers.

1 Instructor's Comments

Your instructor's suggestions for revisions can come in a conference or in comments on your paper. Your instructor can also use *Word*'s Comment tool to make comments electronically on a draft that you have emailed to him or her. When you revise, you can incorporate these suggestions into your revision, as Rebecca did.

Draft with Instructor's Comments (Excerpt)

Emory University English professor Mark Bauerlein asserts that *Wikipedia* articles are written in a "flat, featureless, factual style" (153). Even though *Wikipedia* has instituted a coding system in which it labels the shortcomings of its less-developed articles, a warning about an article's poor writing style is likely to go unnoticed by the typical user.

Comment [JB1]: You need a transition sentence before this one to show that this ¶ is about a new idea. See 13b2.

Comment [JB2]: Wordy. See 17a.

Revision (Incorporating Instructor's Suggestions)

Because they can be edited by anyone, *Wikipedia* articles are often poorly written. Emory University English professor Mark Bauerlein asserts that *Wikipedia* articles are written in a "flat, featureless, factual style" (153). Even though *Wikipedia* has instituted a coding system to label the shortcomings of its less-developed articles, a warning about an article's poor writing style is likely to go unnoticed by the typical user.

& 2 Peer Review

See 5c2

Feedback you get from **peer review**—other students' comments, handwritten or electronic—can also help you revise. As you incorporate your classmates' suggestions, as well as your own changes and any suggested by your instructor, you can use *Microsoft Word*'s Track Changes tool to help you keep track of the revisions you make on your draft.

Following are two versions of an excerpt from Rebecca's paper. The first version includes comments (inserted with *Microsoft Word*'s Comment tool) from three peer reviewers. The second uses the Track Changes tool to show the revisions Rebecca made in response to these comments.

Draft with Peer Reviewers' Comments (Excerpt)

Because users can update articles in real time from any location, *Wikipedia* offers up-to-the-minute coverage of political and cultural events as well as timely information on popular culture topics that receive little or no attention in other reference sources. In addition, because *Wikipedia* has such a broad user base, more topics are covered in *Wikipedia* than in other online resources. Even when there is little information on a particular topic, *Wikipedia* allows users to create "stub" articles, which provide minimal information that users can expand over time. Thus, *Wikipedia* can be a valuable first step in finding reliable research sources.

> Comment [RS1]: I think you need a better transition here.

> Comment [TG2]: I think some examples here would really help.

> Comment [DL3]: I agree. Maybe talk about a useful *Wikipedia* article you found recently.

> Comment [RS4]: Why?

Revision with Track Changes

Wikipedia has advantages over other online encyclopedias. Because users can update articles in real time from any location, *Wikipedia* offers up-to-the-minute coverage of political and cultural events as well as timely information on popular culture topics that receive little or no attention in other reference sources. In addition, because *Wikipedia* has such a broad user base, more topics are covered in *Wikipedia* than in other online resources. For example, a student researching the history of video gaming would find *Wikipedia*'s "Wii U" article, with its numerous pages of information and nearly two hundred references, to be a valuable resource. *Encyclopedia Britannica* does not contain a comparable article on this popular game console. Even when there is little information on a particular topic, *Wikipedia* allows users to create "stub" articles, which provide minimal information that users can expand over time. Thus, by offering immediate access to information on relatively obscure topics, *Wikipedia* can be a valuable first step in finding reliable research sources on such topics.

See
5c4, 41i

3 Outlining

As you move closer to a final draft, you can make a formal outline of your paper-in-progress to check the logic of its organization and the relationships among sections. An excerpt from the **sentence outline** Rebecca constructed to check the structure of her paper is shown below.

Sentence Outline (Excerpt)

Thesis statement: All in all, the debate over *Wikipedia* has been a positive development because it has led the academic community to confront the challenges of open, collaborative software on the web.

I. *Wikipedia* is the most popular wiki.

    A. Users can edit existing articles and add new articles using *Wikipedia*'s editing tools.

    B. *Wikipedia* has grown into a huge database.

II. *Wikipedia* has several shortcomings that limit its trustworthiness.

    A. *Wikipedia*'s "Researching with *Wikipedia*" page acknowledges existing problems.

    B. *Wikipedia*'s "Reliability of *Wikipedia*" page presents criticisms.

    C. Academics have objections.

CHECKLIST

Revising a Research Paper

As you revise, consider the following questions:

❑ Should you do more research to find support for certain points?

❑ Do you need to reorder the major sections of your paper?

❑ Should you rearrange the order in which you present your points within sections?

❑ Do you need to add section headings? Transitional paragraphs?

See
44d

❑ Have you integrated source material smoothly into your paper?

❑ Have you chosen visuals carefully and integrated them smoothly into your paper?

❑ Are quotations blended with paraphrase, summary, and your own observations and reactions?

See
Ch. 46

❑ Have you avoided plagiarism by carefully documenting all borrowed ideas?

❑ Have you analyzed and interpreted the ideas of others rather than simply stringing those ideas together?

❑ Do your own ideas—not those of your sources—define the focus of your discussion?

III. *Wikipedia* is not always reliable or accurate.

  A. Many *Wikipedia* articles do not include citations.

  B. *Wikipedia* articles can be inaccurate or biased.

  C. *Wikipedia* articles can be targets for vandalism.

Note: You will probably take your paper through several drafts, changing different parts of it each time or working on one part over and over again. After revising each draft thoroughly, print out a corrected version, and label it *First Draft, Second Draft,* and so on. Then, make additional corrections by hand on that draft before typing in your changes to create the next draft. Be sure to save and clearly label every electronic draft so you can go back to a previous draft if necessary.

When you finish revising your paper, copy the file that contains your working bibliography and insert it at the end of your paper. Keep the original file for your working bibliography as a backup in case any data is lost in the process. Delete any irrelevant entries, and then create your works-cited list. (Make sure the format of the entries in your works-cited list conforms to the documentation style you are using.)

If you save multiple drafts of your works-cited list, be sure to name each file with the date or some other label so that it is readily identifiable. Keep all files pertaining to a single project in a folder dedicated to that paper or assignment.

Close-Up USING CITATION TOOLS

Use citation tools such as the following to create your bibliography and to make sure all the sources you used—and only those sources—appear in your works-cited list.

BibMe

- Free and easy to use: made for quick copying and pasting of citations anywhere; allows saving for later use
- Entirely web-based
- Supports MLA, APA, and other documentation styles

EasyBib

- Free and easy to use: made for quick copying and pasting of citations anywhere; allows saving for later use
- Entirely web-based
- Supports MLA, APA, and other documentation styles

EndNote

- Purchase required (consult with your college library or bookstore for free institutional access or student discounts; if you access through your institution's license, you may not be able to access your citations after graduation)

(continued)

USING CITATION TOOLS *(continued)*

- Easy to use: Allows you to collect citations and add notes with unlimited storage. Cite While You Write feature allows you to cite within a document. Compatible with *Microsoft Office, OpenOffice*, and *iWork Pages*.

- Works on both Mac and PC either offline or online, but more robust when used on a local computer. Syncs with *EndNote Basic* for web access.

- Supports MLA, APA, and many other documentation styles

EndNote Basic/EndNote Web

- Free and easy to use: Allows sharing of citations with others, as in group projects. Compatible with *Microsoft Word*.

- Entirely web-based (Internet connection needed to access citations). Syncs with *EndNote* (on a local computer).

Mendeley

- Free (unless large-capacity online storage space is needed)

- Easy to use: Allows you to collect citations and add notes. Citations can be shared privately with up to two additional users or open to public viewing. Retains PDFs alongside citations with easy organization and retrieval. Compatible with *Microsoft Word, OpenOffice*, and *LaTeX*.

- Works on both Mac and PC either offline or online, but more robust when used on a local computer. Can be synced with multiple devices, allowing access to citations from anywhere.

- Supports MLA, APA, and many other documentation styles

Qiqqa

- Free and easy to use: Allows you to collect citations and add notes. InCite feature allows you to cite within a document. Retains PDFs alongside citations with easy organization and retrieval.

- PC-compatible only

- Supports MLA, APA, and many other documentation styles

RefWorks

- Purchase required (consult with your college library or bookstore for free institutional access or student discounts; if you access through your institution's license, you may not be able to access your citations after graduation)

- Easy to use: Allows you to collect citations and add notes. Write-N-Cite feature allows you to cite within a document. *RefShare* (a companion to *RefWorks*) allows you to share citations with others.

- Entirely web-based

- Supports MLA, APA, and many other documentation styles

Zotero

- Free (unless large-capacity online syncing storage space is needed)

- Easy to use: Allows you to collect citations and add extensive review notes. Plugin automatically inserts footnotes or parenthetical citations into a word-processing document. Quick Copy function allows you to drag and drop a citation in any text field in your document. "Scrapes" websites for citation information by taking a snapshot (some data may need to be added if *Zotero* cannot identify a particular field). Allows sharing of citations with others, as in group projects. Retains PDFs alongside citations with easy organization and retrieval. Compatible with *Microsoft Word*, *OpenOffice*, and *Google Drive*.

- Works on both Mac and PC either offline or online, but more robust when used on a local computer. Can be synced with multiple devices, allowing access to citations from anywhere. Prefers *Firefox* browser.

- Supports MLA, APA, and many other documentation styles

EXERCISE 41.8

Following the guidelines in **41k** and **5c,** revise your research project until you are ready to prepare your final draft.

41l Preparing a Final Draft

Before you submit the final version of your paper, **edit and proofread** hard copy of both the paper itself and your works-cited list. Next, consider (or reconsider) your **title**. It should be descriptive enough to tell your readers what your paper is about, and it should create interest in your subject. Your title should also be consistent with your **purpose** and tone. (You would hardly want a humorous title for an essay about famine in Sub-Saharan Africa or inequities in the American judicial system.) Finally, your title should be engaging and to the point—perhaps even provocative. Often, a quotation from one of your sources will suggest a likely title.

See 5d

See 2b

When you are satisfied with your title, read your paper one last time, proofreading for grammar, spelling, or typing errors you may have missed. Pay particular attention to parenthetical documentation and works-cited entries. (Remember that every error undermines your credibility.) Once you are satisfied that your paper is as accurate as you can make it, print out your final draft or email it to your instructor, following all established guidelines. (For the final draft of Rebecca's research paper, along with her works-cited list, **see 47c**.)

EXERCISE 41.9

Prepare a works-cited list for your research paper. Then, edit your paper and your works-cited list, decide on a title, and check to make sure your paper follows the format your instructor requires. Proofread your final draft carefully before you hand it in.

C H A P T E R   **42**

Finding Information

42a   Finding Information in the Library

When it comes to finding trustworthy, high-quality, and authoritative sources, nothing beats your college library. A modern college library offers resources that you cannot find anywhere else—even on the Internet. In the long run, you will save a good deal of time and effort as well as gain a deeper understanding of your topic if you begin your research by consulting your library's electronic and print resources.

1 Searching the Library's Online Catalog or Discovery Service

The best way to start your research is by visiting your college library's **website**. The website's home page is a gateway to a vast amount of information—for example, the library's catalog or discovery service, the databases the library makes available, special library services, and general information about the library. Many libraries also offer online help to students—for example, study guides on a wide variety of topics and email answers to questions. Figure 42.1 shows the home page of a library's website.

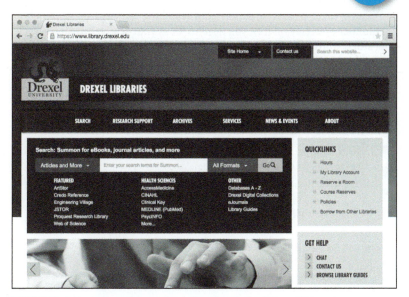

FIGURE 42.1 Home page of an academic library's website. © Drexel University.

Your next step is to search the library's **online catalog**, a comprehensive database that lists the journal titles (but not the articles themselves), books, and multimedia held in the library's collections. When you search the online catalog or discovery service for information, you may do either a *keyword search* or a *subject search*.

Close-Up A DISCOVERY SERVICE

Many libraries have a **discovery service**, which includes not only the physical items held by a library but also e-books and journal articles, including those from electronic databases, as well as articles and books held at other libraries. These items may be obtained through interlibrary loan.

Doing a Keyword Search When you do a **keyword search**, you enter into the search box of the online catalog or discovery service a word (or words) associated with your topic. The computer then displays a list of entries (called **hits**) that contain these words. The more precise your keywords, the more specific and useful the information you retrieve will be. For example, *Civil War* will yield thousands of hits; *The Wilderness Campaign* will yield far fewer.

Because vague or inaccurate keyword searching can yield an overwhelming number of irrelevant hits, you need to focus your search by using **search operators**, words or symbols that can narrow (or broaden) your query. One way to do this is to carry out a **Boolean search**, which combines keywords with the search operators *and, or,* or *not.*

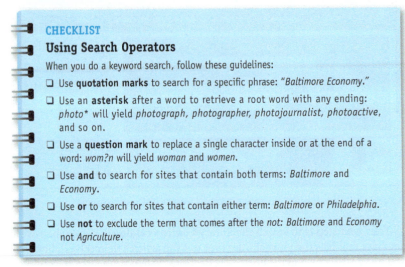

CHECKLIST

Using Search Operators

When you do a keyword search, follow these guidelines:

❑ Use **quotation marks** to search for a specific phrase: "*Baltimore Economy.*"

❑ Use an **asterisk** after a word to retrieve a root word with any ending: *photo** will yield *photograph, photographer, photojournalist, photoactive,* and so on.

❑ Use a **question mark** to replace a single character inside or at the end of a word: *wom?n* will yield *woman* and *women.*

❑ Use **and** to search for sites that contain both terms: *Baltimore* and *Economy.*

❑ Use **or** to search for sites that contain either term: *Baltimore* or *Philadelphia.*

❑ Use **not** to exclude the term that comes after the *not: Baltimore* and *Economy* not *Agriculture.*

Doing a Subject Search When you do a **subject search**, you enter a subject heading into the search box of the online catalog or discovery service. The resources in an academic library are classified under specific subject headings. Many online catalogs list these subject headings to help you identify the exact words that you need for your search. Figure 42.2 shows the results of a subject search in a university library's discovery service.

Note: *WorldCat* and *WorldCat Local* are "super" catalogs of millions of items. If your college library provides access to these resources, you can locate books, DVDs, music, photographs, and specialized databases from thousands of participating libraries around the world and in your community. Check with your reference librarian for information about these resources.

2 Searching the Library's Databases

Through your college library's website, you can access a variety of databases to which the library subscribes. **Online databases** are collections of digital information—such as newspaper, magazine, and journal articles—

arranged for easy access and retrieval. (You search these databases the same way you search the library's online catalog—by doing a **keyword search** or a subject search.)

See
42a1

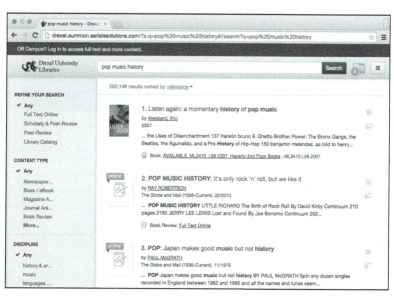

FIGURE 42.2 Discovery service search results for the subject heading *pop music history*.
© Drexel University.

Close-Up KEYWORD SEARCHING VERSUS SUBJECT SEARCHING

When deciding whether to do a keyword search or a subject search, consider the strengths and weaknesses of each method.

Keyword Searching	Subject Searching
• Searches many subject areas	• Searches only a specific subject area
• Can use any significant word or phrase	• Can use only specific subject headings
• Retrieves a large number of items	• Retrieves a smaller number of items
• May retrieve many irrelevant items	• Retrieves few irrelevant items

One of the first things you should do is find out which databases your library subscribes to. You can usually access a list of these databases through the library's website; if necessary, you can ask a reference librarian for more information. Figure 42.3 shows a partial list of databases to which one library subscribes.

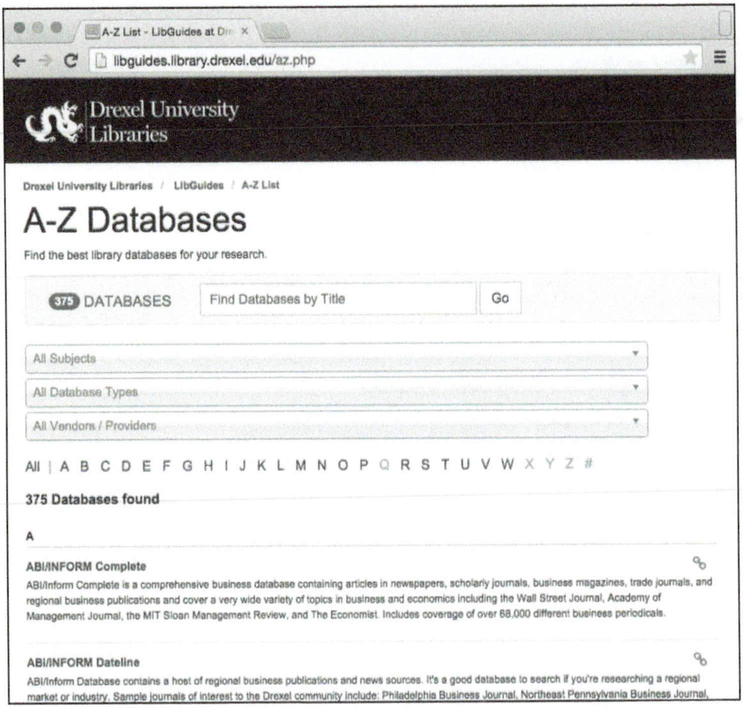

FIGURE 42.3 Excerpt from list of databases to which one academic library subscribes. © Drexel University.

College libraries subscribe to information service companies, such as Gale Cengage Learning, which provide access to hundreds of databases not available for free on the Internet. These databases enable you to access current information from scholarly journals, abstracts, books, reports, case studies, government documents, magazines, and newspapers. Most libraries subscribe to databases that cover many subject areas (*Expanded Academic ASAP*, EBSCOhost's *Academic Search*, and *LexisNexis Academic Universe*, for example); others cover a single subject area in great detail (*PsycINFO* or *Sociological Abstracts*, for example).

Assuming that your library offers a variety of databases, how do you know which ones will be best for your research? First, you should determine the level of the periodical articles listed in the database. A **periodical** is a scholarly journal, magazine, newspaper, or other publication that appears at regular intervals (weekly, monthly, or quarterly, for example). **Scholarly journals** are often the most reliable sources you can find on a subject. They contain articles written by experts in a field, and because journals focus on a particular subject area, they usually provide in-depth analysis. However, because journal articles are aimed at experts, they can be difficult for general readers to understand. **Popular periodicals** are magazines and newspapers that publish articles aimed at general readers. These periodicals are more accessible, but they are less reliable than scholarly journals because they can vary greatly in quality. Some articles might conform to academic standards of reliability, but others may be totally unsuitable as sources. (See **43a** for a discussion of scholarly versus popular publications.)

Next, you should look for a database that is suitable for your topic. Most libraries list databases alphabetically by title or arrange them by subject area. Some offer online study guides (also called research guides or subject guides) that were designed by reference librarians and that list databases (as well as other resources) that are appropriate for research in a given subject area. If you know what database you are looking for, you can find it in the alphabetical listing. If you don't, go to the subject list and locate your general subject area—*History, Nursing,* or *Linguistics,* for example. Then, review the databases that are listed under this heading.

You can begin with a multisubject **general database** such as *Expanded Academic ASAP* or EBSCOhost's *Academic Search* that includes thousands of full-text articles. Then, you can move on to more **specialized databases** that examine your specific subject in detail. The specialized databases include a far greater number of discipline-specific sources than do general-interest databases.

Close-Up   USING MULTI SEARCH

Check to see if your library uses EBSCO Discovery Service, which enables you to search many library databases at one time. Libraries often call it "One Search," "Quick Search," or "Multi Search," and it typically appears as one search box on the home page, as in this example.

| Quick Search | Books & DVD's | Databases | Journals |

Search many online library resources at once

Search

University of Arkansas

Frequently Used General Databases

Database	Description
Academic OneFile	Articles from journals and reference sources in a number of disciplines
Credo Reference	A database of several hundred reference books
EBSCOhost's *Academic Search*	Thousands of periodical articles on many subjects
Expanded Academic ASAP	Articles from journals in the humanities, social sciences, and the natural and applied sciences
JSTOR	Full-text articles from older issues (typically three to five years out) of hundreds of peer-reviewed journals spanning all disciplines from major academic presses, such as Stanford University and University of Chicago
LexisNexis Academic Universe	Full-text articles from national, international, and local news publications as well as legal and business publications
Opposing Viewpoints Resource Center	A library of debates on current topics
Project MUSE	Articles from dozens of major peer-reviewed journals with an emphasis on the humanities
ProQuest Research Library	An index of journal articles in various disciplines, many full text

Close-Up CHOOSING A LIBRARY DATABASE

Consulting with a reference librarian is an excellent way to get connected to the best databases for your topic. You could also ask your instructor if your class will be visiting the library for a research session conducted by a reference librarian. Such hands-on sessions can help guide you through the maze of resources to the best ones for your topic.

Specialized Databases

Database	Description
Arts	
Art Abstracts	Articles in art magazines and journals
Communication	
Communication & Mass Media Complete	Index and abstracts for more than four hundred journals and coverage of two hundred more
History	
America: History and Life	Articles on North American history
Historical Abstracts	Articles on world history
History Reference Center	Full-text articles and other resources for the study of history
Literature	
MLA International Bibliography	An index for books, articles, and websites focusing on literature, language, and film studies
Gale Literature Criticism Online	Full-text articles on literary criticism and analysis
Philosophy	
Philosopher's Index	Index and abstracts from over five hundred fifty journals from forty countries
Religion	
ATLA Religion	Articles in religion studies journals

Database	Description
Business	
ABI/INFORM Global	A ProQuest collection of over eighteen hundred journals and company profiles
Business Source Premier	Indexes more than seventy-eight hundred publications
Economics	
EconLit	Offers a wide range of economics-related resources
Education	
Education Research Complete	*The world's largest collection of full-text education journals*

Specialized Databases (continued)

Psychology

PsycINFO   Indexes books and journal articles in the
                                    psychological and behavioral sciences

Sociology and Social Work

Sociological Abstracts   An index of literature in sociology
Social Work Abstracts   An index of current research in social work

NATURAL AND APPLIED SCIENCES

Database	Description
Biology	
Biological Sciences	Abstracts and citations from a wide range of biological research
Chemistry	
American Chemical Society Publications	Articles from over thirty peer-reviewed journals
Computer Science	
ACM Guide to Computing Literature	Over 750,000 citations and abstracts of literature about computing

NATURAL AND APPLIED SCIENCES

Database	Description
Engineering	
IEEE Xplore	Full-text access to all IEEE journals, magazines, and conference proceedings
Environmental Science	
Environmental Science Database	Information on environmental subjects
Nursing	
ProQuest Nursing & Allied Health Source	Resources for nursing and the allied health fields

3 Finding Books

The library's online catalog or discovery service also give you the information you need for locating specific books. Entries for books include the author's name, the title, the subject, publication information, and a call number. A **call number** is like a book's address in the library: it tells you exactly where to find the book you are looking for. (Figure 42.4 shows the results of an author search in a university library's online catalog.)

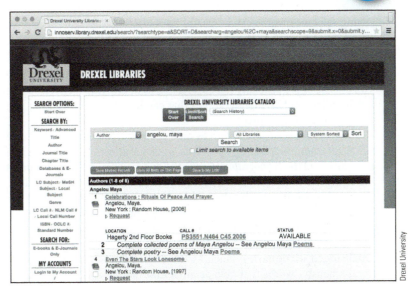

Drexel University

FIGURE 42.4 Online catalog search results for the author *Maya Angelou*.

CHECKLIST

Tracking Down a Missing Source

Problem	**Possible solution**
1. Book is checked out of the library.	❑ Consult the person at the circulation desk.
2. Book is not in the library's collection.	❑ Ask your instructor if you can borrow a copy.
	❑ Arrange for an interlibrary loan (if time permits).
3. Periodical is not in the library's collection.	❑ See if the article is available in a full-text database.
	❑ Check *WorldCat* (worldcat.org) to see if other local libraries have what you need.
	❑ Arrange for an interlibrary loan (if time permits).
	❑ Ask a librarian if the article has been reprinted as part of a collection.

---

4 Consulting Reference Sources

Reference sources—online and print dictionaries, encyclopedias, almanacs, atlases, bibliographies, and so on—can provide an overview of your topic as well as essential background and factual information. Even though they do not discuss your topic in enough depth to be used as research sources, the following reference works can be useful for gathering information and for focusing your research on the specific issues you want to explore in depth.

- **Encyclopedias**—such as the *Encyclopedia Americana* and *The New Encyclopaedia Britannica*—provide an introduction to your topic and give you a sense of the scholarly debates related to it. Individual encyclopedia entries often contain bibliographies that can lead you to works that you can use as research sources.
- **Bibliographies** are lists of sources on a specific topic. For example, the *MLA International Bibliography* lists books and articles published in literature, and the *Bibliographic Guide to Education* lists published sources on all aspects of education. Bibliographic entries often include abstracts.
- **Biographical reference books**—such as *Who's Who in America*, *Who's Who*, and *Dictionary of American Biography*—provide information about people's lives as well as bibliographic listings. They can also provide general information about the times in which people lived.
- **Unabridged dictionaries**—such as the *Oxford English Dictionary*—are comprehensive works that give detailed information about words. They give the history of words and show how their connotations and denotations have changed over time.
- Some **special dictionaries** focus on topics such as synonyms, slang and idioms, rhyming, symbols, proverbs, sign language, and foreign phrases. Other special dictionaries concentrate on specific academic disciplines, such as law, medicine, and computing.
- A **yearbook or almanac** is an annual publication that updates factual and statistical information—for example, *Facts on File*, *Information Please Almanac*, and *World Almanac*. An **atlas** contains maps and charts as well as historical, cultural, and economic information—for example, *National Geographic Atlas of the World*.

5 Using Special Library Services

In addition to their standard services, libraries provide a number of special services. As you do your research, consult a librarian if you would like to take advantage of any of the following special services.

Close-Up SPECIAL LIBRARY SERVICES

- **Interlibrary Loans**   Your library may be part of a system that allows you to borrow books from other libraries.
- **Document Delivery**   Some libraries are able to request the electronic delivery of journal articles and book chapters.
- **Online Communication**   Many libraries answer student questions by chat or email.

- **Services for the Visually Impaired**   Many libraries offer special services—for example, large print books, braille texts, or audio-described video—to students with reading impairments or other disabilities.
- **Special Collections**   Your college library may house special collections of books, manuscripts, or documents. These items are usually listed on the library's website.
- **Government Documents**   A large university library may have a separate area, with its own listing or index, for government documents.
- **Vertical File**   The vertical file includes pamphlets from a variety of organizations and interest groups, reprints, newspaper clippings, and other miscellaneous material collected by librarians. These can be idiosyncratic but useful in certain cases.

EXERCISE 42.1

Which library research sources would you consult to find the following information?

1. A review of the movie *Wild* (2014), based on Cheryl Strayed's memoir
2. A government publication about how to heat your home with solar energy
3. Biographical information about the American anthropologist Margaret Mead
4. Books about Margaret Mead and her work
5. Information about what is being done to prevent the killing of wolves in North America
6. Information about the theories of Albert Einstein
7. Current information about the gun lobby
8. The email address at which to contact Celeste Ng, an American writer
9. Whether your college library has *The Human Use of Human Beings* by Norbert Wiener
10. Current information about AmeriCorps

42b   Finding Information on the Internet

The **web** (which is part of the Internet) is the research tool of choice for most college students. This strategy is not without its drawbacks, however. Because no one is responsible for checking web documents to make sure they are trustworthy, factually accurate, or current, you have to use them with care.

Of course, there are many trustworthy sources of information on the Internet. You can learn to use the search engine *Google* in ways to better find trustworthy materials, and *Google Scholar* provides links to scholarly and academic sources that can also be found in your college's online library databases. In addition, the *Directory of Open Access Journals* (doaj.org) lists almost ten thousand open-access scientific and scholarly journals—many of which are highly respected—in its directories.

Even though the Internet can be a valuable resource for research, you must be able to search effectively for, keep track of, and carefully evaluate materials you find. To carry out a web search, you need a **web browser**, an application—such as *Google Chrome, Mozilla Firefox, Microsoft Internet Explorer,* or *Safari*—that enables you to view information on the web.

CHECKLIST

Using a Browser to Manage Your Research

In addition to connecting you to the web, a browser can help you keep track of your research.

❏ Use browser-based tools, extensions, and apps to bookmark, annotate, and organize your research (see **41a3**).

❏ Use the browser Bookmark function to save useful URLs.

❏ Use the browser History function to view a list of sites you have accessed during your research.

You access information on the web by either entering a URL into your browser's search field or using your search engine to carry out a keyword search.

❶ Pasting a URL

Every page and document on the web has an electronic address called a **URL** (uniform resource locator). When you paste a URL into your browser's location field and click Search, you will be connected to the website you want. (Figure 42.5 shows a location field.)

FIGURE 42.5 Where to copy and paste an address (URL) in *Google Chrome.* © Google

2 Doing a Keyword Search

Once you are connected to the web, use your browser to access a **search engine**, an application such as *Google* or *Google Scholar* that searches for and provides links to documents. You carry out a **keyword search** by entering a keyword (or keywords) into your search engine's search field. (Figure 42.6 shows a search engine's keyword search page.) The search engine will identify any site in its database on which the keyword (or keywords) you have typed appears. (These are called **hits**.)

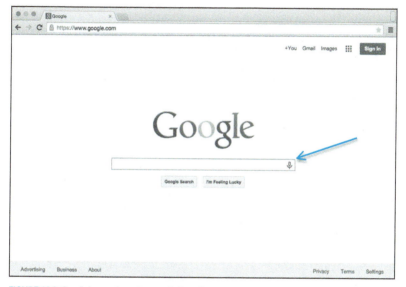

FIGURE 42.6 *Google* keyword search page. © Google

You can develop a list of useful keywords by looking at your college library's online catalog or discovery service and using its headings as keywords. You can also find keywords by looking at the list of Library of Congress Subject Headings (id.loc.gov/authorities/subjects.html). Finally, you can access an online general encyclopedia, such as *Wikipedia*, and look at the category list that follows each article. These categories make excellent keywords that you can use as you search. (Keep in mind, however, that articles from general encyclopedias are typically not acceptable for including as sources in your writing for college-level research unless your assignment states otherwise.)

Many search engines have advanced options that enable you to limit the number of irrelevant results. For example, you can tailor your search so that it retrieves only documents from a particular type of site (*.edu* or *.org*, for example) or documents containing certain keywords in the title or URL. For more on *Google* search operators, see *googleguide.com/advanced_operators_reference.html*.

3 Choosing the Right Search Engine

General-Purpose Search Engines   The most widely used search engines are **general-purpose search engines** that focus on a wide variety of topics. Some of these search engines are more user-friendly than others; some allow for more sophisticated searching functions; some are updated more frequently; and some are more comprehensive than others. As you try out various search engines, you will probably settle on a favorite that you will turn to first whenever you need to find information.

Close-Up   POPULAR SEARCH ENGINES

Ask.com (ask.com): Allows you to narrow your search by asking questions, such as *Are dogs smarter than pigs?*

Bing (bing.com): Developed by Microsoft, *Bing* is a solid competitor to *Google*. *Bing* offers suggestions for follow-up searches, called "Also Try" and "Related Searches." *Bing* favors *.edu, .gov,* and *.mil* sites more than *Google*, paying close attention to top-level domain names, while *Google* pays more attention to PageRank (see the *Google* description below). *Bing* has excellent image and video functions.

Google (google.com): Arguably the best search engine available, it accesses a large database that includes both text and graphics. It is easy to navigate, and searches usually yield a high percentage of useful hits. *Google* purportedly ranks its results using an algorithm called PageRank, based on the number of times a page is linked to other sites. The more a page is linked, the higher it will rise to the top of the results list. (See page 377 for more information about *Google* resources.)

Yahoo*! (yahoo.com): *Yahoo!* relies heavily on the titles of pages. If your keywords appear in the title of a page, that page is likely to rise to the top of the results list. *Yahoo!* also favors more popular pages, measured by the number of times a page is clicked.

Because even the best search engines search only a fraction of the material available on the web, if you use only one search engine, you will most likely miss much valuable information. In addition, search engines vary widely in the way they rank results; this means that the results displayed on the first few pages of one search engine may be completely different from those displayed in another search engine. It is therefore a good idea to repeat each search with several different search engines or to use a **metasearch** or **metacrawler** engine that uses several search engines simultaneously.

Close-Up — METASEARCH ENGINES

Dogpile (dogpile.com)

Ixquick (ixquick.com)

Kartoo (kartoo.com)

Mamma (mamma.com)

SurfWax (surfwax.com)

Yippy (yippy.com)

Zoo (zoo.com)

Specialized Search Engines In addition to the popular general-purpose search engines and metasearch engines, there are also numerous **specialized search engines** devoted entirely to specific subject areas, such as literature, business, sports, and women's issues. Hundreds of specialized search engines are indexed at *listofsearchengines.info*. These search engines are especially useful when you are looking for in-depth information about your topic.

Close-Up — *GOOGLE* RESOURCES

Google is the most-used search engine on the Internet. Most people who use *Google*, however, do not actually know its full potential. Following are just a few of the resources that *Google* offers:

- *Blogger* (blogger.com)   A tool for creating and posting blogs online
- *Book Search* (books.google.com)   A database that allows users to access millions of books that they can either preview or read for free
- *Google Earth* (earth.google.com)   A downloadable, dynamic global map that enables users to see satellite views of almost any place on the planet
- *Finance* (google.com/finance)   Business information, news, and interactive charts
- *News* (news.google.com)   Enables users to search thousands of news stories
- *Patent Search* (google.com/patents)   Enables users to search the full text of US patents
- *Google Scholar* (scholar.google.com)   Searches scholarly literature, including peer-reviewed papers, books, and abstracts
- *Google Translate* (translate.google.com)   A free online language translation service that instantly translates text and web pages

4 Using *Wikipedia* as a Research Source

Although **no encyclopedia**—electronic or print—should be used as a research source, *Wikipedia* requires an extra level of scrutiny.

Wikipedia is an open-source, online general encyclopedia created through the collaborative efforts of its users. Anyone (not necessarily experts) registered with the site can write an article, and in most cases, anyone who views the site can edit an article. The theory is that if enough people contribute, over time, entries will become more and more accurate. Needless to say, *Wikipedia* has its critics—especially in academia. Many instructors point out that the coverage in *Wikipedia* is uneven; some articles follow acceptable standards of academic research, but many others do not. Because some articles have little or no documentation, it is difficult to judge their merit. In addition, because *Wikipedia* does not have an editorial staff responsible for checking entries for accuracy, it is not necessarily a reliable source of information. Finally, critics point out that there is no foolproof way that *Wikipedia* can guard against **vandalism**—the purposeful addition of false or misleading information into an article.

Still, *Wikipedia* does have its strengths. Currently, it contains almost four million entries, and many of its articles focus on subjects not covered in other encyclopedias. Because it is constantly being revised, it can be more up to date than other reference sources. In addition, many articles contain bibliographic citations that enable users to link to reliable sources of information. Keep in mind, however, that even though you can use *Wikipedia* to get a general overview of your topic, most instructors do not consider it a trustworthy, let alone authoritative, research source.

EXERCISE 42.2

Choose a topic that interests you—for example, alternate energy sources or student loans. Then, choose two popular search engines listed in the box on page 376 and do a search of your topic on each. When you finish, compare the results, and answer the following questions:

1. How many results did you get from each search engine?
2. How useful were the results?
3. How easy is it to access visuals about your topic? Video? Blogs? News?
4. Which search engine seemed the most helpful? Why?
5. Which search features were similar, and which were different?

42c Doing Field Research

In addition to using the library's resources, you can find valuable information by doing **field research** (sometimes called **primary research**). Field research involves gathering your own information by making observations (of people, places, objects, and events); by conducting an interview; or by conducting a survey.

1 Making Observations

Your own observations can be a useful source of information. For example, an art or music essay can be enriched by information gathered during a visit to a museum or attending a concert. An education essay may include an account of a classroom visit, and a psychology or sociology essay may include observations (as well as photographs) of an individual's or a group's behavior.

2 Conducting an Interview

Interviews (conducted in person or by email) often give you material that you cannot find in a library—for instance, biographical information, a first-hand account of an event, or the opinions of an expert.

The kinds of questions you ask in an interview depend on the information you want. **Open-ended questions**—questions designed to elicit general information—allow a respondent great flexibility in answering: *"Do you think students today are motivated? Why or why not?"* **Closed-ended questions**—questions intended to elicit specific information—zero in on a particular detail about a subject: *"How much money did the government's cost-cutting programs actually save?"*

Close-Up CONDUCTING AN EMAIL INTERVIEW

Using email to conduct an interview can save you a great deal of time. Before you email your questions, make sure the person is willing to cooperate. If the person agrees to be interviewed, send a short list of specific questions. After you have received the answers, send an email thanking the person for cooperating. When you conduct an email interview, make sure you follow the guidelines for writing emails.

See 12b1

---

3 Conducting a Survey

If your research project is examining a contemporary social, political, or economic issue, a **survey** of attitudes or opinions could be very useful. You begin conducting a survey by identifying the group of individuals that you will poll. This group can be a **convenient sample**—for example, people in your composition class—or a **random sample**—names chosen from the campus directory or a class roster. When you identify a sample, your goal is to select a population that is both *representative*—that accurately reflects the group you are studying—and *significant*—that includes enough respondents to convince people that your results are valid. If you poll ten people in your French class about a college policy and your school has thousands of students, you cannot expect your conclusion to be valid.

You should also make sure that your questions are clearly worded and designed to elicit the information you want. For example, multiple-choice questions or closed-ended questions that require a simple "yes" or "no" will yield more usable data than questions that call for paragraph-length answers. Also, be sure that you do not ask so many questions that respondents lose interest and stop answering. Finally, be careful not to ask biased or **leading questions**—questions asked in a way that suggests an answer.

For an example of a student essay that uses information from a survey, **see 48c.**

Evaluating Sources

The sources you use in your essays help you to establish credibility. If you use high-quality, reliable sources, your readers are likely to assume that you have more than a superficial knowledge of your subject. If, however, you use questionable sources, readers will begin to doubt your credibility, and they may dismiss your ideas. For these reasons, it is very important to **evaluate** your research sources.

43a Evaluating Library Sources

The fact that something is in the library does not necessarily mean that it meets the standards for academic research or that it is appropriate for your essay. For example, an article in a popular magazine in the library's browsing room may not include documentation, and an article in a scholarly journal may present only one side of a debatable issue.

Before you decide to use a library source (print or electronic), you should assess its suitability according to the following criteria:

- **Reliability:** *Is the source trustworthy?* Does the writer support conclusions with facts and expert opinion, or does the source rely on unsupported opinion? Is the information accurate and free of factual errors? Does the writer include documentation and a bibliography?

- **Credibility:** *Is the source respected?* A contemporary review of a source can help you make this assessment. (*UlrichsWeb* is a subject-specific database that your library may subscribe to that includes reviews of books and journals that have received attention in a particular field.) Is the writer well known in the field? Can you check the writer's credentials? Is the article **refereed** (that is, chosen by experts in the field)?

- **Currency:** *Is the source up to date?* The date of publication tells you whether the information in a book or article is current. A source's currency is particularly important for scientific and technological subjects, but even in the humanities, new discoveries and new ways of thinking lead scholars to reevaluate and modify their ideas.

- **Objectivity:** *Does the writer strive to present a balanced discussion?* Sometimes a writer has a particular agenda to advance. Compare a few statements from the source with a neutral source—a textbook or an encyclopedia, for example—to see whether the writer seems to be exhibiting bias or slanting facts.

- **Scope of coverage:** *Does the source treat your topic in enough detail?* To be useful, a source should treat your topic comprehensively. For example, a book should include a section or chapter on your topic, not simply a brief reference or a note. To evaluate an article, either read the abstract or skim the entire article for key facts, looking closely at section headings, information set in boldface type, and topic sentences. An article should have your topic as its central subject (or at least one of its main concerns).

In general, **scholarly publications**—peer-reviewed books and journals aimed at an audience of expert readers—are more reliable than **popular publications**—books, magazines, and newspapers aimed at an audience of general readers. However, assuming they are current, written by reputable authors, and documented, articles from substantive popular publications (such as *The Atlantic* and *Scientific American*) may be appropriate for your research. Other popular publications—especially sensational tabloids such as the *Globe* and the *National Enquirer*—are almost never appropriate for your research. Check with your instructor to be sure.

FIGURE 43.1 Scholarly (left) and popular (right) publications.

Scholarly versus Popular Publications

Scholarly Publications	Popular Publications
Report the results of research	Entertain and inform
Are often published by a university press or have some connection with a university or other academic organization	Are published by commercial presses

Scholarly Publications	Popular Publications
Are usually peer reviewed—that is, reviewed by other experts in the author's field before they are published	Are usually not peer reviewed
Are usually written by someone who is a recognized authority in the field	May be written by experts in a particular field but more often are written by freelance or staff writers
Are written for a scholarly audience so often use technical vocabulary and include challenging content	Are written for general readers so tend to use an accessible vocabulary and do not include challenging content
Nearly always contain extensive documentation as well as a bibliography of works consulted	Rarely cite sources or use documentation
Are published primarily because they make a contribution to a particular field of study	Are published primarily to make a profit

Close-Up   EVALUATING SOURCES

You can use the following ranking system (with the least authoritative source types listed last) to help determine the verifiability of sources.*

1. Academic peer-reviewed journal articles and academic peer-reviewed books
2. University-level textbooks
3. Books by respected publishing houses
4. Mainstream magazines respected in the field
5. Mainstream newspapers
6. Self-published blogs and opinion pieces
7. Non-published materials

*adapted from "*Wikipedia*: Verifiability"

EXERCISE 43.1

Read the following paragraphs carefully, paying close attention to the information provided about their sources and authors as well as to their content. Decide which sources would be most useful and reliable in supporting the thesis "Winning the right to vote has (or has not) significantly changed the role of women in national politics." Which sources, if any, should be disregarded? Which would you examine first? Why?

1. Woman has been the great unpaid laborer of the world, and although within the last two decades a vast number of new employments have been opened to her, statistics prove that in the great majority of these, she is not paid according to the value of the work done, but according to sex. The opening of all industries to women, and the wage question as connected with her, are the most subtle and profound questions of political economy, closely interwoven with the rights of self-government. (Susan B. Anthony; first appeared in Vol. I of *The History of Woman Suffrage;* reprinted in *Voices from Women's Liberation,* ed. Leslie B. Tanner, NAL, 1970. *An important figure in the battle for women's suffrage, Susan B. Anthony* [1820–1906] *also lectured and wrote on abolition and temperance.*)

2. Nineteen eighty-two was the year that time ran out for the proposed equal rights amendment. Eleanor Smeal, president of the National Organization for Women, the group that headed the intense 10-year struggle for the ERA, conceded defeat on June 24. Only 24 words in all, the ERA read simply: "Equality of rights under the law shall not be denied or abridged by the United States or by any state on account of sex." Two major opinion polls had reported just weeks before the ERA's defeat that a majority of Americans continued to favor the amendment. (June Foley, "Women 1982: The Year That Time Ran Out," *The World Almanac & Book of Facts,* 1983.)

3. It won't happen this year. But the next chance at the White House is only four years away, and more women than you might think are already laying the groundwork for their own presidential bids. Bolstered by changing public attitudes, women in politics no longer assume that the Oval Office will always be a male bastion. In 1936, when George Gallup first asked people whether they would "vote for a woman for president if she qualified in every other respect," 65 percent said they would not. Back then, women were only slightly more open to the idea than men. Things are far different today. A recent poll shows that 90 percent of Americans, men included, say they could support a woman for president. (Eleanor Clift and Tom Brazaitis, *Madam President,* © 2000 by Eleanor Clift and Tom Brazaitis. *The authors profile the women who they say are positioning themselves to be president.*)

4. Women have had an impact in the voting booth since Lydia Taft cast a ballot in Uxbridge, Mass., on whether the town should spend money on troops in the French and Indian War. The year was 1756. Taft was allowed to vote on her dead husband's behalf because of the considerable wealth and land she inherited from him. Women certainly have made strides since then, says Lara Brown, a political scientist at Villanova University. "But I think it is important to remember

that we've had 55 presidential elections and we've only ever had men as the major-party presidential nominees." Only two women have been major-party vice-presidential picks: the late Geraldine Ferraro, a New York Democrat and congresswoman, and Sarah Palin, Alaska's Republican governor. (Salena Zito, "Women's Impact Grows," *Pittsburgh Tribune-Review,* 2011. *The author examines American women's voting habits since they gained the right to vote.*)

43b Evaluating Internet Sources

Because anyone can post anything on the Internet, you can easily be overwhelmed by unreliable material. As you sort through and attempt to evaluate this information, there are some general guidelines you can follow.

If you use the library's databases to find digital versions of print journal articles, you can assume that they conform to standards for academic research (even so, you still have to evaluate them). To a lesser degree, the same is true for digital versions of print newspaper or magazine articles. You still have to check the credentials of the authors, the reputation of the periodicals, and possibly the accuracy of the information, but these publications usually give you the information you need to do this checking.

Many Internet sources, however—for example, anonymous blog posts, e-zines that post no standards for publication, and personal and commercial websites—often lack the specific information you need to fully evaluate them. For this reason, you should not use them as research sources unless you are able to assess the quality of the information they contain.

Close-Up ACCEPTABLE VERSUS UNACCEPTABLE INTERNET SOURCES

Acceptable

- Websites sponsored and maintained by reliable organizations
- Articles in established online encyclopedias, such as *britannica.com.*
- Websites sponsored by reputable newspapers and magazines
- Blogs by reputable authors

Unacceptable

- Information from anonymous sources (on blogs, websites, and so on)
- Information found in chat rooms and on discussion boards
- Articles in e-zines and other questionable online publications
- Personal and commercial websites that post no standards for publication

Before you use an Internet source, you should evaluate it for *reliability*, *credibility*, *currency*, *objectivity*, and *scope of coverage*.

Reliability **Reliability** refers to the accuracy of the material itself and to its use of proper documentation.

Factual errors—especially errors in facts that are central to the main idea of the source—should cause you to question the reliability of the material you are reading. To evaluate a site's reliability, ask these questions:

- Is the text free of basic grammatical and mechanical errors?
- Does the site contain factual errors?
- Does the site provide a list of references?
- Are working links available to other sources?
- Can information be verified by print or other sources?

Credibility **Credibility** refers to the credentials of the person or organization responsible for the site.

Websites operated by well-known institutions (the Smithsonian or the Library of Congress, for example) have a high degree of credibility. Those operated by individuals (personal web pages or blogs, for example) are often less reliable. To evaluate a site's credibility, ask these questions:

- Does the site list an author (or authors)? Are credentials (for example, professional or academic affiliations) provided for the author?
- Is the author a recognized authority in the field?
- Is the site **refereed**? That is, does an editorial board or a group of experts determine what material appears on the website?
- Can you determine how long the website has existed?

Currency **Currency** refers to how up to date the website is.

The easiest way to assess a site's currency is to see when it was last updated. Keep in mind, however, that even if the date on the site is current, the information that the site contains may not be. To evaluate a site's currency, ask these questions:

- Does the site include the date when it was last updated?
- Are all the links to other sites still functioning?
- Is the actual information on the page up to date?
- Does the site clearly identify the date it was created?

Objectivity **Objectivity** refers to the degree of bias that a website exhibits.

Some websites strive for objectivity, but others make no secret of their biases. They openly advocate a particular point of view or action, or they clearly try to sell something. Some websites may try to hide their biases. For example, a website may present itself as a source of factual information when it is actually advocating a political point of view. To evaluate a site's objectivity, ask these questions:

- Does advertising appear in the text?
- Does a business, a political organization, or a special interest group sponsor the site?
- Does the site express a particular viewpoint?
- Does the site contain links to other sites that express a particular viewpoint?

CHECKLIST

Determining the Legitimacy of an Anonymous or Questionable Web Source

When a web source is anonymous (or has an author whose name is not familiar to you), you have to take special measures to determine its legitimacy:

❏ **Follow the links.** Follow the hypertext links in a document to other documents. If the links take you to legitimate sources, you know that the author is aware of these sources of information.

❏ **Find out what web pages link to the site.** You can go to *alexa.com* to find information about a website. Type the website's URL into *Alexa*'s search box, and you will be given the volume of traffic to the site, the ownership information for the site, and the other sites visited by people who visited the URL. In addition, you will also be given a link to the "Wayback Machine," *archive.org/web/web.php*, an archive that shows what the page looked like in the past.

❏ **Do a keyword search.** Do a search using the name of the sponsoring organization or the author as keywords. Other documents (or citations in other works) may identify the author.

❏ **Verify the information.** Check the information you find against a reliable source—a textbook or a reputable website, for example. Also, see if you can find information that contradicts what you have found.

❏ **Check the quality of the writing.** Review the writing on the website to see if there are typos, misspellings, and errors in grammar or word choice. Writers who are careless about these things have probably not spent much time checking facts.

❏ **Look at the URL.** Although a website's URL is not a foolproof guide to the site's purpose, it does give you some useful information. The last part of a website's URL (immediately following the **domain name**) can often tell you whether the site is sponsored by a commercial entity (*.com*), a nonprofit organization (*.org*), an educational institution (*.edu*), the military (*.mil*), or a government agency (*.gov*). Knowing this information can help you assess its legitimacy.

Scope of Coverage **Scope of coverage** refers to the comprehensiveness of the information on a website.

More coverage is not necessarily better, but some sites may be incomplete. Others may provide information that is no more than common knowledge. Still others may present discussions that are not suitable for college-level research. To evaluate the scope of a site's coverage, ask these questions:

- Does the site provide in-depth coverage?
- Does the site provide information that is not available elsewhere?
- Does the site identify a target audience? Does this target audience suggest the site is appropriate for your research needs?

Close-Up EVALUATING MATERIAL FROM ONLINE FORUMS

Be especially careful with material posted on discussion boards, blogs, newsgroups, and other online forums. Unless you can adequately evaluate this material—for example, determine its accuracy and the credibility of the author or authors—you should not use it in your essay. In most cases, online forums are not good sources of high-quality information because they are published without formal review.

EXERCISE 43.2

Working in a group of three or four students, examine the home page of *National Geographic*'s website. Using the criteria discussed in **43b**, write a paragraph in which you evaluate the site's content in terms of reliability, credibility, currency, objectivity, and scope of coverage.

CHAPTER 44

Summarizing, Paraphrasing, and Quoting Sources

Experienced researchers know that copying down the words of a source is the least efficient way of **taking notes**. A better approach is to take notes that combine summaries, paraphrases, and quotations. This strategy ensures that you understand your source material and see its relevance to your research.

See 41g

44a Writing a Summary

A **summary** is a brief restatement, *in your own words*, of the main idea of a passage or an article. It is always much shorter than the original because it omits the examples, asides, analogies, and rhetorical strategies that writers use to add interest.

When you summarize, use your own words, not the language or phrasing of your source. Remember that your summary should accurately represent the writer's ideas and should include only the ideas of your source, not your interpretations or opinions. Finally, be sure to document the summary.

Close-Up SUMMARIES

- **Summaries are original.** They should use your own language and phrasing, not the language and phrasing of your source.
- **Summaries are concise.** They should always be much shorter than the original.
- **Summaries are accurate.** They should precisely and accurately express the main idea of your source.
- **Summaries are objective.** They should not include your opinions.

Compare the following three passages. The first is an original source; the second, an acceptable summary; and the third, an unacceptable summary.

Original Source
   Today, the First Amendment faces challenges from groups who seek to limit expressions of racism and bigotry. A growing number of legislatures have passed rules against "hate speech"—[speech] that is offensive on the basis of race,

ethnicity, gender, or sexual orientation. The rules are intended to promote respect for all people and protect the targets of hurtful words, gestures, or actions.

Legal experts fear these rules may wind up diminishing the rights of all citizens. "The bedrock principle [of our society] is that government may never suppress free speech simply because it goes against what the community would like to hear," says Nadine Strossen, president of the American Civil Liberties Union and professor of constitutional law at New York University Law School. In recent years, for example, the courts have upheld the right of neo-Nazis to march in Jewish neighborhoods; protected cross-burning as a form of free expression; and allowed protesters to burn the American flag. The offensive, ugly, distasteful, or repugnant nature of expression is not reason enough to ban it, courts have said.

But advocates of limits on hate speech note that certain kinds of expression fall outside of First Amendment protection. Courts have ruled that "fighting words"—words intended to provoke immediate violence—or speech that creates a clear and present danger are not protected forms of expression. As the classic argument goes, freedom of speech does not give you the right to yell "Fire!" in a crowded theater. (Phil Sudo, "Freedom of Hate Speech?")

The following acceptable summary gives an accurate, objective overview of the original without using its exact language or phrasing.

Acceptable Summary

Some people think that stronger laws against the use of hate speech weaken the First Amendment, but others argue that some kinds of speech should be exempt from this protection (Sudo 17).

The following unacceptable summary uses words and phrases from the original. In addition, the unacceptable summary includes the student writer's opinion (**Other people have the sense to realize . . .**).

Unacceptable Summary

Today, the First Amendment faces challenges from lots of people. Some of these people are legal experts who want to let Nazis march in Jewish neighborhoods. Other people have the sense to realize that some kinds of speech fall outside of First Amendment protection because they create a clear and present danger (Sudo 17).

PLANNING GUIDE

SUMMARY

- Reread the source until you understand it.
- Write a one-sentence restatement of the main idea.
- Write your summary, using the one-sentence restatement as your topic sentence.
- Use your own words and phrasing, not those of your source.
- Include quotation marks for all quoted material.
- Add appropriate documentation.
- Proofread to make sure that you have not inadvertently plagiarized.

44b **Writing a Paraphrase**

A summary conveys just the main idea of a source; a **paraphrase**, however, gives a *detailed* restatement of a source's important ideas. It not only indicates the source's main points, but it also reflects its tone and emphasis. For this reason, a paraphrase can sometimes be as long as—or even longer than—the source itself. Keep in mind that a paraphrase should convey only the ideas of the source—not the writer's analysis or interpretation of those ideas.

When you paraphrase, use your own words, except when you want to quote to give readers a sense of the original. If you do include quotations, circle the quotation marks in your draft so that you will not think that they are your own words later on. Try not to look at the source as you write, use language and syntax that come naturally to you, and avoid duplicating the phrasing or sentence structure of the original. Whenever possible, use synonyms that accurately convey the meaning of the original word or phrase. If you cannot think of a synonym for an important term, quote it. Finally, be sure to document the paraphrase.

Close-Up PARAPHRASES

- **Paraphrases are original.** They should use your original language and phrasing, not the language and phrasing of your source.
- **Paraphrases are accurate.** They should precisely reflect both the ideas and the emphasis of your source.
- **Paraphrases are objective.** They should not include your opinions or interpretations.
- **Paraphrases are complete.** They should include all the important ideas in your source.

Compare the following three passages. The first is an original source, the second is an acceptable paraphrase, and the third is an unacceptable paraphrase.

Original Passage

When you play a video game, you enter into the world of the programmers who made it. You have to do more than identify with a character on a screen. You must act for it. Identification through action has a special kind of hold. Like playing a sport, it puts people into a highly focused and highly charged state of mind. For many people, what is being pursued in the video game is not just a score, but an altered state.

The pilot of a race car does not dare to take . . . attention off the road. The imperative of total concentration is part of the high. Video games demand the same level of attention. They can give people the feeling of being close to the edge because, as in a dangerous situation, there is no time for rest and the consequences of wandering attention [are] dire. With pinball, a false move can be recuperated. The machine can be shaken, the ball repositioned. In a video game, the program has no tolerance for error, no margin for safety. Players experience their every movement as instantly translated into game action. The game is relentless in its demand that all other time stop and in its demand that the player take full responsibility for every act, a point that players often sum up [with] the phrase "One false move and you're dead." (Sherry Turkle, *The Second Self: Computers and the Human Spirit*)

The following acceptable paraphrase conveys the key ideas of the source and maintains an objective tone. Although it follows the emphasis of the original—and even quotes a key phrase—its wording and sentence structure are very different from those of the source.

Acceptable Paraphrase

According to Turkle, the programmer defines the reality of the video game. The game forces a player to merge with the character who is part of the game. The character becomes an extension of the player, who determines how the character will think and act. Like sports, video games put a player into a very intense state of mind that is the most important part of the activity.

For Turkle, the total involvement video games demand is what attracts many people to them. These games can simulate the thrill of participating in a dangerous activity without any of the risks. Players cannot stop to rest, and there is no opportunity to correct errors of judgment. Unlike video games, pinball games are forgiving. A player can—within certain limits—manipulate a pinball game to correct minor mistakes. With video games, however, every move has immediate consequences. The game forces a player to adapt to its rules and to act carefully. One mistake can cause the "death" of the character on the screen and the end of the game (84).

See
Ch. 46

The following unacceptable paraphrase mirrors the phrasing and syntax of the original, borrowing words and expressions without enclosing them in quotation marks. This constitutes plagiarism. In addition, the paraphrase gives the student writer's own views about the relative merits of pinball and video games (**That is why I like . . .**).

Unacceptable Paraphrase

Playing a video game, you enter into a new world—one the programmer of the game made. You can't just play a video game; you have to identify with it. You go to a new level, and you are put into a highly focused, highly charged state of mind.

Just as you would if you were driving a race car or piloting a plane, you must not let your mind wander. Video games demand complete attention. But the sense that at any time you could make one false move and lose is their attraction—at least for me. That is why I like video games more than pinball. Pinball is just too easy. You can always recover. By shaking the machine or quickly operating the flippers, you can save the ball. Video games, however, are not so easy to control. Usually, one slip and you're dead (Turkle 84).

PLANNING GUIDE

PARAPHRASE

- Reread the source until you understand it.
- Write your paraphrase, following the tone and emphasis of the original.
- Avoid using the words or phrasing of the original.
- Include quotation marks for all quoted material.
- Add appropriate documentation.
- Proofread to make sure that you have not inadvertently plagiarized.

44c Quoting Sources

Quote when you want to use a source's unique wording in your essay. When you **quote**, you copy a writer's statements exactly as they appear in a source, word for word and punctuation mark for punctuation mark, enclosing the borrowed material in quotation marks.

As a rule, you should not quote extensively in a research paper. Numerous quotations interrupt the flow of your discussion and give readers the impression that your essay is just a collection of other people's ideas.

CHECKLIST
When to Quote

Quote a source only in the following situations:

❑ Quote when a source's wording or phrasing is so distinctive that a summary or paraphrase would diminish its impact.

❑ Quote when a source's words will lend authority to your discussion.

❑ Quote when a writer's words are so concise that paraphrasing would change the meaning of the original.

❑ Quote when you go on to disagree with a source. Using a source's exact words helps convince readers you are being fair.

Note: Remember to document all quotations that you use in your essay.

EXERCISE 44.1

Assume that in preparation for an essay on the effects of the rise of the suburbs, you read the following paragraph from the book *Great Expectations: America and the Baby Boom Generation*, by Landon Y. Jones. Reread the paragraph, and write a brief summary. Then, write a paraphrase of the paragraph, quoting only those words and phrases you consider especially distinctive.

As an internal migration, the settling of the suburbs was phenomenal. In the twenty years from 1950 to 1970, the population of the suburbs doubled from 36 million to 72 million. No less than 83 percent of the total population growth in the United States during the 1950s was in the suburbs, which were growing fifteen times faster than any other segment of the country. As people packed and moved, the national mobility rate leaped by 50 percent. The only other comparable influx was the wave of European immigrants to the United States around the turn of the century. But as *Fortune* pointed out, more people moved to the suburbs every year than had ever arrived on Ellis Island.

44d Integrating Source Material into Your Writing

Weave quotations, paraphrases, and summaries smoothly into your discussion, adding your own analysis or explanation to increase coherence and to show the relevance of your source material to the points you are making.

Close-Up INTEGRATING SOURCE MATERIAL INTO YOUR WRITING

To make sure your sentences do not all sound the same, experiment with different methods of integrating source material into your essay:

- Vary the verbs you use to introduce a source's words or ideas (instead of repeating *says*).

acknowledges	discloses	implies
suggests	observes	notes
concludes	believes	comments
insists	explains	claims
predicts	summarizes	illustrates
reports	finds	proposes
warns	concurs	speculates
admits	affirms	indicates

- Vary the placement of the **identifying tag** (the phrase that identifies the source), putting it in the middle or at the end of the quoted material instead of always at the beginning.

Quotation with Identifying Tag in Middle: "A serious problem confronting Amish society from the viewpoint of the Amish themselves," observes Hostetler, "is the threat of absorption into mass society through the values promoted in the public school system" (193).

Paraphrase with Identifying Tag at End: The Amish are also concerned about their children's exposure to the public school system's values, notes Hostetler (193).

1 Integrating Quotations

Be sure to work quotations smoothly into your sentences. Quotations should never be awkwardly dropped into your essay, leaving the exact relationship between the quotation and your point unclear. Use a brief introductory remark to provide a context for the quotation, and quote only those words you need to make your point.

Acceptable: For the Amish, the public school system is a problem because it represents "the threat of absorption into mass society" (Hostetler 193).

Unacceptable: For the Amish, the public school system represents a problem. "A serious problem confronting Amish society from the viewpoint of the Amish themselves is the threat of absorption into mass society through the values promoted in the public school system" (Hostetler 193).

Whenever possible, use an identifying tag to introduce the source of the quotation.

Identifying Tag: As John Hostetler points out, the Amish see the public school system as a problem because it represents "the threat of absorption into mass society" (193).

Close-Up PUNCTUATING IDENTIFYING TAGS

Whether or not to use a comma with an identifying tag depends on where you place the tag in the sentence. If the identifying tag immediately precedes a quotation, use a comma.

As Hostetler points out, "The Amish are successful in maintaining group identity" (56).

(continued)

PUNCTUATING IDENTIFYING TAGS *(continued)*

If the identifying tag does not immediately precede a quotation, do not use a comma.

> Hostetler points out that the Amish frequently "use severe sanctions to preserve their values" (56).

Note: Never use a comma after *that*: Hostetler says that,/ Amish society is "defined by religion" (76).

Substitutions or Additions within Quotations Indicate changes or additions that you make to a quotation by enclosing your changes in brackets.

Original Quotation: "Immediately after her wedding, she and her husband followed tradition and went to visit almost everyone who attended the wedding" (Hostetler 122).

Quotation Edited to Make Verb Tenses Consistent: Nowhere is the Amish dedication to tradition more obvious than in the events surrounding marriage. Right after the wedding celebration, the Amish bride and groom "visit almost everyone who [has] attended the wedding" (Hostetler 122).

Quotation Edited to Supply an Antecedent for a Pronoun: "Immediately after her wedding, [Sarah] and her husband followed tradition and went to visit almost everyone who attended the wedding" (Hostetler 122).

Quotation Edited to Change an Uppercase to a Lowercase Letter: The strength of the Amish community is illustrated by the fact that "[i]mmediately after her wedding, she and her husband followed tradition and went to visit almost everyone who attended the wedding" (Hostetler 122).

Omissions within Quotations When you delete unnecessary or irrelevant words, substitute an ellipsis (three spaced periods) for the deleted words.

See 34f1

Original Quotation: "Not only have the Amish built and staffed their own elementary and vocational schools, but they have gradually organized on local, state, and national levels to cope with the task of educating their children" (Hostetler 206).

Quotation Edited to Eliminate Unnecessary Words: "Not only have the Amish built and staffed their own elementary and vocational schools, but they have gradually organized . . . to cope with the task of educating their children" (Hostetler 206).

Close-Up OMISSIONS WITHIN QUOTATIONS

Be sure you do not misrepresent or distort the meaning of quoted material when you shorten it. For example, do not say, "the Amish have managed to maintain . . . their culture" when the original quotation is "the Amish have managed to maintain *parts* of their culture."

Note: If the passage you are quoting already contains ellipses, MLA style requires that you place brackets around any ellipses that you add.

See Ch. 47

Long Quotations Set off a quotation of more than four typed lines of prose (or more than three lines of poetry) by indenting it one-half inch from the margin. Double-space, and do not use quotation marks. If you are quoting a single paragraph, do not indent the first line. If you are quoting more than one paragraph, indent the first line of each complete paragraph an additional one-quarter inch. Integrate the quotation into your essay by introducing it with a complete sentence followed by a colon. Place parenthetical documentation one space after the end punctuation.

See 33b

> According to Hostetler, the Amish were not always hostile to public education:
>
>> The one-room rural elementary school served the Amish community well in a number of ways. As long as it was a public school, it stood midway between the Amish community and the world. Its influence was tolerable, depending upon the degree of influence the Amish were able to bring to the situation. (196)

2 Integrating Paraphrases and Summaries

Introduce your paraphrases and summaries with identifying tags, and end them with appropriate documentation. By doing so, you enable your readers to differentiate your ideas from those of your sources.

Correct (Identifying Tag Differentiates Ideas of Source from Ideas of Writer): Art can be used to uncover many problems that children have at home, in school, or with their friends. For this reason, many therapists use art therapy extensively. According to William Alschuler in *Art and Self-Image*, children's views of themselves in society are often reflected by their art style. For example, a cramped, crowded art style using only a portion of the paper shows a child's limited role (260).

Misleading (Ideas of Source Blend with Ideas of Writer): Art can be used to uncover many problems that children have at home, in school, or with their friends. For this reason, many therapists use art therapy extensively. Children's views of themselves in society are often reflected by their art style. For example, a cramped, crowded art style using only a portion of the paper shows their limited role (Alschuler 260).

EXERCISE 44.2

Look back at the summary and paraphrase that you wrote for Exercise 44.1. Write three possible identifying tags for each, varying the verbs you use for attribution and the placement of the identifying tags. Be sure to include appropriate documentation at the end of each passage.

EXERCISE 44.3

Choose a debatable issue from the following list.

- Illegal immigrants' rights to medical care
- Helmet requirements for cyclists
- Community service requirements for college students

Write a one-sentence summary of your own position on the issue. Then, interview a classmate and write a one-sentence summary of your classmate's position on the same issue. Finally, locate a source that discusses your issue, and write a paraphrase of the writer's position.

CHAPTER **45**

Synthesizing Sources

To *synthesize* means to combine two or more things to form something new. In academic settings, writers must often synthesize information, combining borrowed material with their own ideas in order to express an original viewpoint. **Synthesis** allows writers to explore relationships among ideas and to discuss those ideas in a logical and meaningful way.

45a Understanding Synthesis

Summaries and paraphrases rephrase a source's main ideas, and quotations reproduce a source's exact language. **Synthesis** combines summary, paraphrase, and quotation to create a paragraph or essay that expresses your original viewpoint about a topic. An effective synthesis creates a context for your source material, showing the relevance of each source to your ideas.

The following synthesis was written by a student as part of a research paper. The student effectively uses summary, paraphrase, and quotation to define the term *outsider art* and to explain it in relation to a particular artist's life and work.

Sample Student Synthesis

> Bill Traylor is one of America's leading outsider artists. **[Topic sentence states student's main point]** According to *Raw Vision* magazine, Traylor is one of the foremost artists of the twentieth century (Karlins). **[Summary of online Karlins article]** Born on a cotton plantation as a slave in the 1850s and illiterate all his life, Traylor was self-taught and did not consider himself an artist. He created works for himself rather than for the public (Glueck). **[Paraphrase from one-page Glueck article]** The term *outsider art* refers to works of art created by individuals who are by definition outside society. Because of their economic condition, lack of education, criminal behavior, or physical handicaps, they are not part of mainstream society. According to Louis-Dreyfus, in the United States, "'Outsider Art' . . . refers to work done by the poor, illiterate, and self-taught African Americans whose artistic product **[Quotation from introduction to exhibit pamphlet]** is . . . [a reflection] of their untaught and impoverished social conditions" (iv). As a Southern African American man with few resources and little formal training, Traylor fits the definition **[Conclusion summarizes student writer's position]** of an outsider artist whose works are largely defined by the hardships he faced.

As this example demonstrates, an effective synthesis weaves information from different sources into the discussion, establishing relationships between the sources and the writer's own ideas.

45b Planning a Synthesis

To synthesize source material, you need to discover connections among sources that may seem unrelated. For this reason, you need to think critically about your topic and your sources, trying to understand both your topic and your own point of view.

The first step in synthesizing material is to determine how your sources are alike and how they are different, where they agree and disagree, and whether they reach the same conclusions. As you identify connections between one source and another or between a source and your own ideas, you will develop your own perspective on your subject. It is this viewpoint, summarized in a thesis statement (in the case of an entire essay) or in a topic sentence (in the case of a paragraph), that becomes the focus of your synthesis.

Close-Up   QUESTIONS FOR MAKING CONNECTIONS BETWEEN AND AMONG SOURCES

As you plan your synthesis, ask yourself these questions:

- What positions do the sources take on the issue?
- What key terms do the sources identify and define?
- What background information do the sources provide?
- How do the sources address their audiences?
- How do the sources agree?
- How do the sources disagree?
- What evidence do the sources use to support their assertions?
- How do the sources address opposing points of view?
- How do the sources organize their main ideas?

PLANNING GUIDE

SYNTHESIS

- Analyze and interpret your source material.
- Begin with a statement that sums up the main idea you want your synthesis to convey.
- Blend sources carefully, identifying each source and naming its author(s) and title.
- Identify key similarities and differences among your sources.
- Use identifying tags and transitional words and phrases to help readers follow your discussion.
- Be sure to clearly differentiate your ideas from those of your sources.
- Document all paraphrased and summarized material as well as all quotations.
- Proofread to make sure that you have not inadvertently plagiarized.

45c Writing a Synthesis

In a first-semester composition class, Jay Gilman, a computer science major, was given the following assignment prompt:

Choose an area that you think others would benefit from learning more about. Then, using three sources as support, write a paragraph that explains this topic to an audience unfamiliar with the field. Summarize, paraphrase, and quote source material as appropriate, using MLA documentation style.

After carefully reading his sources and thinking critically about them, Jay wrote the following synthesis.

Effective Synthesis

Computers perform many tasks that make our way of life possible. For example, computer billing makes modern business possible, and without computers we would not have access to the cellular services and cable or satellite television that we take for granted. But computers are more than fast calculators; some also have artificial intelligence (AI), which has transformed fields such as medicine, agriculture, and manufacturing. One technology writer defines artificial intelligence as "a field that attempts to provide machines with humanlike reasoning and language-processing capabilities" (Havenstein). Farming is an industry

Topic sentence states student's main point

Quotation from Havenstein article

Source

There's no precise definition of AI, but broadly, it's a field that attempts to provide machines with humanlike reasoning and language-processing capabilities.

Source

Paraphrase of unsigned article's text and visual content

that is now using AI technology: with new, high-tech agricultural sprayers that "decide" how to treat crops, farmers are able to improve the output and quality of their yield ("More Machine Intelligence"). AI has also made possible numerous medical advances—for example, helping scientists

Effective synthesis of source material to explain application of AI

Summary of Howell article

Researchers at Oklahoma State University, meanwhile, have demonstrated the potential for adding machine intelligence to agricultural sprayers (photo). Enhanced with sensors and computers, the field sprayers dramatically increased the application efficiency by applying fertilizers and herbicides only where needed, reports John B. Solie, professor, power and machinery at Oklahoma State.

© F. Schussler/PhotoLink/Getty Images

—to generate human tissue, bone, and organs for patients in need (Howell). Given the importance of AI technology, computers will certainly change our lives even more in the future.

Conclusion summarizes student writer's position

Source

> **Human 2.0**
> News that an artificial pancreas has been developed, which could help millions of diabetes patients, is only the tip of the iceberg as far as augmentation of the human body goes. We can already grow skin, cartilage, bone, ears and bladders.

This synthesis effectively defines the term *artificial intelligence* and uses information from three short articles to explain AI and briefly describe its use in various fields. The writer introduces his paragraph with a summary of computer applications familiar to his readers and then moves into a discussion of AI.

The sources selected for the synthesis above could have been used far less carefully and effectively. In the following ineffective synthesis, the source material dominates the discussion, all but eliminating the writer's own voice.

Ineffective Synthesis

Begins with out-of-context quotation from source, not student writer's own position

Heather Havenstein defines artificial intelligence (AI) as "a field that attempts to provide machines with humanlike reasoning and language-processing capabilities." As reported in *IndustryWeek* magazine, the farming community is using AI technology by adding machine intelligence to agricultural sprayers, dramatically increasing their application efficiency and improving the output and quality of crops ("More Machine Intelligence"). In the medical field, scientists have used AI to "grow skin, cartilage, bone, ears and bladders" (Howell). AI technology has changed our lives in important ways, and it seems obvious that it will continue to do so in the future.

Source's exact words used without quotation marks, resulting in plagiarism

Quotation used where paraphrase is more appropriate

Vague conclusion

This example does not include a topic sentence that states the writer's position; it also lacks supporting examples and has a vague conclusion. Moreover, the writer commits plagiarism by using the source's exact words.

See Ch. 46

EXERCISE 45.1

Examine a group of advertisements (in print, online, on television, or out in the world—on buildings, buses, billboards, or benches) that either target the same group of consumers (such as parents) or focus on a similar product (such as teeth whiteners or mobile service providers). Then, integrate the information from at least three ads in a paragraph-length synthesis that explains the message the ads are trying to convey.

EXERCISE 45.2

Read the following three sources. Then, write an essay that synthesizes the sources. Summarize, paraphrase, and quote from the sources, using MLA documentation style.

Source A

The following is excerpted from a study analyzing the depiction of women in magazine advertisements since 1955.

> This study was designed to examine the portrayal of women in adver-tisements in a general interest magazine (i.e., *Time*) and a women's fashion magazine (i.e., *Vogue*) over the last 50 years. The coding scheme used for this analysis was based on the one developed by sociologist Erving Goffman in the 1970s, which focuses primarily on the subtle and underlying clues in the picture content of advertisements that contain messages in terms of (stereotypical) gender roles. The results of this study show that, overall, advertisements in *Vogue*, a magazine geared toward a female audience, depict women more stereotypically than do those in *Time*, a magazine with the general public as a target audience. In addition, only a slight decrease in the stereotypical depiction of women was found over time, despite the influence of the Women's Movement. . . .
>
> In this study, a longitudinal approach was taken to analyze the portrayal of women in a general interest magazine and a women's fashion magazine from 1955 to 2002. The sample consisted of the issues of *Time* in the first 4 weeks of January and June in the years 1955, 1965, 1975, 1985, 1995, and 2002 as well as the January and June issues of *Vogue* in the same years. The months of January and June were selected to avoid a bias in the sample based on the time of the year the advertisements were published. (It could be expected, for example, that advertisements in magazine issues of the summer months include more instances of "body display.") By including summer as well as winter issues, the sample was expected to reveal greater insight regard-ing the overall picture of the way women are portrayed. (Lindner, Katharina. "Images of Women in General Interest and Fashion Magazine Advertisements from 1955 to 2002." *Sex Roles*, vol. 51, no. 8, 2004, pp. 409–21.)

Source B

The following passage is excerpted from a book exploring the relationship between advertising and consumer behavior.

> The gap between boys and girls is closing, but this is not always for the best. According to a 1998 status report by a consortium of universities and research centers, girls have closed the gap with boys in math performance and are coming close in science. But they are also now smoking, drinking, and using drugs as often as boys their own age. And, although girls are not nearly as violent as boys, they are committing more crimes than ever before and are far more often physically attacking each other.
>
> It is important to understand that these problems go way beyond indi-vidual psychological development and pathology. Even girls who are raised in

loving homes by supportive parents grow up in a toxic cultural environment, at risk for self-mutilation, eating disorders, and addictions. The culture, both reflected and reinforced by advertising, urges girls to adopt a false self, to bury alive their real selves, to become "feminine," which means to be nice and kind and sweet, to compete with other girls for the attention of boys, and to value romantic relationships with boys above all else. Girls are put into a terrible double bind. They are supposed to repress their power, their anger, their exuberance and be simply "nice," although they also eventually must compete with men in the business world and be successful. They must be overtly sexy and attractive but essentially passive and virginal. It is not surprising that most girls experience this time as painful and confusing, especially if they are unconscious of these conflicting demands. (Kilbourne, Jean. *Can't Buy My Love: How Advertising Changes the Way We Think and Feel.* Simon, 1999, pp. 129–30.)

Source C

The following is excerpted from a book about the impact of popular notions of feminine beauty.

When this book first came out [in 1991], general public opinion considered anorexia and bulimia to be anomalous marginal behavior, and the cause was not assumed to be society's responsibility, insofar as it created ideals and exerted pressure to conform to them—but rather personal crises, perfectionism, poor parenting, and other forms of individual psychological maladjustment. In reality, however, these diseases were widely suffered by many ordinary young women from unremarkable backgrounds, women and girls who were simply trying to maintain an unnatural "ideal" body shape and weight. I knew from looking around me in high school and at college that eating disorders were widespread among otherwise perfectly well balanced young women, and that the simple, basic social pressure to be thin was a major factor in the development of these diseases. . . . Disordered eating, which was understood to fit a disordered ideal, was one of the causes of the disease, and not necessarily, as popular opinion of the day held, a manifestation of an underlying neurosis.

Now, of course, education about the dangers of obsessive dieting or exercise is widespread, and information about eating disorders, their addictive nature, and how to treat them is available in every bookstore, as well as in middle schools, doctors' offices, gyms, high schools, and sororities. *This*, now, is progress.

Yet, on the down side, those very disorders are now so widespread, in fact, almost destigmatized by such intense publicity that they have become virtually normal. Not only do whole sororities take for granted that bulimia is mainstream behavior, but models now openly talk to *Glamour* magazine about their starvation regimes. A newspaper feature about a group of thin, ambitious young women talking about weight quotes one of them as saying, "Now what's wrong with throwing up?" And "pro-an" Web sites have appeared on the Internet, indicating a subculture of girls who are "pro-anorexia," who find the anorexic look appealing and validate it. This is definitely *not* progress. (Wolf, Naomi. *The Beauty Myth: How Images of Beauty Are Used against Women.* Harper, 2002, pp. 5–6.)

CHAPTER **46**

Using Sources Ethically

46a   Defining Plagiarism

When you do a research project, you use information from your sources. It is your ethical responsibility to present this material fairly and to make sure that you document it appropriately.

Plagiarism occurs when a writer (intentionally or unintentionally) uses the words, ideas, or distinctive style of others without acknowledging the source. For example, you plagiarize when you submit someone else's work as your own or fail to document appropriately.

The harm plagiarism does extends beyond the act itself. Instructors assign research for a reason; they want students to become part of a community of scholars and to take part in the conversations that define this community. When you misappropriate the work of others, you deprive yourself of a unique opportunity to learn. Moreover, by plagiarizing, you devalue the work of other students who have acted ethically and responsibly. Finally, plagiarism (as well as other forms of academic dishonesty) compromises the academic mission of your school, weakens the intellectual foundation on which all colleges and universities rest, and undermines the climate of mutual trust and respect that must exist for learning to take place.

Most plagiarism is **unintentional plagiarism**—for example, a student might paste a quoted passage into a paper and forget to include the quotation marks and documentation. There is a difference, however, between an honest mistake and **intentional plagiarism**—for example, copying a passage word for word from a journal article or submitting a paper that someone else has written. The penalties for unintentional plagiarism may sometimes be severe, but intentional plagiarism is almost always dealt with harshly: students who intentionally plagiarize can receive a failing grade for the paper (or the course) and can even be expelled from school.

Close-Up

DETECTING PLAGIARISM

The same technology that has made unintentional plagiarism more common has also made plagiarism easier to detect. By doing a *Google* search, an instructor can quickly find the source of a phrase that has been plagiarized from an Internet source. In addition, plagiarism detection services, such as *Turnitin.com*, can search scholarly databases and identify plagiarized passages in student essays.

46b Avoiding Unintentional Plagiarism

See
Chs.
47–48

MULTILINGUAL TIP

Although you may be tempted to closely follow the syntax and word choice of your sources, be aware that this practice constitutes plagiarism.

The most common cause of unintentional plagiarism is sloppy research habits. To avoid this problem, start your research paper early. Do not cut and paste text from a website or full-text database directly into your essay. If you paraphrase, do so correctly by following the advice in **44b**.

In addition, make sure to keep track of your sources—especially those you scan, download, or otherwise save electronically—so that they do not overwhelm you (**see 41c**). Unintentional plagiarism often occurs when students use source material thinking that it is their own.

Another cause of unintentional plagiarism is failure to use proper <u>documentation</u>. In general, you must document the following information:

- Direct quotations, summaries, and paraphrases of material in sources (including web sources)
- Images that you borrow from a source (print or electronic)
- Facts and opinions that are another writer's original contributions
- Information that is the product of an author's original research
- Statistics, charts, graphs, or other compilations of data that are not yours

Material that is considered **common knowledge** (information most readers probably know) need not be documented. This includes facts available from a variety of reference sources, familiar sayings, and well-known quotations. Your own original research (interviews and surveys, for example) also does not require documentation.

So, although you do not have to document the fact that John F. Kennedy graduated from Harvard in 1940 or that he was elected president in 1960, you do have to document information from a historian's evaluation of his presidency. The best rule to follow is if you have doubts, document.

Close-Up WHY DOCUMENT SOURCES?

There are a number of reasons to document sources:

- **To give credit** By documenting your sources, you acknowledge the original work of others.
- **To become part of a conversation** When you discuss the work of other scholars, you join an ongoing intellectual discussion.
- **To establish your credibility** By indicating what sources you have consulted, you show readers that your conclusions should be taken seriously.
- **To differentiate your ideas from the ideas of your sources** Documentation enables readers to identify the original ideas you have contributed to the discussion. Readers can then locate those cited sources if they wish to collect more information on the subject.

46c Avoiding Intentional Plagiarism

When students plagiarize **intentionally**, they make a decision to misappropriate the ideas or words of others—and this is no small matter. Because academic honesty is absolutely central to any college or university, intentional plagiarism is a very serious breach of trust.

So why do some students engage in this unethical (and risky) behavior? Research has shown that many students who intentionally plagiarize do so out of procrastination and fear. They put off working on their writing projects until they have no time to complete them. Or, they have trouble finding source materials. Some students find that as they do their research, their ideas change. As a result, they discover at the last minute that they have to shift the focus of their essays, and they panic.

Of course, some students plagiarize out of laziness or because they mistakenly believe that buying an essay from an essay mill or paying someone to write an essay is "no big deal." Whatever the reason, there is simply no excuse. Plagiarism is wrong.

46d   Avoiding Other Kinds of Plagiarism

When instructors assign a research paper, they expect it to be your original work. They also expect your essay to be written in response to specific assignments they give. For this reason, you should not submit an essay that you have written for another course. If you intend to substantially rework or expand the essay, however, you may be able to use it. Check with your instructor before doing so.

An essay prepared in collaboration with other students can also present challenges. It is not uncommon in some courses to do work as part of a team. This collaborative work is acceptable in the course for which it was assigned. Even so, you should be clear about who wrote each section.

Finally, although your instructors may encourage you to go the writing center for help, they do not expect your essay to include passages written by a tutor. Passages written (or revised and edited) by a friend or a family member are also unacceptable. If you present material contributed by others as if it were your own, you are committing plagiarism.

46e   Revising to Eliminate Plagiarism

You can avoid plagiarism by using documentation wherever it is required and by following these guidelines.

1   Enclose Borrowed Words in Quotation Marks

Original: Historically, only a handful of families have dominated the fireworks industry in the West. Details such as chemical recipes and mixing procedures were cloaked in secrecy and passed down from one generation to the next. . . . One effect of familial secretiveness is that, until recent decades, basic pyrotechnic research was rarely performed, and even when it was, the results were not generally reported in scientific journals. (Conkling, John A. "Pyrotechnics.")

Plagiarism: John A. Conkling points out that until recently, little scientific research was done on the chemical properties of fireworks, and when it was, the results were not generally reported in scientific journals (96).

Even though the preceding example includes documentation, the student writer uses the source's exact words without placing them in quotation marks.

The writer can correct this problem either by putting the borrowed words in quotation marks or by paraphrasing them.

> **Correct (Borrowed Words in Quotation Marks):** John A. Conkling points out that until recently, little scientific research was done on the chemical properties of fireworks, and when it was, "the results were not generally reported in scientific journals" (96).

> **Correct (Paraphrase):** John A. Conkling points out that the little research conducted on the chemical composition of fireworks was seldom reported in the scientific literature (96).

Close-Up PLAGIARISM AND INTERNET SOURCES

Any time you download text from the Internet, you run the risk of committing unintentional plagiarism. To avoid the possibility of plagiarism, follow these guidelines:

- Download or otherwise collect information into individual files so that you can keep track of your sources.
- Do not cut and paste blocks of downloaded text directly into your essay; first summarize or paraphrase this material.
- If you record the exact words of your source, enclose them in quotation marks.
- Even if your information is from emails, online discussion groups, blogs, or websites, provide appropriate documentation.
- Always document figures, tables, charts, and graphs obtained from the Internet or from any other electronic source.

2 Do Not Imitate a Source's Syntax and Phrasing

> **Original:** If there is a garbage crisis, it is that we are treating garbage as an environmental threat and not what it is: a manageable—though admittedly complex—civic issue. (Patricia Poore, "America's 'Garbage Crisis'")

> **Plagiarism:** If a garbage crisis does exist, it is that people see garbage as a menace to the environment and not what it actually is: a controllable—if obviously complicated—public problem (Poore 39).

Although this student does not use the exact words of her source, she closely follows the original's syntax and phrasing, simply substituting synonyms for the author's words.

Correct (Paraphrase in Writer's Own Words; One Distinctive Phrase Placed in Quotation Marks): Patricia Poore argues that America's "garbage crisis" is exaggerated; rather than viewing garbage as a serious environmental hazard, she says, we should look at garbage as a public problem that may be complicated but that can be solved (39).

3 Document Statistics Obtained from a Source

Although many people assume that statistics are common knowledge, they are usually the result of original research and must, therefore, be documented. Moreover, providing the source of the statistics helps readers to assess their validity.

Correct: According to one study, male drivers between the ages of sixteen and twenty-four accounted for the majority of accidents. Of 303 accidents recorded almost one half took place before the drivers were legally allowed to drive at eighteen (Schuman et al. 1027).

4 Differentiate Your Words and Ideas from Those of Your Source

Original: At some colleges and universities traditional survey courses of world and English literature . . . have been scrapped or diluted. At others they are in peril. At still others they will be. What replaces them is sometimes a mere option of electives, sometimes "multicultural" courses introducing material from Third World cultures and thinning out an already thin sampling of Western writings, and sometimes courses geared especially to issues of class, race, and gender. Given the notorious lethargy of academic decision-making, there has probably been more clamor than change; but if there's enough clamor, there will be change. (Howe, Irving. "The Value of the Canon.")

Plagiarism: Debates about expanding the literary canon take place at many colleges and universities across the United States. At many universities, the Western literature survey courses have been edged out by courses that emphasize minority concerns. These courses are "thinning out an already thin sampling of Western writings" in favor of courses geared especially to issues of "class, race, and gender" (Howe 40).

Because the student writer does not differentiate her ideas from those of her source, it appears that only the quotations in the last sentence are borrowed when, in fact, the second sentence also owes a debt to the original.

In the revised passage below, the writer clearly identifies the boundaries of the borrowed material by introducing it with an identifying tag and ending with documentation.

Correct: Debates about expanding the literary canon take place at many colleges and universities across the United States. According to critic Irving Howe, at many universities the Western literature survey courses have been edged out by courses that emphasize minority concerns. These courses, says Howe, are "thinning out an already thin sampling of Western writings" in favor of "courses geared especially to issues of class, race, and gender" (40).

CHECKLIST

Avoiding Plagiarism

The following strategies can help you avoid plagiarism:

☐ **Take careful notes.** Be sure you have recorded information from your sources carefully and accurately.

☐ **Keep track of your sources.** Place all source material, along with pertinent bibliographic information, in the appropriate files.

☐ **In your notes, clearly identify summaries, paraphrases, and quotations.** In handwritten notes, put all words borrowed from your sources inside circled quotation marks. In typed notes, boldface all quotation marks. Always enclose your own comments within brackets.

☐ **In your essay, differentiate your ideas from those of your sources** by clearly introducing borrowed material with an identifying tag and by following it with parenthetical documentation.

☐ **Enclose all direct quotations** used in your essay within quotation marks.

☐ **Review all paraphrases and summaries** in your essay to make certain that they use your own phrasing and syntax and that any distinctive words and phrases from a source are quoted.

☐ **Document all quoted material and all paraphrases and summaries** of your sources.

☐ **Document all information** that is not common knowledge.

☐ **Document all opinions, conclusions, figures, tables, statistics, graphs, and charts** taken from a source.

☐ **Never use sources that you have not actually read (or invent sources that do not exist).**

EXERCISE 46.1

The following paragraph uses material from three sources, but its student author has neglected to cite them. After reading the paragraph and the three sources that follow it, identify the material that has been quoted directly from a source. Compare the wording to the original for accuracy, and insert quotation marks where necessary, making sure the quoted passages fit smoothly into the paragraph. Differentiate the ideas of the student from those of each of the three sources by using identifying tags to introduce any quotations. (If you think the student did not need to quote a passage, paraphrase it instead.) Finally, add parenthetical documentation for each piece of information that requires it.

Student Paragraph

Oral history is an important way of capturing certain aspects of the past that might otherwise be lost. While history books relate the stories of great men and great events, rarely do they include the experiences of ordinary people—slaves, concentration camp survivors, and the illiterate, for example. By providing information about the people and emotions of the past, oral history makes sense of the present and gives a glimpse of the likely future. But because any particular rendition of a life history relies heavily on personal memory, great care must be taken to evaluate and explain the context of an oral history. Like any other historical account, oral history is just one of many possible versions of an individual's past.

Source 1

Oral history relies heavily on memory, a notoriously malleable entity; people remake the past in light of present concerns and knowledge. Yet not all memories are false, and oral history gives us testimony that might otherwise be lost—stories of slaves, of concentration camp survivors, of the illiterate and the obscure, of the legion "ordinary people" who rarely find their way into the history books. Oral history gives us the human element, the thoughts and emotions and confusions that lie beneath the calm surface of written documents. Even when people remake the past because memories are faulty or unbearable, we can learn much about the ways in which the past affects the present. (Freedman, Jean R. "Never Underestimate the Power of a Bus: My Journey to Oral History." *Oral History Review*, vol. 29, no. 2, 2002, p. 30.)

Source 2

[There is a] widely held view that history belongs to great men and great events, not ordinary people or ordinary life. Yet we know that "ordinary" people in our local districts have important stories to tell. . . . Local histories tell us, on the one hand, that things were done differently in the past, but on the other hand, that in essence people and emotions were much the same. We need to learn from the past to make sense of the present, and get a glimpse of the likely future. (Gregg, Alison. "Planning and Managing an Oral History Collection." *Aplis*, vol. 13, no. 4, 2000, p. 174.)

Source 3

One aspect of oral history . . . concerns the way in which any particular rendition of a life history is a product of the personal present. It is well-recognized that chronicles of the past are invariably a product of the present, so that different "presents" inspire different versions of the past. Just as all historical accounts—the very questions posed or the interpretive framework imposed—are informed by the historian's present, so, too, is a life history structured by both the interviewer's and the narrator's present. . . . [O]ral history cannot be treated as a source of some narrative truth, but rather as one of many possible versions of an individual's past. . . . [and] the stories told in an oral history are not simply the source of explanation, but rather require explanation. (Honig, Emily. "Getting to the Source: Striking Lives: Oral History and the Politics of Memory." *Journal of Women's History*, vol. 9, no. 1, 1997, p. 139.)

Directory of MLA Parenthetical References

Directory of MLA Works-Cited List Entries

Entries for Periodicals

Scholarly Journals

Magazines

Newspapers and News Services

Book Reviews, Newsletters, and Encyclopedias

Entries for Books

Parts of Books

Entries for Internet-Specific Sources

Entries for Other Sources

CHAPTER **47**

MLA Documentation Style

Documentation is the formal acknowledgment of the sources you use in your essay. This chapter explains and illustrates the documentation style recommended by the Modern Language Association (MLA). Chapter 48 discusses the documentation style of the American Psychological Association (APA).

Note: **See 41k3** for a list and description of useful digital citation tools.

47a Using MLA Style

MLA style* is required by instructors of English and other languages as well as by many instructors in other humanities disciplines. MLA documentation has three parts: *parenthetical references in the body of the essay (also known as in-text citations), a works-cited list*, and *content notes*.

1 Parenthetical References

MLA documentation uses parenthetical references in the body of the essay keyed to a works-cited list at the end of the essay. A typical parenthetical reference consists of the author's last name and a page number.

> The colony appealed to many idealists in Europe (Kelley 132).

If you state the author's name or the title of the work in your discussion, do not also include it in the parenthetical reference.

> Penn's political motivation is discussed by Joseph J. Kelley in *Pennsylvania, The Colonial Years, 1681-1776* (44).

To distinguish two or more sources by the same author, include a shortened title after the author's name. When you shorten a title, begin with the word by which the work is alphabetized in the list of works cited.

> Penn emphasized his religious motivation (Kelley, *Pennsylvania* 116).

---

*MLA documentation style follows the guidelines set in the *MLA Handbook*, 8th ed. (MLA, 2016).

Close-Up

PUNCTUATING WITH MLA PARENTHETICAL REFERENCES

Paraphrases and Summaries   Parenthetical references are placed *before* the sentence's end punctuation.

> Penn's writings epitomize seventeenth-century religious thought (Dengler and Curtis 72).

Quotations Run In with the Text   Parenthetical references are placed *after* the quotation but *before* the end punctuation.

> As Ross says, "Penn followed his conscience in all matters" (127).

> According to Williams, "Penn's utopian vision was informed by his Quaker beliefs . . ." (72).

Quotations Set Off from the Text   When you quote more than four lines of prose or more than three lines of poetry, parenthetical references are placed one space *after* the end punctuation.

See 33b

> According to Arthur Smith, William Penn envisioned a state based on his religious principles:
>
> > Pennsylvania would be a commonwealth in which all individuals would follow God's truth and develop according to God's law. For Penn, this concept of government was self-evident. It would be a mistake to see Pennsylvania as anything but an expression of Penn's religious beliefs. (314)

Sample MLA Parenthetical References

1. A Work by a Single Author

Fairy tales reflect the emotions and fears of children (Bettelheim 23).

2. A Work by Two Authors

The historian's main job is to search for clues and solve mysteries (Davidson and Lytle 6).

3. A Work by Three or More Authors

List only the first author, followed by **et al.** ("and others").

Helping each family reach its goals for healthy child development and overall family well-being was the primary approach of Project EAGLE (Bartle et al. 35).

4. A Work in Multiple Volumes

If you list more than one volume of a multivolume work in your works-cited list, include the appropriate volume and page number (separated by a colon followed by a space) in the parenthetical citation.

Gurney is incorrect when he says that a twelve-hour limit is negotiable (6: 128).

5. A Work without a Listed Author

Use the full title (if brief) or a shortened version of the title (if long), beginning with the word by which it is alphabetized in the works-cited list.

The group later issued an apology ("Satire Lost" 22).

6. A Work That Is One Page Long

Do not include a page reference for a one-page article.

Sixty percent of Arab Americans work in white-collar jobs (El-Badru).

7. An Indirect Source

If you use a statement by one author that is quoted in the work of another author, indicate that the material is from an indirect source with the abbreviation **qtd. in** ("quoted in").

According to Valli and Lucas, "the form of the symbol is an icon or picture of some aspect of the thing or activity being symbolized" (qtd. in Wilcox 120).

8. More Than One Work

Cite each work as you normally would, separating one citation from another with a semicolon.

The Brooklyn Bridge has been used as a subject by many American artists (McCullough 144; Tashjian 58).

Note: Long parenthetical references distract readers. Whenever possible, present them as **content notes**.

See 47a3

9. A Literary Work

When citing a work of **fiction**, it is often helpful to include more than the author's name and the page number in the parenthetical citation. Follow the page number with a semicolon, and then include any additional information that might be helpful.

In *Moby-Dick*, Melville refers to a whaling expedition funded by Louis XIV of France (151; ch. 24).

Parenthetical references to **poetry** do not include page numbers. In parenthetical references to *long poems*, cite division and line numbers, separating them with a period.

> In the *Aeneid*, Virgil describes the ships as cleaving the "green woods
>
> reflected in the calm water" (8.124).

(In this citation, the reference is to book 8, line 124 of the *Aeneid*.)

When citing *short poems*, identify the poet and the poem in the text of the essay, and use line numbers in the citation.

> In "My mistress' eyes are nothing like the sun," Shakespeare's speaker says,
>
> "I have seen roses damasked red and white, / But no such roses see I in her
>
> cheeks," (lines 5-6).

Note: When citing lines of a poem, include the word **line** (or **lines**) in the first parenthetical reference; use just the line numbers in subsequent references.

When citing a **play**, include the act, scene, and line numbers (in arabic numerals), separated by periods. Titles of classic literary works (such as Shakespeare's plays) are often abbreviated (**Mac. 2.2.14-16**).

10. Sacred Texts

When citing sacred texts, such as the Bible or the Qur'an, include the version (italicized) and the book (abbreviated if longer than four letters, but not italicized or enclosed in quotation marks), followed by the chapter and verse numbers (separated by a period).

> The cynicism of the speaker is apparent when he says, "All things are
>
> wearisome; no man can speak of them all" (*New English Bible*, Eccles. 1.8).

Note: The first time you cite a sacred text, include the version in your parenthetical reference; after that, include only the book. If you are using more than one version of a sacred text, however, include the version in each in-text citation.

11. An Entire Work

When citing an entire work, include the author's name and the work's title in the text of your essay rather than in a parenthetical reference.

> Lois Lowry's *Gathering Blue* is set in a technologically backward village.

12. Two or More Authors with the Same Last Name

To distinguish authors with the same last name, include their initials in your parenthetical references.

> Increases in crime have caused thousands of urban homeowners to install
>
> alarms (L. Cooper 115). Some of these alarms use sophisticated sensors that
>
> were developed by the army (D. Cooper 76).

13. A Government Document or a Corporate Author

Cite such works using the organization's name followed by the page number (**American Automobile Association 34**). You can avoid long parenthetical references by working the organization's name into your discussion.

> According to the President's Commission for the Study of Ethical Problems in Medicine and Biomedical and Behavioral Research, the issues relating to euthanasia are complicated (76).

14. A Legal Source

Titles of acts or laws that appear in the text of your essay or in the works-cited list should not be italicized or enclosed in quotation marks. In the parenthetical reference, titles are usually abbreviated, and the act or law is referred to by sections. Include the USC (United States Code) and the year the act or law was passed (if relevant).

> Such research should include investigations into the cause, diagnosis, early detection, prevention, control, and treatment of autism (42 USC 284q, 2000).

Names of legal cases are usually abbreviated (**Roe v. Wade**). They are italicized in the text of your essay but not in the works-cited list.

> In *Goodridge v. Department of Public Health*, the court ruled that the Commonwealth of Massachusetts had not adequately provided a reasonable constitutional cause for barring same-sex couples from civil marriages (2003).

15. An Electronic Source

If a reference to an electronic source includes paragraph numbers rather than page numbers, use the abbreviation **par.** or **pars.** followed by the paragraph number or numbers.

> The earliest type of movie censorship came in the form of licensing fees, and in Deer River, Minnesota, "a licensing fee of $200 was deemed not excessive for a town of 1000" (Ernst, par. 20).

If the electronic source has no page or paragraph numbers, cite the work in your discussion rather than in a parenthetical reference. By consulting your works-cited list, readers will be able to determine that the source is electronic and may therefore not have page numbers.

> In her article "Limited Horizons," Lynne Cheney observes that schools do best when students read literature not for practical information but for its insights into the human condition.

2 Works-Cited List

The works-cited list, which appears at the end of your essay, is an alphabetical listing of all the research materials you cite. An effective works-cited entry helps your readers locate its source, primarily by citing traits (like author, title, and location) shared across most sources. These traits are referred to as the nine *core elements*, and every source contains some combination (but not necessarily all) of them. Here is an overview of these elements.

1. Author.

The person or people who wrote or otherwise created the source—or whose work on the source you are choosing to emphasize. This could mean an author, an editor (for a work with no author), a director, a composer, a director, a performer, or a narrator. It might be a full name or a Twitter handle.

- **One author:** Ng, Celeste.
- **Two authors:** Miller, Brenda, and Suzanne Paola.
- **Three or more authors:** Raabe, William A., et al.

2. Title of Source.

The title of the specific source you are citing. This could be a whole book or a short poem within it, if your focus is on that poem. This could be a specific blog entry or an entire album. Shorter works or works that are part of a larger whole usually use quotation marks, while longer or stand-alone works use italics.

- **Essay:** "Once More to the Lake."
- **Television episode:** "Stolen Phone."
- **Play:** *The Tragedy of Hamlet, Prince of Denmark.*
- **Book:** *The Dirty Dust.*

3. Title of Container,

A larger source containing the source you are citing. When citing a full, stand-alone source, element 3 = element 2. However, when citing an essay within a book or an episode of a television show, the container is the book or show. Italicize most containers.

- **Book:** *Frames of Mind: A Rhetorical Reader,*
- **Television show:** *Broad City,*
- **Website:** *The Toast,*

4. Other Contributors,

Noteworthy contributors to the work not listed in element 1. These may include editors, translators, performers, etc. Introduce each name (or set of names) with a description of the role played. If listed after element 2, capitalize the description; if listed after element 3, do not.

- , adapted by Spike Lee,
- , performance by Octavia Spencer,
- , translated by Alan Titley,

5. Version,

Description of a source that appears in more than one version. This appears most frequently for books that exist in multiple editions, whether these are numbered or indicated merely as "revised," "expanded," or similar. It may also apply to the "director's cut" of a film, a version of software, or similar.

- director's cut,
- 15th ed.,

6. Number,

Number indicating source's place in a sequence. This could refer to a volume and/or issue number for journals, to volume numbers for books that appear in multiple volumes, or to season and episode numbers for shows.

- **Television episode:** season 2, episode 1,
- **Book:** vol. 6,
- **Journal Article:** vol. 119, no. 3,

7. Publisher,

Organization that delivers the source to the public. Publishers should be listed for books, films, television shows, and similar, but **not** for periodicals, works published directly by authors or editors, Websites for which the publisher's name is the same as the title, or Websites that do not produce the works they house (examples: *YouTube, EccoHost,* or *WordPress*).

- U of Chicago P,
- Metropolitan Museum of Art,
- Lucasfilm,

8. Publication date,

When the source was made available to the public. This could mean when a work was published or republished in print or online, or when it was released in theaters or on *iTunes*, broadcast on television, or performed live. It might be a year, a month, a specific date, or even a specific time.

- 2016,
- Spring 2016,
- 24 Mar. 2015,
- 10 Jan. 2016, 9:30 p.m.,

9. Location.

Where to find the specific source. This could be a page number or range for print sources; a direct URL or DOI for online sources; or another type of identifier for specific source types. This is also the place to record the location of a lecture, live performance, or similar.

- pp. 30-36.
- www.newyorker.com/magazine/2015/07/20/the-really-big-one/.
- doi:10.1002/cplx.21590.
- Sheraton Hotel, New Orleans.

Not all sources contain all of the nine core elements, and some of them contain additional or optional elements, which you'll learn about in the sections that follow.

Containers within Containers

Some sources are housed in containers within larger containers. For instance, if you cite an article (source) from a journal (container #1) that you accessed through a service like *ProQuest* (container #2), or if you discuss an episode (source) of a television show (container #1) that you accessed on a service like *Netflix* (container #2), then you will need to include information about that larger container, too. This will help readers retrace your steps.

To create a works-cited entry for a source found in a container within a container, do the following:

- List core elements 1 (author) and 2 (title of source).
- List core elements 3-9 that provide information about the first container.
- List core elements 3-9 that provide information about the second container.

In the following example, a writer has identified and ordered source information for a television episode using the core elements. She used this process to create the works-cited entry that follows.

SOURCE

1. Author.	Dan Nowak.
2. Title of Source.	"Unraveling."
CONTAINER 1	
3. Title of Container,	*The Killing,*
4. Other Contributors,	directed by Lodge Kerrigan,
5. Version,	
6. Number,	season 4, episode 2,
7. Publisher,	AMC,
8. Publication date,	1 Aug. 2014.
9. Location.	
CONTAINER 2	
1. Title of Container,	*Netflix,*
2. Other Contributors,	
3. Version,	
4. Number,	

5. Publisher,
6. Publication date,
7. Location.   www.netflix.com/watch/70306003.

WORKS-CITED ENTRY

Nowak, Dan. "Unraveling." *The Killing*, directed by Lodge Kerrigan, season 4,

episode 2, AMC, 1 Aug. 2014. *Netflix*, www.netflix.com/watch/70306003.

The sections that follow will examine how to format these elements for specific source types. For every entry that is listed on your works-cited page, double-space within and between entries on the list, and indent the second and subsequent lines of each entry one-half inch. (**See 47b** for full manuscript guidelines.)

MLA Entries for Periodicals

Periodicals include scholarly journals, magazines, and newspapers. For each works-cited entry, include as many of the nine core elements (described at the beginning of this section) as possible. Figure 47. 1 shows where you can find this information in a print scholarly journal. Figure 47.2 shows where you can find the information in an online scholarly journal.

Scholarly Journals

1. An Article in a Scholarly Journal

When citing a print text, include the volume number (**vol.**) and issue number (**no.**) and be sure to include "**p.**" or "**pp.**" before page numbers.

Harriss, M. Cooper. "One Blues Invisible: Civil Rights and Civil Religion in

Ralph Ellison's Second Novel." *African American Review,* vol. 47,

no. 2, 2014, pp. 247-66.

When citing an online text, include page numbers (if available) and be sure to include the full URL or DOI for the article, followed by a period.

Maeseele, Thomas. "From Charity to Welfare Rights? A Study of Social Care

Practices." *Social Work and Society: The International Online-Only Journal,*

vol. 10, no. 1, 2010, www.socwork.net/sws/article/view/35/90.

2. An Article in a Scholarly Journal from an Online Database

Indicate the database you used to access the source and include the full URL or DOI, followed by a period.

Kerness, Bonnie, et al. "Race and the Politics of Isolation in U.S. Prisons."

Atlantic Journal of Communication, vol. 22, no. 1, 2014, pp. 21-41.

Academic Search Complete, doi:10.1080/15456870.2014.860146.

3. An Article with a Title within Its Title

If the article you are citing contains a title that is normally enclosed in quotation marks, use single quotation marks for the interior title.

> Zimmerman, Brett. "Frantic Forensic Oratory: Poe's 'The Tell-Tale Heart.'"
>
> > *Style,* vol. 35, 2001, pp. 34-50.

If the article you are citing contains a title that is normally italicized, use italics for the title in your works-cited entry.

> Zhang, Mingquan. "The Technological Diegesis in *The Great Gatsby.*"
>
> > *English Language Teaching,* vol. 1, no. 2, Dec. 2008, pp. 86-89.
> >
> > *ERIC,* files.eric.ed.gov/fulltext/EJ1082800.pdf.

FIGURE 47.1 First page of a journal article showing the location of the information needed for documentation. © College Composition and Communication/National Council of Teachers of English.

Author   Title of source (poem)   Title of container 1   Publication date
(last name, first name)

Plumly, Stanley. "Nineteen Species of Sandpipers." *The Atlantic,* Mar. 2015,

     p. 67. *Academic Search Complete,* eds.a.ebscohost.com/proxy/lib.

     miamich.edu/ehost/detail/detail?vid=13&sid=d75be137-2884-4703-

     811a-5b8529257eda%40se.

Location of container 1   Location of container 2

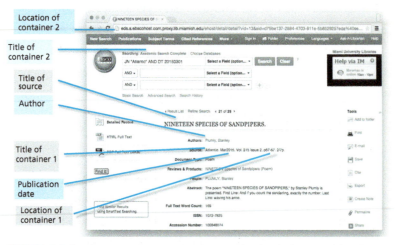

FIGURE 47.2 Opening screen from an online database showing the location of the information needed for documentation. © EBSCO.

Magazines

4. An Article in a Magazine

"Ronald Reagan." *National Review,* 28 June 2004, pp. 14–17.

Jackowe, David J. "Poison Gas Comes to America." *American History,* Dec.

     2014, www.historynet.com/poison-gas-comes-to-america.htm.

If the article begins on one page (say, page 186), but then skips to page 189, include the abbreviation "**pp.**" followed by the first page number and a plus sign.

Di Giovanni, Janine. "The Shiites of Iraq." *National Geographic,* June 2004, pp. 1+.

5. An Article in a Magazine from an Online Database

For all periodical titles, include the initial article (usually "The") prior to the periodical title, as in the following example (***The*** before ***Atlantic***).

Khazan, Olga. "The Bro Whisperer: Michael Kimmel's Quest to Turn College

     Boys into Gentlemen—and Improve Sex on Campus." *The Atlantic,*

     Jan. 2015, pp. 20–21. *Academic OneFile,* connection.ebscohost.com/c/

     articles/99854172/bro-whisperer.

Newspapers and News Services

6. An Article in a Newspaper

Include the version of a text if there is more than one form for it (such as "expanded ed." or "2nd ed.").

> "Suicide Finding is Disputed." *The New York Times,* late ed., 11 Feb. 2015, p. B14.
>
> Jones, Chris. "Don't Overlook the Need for Avant-Garde, Even in Chicago." *The Chicago Tribune,* 11 Feb. 2015. www.chicagotribune.com/ entertainment/theater/ct-avante-garde-theater-tuta-column.html.

7. An Article in a Newspaper from an Online Database

> Spiegel, Peter. "Third Time Lucky? The Latest Plan to Rescue Greece." *The Financial Times*, 17 Sep. 2013, p. 17. *Academic OneFile,* go.galegroup.com.eduproxy.tc-library.org:8080/ps/i.do?id=GALE% 7CA343076709&sid=summon&v=2.1&u=new30429&it=r&p=AONE&sw= w&asid=d9006f47ca3d73b0a937c7b23f0636da.

8. A News Service

> Ryan, Desmond. "Some Background on the Battle of Gettysburg." *Knight Ridder / Tribune Media Service,* 7 Oct. 1993. *Academic OneFile,* search.proquest.com.ezproxy.cul.columbia.edu/docview/259995964.
>
> "Russians Make Giant Snow Portrait of First Astronaut." *Reuters*, 11 Apr. 2016, www.reuters.com/article/us-russia-gagarin-idUSKCN0X81PE? feedType=RSS&feedName=lifestyleMolt.

9. An Editorial or Letter to the Editor in a Newspaper

Insert a descriptor (such as **"Editorial."** or **"Letter."**) to stand in place of a title (if none is given) or after a title. A descriptor designates a particular section of a text.

> "Lynching as Racial Terrorism." Editorial. *The New York Times,* late ed., 11 Feb. 2015, p. A26.
>
> Rossi, Claire. Letter. *The New York Times,* 21 Mar. 2016, www. nytimes.com/2016/03/21/opinion/women-in-science. html?partner=rssnyt&emc=rss&_r=0.

Book Reviews, Newsletters, and Encyclopedias

10. A Book Review

> DeSanctis, Maria. "Small Comforts." Review of *A Motor-Flight through France,* by Edith Wharton. *Tin House,* vol. 16, no. 2, 2014.
>
> Molzhan, Laura. Review of *The Incidents,* by Ayaka Kato. *The Chicago Tribune,* 8 June 2014, www.chicagotribune.com/entertainment/ theater/dance/chi-incidents-dance-review-20140608-story.html.

11. An Article in a Newsletter

Cappucci, Karen. "The Importance of Updated CORIs." *Glenwood News*, 8
Apr. 2016, p. 1.

"The Viking in Scandinavia." *HAAS Recycling Newsletter,* May 2014,
www.haas-recycling.com/tl_files/downloads/newsletter/en/HAAS-
Newsletter-Issue-No.8_04-2014.pdf.

12. An Article in an Encyclopedia

"Hawthorne, Nathaniel." *Encyclopaedia Britannica Online,* 20 Apr. 2015,
www.britannica.com/biography/Nathaniel-Hawthorne.

MLA Entries for Books

Books follow the same guidelines as periodicals. For each works-cited entry,
include as many of the nine core elements (described at the beginning of this
section) as possible. Figures 47.3 and 47.4 show where you can find this information in a print book.

Authors

13. A Book by One Author

Miller, Laura. *The Magician's Book: A Skeptic's Guide to Narnia.* Back Bay,
2009.

Douglass, Frederick. My Bondage and My Freedom, 1855. *Project
Gutenberg,* www.gutenberg.org/files/202/202-h/202-h.htm.

14. A Book by Two Authors

List the first author with last name first, followed by a comma and the word
and. Then list the second author with the first name first.

Gulati, Varun, and Mythili Anoop. *Contemporary Women's Writing in
India.* Lexington, 2014.

Close-Up　PUBLISHERS' NAMES

MLA requires that you use abbreviated forms of certain publishers names
in the works-cited list. In general, note the full publisher's name, but omit
words such as *Incorporated, Company, Limited,* and *Corporation.* Finally,
use the abbreviation *U* for University and *P* for Press.

Name	Abbreviation
Craftsman Book Company	Craftsman Book
Oxford University Press	Oxford UP
Greenleaf Publishing Ltd.	Greenleaf Publishing
Cloverdale Corporation	Cloverdale
University of Chicago Press	U of Chicago P

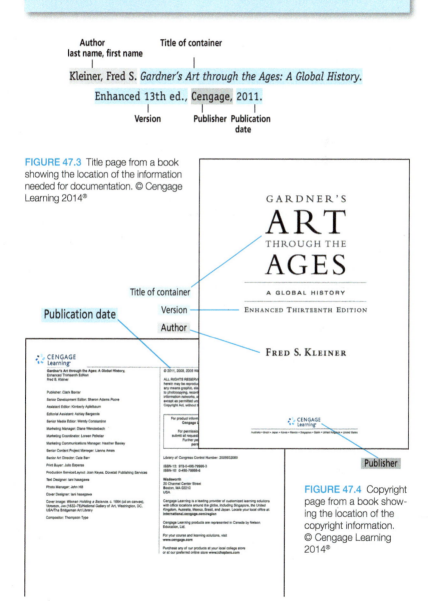

Author
last name, first name

Title of container

Kleiner, Fred S. *Gardner's Art through the Ages: A Global History.*

Enhanced 13th ed., Cengage, 2011.

Version   **Publisher** **Publication date**

FIGURE 47.3 Title page from a book showing the location of the information needed for documentation. © Cengage Learning 2014®

Title of container

Publication date

Version

Author

GARDNER'S

ART

THROUGH THE

AGES

A GLOBAL HISTORY

ENHANCED THIRTEENTH EDITION

FRED S. KLEINER

CENGAGE
Learning

Australia • Brazil • Japan • Korea • Mexico • Singapore • Spain • United Kingdom • United States

Publisher

FIGURE 47.4 Copyright page from a book showing the location of the copyright information. © Cengage Learning 2014®

CENGAGE
Learning

Gardner's Art through the Ages: A Global History, Enhanced Thirteenth Edition
Fred S. Kleiner

Publisher: Clark Baxter
Senior Development Editor: Sharon Adams Poore
Assistant Editor: Kimberly Apfelbaum
Editorial Assistant: Ashley Bargende
Senior Media Editor: Wendy Constantine
Marketing Manager: Diane Wenckebach
Marketing Coordinator: Lorean Pelletier
Marketing Communications Manager: Heather Baxley
Senior Content Project Manager: Lianne Ames
Senior Art Director: Cate Barr
Print Buyer: Julio Esperas
Production Service/Layout: Joan Keyes, Dovetail Publishing Services
Text Designer: tani hasegawa
Photo Manager: John Hill
Cover Designer: tani hasegawa
Cover Image: *Woman Holding a Balance*, c. 1664 (oil on canvas), Vermeer, Jan (1632–75)/National Gallery of Art, Washington, DC, USA/The Bridgeman Art Library
Compositor: Thompson Type

© 2011, 2009, 2006 Wadsworth

ALL RIGHTS RESERVED. No part of this work covered by the copyright herein may be reproduced, transmitted, stored, or used in any form or by any means graphic, electronic, or mechanical, including but not limited to photocopying, recording, scanning, digitizing, taping, Web distribution, information networks, or information storage and retrieval systems, except as permitted under Section 107 or 108 of the 1976 United States Copyright Act, without the prior written permission of the publisher.

For product information and technology assistance, contact us at Cengage Learning Customer & Sales Support, 1-800-354-9706

For permission to use material from this text or product, submit all requests online at www.cengage.com/permissions
Further permissions questions can be e-mailed to permissionrequest@cengage.com

Library of Congress Control Number: 2009932089

ISBN-13: 978-0-495-79986-3
ISBN-10: 0-495-79986-6

Wadsworth
20 Channel Center Street
Boston, MA 02210
USA

Cengage Learning is a leading provider of customized learning solutions with office locations around the globe, including Singapore, the United Kingdom, Australia, Mexico, Brazil, and Japan. Locate your local office at: international.cengage.com/region

Cengage Learning products are represented in Canada by Nelson Education, Ltd.

For your course and learning solutions, visit www.cengage.com

Purchase any of our products at your local college store or at our preferred online store www.ichapters.com

For books that are published by a university press (such as Cambridge University Press), use the abbreviation "**UP**."

> Slaughter, Sheila, and Gary Rhodes. *Academic Capitalism and the New*
>
> *Economy: Markets, State, and Higher Education.* Johns Hopkins UP,
>
> 2009, jhupbooks.press.jhu.edu/content/academic-capitalism-and-
>
> new-economy.

15. A Book by Three or More Authors

Include only the name of the first author (last name first), followed by a comma and **et al.** ("and others").

> Orr, Catherine M., et al. *Rethinking Women's and Gender Studies.*
>
> Routledge, 2011.

The following text is published by National Academies Press; the word "Press" is abbreviated with the letter **"P."**

> Beatty, Alexandra S., et al. *Climate Change Education.* The National
>
> Academies P, 2014, www.nap.edu/read/18807/.

16. Two or More Books by the Same Author

List books by the same author in alphabetical order by title. After the first entry, use three unspaced hyphens followed by a period in place of the author's name.

> Ede, Lisa. *Situating Composition: Composition Studies and the Politics of*
>
> *Location.* Southern Illinois UP, 2004.
>
> ---. *Work in Progress.* 6th ed., Bedford, 2004.

17. A Book by a Corporate Author

If a text is both authored and published by the same organization, begin with the title of the text. If the corporate author is not the same as the publisher, begin with the name of the corporate author.

> *Grade Expectations: How Marks and Education Policies Shape Students'*
>
> *Ambitions.* Organisation for Economic Cooperation and Development,
>
> 2012, doi:10.1787/19963777.
>
> The Home Depot. *Home Improvement 1-2-3.* 2nd ed., Meredith Books, 2003.

18. An Edited Book

An edited book is a work prepared for publication by a person other than the author. If your focus is on the *author's* work, begin your citation with the author's name.

Twain, Mark. *The Adventures of Huckleberry Finn*. Edited by Michael

Patrick Hearn, Norton, 2001.

If your focus is on the *editor's* work, begin your citation with the editor's name, followed by a comma and the word "**editor.**" (For two editors, treat the entry as you would a book by two authors, but include the word "editors" after the second name. For three or more editors, include only the first editor's name (last name first), followed by a comma and the words "**et al., editors.**")

Hearn, Michael Patrick, editor. *The Adventures of Huckleberry Finn*. By

Mark Twain, Norton, 2001.

19. A Translation

If your focus is on the *translator's* work, place that name first in your citation, followed by the word "**translator.**" If your focus is on the *author's* work, follow the first entry under "An Edited Book."

Rabassa, Gregory, translator. *One Hundred Years of Solitude*. By Gabriel

García Márquez, Avon, 1991.

20. A Subsequent Edition of a Book

When citing an edition other than the first, include the edition number after the title of the book. The edition number usually appears on the work's cover and title page.

Yaghijian, Lucretia B. *Writing Theology Well: A Rhetoric for Theological and*

Biblical Writers. 2nd ed., Bloomsbury, 2015.

Miner, Dorothy, et al., editors. *Teaching Chemistry to Students with Disabilities: A*

Manual for High Schools, Colleges, and Graduate Programs. 4th ed., American

Chemical Society, 2001. *ERIC*, files.eric.ed.gov/fulltext/ED476798.pdf.

21. A Republished Book

Include the original publication date after the title of a republished book.

Wharton, Edith. *The House of Mirth*. 1905. Scribner's, 1975.

22. A Book in a Series

If the cover or title page indicates that the book is part of a series, include the series name, neither italicized nor enclosed in quotation marks, and the series number (if applicable) after the publication information.

Davis, Bertram H. *Thomas Percy*. Twayne, 1981. Twayne's English Authors 313.

23. A Multivolume Work

When all volumes of a multivolume work have the same title, include the number of the volume you are using.

Writings of Charles S. Peirce: A Chronological Edition. Vol. 4, edited by

Max H. Fisch, Indiana UP, 2000.

If you use two or more volumes that have the same title, cite the entire work.

Writings of Charles S. Peirce: A Chronological Edition. Edited by Max H.

Fisch, Indiana UP, 2000. 6 vols.

24. An Illustrated Book or a Graphic Narrative

An illustrated book is a work in which illustrations accompany the text. If your focus is on the *author's* work, begin your citation with the author's name. After the title, include the words "**illustrated by**" followed by the illustrator's name and the publication information.

Frost, Robert. *Stopping by Woods on a Snowy Evening,* illustrated by Susan

Jeffers, Penguin, 2001.

If your focus is on the *illustrator's* work, begin your citation with the illustrator's name followed by a comma and the word "**illustator.**" After the title of the work, provide the author's name, preceded by the word "**By.**"

Jeffers, Susan, illustrator. *Stopping by Woods on a Snowy Evening.* By

Robert Frost, Penguin, 2001.

For a graphic novel, where the text and illustrations work together to tell a story, use the same citation you would for a book. If the author and illustrator are different people, cite them in one of the two ways described for an illustrated book.

Bechdel, Alison. *Fun Home: A Family Tragicomic*. Houghton, 2006.

25. The Foreword, Preface, or Afterword of a Book

Campbell, Richard. Preface. *Media and Culture: An Introduction to Mass*

Communication, by Bettina Fabos, Bedford, 2005, pp. vi-xi.

26. A Book with a Title within Its Title

If the book you are citing contains a title that is normally italicized (a novel, play, or long poem, for example), do not italicize the interior title.

Fulton, Joe B. *Mark Twain in the Margins: The Quarry Farm Marginalia and*

A Connecticut Yankee in King Arthur's Court. U of Alabama P, 2000.

If the book you are citing contains a title that is normally enclosed in quotation marks (a short story or poem), keep the quotation marks.

Hawkins, Hunt, and Brian W. Shaffer, editors. *Approaches to Teaching*

Conrad's "Heart of Darkness" and "The Secret Sharer." MLA, 2002.

27. Sacred Texts

The New English Bible with the Apocrypha. Oxford Study ed., Oxford UP, 1976.

Holy Qur'an. Translated by M. H. Shakir, Tahrike Tarsile Qur'an, 1999.

28. A Book Accessed through an E-reader

Sonnenberg, Brittani. *Home Leave: A Novel.* Kindle ed., Hachette, 2014.

Parts of Books
29. A Short Story, Play, or Poem in a Collection

Bukowski, Charles. "lonely hearts." *The Flash of Lightning behind the Mountain: New Poems,* Ecco, 2004, pp. 115-16.

30. An Essay in an Anthology or Edited Collection

Crevel, René. "From *Babylon.*" *Surrealist Painters and Poets: An Anthology,* edited by Mary Ann Caws. MIT P, 2001, pp. 175-77.

31. More than One Work from the Same Anthology

Provide a complete citation for the anthology, but list each work from that anthology separately (with a cross-reference to the entire anthology). Entries should appear in alphabetical order.

Agar, Eileen. "Am I a Surrealist?" Caws, *Surrealist Painters,* pp. 3-7.

Caws, Mary Ann, editor. *Surrealist Painters and Poets: An Anthology.* MIT P, 2001.

Crevel, René. "From *Babylon.*" Caws, *Surrealist Painters,* pp. 175-77.

32. A Scholarly Article Reprinted in a Collection

Booth, Wayne C. "Why Ethical Criticism Can Never Be Simple." *Style,* vol. 32, no. 2, 1998, pp. 351-64. Reprinted in *Mapping the Ethical Turn: A Reader in Ethics, Culture, and Literary Theory,* edited by Todd F. Davis and Kenneth Womack. UP of Virginia, 2001, pp. 16-29.

33. An Article in a Reference Book

For a signed article, begin with the author's name.

Birch, Dinah. "Expressionism." *The Oxford Companion to English Literature.* 7th ed., Oxford UP, 2009.

For an unsigned article, begin with the title.

"Cubism." *The Encyclopedia Americana.* 2012 ed.

MLA Entries for Internet-Specific Sources

When citing Websites, podcasts, *YouTube* videos, and blogs, include as many of the nine core elements (described at the beginning of this section) as possible. Figure 47.5 shows where you can find this information on a Website.

34. An Entire Website

When citing a Website, include the full URL for that site.

> Nelson, Cary, and Bartholomew Brinkman, editors. *Modern American*
>
> > *Poetry*. Dept. of English, U of Illinois, Urbana-Champaign, 2014,
> >
> > www.english.illinois.edu/maps/poets.htm.

35. A Document within a Website

When citing a document or an article within a Website, include the full URL for the document or article.

> Nix, Elizabeth. "6 Viking Leaders You Should Know." *History.com*, A&E
>
> > Television Networks, 6 Feb. 2014, www.history.com/news/history-
> >
> > lists/6-viking-leaders-you-should-know.

36. A Home Page for a Course

> Davis, Brian. Home page. Dept. of Physics and Physical Oceanography, U
>
> > of North Carolina, Wilmington, Fall 2015, www.people.uncw.edu/
> >
> > davis/phy201.html.

37. A Podcast or a Radio Program Accessed Online

> "Teenage Skeptic Takes on Climate Scientists." *Morning Edition*, narrated
>
> > by David Kestenbaum, National Public Radio, 15 Apr. 2008,
> >
> > www.npr.org/templates/story.php?storyId=89619306.

38. An Online Video (*YouTube*)

Because videos posted to online sites can be removed at any time, you should provide as much information as possible in your citation. In the following example, a date of access in included after the full URL for the video.

> Mohr, Nicole. "How to Analyze a Poem." Y*ouTube*, 27 Oct. 2013, www.
>
> > youtube.com/watch?v=5lVHsfkOvV8. Accessed 22 Mar. 2016.

39. A Television Program Streamed via *Netflix* or *Amazon*

Shows that are streamed through online services are often available for a certain period of time. For this reason, you may want to include the date you accessed a program that is streamed online.

> "Episode 4." *Call the Midwife*, season 4, BBC One, 8 Feb. 2015. *Netflix*,
>
> > www.netflix.com/search/call%20the%20midwife?jbv=70245163&jbp
> >
> > =0&jbr=0. Accessed 22 Mar. 2016.

Author
last name, first name | Title of source | Title of container

Keim, Brandon. "What's in a Hurricane Name?" *Wired Science*,

26 Aug. 2009, www.wired.com/2009/08/hurricanename/.

Publication date | Location

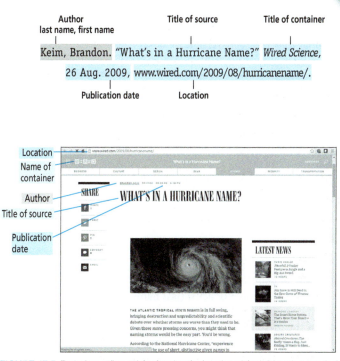

Location
Name of container
Author
Title of source
Publication date

FIGURE 47.5 Part of an online article showing the location of the information needed for documentation. Wired.com © 2011 Condé Nast Digital. All rights reserved. Image from NOAA.

40. A Blog, Tweet, or Social Networking Post

O'Connor, Brendan. "The Downtown Void." *The Awl*, 17 Mar. 2016, www.

theawl.com/2016/03/the-downtown-void.

For a tweet, use the full tweet as the title. Include the date and time, as well as the full tweet's URL.

@tim_cook. "Andy Grove was one of the giants of the technology world.

He loved our country and epitomized America at its best. Rest in

peace." *Twitter*, 21 March 2016, 10:35 p.m., twitter.com/tim_cook/

status/712073584194105344.

41. A Comment on a Blog, Tweet, or Other Online Forum

Often commenters use screen names or pseudonyms to identify themselves. Treat the name exactly as it appears onscreen.

foxinthe_snow. Comment on "My Other Parent," by Nicole Soojung

Callahan. *The Toast*, 22 Dec. 2014, www.aka-sf.org/my-other-parent-

by-nicole-soojung-callahan/.

42. An App (or any Computer Software)

Paper—*Stories from Facebook,* version 1.2.6. *Facebook*, 11 Mar. 2016,
www.facebook.com/paper.

43. A Source Accessed through an App

Dolce, Chris. "Winter Storm Selene: 2,000-Mile-Plus Snow Swath." *The
Weather Channel,* version 7.3.2, 22 Mar. 2016, 8:45 a.m.

44. Email

Mauk, Karen R. "Today." Received by Stephen R. Mandell,
28 June 2015.

MLA Entries for Other Sources

45. A Photograph or Painting

For a photograph or painting viewed at a museum or other location, provide
the name of the photographer or artist (last name first), followed by the title
of the work in italics. Note the year in which the work was created, as well
as the name of the place where it was viewed and its city. If the name of the
museum contains the city name, omit the city.

Stieglitz, Alfred. *The Steerage.* 1907, Los Angeles County Museum of Art.

A photograph or painting without a title is treated the same, but in place of
the italicized title, add a brief description of the work. If the work was accessed online, include the full URL where the work was viewed.

Burns, Patrick. Panoramic print of Providence, Rhode Island. 1988,
Worcester Art Museum, vps343.pairvps.com:8080/emuseum/view/
objects/asitem/search@/15/title-desc?t:state:flow=d8ad95ba-419f-
450a-a5dc-8214e37e7e6f.

46. A Cartoon/Comic Strip

Trudeau, Gary. "Doonesbury." *The Philadelphia Inquirer*, 15 Sept. 2003,
p. E13.

Stossel, Sage. "Star Wars: The Next Generation." *The Atlantic Online,*
20 May 1999, www.theatlantic.com/past/unbound/sage/
ss990519.htm.

47. An Advertisement

If the source you use is not one that readers would be able to identify, include a description in your citation.

Microsoft. Advertisement. *National Review*, 8 June 2010.

48. A Map

Like the previous example, include a description in your citation if readers might not be able to identify the source.

"Philadelphia, Pennsylvania." Map. *U.S. Gazetteer,* 2016, pennsylvania.

hometownlocator.com/maps/countymap,cfips,101,c,philadelphia.cfm.

49. A Film

Include the title of the film (italicized), the distributor, and the date, along with other information that may be useful to readers, such as the name of the director, names of performers, and the screenwriter.

If you focus on the film, place it first in the citation.

Citizen Kane. Directed by Orson Welles, performances by Welles and Agnes

Moorehead, RKO, 1941.

If you focus on the contribution of a particular person, begin with the person's name.

Welles, Orson, director. *Citizen Kane.* RKO, 1941.

If you cite a film on DVD or Blu-ray, include the original release date.

Cowperthwaite, Gabriela, director. *Blackfish.* Magnolia Home

Entertainment, 2013.

50. A Television Program

If the program is part of a series, begin with the episode title. Include the original air date.

"War Feels Like War." *P.O.V.,* PBS, 6 Jul. 2004.

If you accessed the program online, provide the previous information and include the season and episode number, as well as the full URL for the episode.

"The Miseducation of Susan Ross." *Scandal,* season 5, episode 6, ABC, 31

Mar. 2016, abc.go.com/shows/scandal/episode-guide/season-05/16-

the-miseducation-of-susan-ross.

51. An Audio Recording

Malloy, Dave. "No One Else." *Natasha, Pierre, and the Great Comet of 1812,*

Sh-K-Boom, 2013.

Adele. "When We Were Young." *25,* Sony, 2015. *iTunes,* itun.es/us/HIPQp.

52. An Image or Video on a Website

Einspruch, Franklin. "View Out the Window." *The Boston Globe,* 21 Feb.

2015, www.bostonglobe.com/arts/2015/02/21-the- poetry-boston-

snowfall/maV2CoJKQfkbFAAdnh08tL/story.html.

53. A Dissertation

For a published dissertation, place the title in italics and be sure to include the full URL or DOI for the work.

Rodriguez, Jason Anthony. *Bureaucracy and Altruism: Managing the*

Contradictions of Teaching. Dissertation. U of Texas, Arlington,

2003. *ProQuest,* search.proquest.com.ezproxy.cul.columbia.edu/

docview/305227623.

For an unpublished dissertation, place the title in quotation marks.

Pfeffer, Miki. "An 'Enlarging Influence': Women of New Orleans, Julia

Ward Howe, and the Women's Department at the Cotton Centennial

Exposition, 1884-1885." Dissertation. U of New Orleans, 2011.

54. A Government Publication

For a work by a government agency, begin the citation with the name of the government, followed by a comma and the name of the organizational unit (if applicable), followed by the agency. These entities are arranged from largest to smallest, as shown in the following examples. Do not abbreviate words such as "Department" or "Government Printing Office."

United States, Congress, Senate, Office of Consumer Affairs. *2014*

Consumer's Resource Handbook, Government Printing Office,

2014.

United States, Department of Justice, Office of Justice Programs. *Violence*

Against Women: Estimates from the Redesigned National Crime

Victimization Survey, by Ronet Bachman and Linda E. Salzman, Aug.

1995. *Bureau of Justice Statistics,* www.bjs.gov/content/pub/pdf/

FEMVIED.PDF.

If you cite legislation of the United States Congress, include the number and session. If there is a document type (such as a report) and number, include that information, as well.

United States, Congress, Senate, Committee on Energy and Natural

Resources. *Keystone XL Pipeline.* Government Printing Office, 2015.

114th Congress, 1st session, Report 114-1.

55. A Pamphlet

Cite a pamphlet as you would a book. If no author is listed, begin with the title (italicized).

The Darker Side of Tanning. American Academy of Dermatology,

2010.

56. A Lecture

If you attend a lecture or other public address, state that at the end of your citation with the word "**Lecture**" or "**Address**."

Grimm, Mary. "An Afternoon with Mary Grimm." Visiting Writers Program,

Dept. of English, Wright State U, 16 Apr. 2004. Lecture.

57. A Personal Interview or Letter

For a personal interview, begin with the interview subject and use the phrase "**Personal Interview**," followed by the date of the interview.

Tannen, Deborah. Personal Interview. 8 June 2015.

When citing a letter, begin with the letter writer's name and use the phrase "**Personal Letter**," followed by the date of the letter.

Tan, Amy. Personal Letter. 7 Apr. 2016.

58. A Published Interview

Include the phrase "**Interview by**" after the title of the interview. For an interview accessed online, include the full URL for the piece.

"Bill Gates: The *Rolling Stone* Interview." Interview by Jeff Goodell, 13

Mar. 2014, *RollingStone.com,* www.rollingstone.com/culture/news/

bill-gates-the-rolling-stone-interview-20140313.

59. A Published Letter

Joyce, James. "Letter to Louis Gillet." *James Joyce*, by Richard Ellmann,

Close-Up   HOW TO CITE SOURCES NOT LISTED IN THIS CHAPTER

The examples listed in this chapter represent the sources you will most likely encounter in your research. If you encounter a source that is not listed here, find the model that most closely matches it, and adapt the guidelines for your use.

For example, suppose you wanted to include **an obituary** from a print newspaper in your list of works cited. The models that most closely resemble this type of entry are *an editorial in a newspaper* and *a letter to the editor* (entry 9). If you used these models as your guide, your entry would look like this:

Boucher, Geoff, and Elaine Woo. "Michael Jackson's Life Was

Infused with Fantasy and Tragedy." Obituary. *The Los Angeles*

Times, 2 Jul. 2009, p. 4.

Oxford UP, 1965, p. 631.

EXERCISE 47.1

Each of these notes identifies a source used in an essay about online censorship. Determine which information is required to cite each source. Then, following the guidelines and proper format for MLA documentation, create a parenthetical reference for each source, and then create a works-cited list, arranging sources in the proper order. Be sure to format source information correctly, adding quotation marks and italics as needed.

1. Page 72 in a book called Banned in the USA by Herbert N. Foerstel. The book was published in a third edition in 2006 by Greenwood Press. The author's name appears in the text of your essay.

2. A historic statement made by Esther Dyson in her keynote address at the Newspapers 1996 Conference. Her statement is quoted in an article by Jodi B. Cohen called Fighting Online Censorship. The speech has not been printed in any other source. The article is in the April 13, 1996, edition of the weekly business journal Editor & Publisher. Dyson's quotation appears on page 44. The article begins on page 44 and continues on page 60. Dyson's name is mentioned in the text of your essay.

3. An article called Trust Darknet: Control and Compromise in the Internet's Certificate Authority Model by authors Steven B. Roosa and Stephen Schultze. It appears in the online open-access collection Internet Censorship and Control, edited by Steven J. Murdoch and Hal Roberts. The article was published on April 11, 2013. It can be downloaded as a fourteen-page PDF, with numbered pages, from the site. The sponsor is Social Science Electronic Publishing. You summarize the article's findings in your essay.

4. An essay by Nat Hentoff titled Speech Should Not Be Limited on pages 22–26 in the book Censorship: Opposing Viewpoints, edited by Terry O'Neill. The book is published by Greenhaven Press. The publication year is 2005. The quotation you have used is from page 24, and the author is mentioned in the text of your essay.

5. An online essay by Gianna Palmer titled Supervising Kids Online: McAfee Survey Shows Disconnect between Parents and Tweens. The essay was posted to The Huffington Post's Huffpost Screen Sense column. The essay was posted on June 4, 2013, and updated August 4, 2013. Although the essay prints out on two pages, the pages are not numbered onscreen. In your essay, you summarize information from the second page of the document. You accessed the information on June 20, 2015, from the online database Expanded Academic ASAP.

3 **Content Notes**

Content notes—multiple bibliographic citations or other material that does not fit smoothly into your essay—are indicated by a **superscript** (raised numeral) in the text. Notes can appear either as footnotes at the bottom of the page or as endnotes on a separate sheet entitled **Notes**, placed after the last page of the essay and before the works-cited list. Content notes are double-spaced within and between entries. The first line is indented one-half inch, and subsequent lines are typed flush left.

For Multiple Citations

In the Essay

Many researchers emphasize the necessity of having dying patients share their experiences.[1]

In the Note

1. Kübler-Ross 27; Stinnette 43; Poston 70; Cohen and Cohen 31-34; Burke 1: 91-95.

For Other Material

In the Essay

The massacre during World War I is an event the survivors could not easily forget.[2]

In the Note

2. For a firsthand account of these events, see Bedoukian 178-81.

47b MLA-Style Manuscript Guidelines

Although MLA essays do not usually include abstracts or internal headings, this situation is changing. Be sure you know what your instructor expects.

The guidelines in the three checklists that follow are based on the *MLA Handbook* 8th edition.

47c Model MLA-Style Research Paper

The following student essay, "The Great Debate: *Wikipedia* and College-Level Research," uses MLA documentation style. It includes MLA-style in-text citations, three charts, a notes page, and a works-cited list.

CHECKLIST

Typing Your Essay

When typing your essay, use the student essay in **47c** as your model.

❏ Leave a one-inch margin at the top and bottom and on both sides of the page. Double-space your essay throughout.

❏ Capitalize all important words in your title, but not prepositions, articles, coordinating conjunctions, or the *to* in infinitives (unless they begin or end the title or subtitle). Do not italicize your title or enclose it in quotation marks. Never put a period after the title.

❏ Number all pages of your essay consecutively—including the first—in the upper right-hand corner, one-half inch from the top, flush right. Type your last name followed by a space before the page number on every page.

❏ Set off quotations of more than four lines of prose or more than three lines of poetry by indenting the whole quotation one-half inch. If you quote two or more paragraphs, indent the first line of each paragraph an additional quarter inch. (If the first sentence does not begin a paragraph, do not indent it. Indent the first line only in successive paragraphs.)

See 47a

❏ Citations should follow MLA documentation style.

CHECKLIST

Using Visuals

See 11d

❏ Insert visuals into the text as close as possible to where they are discussed.

❏ For **tables,** follow these guidelines: *Above the table,* label each table with the word **Table** followed by an arabic numeral (for instance, **Table 1**). Double-space, and type a descriptive caption, with the first line flush with the left-hand margin; indent subsequent lines one-quarter inch. Capitalize the caption as if it were a title.
Below the table, type the word **Source,** followed by a colon and all source information. Type the first line of the source information flush with the left-hand margin; indent subsequent lines one-quarter inch.

❏ Label other types of visual material—graphs, charts, photographs, drawings, and so on—**Fig.** (Figure) followed by an arabic numeral (for example, **Fig. 2**). Directly below the visual, type the label and a title or caption on the same line, followed by source information. Type all lines flush with the left-hand margin.

❏ Do not include the source of the visual in the works-cited list unless you use other material from that source elsewhere in the essay.

CHECKLIST

Preparing the MLA Works-Cited List

When typing your works-cited list, follow these guidelines:

❑ Begin the works-cited list on a new page after the last page of text or content notes, numbered as the next page of the essay.

See 47a3

❑ Center the title **Works Cited** one inch from the top of the page. Double-space between the title and the first entry.

❑ List entries alphabetically, with last name first. Use the author's full name as it appears on the title page. If a source has no listed author, alphabetize it by the first word of the title (not counting the article).

❑ Type the first line of each entry flush with the left-hand margin; indent subsequent lines one-half inch.

❑ Double-space within and between entries.

Title Pages

Although MLA does not require a separate title page, some instructors prefer that you include one. If so, follow this format:

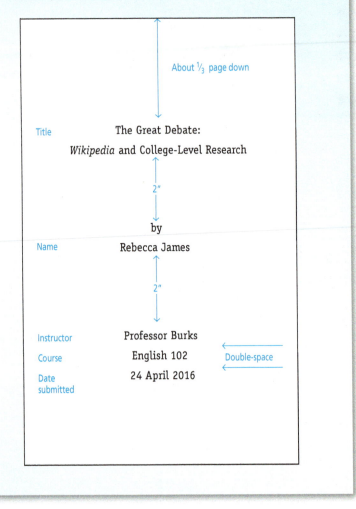

About ⅓ page down

Title

The Great Debate:
Wikipedia and College-Level Research

2″

by

Name

Rebecca James

2″

Instructor

Professor Burks

Course

English 102

Double-space

Date
submitted

24 April 2016

½"
James 1

1"

Rebecca James

Professor Burks

English 102

24 April 2016

Center title →
The Great Debate: *Wikipedia*
and College-Level Research

Indent ½" → When confronted with a research assignment, students

and professionals alike often turn first to *Wikipedia,* the

popular free online encyclopedia. With over 26,000,000 articles,

Double space
Wikipedia is a valuable resource for anyone seeking general

information on a topic. In the academic community, however,

Wikipedia has become a source of controversy. Many college

instructors say that students should not rely on *Wikipedia* as an

authoritative research source or cite it in their bibliographies;

1" → they say that *Wikipedia* (like other encyclopedias) should be used ← 1"

only as a starting point for in-depth research. Some academics,

troubled by the site's lack of reliability, even discourage the use

of *Wikipedia* as a source of factual information. On the other hand,

some instructors (along with some college librarians) believe that

the issue is not so clear-cut. They say that *Wikipedia* is here to

stay and that if the site has problems, it is their responsibility

to help improve it. All in all, the debate over *Wikipedia* has

Thesis statement
been a positive development because it has led to the academic

community to confront the challenges of open, collaborative

software on the web.

Outline point I: Definition of wiki and explanation of *Wikipedia*

Wikipedia is the most popular wiki, an open-source

website that allows users to edit as well as contribute content.

Derived from a Hawaiian word meaning "quick," the term *wiki*

Parenthetical documentation refers to material accessed from a website
suggests the swiftness and ease with which users can access

information on and contribute content to a site ("Wiki").

1"

James 2

In accordance with the site's policies, users can edit existing articles and add new articles using *Wikipedia*'s editing tools, which do not require specialized programming knowledge or expertise. Since its creation in 2001 by Jimmy Wales, *Wikipedia* has grown into a huge database of articles on topics ranging from contemporary rock bands to obscure scientific and technical concepts. Because anyone can edit or add content to the site, however, many members of the academic community consider *Wikipedia* unreliable.

Without a professional editorial board to oversee its development, *Wikipedia* has several shortcomings that limit its trustworthiness. As *Wikipedia*'s own "Researching with *Wikipedia*" page concedes, "not everything in *Wikipedia* is accurate, comprehensive, or unbiased." "Reliability of *Wikipedia*," an article on *Wikipedia*, discusses the many problems that have been identified, presenting criticisms under categories such as "areas of reliability," "susceptibility to bias," and "false biographical information." Academics have similar objections. Villanova University communication department chair Maurice L. Hall has reservations about *Wikipedia*:

> As an open source that is not subjected to traditional forms of peer review, *Wikipedia* must be considered only as reliable as the credibility of the footnotes it uses. But I also tell students that the information can be skewed in directions of ideology or other forms of bias, and so that is why it cannot be taken as a final authority. (qtd. in Burnsed)

In fact, in 2007, *Wikipedia*'s unreliability led Middlebury College's history department to prohibit students from citing *Wikipedia* as a research source—although it does not prohibit

---

Annotations (left margin):

Student's original conclusions; no documentation necessary

Quotations from Internet source, introduced by author's name, are not followed by a paragraph or page number because this information was not provided in the electronic text

Quotation of more than four lines is typed as a block, indented 1/2", and double-spaced, with no quotation marks

Qtd. in indicates that Hall's comments were quoted in Burnsed's article

Annotations (right margin):

Outline point II: Introduction to *Wikipedia*'s drawbacks

James 3

them from using the site for reference. Since then, however, many academics have qualified their criticisms of *Wikipedia*, arguing that although the site is not a reliable research source, it is a valuable stepping stone to more in-depth research. As retired reference librarian Joe Schallan explains, "*Wikipedia* can be useful, especially as a starting point for information on offbeat topics or niche interests that traditional encyclopedias omit." However, he believes that information from *Wikipedia* should be taken "with a very large grain of salt."

Outline point III: Wikipedia's unreliability

Because it is an open-source site, *Wikipedia* is not always reliable or accurate. Although many *Wikipedia* articles include citations, many others—especially those that are underdeveloped—do not. In addition, because anyone can create or edit them, *Wikipedia* articles can be inaccurate, biased, and even targets for vandalism. For example, some *Wikipedia* users tamper with the biographies of especially high-profile political or cultural figures.[1] According to the article "*Wikipedia* Vandalism Detection," seven percent of *Wikipedia*'s articles are vandalized in some way (Adler et al. 277). Although *Wikipedia* has an extensive protection policy that restricts the kinds of edits that can be made to its articles ("*Wikipedia*: Protection Policy"), there are limitations to *Wikipedia*'s control measures.

Superscript number identifies content note

Outline point IV: Wikipedia's poor writing

Because they can be edited by anyone, *Wikipedia* articles are often poorly written. Emory University English professor Mark Bauerlein asserts that *Wikipedia* articles are written in a "flat, featureless, factual style" (153). Even though *Wikipedia* has instituted a coding system to label the shortcomings of its less-developed articles, a warning about an article's poor writing style is likely to go unnoticed by the typical user. Bauerlein argues that the poor writing of many *Wikipedia* articles reaffirms to students

James 4

that sloppy writing and grammatical errors are acceptable in their own writing as well:

Parenthetical documentation is placed one space after end punctuation

> Students relying on *Wikipedia* alone, year in and year out, absorb the prose as proper knowledge discourse, and knowledge itself seems blank and uninspiring. (153-54)

Thus, according to Bauerlein, *Wikipedia* articles have actually lowered the standards for what constitutes acceptable college-level writing.

Despite *Wikipedia*'s drawbacks, there is no denying the popularity of the site among both college students and professionals, who turn to it first for general factual information on a variety of topics. According to Jodi L. Wilson, more than seventy percent of *Wikipedia* contributors are at least twenty-two years old, with the majority of users having higher-education degrees (885–87).² Figs. 1 and 2 show a breakdown of the people who most commonly consult *Wikipedia*.

Outline point V. A: *Wikipedia*'s popularity and benefits; Wilson's findings (charts)

Superscript number identifies content note

Figures summarize relevant data. Source information is typed directly below the figures.

Age Distribution as Reflected in the 2011 Surveys

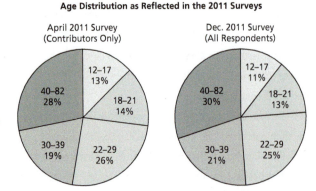

Fig. 1. Jodi L. Wilson, "Proceed with Extreme Caution: Citation to *Wikipedia* in Light of Contributor Demographics and Content Policies." *Vanderbilt Journal of Entertainment & Technology Law*, vol. 16, no. 4, 2014, p. 886. *Academic Search Complete*, web.a.ebscohost.com.ezproxy.cul.columbia.edu/ehost/detail/detail?vid=4&sid=14afe0c2-3351-4754-93dc-2371d2724d5d.

James 5

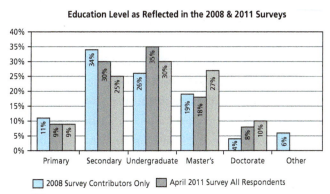

Fig. 2. Jodi L. Wilson, "Proceed with Extreme Caution: Citation to *Wikipedia* in Light of Contributor Demographics and Content Policies." *Vanderbilt Journal of Entertainment & Technology Law*, vol. 16, no. 4, 2014, p. 886. *Academic Search Complete*, web.a.ebscohost.com.ezproxy.cul.columbia.edu/ehost/detail/detail?vid=4&sid=14afe0c2-3351-4754-93dc-2371d2724d5d.

There are good reasons why so many educated adults use *Wikipedia*. Longer *Wikipedia* articles often include comprehensive abstracts that summarize their content. *Wikipedia* articles also often include links to other *Wikipedia* articles, allowing users to navigate quickly through related content. In addition, many *Wikipedia* articles link to other online and print sources, including reliable peer-reviewed sources. Another benefit, noted earlier by Villanova University's Maurice L. Hall, is the inclusion of current and comprehensive bibliographies in some *Wikipedia* articles. According to Alison J. Head and Michael B. Eisenberg, "*Wikipedia* plays an important role when students are formulating and defining a topic."[3] Assuming that *Wikipedia* users make the effort to connect an article's content with more reliable, traditional research sources, *Wikipedia* can be a valuable first step for serious researchers.

Outline point V. B: *Wikipedia's* popularity and benefits: comprehensive abstracts, links to other sources, and current and comprehensive bibliographies

Superscript number identifies content note

James 6

Wikipedia has advantages over other online encyclopedias. Because users can update articles in real time from any location, *Wikipedia* offers up-to-the-minute coverage of political and cultural events as well as timely information on popular culture topics that receive little or no attention in other reference sources. In addition, because *Wikipedia* has such a broad user base, more topics are covered in *Wikipedia* than in other online resources. For example, a student researching the history of video gaming would find *Wikipedia*'s "Wii U" article, with its numerous pages of information and nearly two hundred references, to be a valuable resource. *Encyclopaedia Britannica* does not contain a comparable article on this popular game console. Even when there is little information on a particular topic, *Wikipedia* allows users to create "stub" articles, which provide minimal information that users can expand over time. Thus, by offering immediate access to information on relatively obscure topics, *Wikipedia* can be a valuable first step in finding reliable research sources on such topics.

In their 2014 study, Marcus Messner et al. found that *Wikipedia* has become an even more comprehensive and reliable database of information and that it is gaining increasing acceptance in the academic community. *Wikipedia*'s "About" page claims that the continual editing of articles "generally results in an upward trend of quality and a growing consensus over a neutral representation of information." In fact, *Wikipedia* has instituted control measures to help weed out inaccurate or biased information and to make its content more reliable. For example, evaluating articles on the basis of accuracy, neutrality, completeness, and style, *Wikipedia* ranks its best articles as "featured" and its second-best articles as "good."[4] Although no professional editorial board oversees the

James 7

development of content within *Wikipedia,* experienced users may become editors, and this role allows them to monitor the process by which content is added and updated. Users may also use the "Talk" page to discuss an article's content and make suggestions for improvement. With such controls in place, some *Wikipedia* articles are comparable in scope and accuracy to articles in professionally edited online resources.

Outline point VIII: *Wikipedia*'s content

Although critics argue that the collaborative nature of the wiki format does not necessarily help improve content, the study by Messner et al. seems to suggest the opposite. In examining trends of content development in *Wikipedia* nutritional health articles, Messner et al. affirm that *Wikipedia*'s reliability has improved over time. They explain, "this study's goal was to close a gap in the current research and analyze the online rankings of *Wikipedia* articles on nutritional topics and the types of references they are based on" (Messner et al.).

Messner et al. summarize their findings with a positive conclusion:

> [W]hile *Wikipedia* has grown and expanded over time with reference numbers increasing, the overall quality of articles has at a minimum stayed consistently reliable and has even increased for some of the articles in recent years. This shows that as *Wikipedia* continues to grow, there has been an overall consolidation, creating a better and more reliable source for information on health and nutrition.

Supporting this conclusion, Fig. 3 illustrates how, in recent years, *Wikipedia* articles more consistently include references to reliable sources. In offering increasingly more consistent and well-researched coverage, *Wikipedia* is becoming a more reliable source of information than some of its critics might like to admit.

James 8

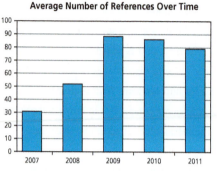

Average Number of References Over Time

Chart summarizes relevant data. Source information is typed directly below the figure.

Fig. 3. Marcus Messner, et al., "Influencing Public Opinion from Corn Syrup to Obesity: A Longitudinal Analysis of the References for Nutritional Entries on *Wikipedia*." *First Monday*, vol. 19, no. 11, 2014. *Google Scholar*, www. firstmonday.dk/ojs/index.php/fm/article/view/4823.

Outline point IX: Academic community's reservations about *Wikipedia*

Some argue that the academic community's reservations about *Wikipedia* have less to do with *Wikipedia*'s shortcomings and more to do with resistance to emergent digital research technologies. Harvard Law professor Jonathan L. Zittrain suggests that academia has, in effect, fallen behind, observing that "so many projects by universities and libraries are about knowledge and information online, . . . [but academics] just couldn't get *Wikipedia* going, or anything like it" (qtd. in Foster). A recent study suggested one reason for *Wikipedia*'s bad reputation among many college instructors: "the perceived detrimental effects of the use of Web 2.0 applications not included in the university suite" (Bayliss 36). Although Jimmy Wales, cofounder of *Wikipedia*, acknowledges that *Wikipedia* should serve only as a starting point for more in-depth research, he calls for the academic community to recognize *Wikipedia* as one of several new, important digital platforms that change the way people learn and disseminate knowledge.

Ellipsis indicates that the student has omitted words from the quotation

James 9

"Instead of fearing the power, complexity, and extraordinary potential of these new platforms," Wales says, "we should be asking how we can gain from their success" (qtd. in Goldstein). As many instructors and librarians argue, members of the academic community are uniquely qualified to improve *Wikipedia* by expanding stub articles and by writing new articles about their areas of expertise.

Outline point X: Instructors' and librarians' efforts to use and improve *Wikipedia*

In recent years, librarians across the country have committed their time and resources to enhancing *Wikipedia* articles that pertain to their own special collections and areas of expertise—and, in general, have become more comfortable with *Wikipedia*. In his research, Colorado Mesa University business professor Johnny Snyder found that "faculty and librarians seem to be using *Wikipedia* more than students . . ." (161). He goes on to explain, "This result was unexpected, as students in the twenty-first century are being classified as 'digital natives' and are embedded in technology and information seeking activities, while librarians and faculty are perceived to be more skeptical about this information source" (Snyder 161). June L. Power, an access service/reference librarian at the University of North Carolina at Pembroke, concedes, "Okay, I am ready for the criticism. What self-respecting librarian turns to *Wikipedia* for reference work? I admit it—this one does" (139). Power describes *Wikipedia*'s value to librarians and students alike: "While I won't complete deep research using only *Wikipedia*, being able to find quick information about a topic is something for which *Wikipedia* is an excellent tool" (139). Snyder, Power, and others believe that it is the responsibility of the academic community to bridge the divide between traditional research sources and the digital

James 10

tools and technologies students are increasingly using to conduct college-level research.

Already, college instructors have found new uses and benefits of *Wikipedia* by incorporating it into their classrooms. In fact, *Wikipedia* has implemented an education program as part of its outreach and collaboration initiative to help instructors around the world build writing assignments based on *Wikipedia*. *Wikipedia*'s "Education Program" page offers guidelines and other resources for incorporating *Wikipedia* into the classroom, noting that this program marks "[t]he end of throwaway assignments and the beginning of real-world impact for student editors." Jeff Byers, a chemistry professor at Middlebury College (where one of the more famous *Wikipedia* "bans" was instituted not long ago), has students in his advanced organic chemistry course write *Wikipedia* entries. Similarly, in her article "Writing for the World: *Wikipedia* as an Introduction to Academic Writing," Christine M. Tardy, an associate professor of writing, rhetoric, and discourse at DePaul University, encourages instructors to use *Wikipedia* in the classroom and outlines some sample writing assignments that can help students "gain a real sense of audience and enjoy the satisfaction of seeing their work published on a high-traffic global website" (18). Instructors like Byers and Tardy emphasize the collaborative nature of *Wikipedia* writing assignments, which offer students a unique opportunity to experience the kinds of writing they are likely to do after college. Additionally, *Wikipedia* writing assignments encourage students to use critical thinking skills, since they require students to evaluate the articles they find on the site and to use *Wikipedia* bibliographies as a starting place to find more suitable research sources.

Outline point XI: *Wikipedia* in the classroom

James 11

Outline point
XII: Academics'
changing view
of Wikipedia

With emerging research on *Wikipedia* use and with new efforts by colleges and universities around the country to incorporate *Wikipedia* into the classroom, the debate surrounding *Wikipedia* seems to be shifting. Although instructors used to seek ways to prevent students from using *Wikipedia* as a research source, some in the academic community are now acknowledging the importance and usefulness of this online resource—at least for general reference. Many former critics are acknowledging that *Wikipedia* offers academics an opportunity to participate in emergent digital technologies that have changed the ways students conduct research. In other words, instructors acknowledge, they need to come to terms with *Wikipedia* and develop guidelines for its use. More and more academics are realizing that improving *Wikipedia* actually benefits students, since the site is often the first place students go when starting a research project. To its credit, *Wikipedia* has taken steps to improve the site's reliability and accuracy, and *Wikipedia*'s outreach and collaboration initiative is building a comprehensive list of best practices for continuing to enhance the quality of *Wikipedia* over time.

Like any encyclopedia, *Wikipedia* is not a suitable source for college-level research. Beyond this fact, however, it may also not yet be as reliable as some other reference sources. Still, it is a valuable starting point for research. As academics and others continue to examine *Wikipedia*'s strengths and weaknesses, they may become more open to its use and more willing to work to improve it. In this sense, the debate over *Wikipedia* is likely to have a positive outcome. Meanwhile, however, students should exercise caution when evaluating general information they find on *Wikipedia* and refrain from citing it as a source.

Conclusion
restates the
thesis and
summarizes
key points

James 12

Center title ————————→ Notes

Indent ½" ————————→ 1. In one well-known example, the reputation of
journalist John Seigenthaler was tarnished when a *Wikipedia*
Double ————→ user edited his biography to claim inaccurately that
space
Seigenthaler was involved in the Kennedy assassination, a
lie that spread to other online sources.

  2. Wilson cautions that, although the majority of
1"
Wikipedia users are educated adults, researchers should
1"
be careful to consider the credibility of the *Wikipedia*
contributors to articles they use in their research.

  3. Head and Eisenberg also note, however, that "when
students are in a deep research mode, . . . it is library
databases, such as *JSTOR* and *PsycINFO*, for instance, that
students use more frequently than *Wikipedia*."

  4. In addition, *Wikipedia*'s policies state that the
information in its articles must be verifiable and must be
based on documented, preexisting research.

James 13

Works Cited

"About *Wikipedia*." *Wikipedia,* 8 Mar. 2016, 3:07,
    en.wikipedia.org/wiki/Wikipedia:About.

Adler, B. Thomas, et al. "*Wikipedia* Vandalism Detection:
    Combining Natural Language, Metadata, and Reputation
    Features." *Lecture Notes in Computer Science*, vol. 6609,
    2011, pp. 277-88. *Google Scholar,* link.springer.com/
    chapter/10.1007/978-3-642-19437-5_23#page-1.

Bauerlein, Mark. *The Dumbest Generation: How the Digital Age
    Stupefies Young Americans and Jeopardizes Our Future (or,
    Don't Trust Anyone Under 30)*. Penguin, 2008.

Bayliss, Gemma. "Exploring the Cautionary Attitude toward
    Wikipedia in Higher Education: Implications for Higher
    Education Institutions." *New Review of Academic
    Librarianship*, vol. 19, no.1, 2013, pp. 36-57. *Academic
    Search Complete,* doi:10.1080/13614533.2012.740439.

Burnsed, Brian. "*Wikipedia* Gradually Accepted in College
    Classrooms." *USNews.com*, 20 June 2011, www.usnews.
    com/education/best-colleges/articles/2011/06/20/
    wikipedia-gradually-accepted-in-college-classrooms.

Foster, Andrea L. "Professor Predicts Bleak Future for the Internet."
    Chronicle of Higher Education, 18 Apr. 2008, p. A29, www.
    chronicle.com/article/Professor-Predicts-Bleak-Fu/31556.

Goldstein, Evan R. "The Dumbing of America?" *Chronicle of
    Higher Education,* 21 Mar. 2008, p. B4, www.chronicle.com/
    article/The-Dumbing-of-America-/22127.

Head, Alison J., and Michael B. Eisenberg. "How Today's College
    Students Use *Wikipedia* for Course-Related Research." *First
    Monday*, vol. 15, no. 3, 2010. *Google Scholar,* papers.ssrn.
    com/sol3/papers.cfm?abstract_id=2281527.

James 14

Messner, Marcus, et al. "Influencing Public Opinion Opinion
from Corn Syrup to Obesity: A Longitudinal Analysis of
the References for Nutritional Entries on *Wikipedia*."
First Monday, vol. 19, no. 11, 2014. *Google Scholar,*
www.firstmonday.dk/ojs/index.php/fm/article/
view/4823.

Power, June L. "Access the Web: Mobile Apps for Librarians."
Journal of Access Services, vol. 10, no. 2, 2013, pp.
138–43. *Academic Search Complete,*
doi:10.1080/15367967.2013.767690.

"Protection Policy." *Wikipedia,* 10 Mar. 2016, 4:23,
en.wikipedia.org/wiki/Protection_policy.

"Reliability of *Wikipedia*." *Wikipedia*, 12 Mar. 2016, 11:02,
en.wikipedia.org/wiki/Reliability_of_Wikipedia.

"Researching with *Wikipedia*." *Wikipedia,* 8 Mar. 2016, 3:25,
en.wikipedia.org/wiki/Wikipedia: Researching_with_
Wikipedia.

Schallan, Joe. "*Wikipedia* Woes." Letter. *American Libraries,*
Apr. 2010, p. 9.

Snyder, Johnny. "*Wikipedia*: Librarians' Perspectives on Its Use
as a Reference Source." *Reference & User Services Quarterly,*
vol. 53, no. 2, 2013, pp. 155-63. *Academic Search
Complete,* go.galegroup.com.eduproxy.tc-library.org:8080/
ps/i.do?id=GALE%7CA361943129.

Tardy, Christine M. "Writing for the World: *Wikipedia* as an
Introduction to Academic Writing." *English Teaching Forum,*
vol. 48, no. 1, 2010, pp. 12+. *ERIC,* eric.ed.gov/?q=Writing+
for+the+World%3a+Wikipedia+%09as+an+Introduction+to+
Academic+Writing&id=EJ914884.

"Wiki." *Encyclopaedia Britannica,* 2014, www.britannica.com/
topic/wiki.

Signed letter to the editor in a monthly magazine

Article in an online encyclopedia

Unsigned document within a website

James 15

"*Wikipedia* Education Program." *Wikipedia,* 10 Mar. 2016,
      5:43, wikimediafoundation.org/wiki/Wikipedia_
      Education_Program.

Wilson, Jodi L. "Proceed with Extreme Caution: Citation to
      Wikipedia in Light of Contributor Demographics and
      Content Policies." *Vanderbilt Journal of Entertainment
      & Technology Law,* vol. 16, no. 4, 2014, pp. 857-908.
      Academic Search Complete, web.a.ebscohost.com.ezproxy.
      cul.columbia.edu/ehost/detail/detail?vid=4&sid=14afe0c2-
      3351-4754-93dc-2371d2724d5d.

Directory of APA In-Text Citations

Directory of APA Reference List Entries

PRINT SOURCES: *Entries for Articles*

Articles in Scholarly Journals

Articles in Magazines and Newspapers

PRINT SOURCES: *Entries for Books*

Authors

Editions, Multivolume Works, and Forewords

CHAPTER 48

APA Documentation Style

48a Using APA Style

APA style* is used extensively in the social sciences. APA documentation has three parts: *parenthetical references in the body of the paper*, a *reference list*, and optional *content footnotes*.

1 Parenthetical References

APA documentation uses short parenthetical references in the body of the essay keyed to an alphabetical list of references at the end of the essay. A typical parenthetical reference consists of the author's last name (followed by a comma) and the year of publication.

> Many people exhibit symptoms of depression after the death of a pet (Russo, 2016).

If the author's name appears in an introductory phrase, include the year of publication in parentheses immediately following the author's name.

> According to Russo (2016), many people exhibit symptoms of depression after the death of a pet.

When quoting directly, include the page number, preceded by **p.** in parentheses after the quotation.

> According to Weston (2015), children from one-parent homes read at "a significantly lower level than those from two-parent homes" (p. 58).

Note: A long quotation (forty words or more) is not set in quotation marks. It is set as a block, and the entire quotation is double-spaced and indented one-half inch from the left margin. Parenthetical documentation is placed one space after the final punctuation.

---

*APA documentation format follows the guidelines set in the *Publication Manual of the American Psychological Association*, 7th ed. Washington, DC: APA, 2020.

Sample APA In-Text Citations

1. A Work by a Single Author

Many college students suffer from sleep deprivation (Anton, 2009).

2. A Work by Two Authors

There is growing concern over the use of psychological testing in elementary schools (Albright & Glennon, 2013).

3. A Work by Three or More Authors

If a work has three or more authors, cite only the first author followed by **et al.** ("and others") and the year.

(Sparks et al., 2015)

4. Works by Authors with the Same Last Name

If your reference list includes works by two or more authors with the same last name, use each author's initials in all in-text citations.

Both F. Bor (2013) and S. D. Bor (2012) concluded that no further study was needed.

5. A Work by a Group Author

If the name of a group author is long, abbreviate it in square brackets after the full name in the first citation, and subsequently use the abbreviation alone.

Close-Up   CITING WORKS BY TWO AUTHORS

When referring to two authors in the text of your essay, join the names with **and**.

According to Albright and Glen (2013). . . .

Parenthetical references (as well as reference list entries) require an **ampersand (&)**.

(Albright & Glen, 2013)

First Reference

(National Institute of Mental Health [NIMH], 2015)

Subsequent Reference

(NIMH, 2015)

6. A Work with No Listed Author

If a work has no listed author, cite the title (followed by a comma) and the year. (If the title is long, use a shortened version of the title.) Use quotation marks around titles of periodical articles and chapters of books; use italics for titles of books, periodicals, brochures, reports, and the like.

("New Immigration," 2014)

7. A Personal Communication

Cite letters, memos, telephone conversations, personal interviews, emails, messages from electronic bulletin boards, and so on only in the text of your essay—*not* in the reference list.

(R. Takaki, personal communication, October 17, 2015)

8. An Indirect Source

Cogan and Howe offer very different interpretations of the problem (as cited in Swenson, 2015).

9. A Specific Part of a Source

Use abbreviations for the words *page* (**p.**), and *pages* (**pp.**), but spell out *chapter* and *section*.

These theories have an interesting history (Lee, 2013, Chapter 2).

10. An Electronic Source

To cite a specific part of an electronic source that does not show page numbers, use the paragraph number preceded by the abbreviation **para**.

Conversation at the dinner table is an example of a family ritual (Kulp, 2015, para. 3).

In the case of an electronic source that has multiple sections, cite the heading of the section in which the material is located. To be more precise, cite both the section and the paragraph number within the section.

> Healthy eating is a never-ending series of free choices (Shapiro, 2016,
>
> Introduction section, para. 2).

11. Two or More Works within the Same Parenthetical Reference

List works by different authors in alphabetical order, separated by semicolons.

> This theory is supported by several studies (Barson & Roth, 2005; Rose,
>
> 2010; Tedesco, 2014).

List two or more works by the same author or authors in order of date of publication (separated by commas), with the earliest date first.

> This theory is supported by several studies (Rhodes & Dollek, 2011, 2013,
>
> 2015).

For two or more works by the same author published in the same year, designate the work whose title comes first alphabetically *a*, the one whose title comes next *b*, and so on; repeat the year in each citation.

> This theory is supported by several studies (Shapiro, 2014a, 2014b).

12. A Table or Figure

If you use or adapt a table or figure from a source, give credit to the author in a note at the bottom of the table or figure. Also include the work in the reference list.

> *Note.* From "Predictors of Employment and Earnings Among JOBS
>
> Participants," by P. A. Neenan and D. K. Orthner, 1996, *Social Work Research,*
>
> *20*(4), p. 233 (https://doi.org/10.1093/swr/20.4.228). Copyright 1996 by
>
> the National Association of Social Workers.

② Reference List

The **reference list** gives the publication information for all the sources you cite. It should appear at the end of your essay on a new numbered page titled **References** in bold. Entries in the reference list should be arranged alphabetically. Double-space within and between reference list entries. The first line of each entry should start at the left margin, with the second and subsequent lines indented one-half inch. (**See 12b** for full manuscript guidelines.)

APA PRINT SOURCES Entries for Articles

Article citations include the author's name (last name first); the date of publication (in parentheses); the title of the article; the title of the periodical (italicized); the volume number (italicized); the issue number, if any (in parentheses); and the inclusive page numbers (including all digits). Figure 48.1 below shows where you can find this information.

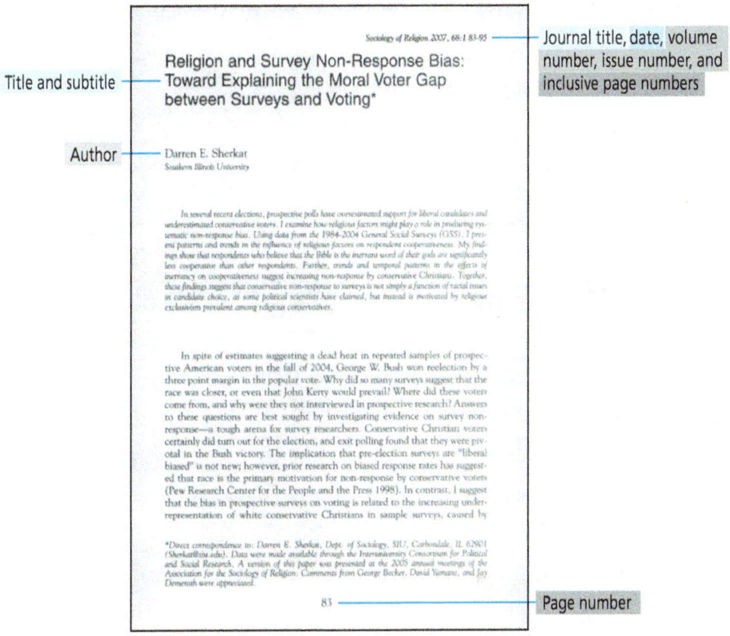

Sociology of Religion 2007, 68:1 83-95

Religion and Survey Non-Response Bias: Toward Explaining the Moral Voter Gap between Surveys and Voting*

Darren E. Sherkat
Southern Illinois University

In several recent elections, prospective polls have overestimated support for liberal candidates and underestimated conservative voters. I examine how religious factors might play a role in producing systematic non-response bias. Using data from the 1984-2004 General Social Surveys (GSS), I present patterns and trends in the influence of religious factors on respondent cooperativeness. My findings show that respondents who believe that the Bible is the inerrant word of their gods are significantly less cooperative than other respondents. Further, trends and temporal patterns in the effects of inerrancy on cooperativeness suggest increasing non-response by conservative Christians. Together, these findings suggest that conservative non-response to surveys is not simply a function of racial issues in candidate choice, as some political scientists have claimed, but instead is motivated by religious exclusivism prevalent among religious conservatives.

In spite of estimates suggesting a dead heat in repeated samples of prospective American voters in the fall of 2004, George W. Bush won reelection by a three point margin in the popular vote. Why did so many surveys suggest that the race was closer, or even that John Kerry would prevail? Where did these voters come from, and why were they not interviewed in prospective research? Answers to these questions are best sought by investigating evidence on survey non-response—a tough arena for survey researchers. Conservative Christian voters certainly did turn out for the election, and exit polling found that they were pivotal in the Bush victory. The implication that pre-election surveys are "liberal biased" is not new; however, prior research on biased response rates has suggested that race is the primary motivation for non-response by conservative voters (Pew Research Center for the People and the Press 1998). In contrast, I suggest that the bias in prospective surveys on voting is related to the increasing under-representation of white conservative Christians in sample surveys, caused by

**Direct correspondence to: Darren E. Sherkat, Dept. of Sociology, SIU, Carbondale, IL 62901 (Sherkat@siu.edu). Data were made available through the Interuniversity Consortium for Political and Social Research. A version of this paper was presented at the 2005 annual meetings of the Association for the Sociology of Religion. Comments from George Becker, David Yamane, and Jay Demerath were appreciated.*

83

FIGURE 48.1 First page of an article showing the location of the information needed for documentation. © Association for the Sociology of Religion.

Author's last name | **Initials** | **Date of publication** (in parentheses) | **Title of article** (only first word of title and subtitle capitalized)

Sherkat, D. E. (2007). Religion and survey non-response bias: Toward explaining the moral voter gap between surveys and voting. *Sociology of Religion*, *68*(1), 83–95.

Title of periodical (italicized; all major words captalized) | **Volume number** (italicized) | **Issue number** (in parentheses) | **Inclusive page numbers** (include all digits)

Capitalize the first word of the article's title and subtitle as well as any proper nouns. Do not underline or italicize the title of the article or enclose it in quotation marks. Give the periodical title in full, and capitalize all words except articles, prepositions, and conjunctions of fewer than four letters. Omit the abbreviation **p.** or **pp.** when referring to page numbers in periodicals.

Articles in Scholarly Journals

1. An Article in a Scholarly Journal without an Issue Number

Gentile, D., Bender, P., & Anderson, C. (2017, May). Violent video game effects on salivary cortisol, arousal, and aggressive thoughts in children. *Computers in Human Behavior, 70*, 39–43.

2. An Article in a Scholarly Journal with an Issue Number

Zell, E., Krizan, Z., & Teeter, S. R. (2015). Evaluating gender similarities and differences using metasynthesis. *American Psychologist, 70*(1), 10–20.

Note: Do not leave a space between the volume and issue numbers.

3. A Book Review in a Scholarly Journal

A review should include a description of the reviewed work in brackets immediately following the title of the review.

Gilbert, S. (2008). Coming of age and joining the cult of thinness [Review of the book *The cult of thinness,* by Sharlene Nagy Hesse-Biber]. *Psychology of Women Quarterly, 32*(2), 221–222.

Articles in Magazines and Newspapers

4. A Magazine Article

Drevitch, G. (2014, May–June). Pop psychology. *Psychology Today, 47*(3), 40.

5. A Newspaper Article

If an article appears on nonconsecutive pages, give all page numbers, separated by commas (for example, **A1, A14**). If the article appears on consecutive pages, indicate the full range of pages (for example, **A7–A9**).

Jargon, J. (2010, December 27). On McDonald's menu: Variety, caution. *The Wall Street Journal,* A1, A14.

6. A Newspaper Editorial (Unsigned)

An editorial with no author should be listed by title, followed by the label **Editorial** in brackets.

The plight of the underinsured [Editorial]. (2008, June 12). *The New York Times,* A30.

7. A Letter to the Editor of a Newspaper

> Mania, M. (2015, February 19). Superfluous selfie sticks [Letter to the
> editor]. *The New York Times*, A24.

APA PRINT SOURCES Entries for Books

Book citations include the author's name (last name first); the year of publication (in parentheses); the book title (italicized); and the publisher. Figures 48.2 and 48.3 on page 472 show where you can find this information.

Capitalize only the first word of the title and subtitle and any proper nouns. Include any additional necessary information—edition, report number, or volume number, for example—in parentheses after the title. For the publisher, write out in full the names of associations, corporations, and university presses. Include the words **Book** and **Press**, but do not include terms such as **Co.** or **Inc**.

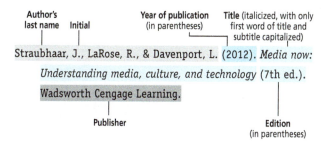

Author's last name | Initial | Year of publication (in parentheses) | Title (italicized, with only first word of title and subtitle capitalized)

Straubhaar, J., LaRose, R., & Davenport, L. (2012). *Media now: Understanding media, culture, and technology* (7th ed.). Wadsworth Cengage Learning.

Publisher | Edition (in parentheses)

Authors

8. A Book with One Author

> Oatley, K. (2011). *Such stuff as dreams: The psychology of fiction*. John
> Wiley & Sons.

9. A Book with More Than One Author

List up to twenty authors by last name and initials, using an ampersand (&) to connect the final two names. For more than twenty authors, insert an ellipsis (three spaced periods) after the nineteenth author and add the final author's name.

> Wolfinger, D., Knable, P., Richards, H. L., & Silberger, R. (2007). *The
> chronically unemployed*. Berman Press.

10. A Book with No Listed Author or Editor

> *Teaching in a wired classroom*. (2012). Drexel Press.

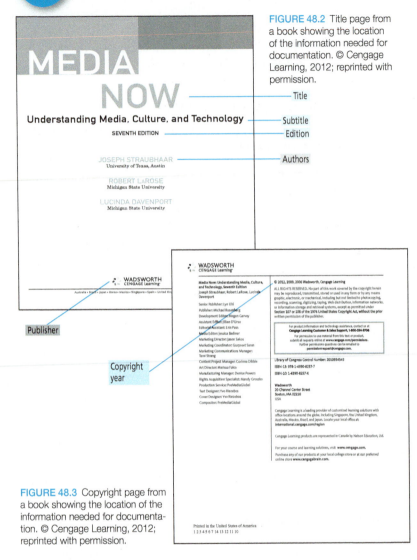

FIGURE 48.2 Title page from a book showing the location of the information needed for documentation. © Cengage Learning, 2012; reprinted with permission.

— Title
— Subtitle
— Edition
— Authors

Publisher

Copyright year

FIGURE 48.3 Copyright page from a book showing the location of the information needed for documentation. © Cengage Learning, 2012; reprinted with permission.

11. A Book with a Group Author

When the author and the publisher are the same, do not repeat the name as the publisher at the end of the citation.

> League of Women Voters of the United States. (2008). *Local league handbook.*

12. An Edited Book

> Wienroth, M., & Rodrigues, E. (Eds.). (2015). *Knowing new biotechnologies: Social aspects of technological convergence.* Routledge.

Editions, Multivolume Works, and Forewords

13. A Volume in a Work of Several Volumes

O'Connor, E. E., & Garofalo, L. (2010). *Documenting Latin America:*

Gender, race, and nation (Vol. 1). Pearson.

14. The Foreword, Preface, or Afterword of a Book

Taylor, T. (1979). Preface. In B. B. Ferencz, *Less than slaves* (pp. ii–ix).

Harvard University Press.

Parts of Books

15. A Selection from an Anthology

Give inclusive page numbers preceded by **pp.** (in parentheses) after the title of the anthology. The title of the selection is not enclosed in quotation marks.

Lorde, A. (1984). Age, race, and class. In P. S. Rothenberg (Ed.), *Racism and*

sexism: An integrated study (pp. 352–360). St. Martin's Press.

Note: If you cite two or more selections from the same anthology, give the full citation for the anthology in each entry.

16. An Article in a Reference Book

Determinism. (2006). In P. Edwards & D. M. Borchert (Eds.), *The encyclopedia*

of philosophy (2nd ed., Vol. 2, pp. 359–373). Macmillan.

Government and Technical Reports

17. A Government Report

National Institute of Mental Health. (2007). *Motion pictures and violence: A*

summary report of research (DHHS Publication No. ADM 91-22187). U.S.

Department of Health and Human Services, National Institutes of Health.

18. A Technical Report

Attali, Y., & Powers, D. (2008). *Effect of immediate feedback and revision*

on psychometric properties of open-ended GRE® subject test items

(ETS GRE Board Research Report No. 04-05). Educational Testing

Service.

APA ENTRIES FOR MISCELLANEOUS PRINT SOURCES

Letters

19. A Personal Letter

References to unpublished personal letters, like references to all other personal communications, should be included only in the text of the essay, not in the reference list.

20. A Published Letter

Joyce, J. (1931). Letter to Louis Gillet. In Richard Ellmann, *James Joyce*
(p. 631). Oxford University Press.

APA ENTRIES FOR OTHER SOURCES

Television Series, Films, Audio Recordings,
Interviews, Speeches, and Software

21. A Television Series

Soloway, J., & Sperling, S. (Executive Producers). (2014–2019).
Transparent [TV series]. Topple; Picrow; Amazon Studios.

22. A Television Series Episode

Bedard, B. (Writer) & Soloway, J. (Writer & Director). (2014 September 26).
Best new girl (Season 1, Episode 8) [TV series episode]. In J. Soloway
& Sperling, S. (Executive Producers), *Transparent*. Topple; Picrow;
Amazon Studios.

23. A Film

DuVernay, A. (Director). (2014). *Selma* [Film]. Pathé; Harpo Films; Plan B
Entertainment; Cloud Eight Films; Ingenious Media.

24. An Audio Recording

Beck. (2014). Don't let it go [Song]. On *Morning phase*. Capitol Records;
Fonograph.

Mozart, W. A. (2008). Requiem mass in D minor, K. 626 [Song recorded by
Royal Philharmonic Orchestra]. On *Mozart: Requiem Mass in D Minor,
K. 626*. (Original work published 1791)

25. A Recorded Interview

Parks, R. (1956, April). *Commentary of a Black Southern Bus Rider*
[Interview]. American Archive of Public Broadcasting. https://
americanarchive.org/catalog/cpb-accip_28-kw57d2qp45

26. A Recorded Speech

Kennedy, J. F. (1961, January 9). *The city upon a hill* [Speech audio
recording]. John F. Kennedy Presidential Library and Museum.
https://www.jfklibrary.org/learn/about-jfk/historic-speeches/the-
city-upon-a-hill-speech

27. Software or an App

Adobe. (2019). *InDesign* (Version 15.0) [Computer software]. https://
www.adobe.com/products/indesign.html

Duolingo. (2020). *Duolingo ABC - Learn to Read* (Version 1.0.11) [Mobile
app]. App Store. https://apple.apple.com/us/app/duolingo-abc-
learn-to-read/id1440502568

APA ELECTRONIC SOURCES   Entries for Sources from
Internet Sites

APA guidelines for documenting electronic sources focus on web sources,
which often do not include all the bibliographic information that print
sources do. For example, web sources may not include page numbers. At a
minimum, a web citation should have a title, a date (the date of publication,
update, or retrieval), and a Digital Object Identifier (DOI) (when available)
or an electronic address (URL). If possible, also include the author(s) of a
source. Figure 48.4 shows where you can find this information.

Both DOIs and URLs should be formatted as hyperlinks beginning with
"http://" or "https://". Do not add a period at the end of a hyperlink.

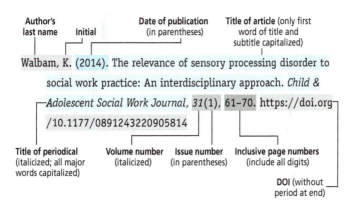

Internet-Specific Sources

28. An Online Article Also Published in a Print Source

If the article has a DOI, do not include the retrieval date or the URL. Always
include the volume number (italicized) and the issue number (in parentheses,
if available).

Rutledge, P. C., Park, A., & Sher, K. J. (2008). 21st birthday drinking:
Extremely extreme. *Journal of Consulting and Clinical Psychology,*
76(3), 511–516. https://doi.org/10.1037/0022-006X.76.3.511

Journal title
Date
Volume number
Inclusive page numbers
DOI
Title and subtitle
Author

Child Adolesc Soc Work J (2014) 31:61–70
DOI 10.1007/s10560-013-0308-2

The Relevance of Sensory Processing Disorder to Social Work Practice: An Interdisciplinary Approach

Katherine M. Walbam

Published online: 7 June 2013
© Springer Science+Business Media New York 2013

Abstract Sensory processing disorder (SPD) is a disruption in the organization of sensory input, and affects up to three million children in the United States. SPD can have a serious impact on the ways that children behave, play, and learn, and yet, it may be overlooked or misunderstood by social work practitioners. The purpose of this article is to inform social work practice regarding SPD, strengthening the biological component of biopsychosocial assessment. After an introduction to the disorder, this article discusses differential diagnosis and practice implications, and concludes with a statement on interdisciplinary treatment.

Keywords Sensory processing disorder · Social work · Children · Interdisciplinary · Differential diagnosis

Sara is a 4 year old girl. Her parents have a hard time getting her to preschool in the mornings because Sara cries and fights with them about getting dressed. She doesn't like the way her shirt feels, and the seams on her socks make her scream. She also has a hard time with breakfast—her parents call her a picky eater, and Sara won't touch most breakfast foods. Oatmeal and eggs are slimy, cereal is too crunchy. Bagels are ok. Sara's mother worries about feeding her daughter a plain bagel every morning, but some days it is just too hard to continue arguing about it. It feels like a constant struggle for Sara to even begin her day. And then she gets to preschool, where the problem only becomes magnified.

Sensory processing disorder (SPD) is a disruption in the organization of sensory input, which shapes our perception of the world and impacts our responses to it. Children with SPD may either get so much information about their world that it

K. M. Walbam (✉)
Simmons College, 300 Fenway, Boston, MA 02115, USA
e-mail: katherine.walbam@simmons.edu

Springer

FIGURE 48.4 Part of an online article showing the location of the information needed for documentation.

29. An Article in an Internet-Only Journal

If the article does not have a DOI, include the URL. Always include the URL (when available) for the archived version of the article. No retrieval date is needed for content that is not likely to be changed or updated, such as a journal article.

> Hill, S. A., & Laugharne, R. (2006). Patient choice survey in general adult psychiatry. *Psychiatry On-Line*. http://www.priory.com/psych/cornwall.pdf

30. A Webpage with an Individual Author

> Moores, S. (2019, November 7). *Pregnant safe sources of omega-3 fats*. Eatright.org. https://eatright.org/health/pregnancy/what-to-eat-when-expecting/pregnant-safe-sources-of-omega-3-fats

31. A Webpage with a Group Author (No Date)

A webpage with no date should include the abbreviation **n.d.** (for no date). If the group author and website are the same, do not repeat the name in the citation.

Investopedia. (n.d.) *Financial analysis*. Retrieved February 16, 2020, from

> https://www.investopedia.com/financial-analysis-4427788

32. An Email

As with all other personal communications, citations for email should be included only in the text of your essay, not in the reference list.

33. A Blog Article or Entry

List the author's name—or, if that is not available, the author's screen name.

Sullivan, A. (2015, February 2). The online conversation that's dying out.

> *The Dish*. http://dish.andrewsullivan.com/2015/02/02/the-online-
>
> conversation-thats-dying-out/

34. A Comment on an Online Article or Post

List the name or username of the commenter as the author. Include the date of the comment, as well as the comment title or up to the first twenty words of the comment. Then, in brackets, provide the information about the original article as shown. If possible, include the URL of the comment. If not, include the URL of the article or post.

Barbara in SC. (2020, January 15). How much more data do climate

> change deniers require to know that we are creating a nightmare
>
> environment for our [Comment on the article "2019 was the
>
> second-hottest year ever, closing out the warmest decade"]. *The New*
>
> *York Times*. https://www.nytimes.com/interactive/2020/01/15/
>
> climate/hottest-year-2019.html

35. An Online Video

Edutopia. (2020, April 10). *Learning to measure the size of a problem*.

> [Video]. YouTube. https://www.youtube.com/watch?v=MufiPWW_uwk

36. A Podcast Episode

Koenig, S. (Host). (2014). The alibi [Audio podcast episode]. In *Serial*.

> WBEZ Chicago. https://serialpodcast.org/season-one/1/the-alibi

37. A Social Networking Post (Facebook post, tweet, etc.)

Provide up to the first twenty words of a Facebook, Twitter, Instagram, or similar post. For a tweet, begin with the author's listed name, followed by the author's Twitter handle in brackets (as in the first example below).

Muna, D. [@DemitriMuna]. (2014, February 21). *Opposed to GM foods?*

> *Stop eating grapefruit; they are genetically modified. There was no*

such thing as a grapefruit before [Tweet]. Twitter. https://twitter
.com/demitrimuna/status/569349630887985152

Psychology Today. (2020, April 22). *Even in the best of times, it's a
struggle to push through a difficult or unpleasant task, but a new*
[Thumbnail with link attached] [Status update]. Facebook. https://
www.facebook.com/psychologytoday/posts/10157436129563845

38. An Online Forum Post

Include the title of the forum post or up to the first twenty words of the post itself.

EvolMedGen. (2020, March 22). *Genetic adaptations can lose their benefit
over time* [Online forum post]. Reddit. https://www.reddit.com/r/
science/comments/fn006y/genetic_adaptations_can_lose_their_
benefit_over_time/

Magazine and Newspaper Articles

39. A Magazine Article

Rodrick, S. (2020, March 26). Greta's world. *Rolling Stone.* https://www
.rollingstone.com/politics/politics-features/greta-thunberg-climate-
crisis-cover-965949/

40. A Newspaper Article

Lowrey, A. (2014, February 20). Study finds greater income inequality
in nation's thriving cities. *The New York Times.* https://www
.nytimes/2013/02/20/business/economy/study-finds-greater-
income-inequality-in-nations-thriving-cities/html

EXERCISE 48.1

Each of these notes identifies a source used in an essay about mental illness and homelessness. Determine which information is required to cite each source. Then, following the guidelines and proper format for APA documentation, create a parenthetical reference for each source, and then create a reference list, arranging sources in the proper order. Be sure to format source information correctly, adding quotation marks and italics as needed.

1. An article called A Primary Care—Public Health Partnership Addressing Homelessness, Serious Mental Illness, and Health Disparities. The authors are listed as Lara Carson Weinstein, Marianna D. LaNoue, James D. Plumb, Hannah King, Brianna Stein, and Sam Tsemberis. The article appears on pages 279–287 of a scholarly journal called Journal of the American Board of Family Medicine. The journal is specifically described as Volume 26, Issue 3, and it was published in May of 2013. You accessed the journal through PubMed, an online

database. The DOI for the article is listed as https://doi.org/10.3122/jabfm.2013.03.120239.

2. Pages 60–64 of a book called Homelessness, Housing, and Mental Illness. The author is Russell K. Schutt. The book was published by Harvard University Press in Boston, Massachusetts, in March of 2011. You referred to the print version of the book.

3. A newspaper article titled Mental Disorders Keep Thousands of Homeless on Streets. The article was written by Rick Jervis and published by USA Today. When you accessed the article, it was available at this URL: <https://www.usatoday.com/story/news/nation/2014/08/27/mental-health-homeless-series/14255283/>. It was posted and last updated on August 27, 2014.

4. A podcast episode titled Dr. Robert L. Okin on Silent Voices: People with Mental Disorders on the Street. The episode is part of a podcast series called The Diane Rehm Show produced by WAMU 88.5, American University Radio. The host is Diane Rehm. When you accessed this podcast, it was streaming at this URL: <http://thedianerehmshow.org/shows/2014-11-24/dr_robert_l_okin_silent_voices_people_with_mental_disorders_on_the_street>. It was posted and last updated on November 24, 2014. You listened to it today.

5. A tweet by the National Homeless Coalition (@Ntl_Homeless) that reads "A heart-wrenching snapshot of the grave physical and mental health conditions of chronically homeless people in LA." The tweet includes a thumbnail with a link to an article from the Los Angeles Times. The tweet was posted on October 31, 2016 and is available at this URL: https://twitter.com/Ntl_Homeless/status/793231121114865664.

3 Content Footnotes

APA format permits content notes, indicated by **superscripts** in the text. Each footnote should appear at the bottom of the page where it is discussed. Alternatively, the footnotes may be listed on a separate numbered page, titled **Footnotes**, after the reference list and before any appendices. If you include the footnotes within the body of your paper, single-space the notes. If you include the footnotes on a separate page, double-space all notes, indenting the first line of each note one-half inch and beginning subsequent lines flush left. Number the notes with superscripts that correspond to the numbers in your text.

48b APA-Style Manuscript Guidelines

Social science essays label sections with headings. Sections may include an introduction (untitled), followed by headings such as **Background**, **Method**, **Results**, and **Conclusion**. Each section of a social science essay is a complete unit with a beginning and an end so that it can be read separately and still make sense out of context. The body of the essay may include charts, graphs, maps, photographs, flowcharts, or tables.

CHECKLIST

Typing Your Essay

When you type your essay, use the student essay in **48c** as your model.

❑ Leave one-inch margins on all sides. Double-space your essay throughout.

❑ Indent the first line of every paragraph one-half inch from the left-hand margin. If you include footnotes on a separate page at the end of your paper, indent those in the same way as well.

❑ Set off a **long quotation** (more than forty words) in a block format by indenting the entire quotation one-half inch from the left-hand margin. Do not indent the first line further.

❑ Number all pages consecutively. Each page should have a **page header** that includes the page number (flush right) and, if required by your instructor, a **running head** (in all capital letters, flush left).

See 11b

❑ Center major headings, and type them with uppercase and lowercase letters. Place headings that are subheadings of a major heading flush left, typed with uppercase and lowercase letters. Use boldface for these levels of headings.

❑ Arrange the pages of the essay in the following order:

  ❑ **Title page** (page 1) with a page header, the title, your name, your affiliation (department and school), the course number and name, the instructor's name, and the assignment due date.

  ❑ **Abstract and keywords** if required by your instructor (page 2)

  ❑ **Text of essay** (beginning on page 3, or on page 2 if an abstract is not included)

  ❑ **Reference list** (new page)

  ❑ **Content footnotes** (new page, if not already included in the body of your paper)

  ❑ **Appendices**, if included (start each appendix on a new page)

See 48a

❑ Citations should follow APA documentation style.

CHECKLIST

Using Visuals

APA style distinguishes between two types of visuals: **tables** and **figures** (charts, graphs, photographs, and diagrams). Tables and figures should either appear on the pages where they are discussed or on separate pages after the reference list.

Tables

Number all **tables** consecutively. Each table should have a *number* and a *title*.

❑ The **number** consists of the word **Table** and an arabic numeral (both in bold), typed flush left above the table.

❑ Double-space and type a brief explanatory **title** for each table (in italics) flush left below the label. Capitalize the first letters of principal words of the title.

Table 7

Frequency of Negative Responses of Dorm Students to Questions Concerning

Alcohol Consumption

Figures

Number all **figures** consecutively. Each figure should have a *number* and a *title*.

❑ The **number** consists of the word ***Figure*** and an arabic numeral (both in bold), typed flush left above the figure.

❑ Double-space and type a brief expanatory **title** for each figure (in italics) flush left below the label. Capitalize the first letters of principal words of the title.

Figure 1

Duration of Responses Measured in Seconds

Note: If necessary, include a note below a table or a figure for clarification or explanation. If you use a table or figure from an outside source, include full source information at the end of the note. See the APA website (apastyle.apa.org) for more details about properly formatting visuals.

CHECKLIST

Preparing the APA Reference List

When typing your reference list, follow these guidelines:

❑ Begin the reference list on a new page after the last page of text, numbered as the next page of the essay.

❑ Center the title **References** in bold at the top of the page.

❑ List the items in the reference list alphabetically (with author's last name first).

❑ Type the first line of each entry at the left margin. Indent subsequent lines one-half inch.

❑ Double-space the reference list within and between entries.

Close-Up ARRANGING ENTRIES IN THE APA REFERENCE LIST

● Single-author entries precede multiple-author entries that begin with the same name.

Field, S. (2015).

Field, S., & Levitt, M. P. (2012).

(continued)

ARRANGING ENTRIES IN THE APA REFERENCE LIST *(continued)*

- Entries by the same author or authors are arranged according to date of publication, starting with the earliest date.

  Ruthenberg, H., & Rubin, R. (2013).

  Ruthenberg, H., & Rubin, R. (2015).

- Entries with the same author or authors and date of publication are arranged alphabetically according to title. Lowercase letters (*a, b, c,* and so on) that indicate the order of publication are placed within parentheses.

  Wolk, E. M. (2016a). Analysis . . .

  Wolk, E. M. (2016b). Hormonal . . .

48c Model APA-Style Research Paper

The following student essay, "Sleep Deprivation in College Students," uses APA documentation style. It includes a title page, an abstract, a reference list, a table, and a bar graph.

½″

Page header

Sleep Deprivation in College Students

Title

Andrew J. Neale

Department of Psychology, University of Texas

PSYC 210: The Psychology of Learning

Dr. Reiss

March 12, 2015

Your name, affiliation (department and school), the course number and name, your instructor's name, and the assignment due date

SLEEP DEPRIVATION IN COLLEGE STUDENTS | 1″ | 2

Abstract

A survey was conducted of 50 first-year college students in an introductory biology class. The survey consisted of five questions regarding the causes and results of sleep deprivation and specifically addressed the students' study methods and the grades they received on the fall midterm. The study's hypothesis was that although students believe that forgoing sleep to study will yield better grades, sleep deprivation may actually cause a decrease in performance. The study concluded that while only 43% of the students who received either an A or a B on the fall midterm deprived themselves of sleep in order to cram for the test, 90% of those who received a C or a D were sleep deprived.

Keywords: sleep disorders, sleep deprivation, grade performance, grades and sleep, forgoing sleep

Include a page header on every page. Check with your instructor to see if a running head is required.

An abstract is a brief summary of your paper in a single paragraph (not indented). Check with your instructor to see if an abstract is required.

An optional list of keywords helps readers find your work in databases.

Center and boldface heading

SLEEP DEPRIVATION IN COLLEGE STUDENTS 3

Sleep Deprivation in College Students

For many college students, sleep is a luxury they feel they cannot afford. Bombarded with tests and assignments and limited by a 24-hour day, students often attempt to make up time by doing without sleep. Unfortunately, students may actually hurt their academic performance by failing to get enough sleep. According to several psychological and medical studies, sleep deprivation can lead to memory loss and health problems, both of which can harm a student's academic performance.

Background

Sleep is often overlooked as an essential part of a healthy lifestyle. Each day, millions of Americans wake up without having gotten enough sleep. This fact indicates that for many people, sleep is viewed as a luxury rather than a necessity. As National Sleep Foundation Executive Director Richard L. Gelula observes, "Some of the problems we face as a society—from road rage to obesity—may be linked to lack of sleep or poor sleep" (National Sleep Foundation, 2002, para. 3). In fact, according to the National Sleep Foundation (2012), sleep deprivation "jolts the immune system into action, reflecting the same type of immediate response shown during exposure to stress" (para. 1).

Sleep deprivation is particularly common among college students, many of whom have busy lives and are required to absorb a great deal of material before their exams. It is common for college students to take a quick nap between classes or fall asleep while studying in the library because they are sleep deprived. Approximately 44% of young adults experience daytime sleepiness at least a few days a month (National Sleep

SLEEP DEPRIVATION IN COLLEGE STUDENTS   4

Foundation, 2002, para. 6). In particular, many students are sleep deprived on the day of an exam because they stayed up all night studying. These students believe that if they read and review immediately before taking a test—even though this usually means losing sleep—they will remember more information and thus get better grades. However, this is not the case.

A study conducted by professors Mary Carskadon at Brown University in Providence, Rhode Island, and Amy Wolfson at the College of the Holy Cross in Worcester, Massachusetts, showed that high school students who got adequate sleep were more likely to do well in their classes (Carpenter, 2001). According to this study, students who went to bed early on both weeknights and weekends earned mainly A's and B's. The students who received D's and F's averaged about 35 minutes less sleep per day than the high achievers (as cited in Carpenter, 2001). The results of this study suggest that sleep is associated with high academic achievement.

Once students reach college, however, many believe that sleep is a luxury they can do without. For example, students believe that if they use the time they would normally sleep to study, they will do better on exams. A survey of 144 undergraduate students in introductory psychology classes disproved this assumption. According to this study, "long sleepers," those individuals who slept 9 or more hours out of a 24-hour day, had significantly higher grade point averages (GPAs) than "short sleepers," individuals who slept less than 7 hours out of a 24-hour day. Therefore, contrary to the belief of many college students, more sleep is often associated with a high GPA (Kelly et al., 2001).

Student uses past tense when discussing other researchers' studies

As cited in indicates an indirect source.

Et al. indicates a source with three or more authors.

SLEEP DEPRIVATION IN COLLEGE STUDENTS   5

Many students believe that sleep deprivation is not the cause of their poor performance, but rather that a host of other factors is to blame. A study in the *Journal of American College Health* tested the effect that several factors have on a student's performance in school, as measured by students' GPAs. Some of the factors considered were exercise, sleep, nutritional habits, social support, time management techniques, stress management techniques, and spiritual health (Trockel et al., 2000). The most significant correlation discovered in the study was between GPA and the sleep habits of students. Sleep deprivation had a more negative impact on GPAs than any other factor (Trockel et al., 2000).

Despite these findings, many students continue to believe that they will be able to remember more material if they do not sleep before an exam. They fear that sleeping will interfere with their ability to retain information. Pilcher and Walters (1997), however, showed that sleep deprivation actually impaired learning skills. In this study, one group of students was sleep deprived, while the other got 8 hours of sleep before the exam. The students in each group estimated how well they had performed on the exam. The students who were sleep deprived believed their performance on the test was better than did those who were not sleep deprived, but actually the performance of the sleep-deprived students was significantly worse than that of those who got 8 hours of sleep prior to the test (Pilcher & Walters, 1997, as cited in Bubolz et al., 2001). This study supports the hypothesis that sleep deprivation harms cognitive performance.

A survey of students in an introductory biology class at the University of Texas, which demonstrated the effects of

Student uses past tense when discussing his own research study sleep deprivation on academic performance, also supported the hypothesis that despite students' beliefs, forgoing sleep does not lead to better test scores.

Method

To determine the causes and results of sleep deprivation, a study of the relationship between sleep and test performance was conducted. Fifty first-year college students in an introductory biology class were surveyed, and their performance on the fall midterm was analyzed.

Each student was asked to complete a survey consisting of the following five questions about their sleep patterns and their performance on the fall midterm:

1. Do you regularly deprive yourself of sleep when studying for an exam?
2. Did you deprive yourself of sleep when studying for the fall midterm?
3. What was your grade on the exam?
4. Do you feel your performance was helped or harmed by the amount of sleep you had?
5. Will you deprive yourself of sleep when you study for the final exam?

To maintain confidentiality, the students were asked not to put their names on the survey. Also, to determine whether the students answered question 3 truthfully, the group grade distribution from the surveys was compared to the number of A's, B's, C's, and D's shown in the instructor's record of the test results. The two frequency distributions were identical.

Results

Analysis of the survey data indicated a significant difference between the grades of students who were sleep

Numbered list is indented ½" and set in block format

SLEEP DEPRIVATION IN COLLEGE STUDENTS   7

deprived and the grades of those who were not. The results of the survey are presented in Table 1.

Table 1 introduced

Table 1

Results of Survey of Students in University of Texas Introduction to Biology Class Examining the Relationship between Sleep Deprivation and Academic Performance

Table placed on page where it is discussed

Grade totals	Sleep deprived	Not sleep deprived	Usually sleep deprived	Improved	Harmed	Continue sleep deprivation?
A = 10	4	6	1	4	0	4
B = 20	9	11	8	8	1	8
C = 10	10	0	6	5	4	7
D = 10	8	2	2	1	3	2
Total	31	19	17	18	8	21

Table created by student; no documentation necessary

The grades in the class were curved so that out of 50 students, 10 received A's, 20 received B's, 10 received C's, and 10 received D's. For the purposes of this survey, an A or B on the exam indicates that the student performed well. A grade of C or D on the exam is considered a poor grade.

Of the 50 students in the class, 31 (or 62%) said they deprived themselves of sleep when studying for the fall midterm. Of these students, 17 (or 34% of the class) reported that they regularly deprive themselves of sleep before an exam.

Statistical findings in table discussed

Of the 31 students who said they deprived themselves of sleep when studying for the fall midterm, only 4 earned A's, and the majority of the A's in the class were received by those students who were not sleep deprived. Even more significant was the fact that of the 4 students who were sleep deprived and got A's, only one student claimed to usually be sleep deprived on the day of an exam. Thus, assuming the students who earn A's in a class do well in general, it is possible that sleep deprivation did not help or harm these students' grades. Not surprisingly, of the 4 students who received A's and were sleep deprived, all said they would continue this behavior pattern.

The majority of those who deprived themselves of sleep received B's and C's on the exam. A total of 20 students earned a grade of B on the exam. Of those students, only 9, or 18% of the class, said they were deprived of sleep when they took the test.

Students who said they were sleep deprived when they took the exam received the majority of the poor grades. Ten students got C's on the midterm, and of these 10 students, 100% said they were sleep deprived when they took the test. Of the 10 students (20% of the class) who got D's, 8 said they were sleep deprived. Figure 1 shows the significant relationship that was found between poor grades on the exam and sleep deprivation.

Figure 1 introduced

Conclusion

For many students, sleep is viewed as a luxury rather than as a necessity. Particularly during exam periods, students use the hours in which they would normally sleep to study. However, this behavior does not seem to be effective. The survey discussed here reveals a definite correlation between sleep deprivation and lower exam scores. In fact, the majority of students who performed well on the exam, earning either A's or B's, were not deprived of sleep. Therefore, students who choose studying over sleep should consider that

SLEEP DEPRIVATION IN COLLEGE STUDENTS   9

sleep deprivation may actually lead to impaired academic
performance.

Figure 1

*Results of a Survey of Students in a University of Texas
Introduction to Biology Class, Examining the Relationship
Between Sleep Deprivation and Academic Performance*

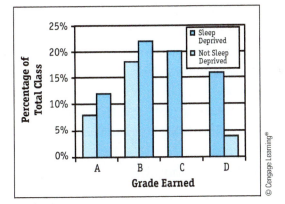

© Cengage Learning®

SLEEP DEPRIVATION IN COLLEGE STUDENTS   1"   10

References

Bubolz, W. C., Brown, F., & Soper, B. (2001). Sleep habits and patterns of college students: A preliminary study. *Journal of American College Health*, *50*(3), 131–135. https://doi.org/10.1080/07448480109596017

Carpenter, S. (2001). Sleep deprivation may be undermining teen health. *Monitor on Psychology*, *32*(9). http://www.apa.org/monitor/oct01/sleepteen.html

Kelly, W. E., Kelly, K. E., & Clanton, R. C. (2001). The relationship between sleep length and grade-point average among college students. *College Student Journal*, *35*(1), 84–90.

National Sleep Foundation. (2002, April 2). Epidemic of daytime sleepiness linked to increased feelings of anger, stress and pessimism. *ScienceBlog*. https://www3.scienceblog.com/community/older/archives/K/4/pub4460.html

National Sleep Foundation. (2012, July 1). *Sleep deprivation effect on the immune system mirrors physical stress*. https://www.sleepfoundation.org/articles/sleep-deprivation-effect-immune-system-mirrors-physical-stress

Trockel, M. T., Barnes, M. D., & Egget, D. L. (2000). Health-related variables and academic performance among first-year college students: Implications for sleep and other behaviors. *Journal of American College Health*, *49*(3), 125–131. https://doi.org/10.1080/07448480009596294

Center and boldface heading

Indent ½"

Double-space

Entries listed in alphabetical order

URL is provided for web citation that does not have a DOI

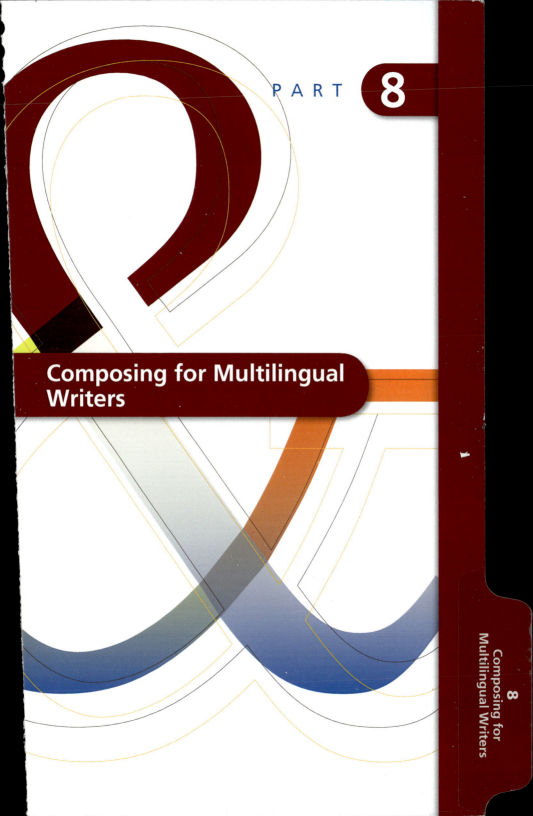

PART 8

Composing for Multilingual Writers

Composing for Multilingual Writers

Grammar and Style for Multilingual Writers

For multilingual writers (as for many native English writers), grammar can be a persistent problem. Grammatical knowledge in a second language usually develops slowly, with time and practice, and much about English is idiomatic (not subject to easy-to-learn rules). This chapter is designed to provide you with the tools you will need to address some of the most common grammatical problems multilingual writers face.

49a Using Verbs

1 Subject-Verb Agreement

English **verbs** change their form according to person, number, and tense. The verb in a sentence must **agree** with the subject in both person and number. Person refers to *who* or *what* is performing the action of the verb (for example, **I**, **you**, or someone else), and number refers to *how many* people or things are performing the action (one or more than one).

See Ch. 22

In English, the rules for **subject-verb agreement** are very important. Unless you use the correct person and number in the verbs in your sentences, you will confuse your English-speaking audience by communicating meanings you do not intend.

See 26a

Close-Up SUBJECT-VERB AGREEMENT

Follow these basic guidelines when selecting verbs for your sentences:

- If the subject consists of only one noun or pronoun, use a singular verb.

  He is at the park.

- If the subject consists of two or more nouns or pronouns connected with the word *and*, use a plural verb.

  Bob and Carol are at the park.

- If the subject contains both a singular and a plural noun or pronoun connected with the word *or*, the verb should agree with the noun that is nearer to it.

(continued)

SUBJECT-VERB AGREEMENT *(continued)*

Either <u>Bob</u> or the boys <u>are</u> at the park.
Either the boys or <u>Bob</u> <u>is</u> at the park.

Note: Don't be confused by phrases that come between the subject and the verb. The verb should agree with the subject of the sentence, not with a noun that appears within an intervening phrase.

The <u>woman</u> with all of the children <u>is</u> at the park.
The <u>coach</u>, as well as the players, <u>is</u> nervous.

For information on subject-verb agreement with **indefinite pronouns**, such as *each, everyone*, and *nobody*, see **26a4**.

② Verb Tense

See 22b

See 22a2

In English, the form of the verb changes to indicate **tense**—when the action of the verb takes place (in the past, present, or future). One problem that many nonnative speakers of English have with English verb tenses results from the large number of **irregular verbs** in English. For example, the first-person singular present tense of *be* is not "I be" but "I am," and the past tense is not "I beed" but "I was."

Note: Multilingual writers whose first language is Chinese, Japanese, Korean, Russian, Thai, or Vietnamese are especially likely to have difficulty with verb tenses.

 Close-Up CHOOSING THE SIMPLEST VERB FORMS

Some nonnative English speakers use verb forms that are more complicated than they need to be. They may do this because their native language uses more complicated verb forms than English does or because they "overcorrect" their verbs into complicated forms. Specifically, nonnative speakers tend to use progressive and perfect verb forms instead of simple verb forms. To communicate your ideas clearly to an English-speaking audience, choose the simplest possible verb form.

③ Auxiliary Verbs

The **auxiliary verbs** (also known as **helping verbs**) *be, have,* and *do* are used to create some present, past, and future forms of verbs in English: "<u>Julio</u> <u>is</u> taking a vacation"; "<u>I</u> <u>have been</u> tired lately"; "<u>He</u> <u>does</u> not <u>need</u> a license."

The auxiliary verbs *be, have,* and *do* change form to reflect the time frame of the action or situation and to agree with the subject.

Note: Multilingual writers whose first language is Arabic, Chinese, Creole, Haitian, or Russian may have difficulty with auxiliary verbs because their first language sometimes omits the *be* verb.

Close-Up AUXILIARY VERBS

Only auxiliary verbs, not the verbs they "help," change form to indicate person, number, and tense.

Present: We <u>have</u> to eat.

Past: We <u>had</u> to eat. (*not* "We had to ate.")

<u>Modal auxiliaries</u> (such as *can* and *should*) do not change form to indicate tense, person, or number.

See 20c1

EXERCISE 49.1

A student wrote the following two paragraphs as part of an essay for his composition class. He was asked to write about several interviews he conducted with people in his future profession, hotel management. The paragraphs contain errors in subject-verb agreement and verb tense, which the student's instructor underlined. Correct the underlined verbs by changing their form: begin by considering when the action took place, and then choose the simplest appropriate verb form to express that time. (Be sure to pay attention to the meaning and context of the sentences to determine which verb form is appropriate.)

In the past, when someone ▶(1) <u>ask</u> me why I was interested in the hotel business, I always ▶(2) <u>have</u> a hard time answering that question. I do not know exactly when and why I ▶(3) <u>decide</u> to be a hotel manager. The only reason I can think of is my father. In his current job, he ▶(4) <u>travel</u> a lot, and I have had a few chances to follow him and see other cities. Every time I went with him on a business trip, we ▶(5) <u>spended</u> the night in a hotel, and I was surprised at how much hotels ▶(6) <u>does</u> to satisfy their customers. All the employees are always friendly and polite. This gave me a positive image of hotels that made me ▶(7) <u>decided</u> that the hotel business would be right for me.

For this essay, I (8) <u>spended</u> almost two weeks interviewing department heads at a local Hilton Hotel. Mr. Andrew Plain, the person who (9) <u>spend</u> the most time with me, (10) <u>share</u> an experience related to when he first got into the business. One of his first jobs was to plan a wedding, and he (11) <u>feel</u> a lot of responsibility because he (12) <u>believe</u> that a wedding is a one-time life experience for most people. So he wanted to take care of everything and make sure that everything was on track. To prepare for the wedding, he (13) <u>need</u> to work almost every Sunday, and one night he even (14) <u>have</u> to sleep in his office to attend the early wedding ceremony the next morning. From my experience with this interview, I realized that the people who are interested in the hotel business (15) <u>needs</u> great dedication to their career.

4 Negative Verbs

The meaning of a verb may be made negative in English in a variety of ways, chiefly by adding the words *not* or *does not* to the verb (is, is *not*; can ski, *can't* ski; drives a car, *does not* drive a car).

Close-Up CORRECTING DOUBLE NEGATIVES

A **double negative** is an error that occurs when the meaning of a verb is made negative not just once but twice in a single sentence.

         any   *has*
Henry doesn't have ~~no~~ friends. (*or* Henry ~~doesn't have~~ no friends.)

I looked for relevant articles, but there weren~~'t~~ none. (*or* I looked for
                                     any
relevant articles, but there weren't ~~none~~.)

Note: Some multilingual writers whose first language is Spanish tend to use double negatives.

---

5 Phrasal Verbs

Many verbs in English are composed of two or more words that are combined to create a new idiomatic expression—for example, *check up on, run for, turn into*, and *wait on*. These verbs are called **phrasal verbs**. It is important to become familiar with phrasal verbs and their definitions so you will recognize these verbs as phrasal verbs instead of as verbs that are followed by prepositions.

Separable Phrasal Verbs Often, the words that make up a phrasal verb can be separated by a direct object. In these **separable phrasal** verbs, the object can come either before or after the preposition. For example, "Ellen <u>turned down</u> the job offer" and "Ellen <u>turned</u> the job offer <u>down</u>" are both correct. However, when the object is a pronoun, the pronoun must come before the preposition. Therefore, "Ellen turned it down" is correct, but "Ellen turned down it" is incorrect.

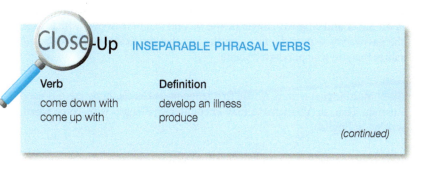

Close-Up   SEPARABLE PHRASAL VERBS

Verb	Definition
call off	cancel
carry on	continue
cheer up	make happy
clean out	clean the inside of
cut down	reduce
figure out	solve
fill in	substitute
find out	discover
give back	return something
give up	stop doing something or stop trying
leave out	omit
pass on	transmit
put away	place something in its proper place
put back	place something in its original place
put off	postpone
start over	start again
talk over	discuss
throw away/out	discard
touch up	repair

Inseparable Phrasal Verbs Some phrasal verbs—such as *look into, make up for*, and *break into*—consist of words that can never be separated. With these **inseparable phrasal verbs**, you do not have a choice about where to place the object; the object must always directly follow the preposition. For example, "Anna cared for her niece" is correct, but "Anna cared her niece for" is incorrect.

Close-Up   INSEPARABLE PHRASAL VERBS

Verb	Definition
come down with	develop an illness
come up with	produce

(continued)

INSEPARABLE PHRASAL VERBS *(continued)*

Verb	Definition
do away with	abolish
fall behind in	lag
get along with	be congenial with
get away with	avoid punishment
keep up with	maintain the same achievement or speed
look up to	admire
make up for	compensate
put up with	tolerate
run into	meet by chance
see to	arrange
show up	arrive
stand by	wait or remain loyal to
stand up for	support
watch out for	beware of or protect

6 Voice

See 22d

Verbs may be in either active or passive voice. When the subject of a sentence performs the action of the verb, the verb is in **active voice**. When the action of the verb is performed on the subject, the verb is in **passive voice**.

Karla and Miguel purchased the tickets. (active voice)

The tickets were purchased by Karla and Miguel. (passive voice)

Because your writing will usually be clearer and more concise if you use the active voice, you should use the passive voice only when you have a good reason to do so. For example, in scientific writing, it is common for writers to use the passive voice in order to convey scientific objectivity (lack of bias).

When deciding whether to use the passive or active voice, you need to consider what you want to focus on. In the first example above, the focus is on Karla and Miguel. However, the second example above, which uses the passive voice, puts the focus on the fact that the tickets were *purchased* rather than on *who* purchased them.

Note: Multilingual writers whose first language is Creole, Japanese, Korean, Russian, Thai, or Vietnamese may encounter challenges with voice when writing in English.

7 Transitive and Intransitive Verbs

Many nonnative English speakers find it difficult to decide whether or not a verb needs an object and in what order direct and indirect objects should appear in a sentence. Learning the difference between transitive verbs and intransitive verbs can help you with such problems.

A **transitive verb** is a verb that has a direct object: "My father asked a question" (subject + verb + direct object). In this example, *asked* is a transitive verb; it needs an object to complete its meaning.

An **intransitive verb** is a verb that does not take an object: "The doctor smiled" (subject + verb). In this example, *smiled* is an intransitive verb; it does not need an object to complete its meaning.

A transitive verb may be followed by a direct object or by both an indirect object and a direct object. (An indirect object answers the question "To whom?" or "For whom?") The indirect object may come before or after the direct object. If the indirect object follows the direct object, the preposition *to* or *for* must precede the indirect object.

s   v   do
Keith wrote a letter. (subject + verb + direct object)

s   v   io   do
Keith wrote his friend a letter. (subject + verb + indirect object + direct object)

s   v   do   io
Keith wrote a letter to his friend. (subject + verb + direct object + *to/for* + indirect object)

Some verbs in English look similar and have similar meanings, except that one is transitive and the other is intransitive. For example, *lie* is intransitive, *lay* is transitive; *sit* is intransitive, *set* is transitive; *rise* is intransitive, *raise* is transitive. Knowing whether a verb is transitive or intransitive will help you with troublesome verb pairs such as these and will help you place words in the correct order. (See the **Glossary of Usage** for more on these verb pairs.)

Note: It is also important to know whether a verb is transitive or intransitive because only transitive verbs can be used in the **passive voice**. To determine whether a verb is transitive or intransitive—that is, to determine whether or not it needs an object—consult the example phrases in a dictionary.

See 22d

8 Infinitives and Gerunds

In English, two verb forms may be used as nouns: **infinitives**, which always begin with *to* (as in *to work, to sleep, to eat*), and **gerunds**, which always end in *-ing* (as in *working, sleeping, eating*).

To bite into this steak <u>requires</u> better teeth than mine. (infinitive used as a noun)

<u>Cooking</u> <u>is</u> one of my favorite hobbies. (gerund used as a noun)

Sometimes the gerund and the infinitive form of the same verb can be used interchangeably. For example, "He continued *to sleep*" and "He continued *sleeping*" convey the same meaning. However, this is not always the case. Saying, "Marco and Lisa stopped *to eat* at Julio's Café" is not the same as saying, "Marco and Lisa stopped *eating* at Julio's Café." In this example, the meaning of the sentence changes depending on whether a gerund or infinitive is used.

Note: Multilingual writers whose first language is Arabic, Chinese, Farsi, French, Greek, Korean, Portuguese, Spanish, or Vietnamese may have difficulty with gerunds.

9 Participles

In English, verb forms called **present participles** and **past participles** are frequently used as adjectives. Present participles usually end in *-ing*, as in *working, sleeping,* and *eating,* and past participles usually end in *-ed, -t,* or *-en,* as in *worked, slept,* and *eaten.*

According to the Bible, God spoke to Moses from a <u>burning</u> bush. (present participle used as an adjective)

Some people think raw fish is healthier than <u>cooked</u> fish. (past participle used as an adjective)

A **participial phrase** is a group of words consisting of the participle plus the noun phrase that functions as the object or complement of the action being expressed by the participle. To avoid confusion, the participial phrase must be placed as close as possible to the noun it modifies.

<u>Having visited San Francisco last week</u>, Jim and Lynn showed us pictures from their vacation. (The participial phrase is used as an adjective that modifies *Jim and Lynn.*)

Note: When a participial phrase falls at the beginning of a sentence, a <u>comma</u> is used to set it off. When a participial phrase is used in the middle of a sentence, commas should be used only if the phrase is not essential to the meaning of the sentence. No commas should be used if the participial phrase is essential to the meaning of the sentence.

See 30d

10 Verbs Formed from Nouns

In English, nouns can sometimes be used as verbs, with no change in form (other than the addition of an *-s* for agreement with third-person singular subjects or the addition of past tense endings). For example, the nouns *chair, book, frame,* and *father* can all be used as verbs.

She <u>chairs</u> a committee on neighborhood safety.

We <u>booked</u> a flight to New York for next week.

I will <u>frame</u> my daughter's diploma after she graduates.

He <u>fathered</u> several children out of wedlock.

49b Using Nouns

<u>Nouns</u> name things: people, animals, objects, places, feelings, ideas. If a noun names one thing, it is singular; if a noun names more than one thing, it is plural.

See 21a

1 Recognizing Noncount Nouns

Some English nouns do not have a plural form. They are called **noncount nouns** because what they name cannot be counted. (**Count nouns** name items that *can* be counted, such as *cat* or *desk.*)

Note: Multilingual writers whose first language is Chinese or Japanese may have trouble with noncount nouns.

Close-Up NONCOUNT NOUNS

The following commonly used nouns are noncount nouns. These words have no plural forms. Therefore, you should never add -s to them.

advice	evidence	knowledge
clothing	furniture	luggage
education	homework	merchandise
equipment	information	revenge

EXERCISE 49.2

A student wrote the following paragraph as part of an essay about her experiences learning English. Read the paragraph, and decide which of the underlined words need to be made plural and which should remain unchanged. If a word should be made plural, make the necessary correction. If a word is correct as is, mark it with a C. If you are not sure whether a noun is countable, look it up in a dictionary.

Visiting Ireland for three ▶(1) <u>month</u> expanded my ▶(2) <u>knowledge</u> of English. I took a part-time English ▶(3) <u>course</u>, which was the key to improving my writing. The ▶(4) course helped me understand the essential ▶(5) rule of English, and I learned a lot of new (6) vocabulary and expressions. In the first three (7) lecture, the teacher, Mr. Nelson, explained the fundamentals of writing in English. My (8) enthusiasm for the English language increased because I realized the importance of this (9) language for my (10) future. Mr. Nelson recommended that I read more English (11) book. I took his advice, and my English got better.

2 Using Articles with Nouns

English has two kinds of **articles**, indefinite and definite.

Use an **indefinite article** (*a* or *an*) with a noun when readers are not familiar with the noun you are naming—for example, when you are introducing the noun for the first time. To say, "Jim entered *a* building," signals to the audience that you are introducing the idea of the building for the first time. The building is indefinite, or not specific, until it has been identified.

The indefinite article *a* is used when the word following it (which may be a noun or an adjective) begins with a consonant or with a consonant sound: *a tree, a onetime offer.* The indefinite article *an* is used if the word following it begins with a vowel (*a, e, i, o,* or *u*) or with a vowel sound: *an apple, an honor.*

Use the **definite article** (*the*) when the noun you are naming has already been introduced, when the noun is already familiar to readers, or when the noun to which you refer is specific. To say, "Jim entered *the* building," signals to readers that you are referring to the same building you mentioned earlier. The building has now become specific and may be referred to by the definite article.

Note: Multilingual writers whose first language is Chinese, Farsi, Russian, or Swahili are likely to have difficulty with articles.

Close-Up USING ARTICLES WITH NOUNS

There are three main exceptions to the rules governing the use of articles with nouns:

1. **Plural nouns** do not require indefinite articles: "I love horses," not "I love a horses." (However, plural nouns do require definite articles if you have already introduced the noun to your readers or if you are referring to a specific plural noun: "I love *the* horses on the carousel in the park near my house.")

2. **Noncount nouns** may or may not require articles.

   "Love conquers all," not "*A* love conquers all" or "*The* love conquers all."

   "*A* good education is important," not "Good education is important."

"*The* homework is difficult" or "Homework is difficult," not "*A* homework is difficult."

To help determine whether or not a noncount noun requires an article, look up that noun in a dictionary and consult the sample sentences provided.

3. **A proper noun**, which names a particular person, place, or thing, sometimes takes an article and sometimes does not. When you use an article with a proper noun, do not capitalize the article unless the article is the first word of the sentence.

"*The Mississippi River* is one of the longest rivers in the world," not "Mississippi River is one of the longest rivers in the world."

"Teresa was born in *the* United States," not "Teresa was born in United States."

"China is the most populous nation on earth," not "*The* China is the most populous nation on earth."

To find out whether or not a proper noun requires an article, look up that noun in a dictionary, and consult the sample sentences provided.

EXERCISE 49.3

The following introductory paragraph of an essay about renewable energy power sources was written for a composition course. Read the paragraph, and decide whether or not each of the underlined noun phrases requires an article. If a noun phrase is correct as is, mark it with a *C*. If a noun phrase needs an article, indicate whether that article should be *a, an,* or *the.*

▶(1) Use of electrical power has increased dramatically over ▶(2) last thirty years and continues to rise. ▶(3) Most ordinary sources of ▶(4) electricity require ▶(5) oil, ▶(6) gas, or ▶(7) uranium, which are not ▶(8) renewable resources. Living without ▶(9) electrical power is not feasible as long as everything in our lives depends on ▶(10) electricity, but (11) entire world will be in (12) big crisis if (13) ignorance regarding renewable energy continues. (14) Renewable energy, including (15) solar energy, (16) wind energy, (17) hydro energy, and (18) biomass energy, needs (19) more attention from (20) scientists.

③ Using Other Determiners with Nouns

Determiners are words that function as **adjectives** to limit or qualify the meaning of nouns. In addition to articles, **demonstrative pronouns, possessive nouns and pronouns, numbers** (both **cardinal** and **ordinal**), and other words indicating number and order can function in this way.

See 20d2

Close-Up   USING OTHER DETERMINERS WITH NOUNS

- **Demonstrative pronouns** (*this, that, these, those*) communicate the following:
  1. the relative distance of the noun from the speaker's position (*this* and *these* for things that are *near*, *that* and *those* for things that are *far*): *this* book on my desk, *that* book on your desk; *these* shoes on my feet, *those* shoes in my closet.
  2. the number of things indicated (*this* and *that* for *singular* nouns, *these* and *those* for *plural* nouns): *this* (or *that*) flower in the vase, *these* (or *those*) flowers in the garden.
- **Possessive nouns** and **possessive pronouns** (*Ashraf's, his, their*) show who or what the noun belongs to: *Maria's* courage, *everybody's* fears, the *country's* natural resources, *my* personality, *our* groceries.
- **Cardinal numbers** (*three, fifty, a thousand*) indicate how many of the noun you mean: *seven* continents. **Ordinal** numbers (*first, tenth, thirtieth*) indicate in what order the noun appears among other items: *third* planet.
- Words other than numbers may indicate **amount** (*many, few*) and **order** (*next, last*) and function in the same ways as cardinal and ordinal numbers: *few* opportunities, *last* chance.

49c   Using Pronouns

See 20b, Ch. 21

Any English noun may be replaced by a **pronoun**. For example, *doctors* may be replaced by *they*, *books* by *them*, and *computer* by *it*.

1   Pronoun Reference

See 21c

Pronoun reference is very important in English sentences, where the noun the pronoun replaces (the **antecedent**) must be easily identified. In general, you should place the pronoun as close as possible to the noun it replaces so the noun to which the pronoun refers is clear. If this is impossible, use the noun itself instead of replacing it with a pronoun.

Unclear: When Tara met Emily, she was nervous. (Does *she* refer to Tara or to Emily?)

Clear: When Tara met Emily, Tara was nervous.

Unclear: Stefano and Victor love his sneaker collection. (Whose sneaker collection—Stefano's, Victor's, or someone else's?)

Clear: Stefano and Victor love Emilio's sneaker collection.

Note: Multilingual writers whose first language is Spanish or Thai may have difficulty with pronoun reference.

2 Pronoun Placement

Never use a pronoun immediately after the noun it replaces. For example, do not say, "Most of my classmates *they* are smart"; instead, say, "Most of my classmates are smart."

The only exception to this rule occurs with an **intensive pronoun**, which ends in *-self* and emphasizes the preceding noun or pronoun: *Marta herself was eager to hear the results.*

3 Indefinite Pronouns

Unlike **personal pronouns** (*I, you, he, she, it, we, they, me, him, her, us, them,* and so on), **indefinite pronouns** do not refer to a particular person, place, or thing. Therefore, an indefinite pronoun does not require an antecedent. **Indefinite pronoun subjects** (*anybody, nobody, each, either, someone, something, all, some*), like personal pronouns, must **agree** in number with the sentence's verb.

See 26a4

> has
> Nobody ₍have₎ failed the exam. (*Nobody* is a singular subject and requires a singular verb.)

4 Appositives

Appositives are nouns or noun phrases that identify or rename an adjacent noun or pronoun. An appositive usually follows the word it explains or modifies but can sometimes precede it.

> My parents, <u>Mary and John</u>, live in Louisiana. (*Mary and John* identifies *parents.*)

Note: The **case** of a pronoun in an appositive depends on the case of the word it identifies.

See 21b3

If an appositive is *not* essential to the meaning of the sentence, use commas to set off the appositive from the rest of the sentence. If an appositive *is* essential to the meaning of the sentence, do not use commas.

> His aunt <u>Trang</u> is in the hospital. (*Trang* is necessary to the meaning of the sentence because it identifies which aunt is in the hospital.)

> Akta's car, <u>a 1994 Jeep Cherokee</u>, broke down last night, so she had to walk home. (*a 1994 Jeep Cherokee* is not essential to the meaning of the sentence.)

5 Pronouns and Gender

A pronoun generally agrees in **gender** with the noun to which it refers.

My *sister* sold *her* old car.

Your *uncle* is walking *his* dog.

Keep in mind that in English, most nonhuman nouns are referred to as *it* because they do not have grammatical gender. However, exceptions are sometimes made for pets. Pets are often referred to as *he* or *she*, depending on their sex.

Note: Multilingual writers whose first language is Bengali, Farsi, Gujarati, or Thai may have problems with pronouns and gender.

EXERCISE 49.4

There are no pronouns in the following passage. The repetition of the nouns again and again would seem strange to a native English speaker. Rewrite the passage, replacing as many of the nouns as possible with appropriate pronouns. Be sure that the connection between the pronouns and the nouns they replace is clear.

► The young couple seated across from Daniel at dinner the night before were newlyweds from Tokyo. ► The young couple and Daniel ate together with other guests of the inn at long, low tables in a large dining room with straw mat flooring. ► The man introduced himself immediately in English, shook Daniel's hand firmly, and, after learning that Daniel was not a tourist but a resident working in Osaka, gave Daniel a business card. ► The man had just finished college and was working at the man's first real job, clerking in a bank. ► Even in a sweatsuit, the man looked ready for the office: chin closely shaven, bristly hair neatly clipped, nails clean and buffed. After a while the man and Daniel exhausted the man's store of English and drifted into Japanese.

The man's wife, shy up until then, took over as the man fell silent. The woman and Daniel talked about the new popularity of hot springs spas in the countryside around the inn, the difficulty of finding good schools for the children the woman hoped to have soon, the differences between food in Tokyo and Osaka. The woman's husband ate busily. From time to time the woman refilled the man's beer glass or served the man radish pickles from a china bowl in the middle of the table, and then returned to the conversation.

49d Using Adjectives and Adverbs

See Ch. 23

Adjectives and adverbs are words that **modify** (describe, limit, or qualify) other words.

1 Position of Adjectives and Adverbs

Adjectives in English usually appear *before* the nouns they modify. A native speaker of English would not say, "*Cars red and black* are involved in more accidents than *cars blue or green*" but would say instead, "*Red and black cars* are involved in more accidents than *blue or green cars*."

However, adjectives may appear *after* linking verbs ("The name seemed *familiar*."), *after* direct objects ("The coach found them *tired* but *happy*."), and *after* indefinite pronouns ("Anything *sad* makes me cry.").

Adverbs may appear before or after the verbs they describe, but they should be placed as close to the verb as possible: not "I *told* John that I couldn't meet him for lunch *politely*," but "I *politely told* John that I couldn't meet him for lunch" or "I *told* John *politely* that I couldn't meet him for lunch." When an adverb describes an adjective or another adverb, it usually comes *before* that adjective or adverb: "The essay has *basically sound* logic"; "You must express yourself *absolutely clearly*."

Never place an adverb between the verb and the direct object.

Incorrect: Rolf *drank quickly* the water.

Correct: Rolf *drank* the water *quickly* (or, Rolf *quickly drank* the water).

Incorrect: Suong *took quietly* the test.

Correct: Suong *quietly took* the test (or, Suong *took* the test *quietly*).

Note: Multilingual writers whose first language is Creole or Haitian may have problems with adverbs.

2 Order of Adjectives

A single noun may be modified by more than one adjective, perhaps even by a whole list of adjectives. Given a list of three or four adjectives, most native speakers would arrange them in a sentence in the same order. If, for example, shoes are to be described as *green* and *big*, numbering *two*, and of the type worn for playing *tennis*, a native speaker would say "two big green tennis shoes." Generally, the adjectives that are most important in completing the meaning of the noun are placed closest to the noun.

Close-Up ORDER OF ADJECTIVES

1. Articles (*a, the*), demonstratives (*this, those*), and possessives (*his, our, Maria's, everybody's*)
2. Amounts (*one, five, many, few*), order (*first, next, last*)

(continued)

> **ORDER OF ADJECTIVES** (continued)
>
> 3. Personal opinions (*nice, ugly, crowded, pitiful*)
> 4. Sizes and shapes (*small, tall, straight, crooked*)
> 5. Age (*young, old, modern, ancient*)
> 6. Colors (*black, white, red, blue, dark, light*)
> 7. Nouns functioning as adjectives to form a unit with the noun (*soccer ball, cardboard box, history class*)

EXERCISE 49.5

Write five original sentences in which two or three adjectives describe a noun. Be sure that the adjectives are in the correct order.

49e Using Prepositions

See 20f

In English, **prepositions** (such as *to, from, at, with, among, between*) give meaning to nouns by linking them with other words and other parts of the sentence. Prepositions convey several kinds of information:

- Relations of **time** (*at* nine o'clock, *in* five minutes, *for* a month)
- Relations of **place** (*in* the classroom, *at* the library, *beside* the chair) and **direction** (*to* the market, *onto* the stage, *toward* the freeway)
- Relations of **association** (go *with* someone, the tip *of* the iceberg)
- Relations of **purpose** (working *for* money)

1 Commonly Used Prepositional Phrases

In English, the use of prepositions is often **idiomatic** rather than governed by grammatical rules. In many cases, therefore, learners of English as a second language need to memorize which prepositions are used in which phrases.

In English, some prepositions that relate to time have specific uses with certain nouns, such as days, months, and seasons:

- *On* is used with days and specific dates: *on* Tuesday, *on* September 11, 2001.
- *In* is used with months, seasons, and years: *in* November, *in* the spring, *in* 1999.
- *In* is also used when referring to some parts of the day: *in* the morning, *in* the afternoon, *in* the evening.
- *At* is used to refer to other parts of the day: *at* noon, *at* night, *at* seven o'clock.

Close-Up DIFFICULT PREPOSITIONAL PHRASES

The following phrases (accompanied by their correct prepositions) sometimes cause difficulties for multilingual writers:

according *to*	*at* least	relevant *to*
apologize *to*	*at* most	similar *to*
appeal *to*	refer *to*	subscribe *to*
different *from*		

2 Commonly Confused Prepositions

The prepositions *to, in, on, into*, and *onto* are very similar and are therefore easily confused.

Close-Up USING COMMON PREPOSITIONS

- **To** is the basic preposition of direction. It indicates movement toward a physical place: "She went *to* the restaurant"; "He went *to* the meeting." (*To* is also used to form the infinitive of a verb: "He wanted *to deposit* his paycheck before noon"; "Irene offered *to drive* Maria to the baseball game.")
- **In** indicates that something is within the boundaries of a particular space or period of time: "My son is *in* the garden"; "I like to ski *in* the winter"; "The map is *in* the car."
- **On** indicates position above or the state of being supported by something: "The toys are *on* the porch"; "The baby sat *on* my lap"; "The book is *on* top of the magazine."
- **Into** indicates movement to the inside or interior of something: "She walked *into* the room"; "I threw the stone *into* the lake"; "He put the photos *into* the box." Although *into* and *in* are sometimes interchangeable, note that usage depends on whether the subject is stationary or moving. *Into* usually indicates movement, as in "I jumped *into* the water." *In* usually indicates a stationary position relative to the object of the preposition, as in "Mary is swimming *in* the water."
- **Onto** indicates movement to a position on top of something: "The cat jumped *onto* the chair"; "Crumbs are falling *onto* the floor." Both *on* and *onto* can be used to indicate a position on top of something (and therefore they can sometimes be used interchangeably), but *onto* specifies that the subject is moving to a place from a different place or from an outside position.

Close-Up PREPOSITIONS IN IDIOMATIC EXPRESSIONS

Many nonnative speakers use incorrect prepositions in idiomatic expressions. Compare the incorrect expressions in the left-hand column below with the correct expressions in the right-hand column.

Incorrect	Correct
according *with*	according *to*
apologize *at*	apologize *to*
appeal *at*	appeal *to*
believe *at*	believe *in*
different *to*	different *from*
for least, *for* most	*at* least, *at* most
refer *at*	refer *to*
relevant *with*	relevant *to*
similar *with*	similar *to*
subscribe *with*	subscribe *to*

EXERCISE 49.6

A student in a composition class wrote the following paragraphs as part of an essay about her experiences learning to write in English. In several cases, she chose the wrong prepositions. The student's instructor has underlined the misused prepositions. Your task is to replace each underlined preposition with a correct preposition. (In some cases, there may be more than one possible correct answer.) If you have trouble, consult a dictionary, and look up a noun or verb that is part of the phrase in question.

My first experience writing ▶(1) of English took place ▶(2) at my early youth. I don't remember what the experience was like, but I do know that I have improved my writing skills since then. The improvement stems from various reasons. One major impact ▶(3) to my writing was the fact that I attended an American school ▶(4) of my country. This helped a lot because the first language ▶(5) to the school was English. Being surrounded (6) in English helped me improve both my verbal skills and my writing skills. Another major factor that helped me develop my English writing skills, especially my grammar and vocabulary, was reading novels.

(7) At the future, I plan to improve my writing skills in English by participating (8) to several activities. I plan to read more novels so I can further develop the grammar and vocabulary skills that will help me earn my degree. I also plan to communicate verbally with native speakers and to listen (9) at public speeches (such as the president's state of the union address), which usually contain rich vocabulary. But my main plan is to keep writing

more essays and discussing my writing (10) <u>to</u> my instructor. The more I write, the more confident I will become and the more my writing will improve. And there is always room for improvement.

49f Understanding Word Order

Word order is extremely important in English sentences. For example, word order may indicate which word is the subject of a sentence and which is the object, or it may indicate whether a sentence is a question or a statement.

1 Standard Word Order

Like Chinese, English is an SVO language, or one in which the most typical sentence pattern is "subject-verb-object." (Arabic, by contrast, is an example of a VSO language.)

2 Word Order in Questions

Word order in questions can be particularly troublesome for speakers of languages other than English, partly because there are so many different ways to form questions in English.

Close-Up WORD ORDER IN QUESTIONS

1. To create a **yes/no question** from a statement whose verb is a form of *be* (*am, is, are, was, were*), move the verb so it precedes the subject.

    <u>Rasheem</u> <u>is</u> in his laboratory.

    <u>Is</u> <u>Rasheem</u> in his laboratory?

    When the statement is *not* a form of *be*, change the verb to include a form of *do* as a helping verb, and then move that helping verb so it precedes the subject.

    <u>Rasheem</u> <u>researched</u> the depletion of the ozone level.

    <u>Did</u> <u>Rasheem</u> <u>research</u> the depletion of the ozone level?

2. To create a **yes/no question** from a statement that includes one or more helping verbs, move the first helping verb so it precedes the subject.

    <u>Rasheem</u> <u>is researching</u> the depletion of the ozone layer.

    <u>Is</u> <u>Rasheem</u> <u>researching</u> the depletion of the ozone layer?

    (continued)

WORD ORDER IN QUESTIONS *(continued)*

3. To create a **question asking for information**, replace the information being asked for with an **interrogative** word (*who, what, where, why, when, how*) at the beginning of the question, and invert the order of the subject and verb as with a yes/no question.

Rasheem is in his laboratory.

Where is Rasheem?

Rasheem is researching the depletion of the ozone layer.

What is Rasheem researching?

Rasheem researched the depletion of the ozone level.

What did Rasheem research?

If the interrogative word is the subject of the question, however, do *not* invert the subject and verb.

Who is researching the depletion of the ozone level?

4. You can also form a question by adding a **tag question** (such as *won't he?* or *didn't I?*) to the end of a statement. If the verb of the main statement is *positive*, then the verb of the tag question is *negative*; if the verb of the main statement is *negative*, then the verb of the tag question is *positive*.

Rasheem is researching the depletion of the ozone layer, isn't he?

Rasheem doesn't intend to write his dissertation about the depletion of the ozone layer, does he?

3 Word Order in Imperative Sentences

Imperative sentences state commands. It is common for the subject of an imperative sentence to be left out because the word *you* is understood to be the subject: "Go to school"; "Eat your dinner." Therefore, the word order pattern in an imperative sentence is usually "verb-object," or VO.

49g Distinguishing Commonly Confused Words

A number of word pairs in English have similar meanings. These word pairs can be confusing to nonnative English speakers because the ways in which the expressions are used in sentences are different although their meanings may be similar.

NO AND NOT

No is an adjective; *not* is an adverb. Therefore, use *no* with nouns, and use *not* with verbs, adjectives, and other adverbs.

She has no desire to go to the football game.

Sergio's sisters are not friendly.

TOO AND VERY

Too is an intensifier. It is used to add emphasis and to indicate excess.

It is too cold outside to go swimming.

Very is also an intensifier. It means "greatly" or "intensely," but not to excess.

It was very cold outside, but not cold enough to keep us from playing in the backyard.

EVEN, EVEN IF, AND EVEN THOUGH

When used as an adverb, *even* is used to intensify or to indicate surprise.

Greta felt even worse than she looked.

Even my little brother knows how to figure that out!

Even if is used where there is a condition that may or may not occur.

Even if it rains tomorrow, I'm going to the park.

Even though is similar in meaning to *although*.

Even though Christopher is a very fast runner, he did not make the national track team.

A FEW/A LITTLE AND FEW/LITTLE

A few and *a little* mean "not much," but "some" or "enough." *A few* is used with count nouns. *A little* is used with noncount nouns.

We have a few screws remaining from the project.

There is a little paint left in the can.

Few and *little* mean "a small number"—there are some, but perhaps not as much as one would like.

Few singers are as talented as Kelly.

I have little hope that this situation will change.

MUCH AND MANY

Both *much* and *many* mean "a great quantity" or "to a great degree." Use *much* to modify noncount nouns: "much experience"; "much money." Use *many* to modify count nouns: "many people"; "many incidents."

MOST OF, MOST, AND THE MOST

Most and *most of* have similar meanings. *Most of* means "nearly all of something." Use *most of* when the noun that follows is a specific plural noun. When you use *most of*, be sure to use the definite article *the* before the noun.

Most of the children had cookies for dessert.

Most is used for more general observations and means "nearly all."

Most houses in the United States have electricity.

The most is used for comparing more than two of something.

Thomas has the most jellybeans.

Pedro is the most experienced of the engineers.

SOME AND ANY

Some denotes an unspecified amount or quantity that may be part of a larger amount. It can modify both count and noncount nouns: "some water"; "some melons." *Any* indicates an unspecified amount, which may be none, some, or all. It can modify both count and noncount nouns: "any person"; "any luggage."

Glossary of Usage

This glossary of usage lists words and phrases that writers often find troublesome and explains how they are used.

a, an   Use *a* before words that begin with consonants and words with initial vowels that sound like consonants: *a* person, *a* historical document, *a* one-horse carriage, *a* uniform. Use *an* before words that begin with vowels and words that begin with a silent *h*: *an* artist, *an* honest person.

MULTILINGUAL TIP

For a list of commonly confused words that present particular challenges for multilingual writers, **see 49g.**

accept, except   *Accept* is a verb that means "to receive"; *except* as a preposition or conjunction means "other than" and as a verb means "to leave out": The auditors will *accept* all your claims *except* the last two. Some businesses are *excepted* from the regulation.

advice, advise   *Advice* is a noun meaning "opinion or information offered"; *advise* is a verb that means "to offer advice to": The broker *advised* her client to take his attorney's *advice*.

affect, effect   *Affect* is a verb meaning "to influence"; *effect* can be a verb or a noun—as a verb it means "to bring about," and as a noun it means "result": We know how the drug *affects* patients immediately, but little is known of its long-term *effects*. The arbitrator tried to *effect* a settlement between the parties.

all ready, already   *All ready* means "completely prepared"; *already* means "by or before this or that time": I was *all ready* to help, but it was *already* too late.

all right, alright   Although the use of *alright* is increasing, current usage calls for *all right*.

allusion, illusion   An *allusion* is a reference or hint; an *illusion* is something that is not what it seems: The poem makes an *allusion* to the Pandora myth. The shadow created an optical *illusion*.

a lot   *A lot* is always two words.

among, between   *Among* refers to groups of more than two things; *between* refers to just two things: The three parties agreed *among* themselves to settle the case. There will be a brief intermission *between* the two acts. (Note that *amongst* is British, not American, usage.)

amount, number   *Amount* refers to a quantity that cannot be counted; *number* refers to things that can be counted: Even a small *amount* of caffeine can be harmful. Seeing their commander fall, a large *number* of troops ran to his aid.

an, a   See **a, an.**

and/or   In business or technical writing, use *and/or* when either or both of the items it connects can apply. In college writing, however, avoid the use of *and/or.*

as, like   *As* can be used as a conjunction (to introduce a complete clause) or as a preposition; *like* should be used as a preposition only: In *The Scarlet Letter*, Hawthorne uses imagery *as* (not *like*) he does in his other works. After classes, Fred works *as* a manager of a fast food restaurant. Writers *like* Carl Sandburg appear once in a generation.

at, to   Many people use the prepositions *at* and *to* after *where* in conversation: *Where* are you working *at*? Where are you going *to*? This usage is redundant and should not appear in college writing.

awhile, a while   *Awhile* is an adverb; *a while*, which consists of an article and a noun, is used as the object of a preposition: Before we continue, we will rest *awhile* (modifies the verb *rest*). Before we continue, we will rest for *a while* (object of the preposition *for*).

bad, badly   *Bad* is an adjective, and *badly* is an adverb: The school board decided that *Adventures of Huckleberry Finn* was a *bad* book. American automobile makers did not do *badly* this year. After verbs that refer to any of the senses or after any other linking verb, use the adjective form: He looked *bad*. He felt *bad*. It seemed *bad*.

being as, being that   These awkward phrases add unnecessary words, thereby weakening your writing. Use *because* instead.

beside, besides   *Beside* is a preposition meaning "next to"; *besides* can be either a preposition meaning "except" or "other than" or an adverb meaning "as well": *Beside* the tower was a wall that ran the length of the city. *Besides* its industrial uses, laser technology has many other applications. Edison invented not only the lightbulb but the phonograph *besides*.

between, among   See **among, between.**

bring, take   *Bring* means "to transport from a farther place to a nearer place"; *take* means "to carry or convey from a nearer place to a farther place": *Bring* me a souvenir from your trip. *Take* this message to the general, and wait for a reply.

can, may   *Can* denotes ability; *may* indicates permission: If you *can* play, you *may* use my piano.

cite, site   *Cite* is a verb meaning "to quote as an authority or example"; *site* is a noun meaning "a place or setting"; it is also a shortened form of *website*:

Jeff *cited* five sources in his research paper. The builder cleared the *site* for the new bank. Marisa uploaded her *site* to the web.

climactic, climatic   *Climactic* means "of or related to a climax"; *climatic* means "of or related to climate": The *climactic* moment of the movie occurred unexpectedly. If scientists are correct, the *climatic* conditions of Earth are changing.

complement, compliment   *Complement* means "to complete or add to"; *compliment* means "to give praise": A double-blind study would *complement* their preliminary research. My instructor *complimented* me on my improvement.

conscious, conscience   *Conscious* is an adjective meaning "having one's mental faculties awake"; *conscience* is a noun that means the moral sense of right and wrong: The patient will remain *conscious* during the procedure. His *conscience* would not allow him to lie.

continual, continuous   *Continual* means "recurring at intervals"; *continuous* refers to an action that occurs without interruption: A pulsar is a star that emits a *continual* stream of electromagnetic radiation. (It emits radiation at regular intervals.) A small battery allows the watch to run *continuously* for five years. (It runs without stopping.)

could of, should of, would of   The contractions *could've*, *should've*, and *would've* are often misspelled as the nonstandard constructions *could of*, *should of*, and *would of*. Use *could have, should have*, and *would have* in college writing.

couple, couple of   *Couple* means "a pair," but *couple of* is often used colloquially to mean "several" or "a few." In your college writing, specify "four points" or "two examples" rather than using "a couple of."

criterion, criteria   *Criteria*, from the Greek, is the plural of *criterion*, meaning "standard for judgment": Of all the *criteria* for hiring graduating seniors, class rank is the most important *criterion*.

data   *Data* is the plural of the Latin *datum*, meaning "fact." In colloquial speech and writing, *data* is often used as the singular as well as the plural form. In college writing, use *data* only for the plural: The *data* discussed in this section *are* summarized in Appendix A.

different from, different than   *Different than* is widely used in American speech. In college writing, use *different from*.

disinterested, uninterested   *Disinterested* means "objective" or "capable of making an impartial judgment"; *uninterested* means "indifferent or unconcerned": The American judicial system depends on *disinterested* jurors. Finding no treasure, Hernando de Soto was *uninterested* in going farther.

don't, doesn't   *Don't* is the contraction of *do not*; *doesn't* is the contraction of *does not*. Do not confuse the two: My dog *doesn't* (not *don't*) like to walk in the rain. (Note that contractions are generally not acceptable in college writing.)

economic, economical *Economic* refers to the economy—to the production, distribution, and consumption of goods. *Economical* means "avoiding waste" or "careful use of resources": There was strong *economic* growth this quarter. It is *economical* to have roommates in this city.

effect, affect See **affect, effect**.

e.g. *E.g.* is an abbreviation for the Latin *exempli gratia,* meaning "for example" or "for instance." In college writing, do not use *e.g.* Instead, use *for example* or *for instance.*

emigrate from, immigrate to To *emigrate* is "to leave one's country and settle in another"; to *immigrate* is "to come to another country and reside there." The noun forms of these words are *emigrant* and *immigrant*: My great-grandfather *emigrated from* Warsaw along with many other *emigrants* from Poland. Many people *immigrate to* the United States for economic reasons, but *immigrants* still face great challenges.

eminent, imminent *Eminent* is an adjective meaning "standing above others" or "prominent"; *imminent* means "about to occur": Oliver Wendell Holmes Jr. was an *eminent* jurist. In ancient times, a comet signaled *imminent* disaster.

enthused *Enthused,* a colloquial form of *enthusiastic,* should not be used in college writing.

etc. *Etc.,* the abbreviation of *et cetera,* means "and the rest." Do not use it in your college writing. Instead, use *and so on*—or, better yet, specify what *etc.* stands for.

everyday, every day *Everyday* is an adjective that means "ordinary" or "commonplace"; *every day* means "occurring daily": In the Gettysburg Address, Lincoln used *everyday* language. She exercises almost *every day.*

everyone, every one *Everyone* is an indefinite pronoun meaning "every person"; *every one* means "every individual or thing in a particular group": *Everyone* seems happier in the spring. *Every one* of the packages had been opened.

except, accept See **accept, except**.

explicit, implicit *Explicit* means "expressed or stated directly"; *implicit* means "implied" or "expressed or stated indirectly": The director *explicitly* warned the actors to be on time for rehearsals. Her *implicit* message was that lateness would not be tolerated.

farther, further *Farther* designates distance; *further* designates degree: I have traveled *farther* from home than any of my relatives. Critics charge that welfare subsidies encourage *further* dependence.

fewer, less Use *fewer* with nouns that can be counted: *fewer* books, *fewer* people, *fewer* dollars. Use *less* with quantities that cannot be counted: *less* pain, *less* power, *less* enthusiasm.

firstly (secondly, thirdly, . . .)   Archaic forms meaning "in the first . . . second . . . third place." Use *first, second, third* instead.

further, farther   See **farther, further**.

good, well   *Good* is an adjective, never an adverb: She is a *good* swimmer. *Well* can function as an adverb or as an adjective. As an adverb, it means "in a good manner": She swam *well* (not *good*) in the meet. *Well* is used as an adjective meaning "in good health" with verbs that denote a state of being or feeling: I feel *well*.

got to   *Got to* is not acceptable in college writing. To indicate obligation, use *have to, has to,* or *must*.

hanged, hung   Both *hanged* and *hung* are past participles of *hang*. *Hanged* is used to refer to executions; *hung* is used to mean "suspended": Billy Budd was *hanged* for killing the master-at-arms. The stockings were *hung* by the chimney with care.

he, she   Traditionally, *he* has been used in the generic sense to refer to both males and females. To acknowledge the equality of the sexes, however, avoid the generic *he*. Use plural pronouns whenever possible. **See 19e2.**

historic, historical   *Historic* means "important" or "momentous"; *historical* means "relating to the past" or "based on or inspired by history": The end of World War II was a *historic* occasion. *Historical* records show that Quakers played an important part in the abolition of slavery.

hopefully   The adverb *hopefully*, meaning "in a hopeful manner," should modify a verb, an adjective, or another adverb. Do not use *hopefully* as a sentence modifier meaning "it is hoped." Rather than "*Hopefully*, scientists will soon discover a cure for AIDS," write "*People hope* scientists will soon discover a cure for AIDS."

i.e.   *I.e.* is an abbreviation for the Latin *id est*, meaning "that is." In college writing, do not use *i.e.* Instead, use its English equivalent.

if, whether   When asking indirect questions or expressing doubt, use *whether*: He asked *whether* (not *if*) the flight would be delayed. The flight attendant was not sure *whether* (not *if*) it would be delayed.

illusion, allusion   See **allusion, illusion**.

immigrate to, emigrate from   See **emigrate from, immigrate to**.

implicit, explicit   See **explicit, implicit**.

imply, infer   *Imply* means "to hint" or "to suggest"; *infer* means "to conclude from": Mark Antony *implied* that the conspirators had murdered Caesar. The crowd *inferred* his meaning and called for justice.

infer, imply   See **imply, infer**.

irregardless, regardless   *Irregardless* is a nonstandard version of *regardless*. Use *regardless* or *irrespective* instead.

is when, is where These constructions are faulty when they appear in definitions: A playoff is (not *is when* or *is where*) an additional game played to establish the winner of a tie.

its, it's *Its* is a possessive pronoun; *it's* is a contraction of *it is*: *It's* no secret that the bank is out to protect *its* assets.

kind of, sort of The use of *kind of* and *sort of* to mean "rather" or "somewhat" is colloquial. These expressions should not appear in college writing: It is well known that Napoleon was rather (not *kind of*) short.

lay, lie See **lie, lay**.

leave, let *Leave* means "to go away from" or "to let remain"; *let* means "to allow" or "to permit": *Let* (not *leave*) me give you a hand.

less, fewer See **fewer, less**.

let, leave See **leave, let**.

lie, lay *Lie* is an intransitive verb (one that does not take an object) meaning "to recline." Its principal forms are *lie, lay, lain, lying*: Each afternoon she would *lie* in the sun and listen to the surf. *As I Lay Dying* is a novel by William Faulkner. By 1871, Troy had *lain* undisturbed for two thousand years. The painting shows a nude *lying* on a couch.

   Lay is a transitive verb (one that takes an object) meaning "to put" or "to place." Its principal forms are *lay, laid, laid, laying*: The Federalist Papers *lay* the foundation for American conservatism. In October 1781, the British *laid* down their arms and surrendered. He had *laid* his money on the counter before leaving. We watched the stonemasons *laying* a wall.

life, lifestyle *Life* is the span of time that a living thing exists; *lifestyle* is a way of living that reflects a person's values or attitudes: Before he was hanged, Nathan Hale said, "I only regret that I have but one *life* to lose for my country." The writer Virginia Woolf was known for her unconventional *lifestyle*.

like, as See **as, like**.

loose, lose *Loose* is an adjective meaning "not rigidly fastened or securely attached"; *lose* is a verb meaning "to misplace": The marble facing of the building became *loose* and fell to the sidewalk. After only two drinks, most people *lose* their ability to judge distance.

lots, lots of, a lot of These words are colloquial substitutes for *many, much*, or *a great deal of*. Avoid their use in college writing: The students had *many* (not *lots of* or *a lot of*) options for essay topics.

man Like the generic pronoun *he*, *man* has been used in English to denote members of both sexes. This usage is being replaced by *human beings, people*, or similar terms that do not specify gender. **See 19e2**.

may, can See **can, may**.

may be, maybe *May be* is a verb phrase: *maybe* is an adverb meaning "perhaps": She *may be* the smartest student in the class. *Maybe* her experience has given her an advantage.

media, medium   *Medium*, meaning "a means of conveying or broadcasting something," is singular; *media* is the plural form and requires a plural verb: The *media have* distorted the issue.

might have, might of   *Might of* is a nonstandard spelling of the contraction of *might have* (*might've*). Use *might have* in college writing.

number, amount   See **amount, number**.

OK, O.K., okay   All three spellings are acceptable, but this term should be avoided in college writing. Replace it with a more specific word or words: The lecture was *adequate* (not *okay*), if uninspiring.

passed, past   *Passed* is the past tense of the verb *pass*; *past* means "belonging to a former time" or "no longer current": The car must have been going eighty miles per hour when it *passed* us. In the envelope was a bill marked *past* due.

percent, percentage   *Percent* indicates a part of a hundred when a specific number is referred to: "*10 percent* of his salary." *Percentage* is used when no specific number is referred to: "a *percentage* of next year's receipts." In technical and business writing, it is permissible to use the % sign after percentages you are comparing. Write out the word *percent* in college writing.

plus   As a preposition, *plus* means "in addition to." Avoid using *plus* as a substitute for *and*: Include the principal, *plus* the interest, in your calculations. Your quote was too high; *moreover* (not *plus*), it was inaccurate.

precede, proceed   *Precede* means "to go or come before"; *proceed* means "to go forward in an orderly way": Robert Frost's *North of Boston* was *preceded* by an earlier volume. In 1532, Francisco Pizarro landed at Tumbes and *proceeded* south.

principal, principle   As a noun, *principal* means "a sum of money (minus interest) invested or lent" or "a person in the leading position"; as an adjective, it means "most important"; a *principle* is a noun meaning a rule of conduct or a basic truth: He wanted to reduce the *principal* of the loan. The *principal* of the high school is a talented administrator. Women are the *principal* wage earners in many American households. The Constitution embodies certain fundamental *principles*.

quote, quotation   *Quote* is a verb. *Quotation* is a noun. In college writing, do not use *quote* as a shortened form of *quotation*: Scholars attribute these *quotations* (not *quotes*) to Shakespeare.

raise, rise   *Raise* is a transitive verb, and *rise* is an intransitive verb—that is, *raise* takes an object, and *rise* does not: My grandparents *raised* a large family. The sun will *rise* at 6:12 tomorrow morning.

real, really   *Real* means "genuine" or "authentic"; *really* means "actually." In college writing, do not use *real* as an adjective meaning "very."

reason is that, reason is because   *Reason* should be used with *that* and not with *because*, which is redundant: The *reason* he left is *that* (not *because*) you insulted him.

regardless, irregardless   See **irregardless, regardless**.

rise, raise   See **raise, rise**.

set, sit   *Set* means "to put down" or "to lay." Its principal forms are *set* and *setting*: After rocking the baby to sleep, he *set* her down carefully in her crib. After *setting* her down, he took a nap.

   Sit means "to assume a sitting position." Its principal forms are *sit, sat,* and *sitting*: Many children *sit* in front of the television five to six hours a day. The dog *sat* by the fire. We were *sitting* in the airport when the flight was canceled.

shall, will   *Will* has all but replaced *shall* to express all future action.

should of   See **could of, should of, would of**.

simple, simplistic   *Simple* means "plain, ordinary, or uncomplicated"; *simplistic* means "overly or misleadingly simplified": Because she had studied, Tanya thought the test was *simple*. His explanation of how the Internet works is *simplistic*.

since   Do not use *since* for *because* if there is any chance of confusion. In the sentence "*Since* President Nixon traveled to China, trade between China and the United States has increased," *since* could mean either "from the time that" or "because." To be clear, use *because*.

sit, set   See **set, sit**.

so   Avoid using *so* as a vague intensifier meaning "very" or "extremely." Follow *so* with *that* and a clause that describes the result: She was *so* pleased with their work *that* she took them out to lunch.

sometime, sometimes, some time   *Sometime* means "at some time in the future"; *sometimes* means "now and then"; *some time* means "a period of time": The president will address Congress *sometime* next week. All automobiles, no matter how reliable, *sometimes* need repairs. It has been *some time* since I read that book.

sort of, kind of   See **kind of, sort of**.

supposed to, used to   *Supposed to* and *used to* are often misspelled. Both verbs require the final *d* to indicate past tense.

take, bring   See **bring, take**.

than, then   *Than* is a conjunction used to indicate a comparison; *then* is an adverb indicating time: The new shopping center is bigger *than* the old one. He did his research; *then*, he wrote a report.

that, which, who   Use *that* or *which* when referring to a thing; use *who* when referring to a person: It was a speech *that* inspired many. The movie, *which* was a huge success, failed to impress her. Anyone *who* (not *that*) takes the course will benefit.

their, there, they're   *Their* is a possessive pronoun; *there* indicates place and is also used in the expressions *there is* and *there are*; *they're* is a contraction of *they are*: Watson and Crick did *their* DNA work at Cambridge University.

I love Los Angeles, but I wouldn't want to live *there*. *There* is nothing we can do to resurrect an extinct species. When *they're* well treated, rabbits make excellent pets.

themselves, theirselves, theirself   *Theirselves* and *theirself* are nonstandard variants of *themselves*.

then, than   See **than, then**.

till, until, 'til   *Till* and *until* have the same meaning, and both are acceptable. *Until* is preferred in college writing. *'Til*, a contraction of *until*, should be avoided.

to, at   See **at, to**.

to, too, two   *To* is a preposition that indicates direction; *too* is an adverb that means "also" or "more than is needed"; *two* expresses the number 2: Last year we flew from New York *to* California. "Tippecanoe and Tyler, *too*" was William Henry Harrison's campaign slogan. The plot was *too* complicated for the average reader. Just north of *Two* Rivers, Wisconsin, is a petrified forest.

try to, try and   *Try and* is the colloquial equivalent of the more formal *try to*: He decided to *try to* (not *try and*) do better. In college writing, use *try to*.

-type   Deleting this empty suffix eliminates clutter and clarifies meaning: Found in the wreckage was an incendiary (not *incendiary-type*) device.

uninterested, disinterested   See **disinterested, uninterested**.

unique   Because *unique* means "the only one," not "remarkable" or "unusual," never use constructions such as *the most unique* or *very unique*.

until   See **till, until, 'til**.

used to   See **supposed to, used to**.

utilize   In most cases, replace *utilize* with *use* (*utilize* often sounds pretentious).

wait for, wait on   To *wait for* means "to defer action until something occurs." To *wait on* means "to act as a waiter": I am *waiting for* (not *on*) dinner.

weather, whether   *Weather* is a noun meaning "the state of the atmosphere"; *whether* is a conjunction used to introduce an alternative: The *weather* will improve this weekend. It is doubtful *whether* we will be able to ski tomorrow.

well, good   See **good, well**.

were, we're   *Were* is a verb; *we're* is the contraction of *we are*: The Trojans *were* asleep when the Greeks attacked. We must act now if *we're* going to succeed.

whether, if   See **if, whether**.

which, who, that   See **that, which, who**.

who, whom   When a pronoun serves as the subject of its clause, use *who* or *whoever*; when it functions in a clause as an object, use *whom* or *whomever*: Sarah, *who* is studying ancient civilizations, would like to visit Greece. Sarah, *whom* I met in France, wants me to travel to Greece with her. **See 21b2**.

who's, whose   *Who's* means "who is" or "who has"; *whose* indicates possession: *Who's* going to take calculus? *Who's* already left for the concert? The writer *whose* book was in the window was autographing copies.

will, shall   See **shall, will.**

would of   See **could of, should of, would of.**

your, you're   *Your* indicates possession; *you're* is the contraction of *you are*: You can improve *your* stamina by jogging two miles a day. *You're* certain to be the winner.

Answers to Selected Exercises

Answers are provided here for exercise items marked with a ▶ throughout the text.

EXERCISE 4.1 (p. 33)

1. An announcement, not a thesis.
2. A subject, not a thesis. Gives no indication of essay's focus or direction, let alone writer's position.
3. A subject, not a thesis. Why should it be avoided? What coast? What kind of development? What constitutes overdevelopment?
4. No position indicated. What aspects will be considered? What patterns of development might be used? What standards of judgment will be used?
5. A good start; however, "but it has a number of disadvantages" is not specific enough.

EXERCISE 6.1 (p. 65)

1. F
2. O
3. F
4. O
5. F

EXERCISE 6.4 (p. 74)

Rewritten statements will vary. Here are the logical fallacies.

1. *Post hoc* fallacy
2. Argument to the person; sweeping generalization
3. Argument to the person
4. Equivocation
5. Begging the question

EXERCISE 13.4 (p. 150)

1. **A.** Give specific examples; exemplification. The paragraph could be developed further by exemplification—that is, by giving examples of words that came into the English language from computer terminology, from popular music, from politics, and from films or TV. If enough examples are given, the paragraph can be expanded into an essay.

EXERCISE 14.1 (p. 157)

1. Isaac Asimov first saw science fiction stories (DO) in the newsstand of his parents' Brooklyn candy store.
2. He practiced writing (DO) by telling his schoolmates (IO) stories (DO).
3. Asimov published his first story (DO) in *Astounding Science Fiction*.
4. The magazine's editor, John W. Campbell, encouraged Asimov (DO) to continue writing.
5. The young writer researched scientific principles (DO) to make his stories more accurate.

EXERCISE 14.2 (p. 159)

1. IC
2. DC
3. P
4. IC
5. IC

EXERCISE 14.3 (p. 161)

1. The average American consumes more than 150 pounds of sugar each year; therefore, most Americans eat much more sugar than any other food additive, including salt.
2. Many of us are determined to reduce our sugar intake; consequently, we have consciously eliminated sweets from our diets.
3. Unfortunately, sugar is found not only in sweets but also in many processed foods.
4. Processed foods such as puddings and cake contain sugar, and foods such as ketchup and spaghetti sauce do too.
5. We are trying to cut down on sugar, yet we find limiting sugar intake extremely difficult.

EXERCISE 14.4 (p. 163)

1. Many high school graduates who are out of work need new skills for new careers.
2. Although talented high school students are usually encouraged to go to college, some high school graduates are now starting to see that a college education may not guarantee them a job.
3. Because a college education can cost a student more than $100,000, vocational education is becoming an increasingly attractive alternative.
4. Because vocational students complete their work in fewer than four years, they can enter the job market more quickly.
5. Nurses' aides, paralegals, travel agents, and computer technicians, who do not need college degrees, have little trouble finding work.

EXERCISE 15.1 (p. 166)

Answers will vary. Here is one revision.

The first modern miniature golf course, built in New York in 1925, was an indoor course with 18 holes. As the game caught on, entrepreneurs Drake

Delanoy and John Ledbetter built 150 more indoor and outdoor courses; Garnet Carter, who made miniature golf a worldwide fad with his elaborate miniature courses, later joined with Delanoy and Ledbetter to build more courses.

EXERCISE 15.2 (p. 167)

Answers will vary. Here are some possibilities.

1. When he was a very young child, Momaday was taken to Devil's Tower, the geological formation in Wyoming that is called Tsoai (Bear Tree) in Kiowa, and given the name Tsoai-talee (Bear Tree Boy). (adverb clause)
2. In the Kiowa myth of the origin of Tsoai, a boy playfully chases his seven sisters up a tree, which rises into the air as the boy is transformed into a bear. (prepositional phrase)

EXERCISE 16.1 (p. 169)

Listening to diatribes by angry callers or ranting about today's news, the talk radio host <u>spreads ideas over the air waves.</u> (climactic order)

<u>Every day at the same time</u>, the political talk show host discusses national events and policies, the failures of the opposing view, and the foibles of the individuals who espouse those views. (beginning)

<u>Listening for hours a day</u>, some callers become recognizable contributors to many different talk radio programs. (beginning)

<u>Other listeners are less devoted</u>, tuning in only when they are in the car and never calling to voice their opinions. (beginning)

EXERCISE 16.2 (p. 170)

1. Because criminals are better armed than ever before, police want to upgrade their firepower.
2. Previously, felons used small-caliber, six-shot revolvers—so-called Saturday night specials.

EXERCISE 16.3 (p. 171)

1. A. <u>However different in their educational opportunities</u>, [both Jefferson and Lincoln as young men became known to their contemporaries as "hard students."] (periodic)
   B. Both Lincoln and Jefferson as young men became known to their contemporaries as "hard students," however different their educational opportunities.

EXERCISE 16.4 (p. 172)

Answers will vary. Here is one revision.

Many readers distrust newspapers, news sites, and magazines; they also distrust what they hear on radio and television. Of these media, newspapers have been the most responsive to audience criticism. Some newspapers even have ombudsmen, who listen to reader complaints and act on these grievances.

EXERCISE 16.5 (p. 173)

Answers will vary. Here is one revision.

Jack Dempsey, the heavyweight champion between 1919 and 1926, had an interesting but uneven career. Many considered him one of the greatest boxers of all time. Dempsey began fighting as "Kid Blackie," but his career did not take off until 1919, when Jack "Doc" Kearns became his manager. Dempsey won the championship when he defeated Jess Willard in Toledo, Ohio, in 1919. Dempsey immediately became a popular sports figure; President Franklin D. Roosevelt was one of his biggest fans.

EXERCISE 17.1 (p. 176)

Answers will vary. Here is one revision.

The shopping mall is no longer so important to American culture. In the 1980s, shopping malls became gathering places where teenagers met, walkers came to get in a few miles, and shoppers looking for selection (not value) went to shop. Several factors have undermined the mall's popularity. First, today's shopper is interested in value and is more likely to shop in discount stores or bulk-buying warehouse stores than in the small, expensive specialty shops in large shopping malls.

EXERCISE 17.2 (p. 177)

Answers will vary. Here is one revision.

For different reasons, people today are choosing a vegetarian diet. Strict vegetarians eat no animal foods; lactovegetarians eat dairy products but no meat, fish, poultry, or eggs; and ovolactovegetarians eat eggs and dairy products but no meat, fish, or poultry. Famous vegetarians include George Bernard Shaw, Leonardo da Vinci, Ralph Waldo Emerson, Henry David Thoreau, and Mahatma Gandhi. Like them, people today have become vegetarians for good reasons.

EXERCISE 17.3 (p. 179)

Answers will vary. Here is one revision.

Some colleges that have supported fraternities for many years are reevaluating the fraternities' positions on campus. Opposing the fraternities are students, faculty, and administrators, who claim that fraternities are inherently sexist and, therefore, are unacceptable in coed institutions that offer equal opportunities. Many members of the college community see fraternities as elitist as well as sexist and favor their abolition.

EXERCISE 18.1 (p. 181)

1. After he completed his engineering degree, Manek returned to India [to visit his large extended family] and [to find a wife].
2. [Unfamiliar with marriage practices in India] and [accustomed to the American notion of marriage for love], Manek's American friends disapproved of his plans.

EXERCISE 18.2 (p. 182)

1. The world is divided between <u>those who wear boots</u> and <u>those who discover continents</u>.
2. <u>World leaders, members of Congress</u>, and <u>religious groups</u> are all concerned about global climate change.

EXERCISE 19.2 (p. 186)

Answers will vary. Here are some examples.

1. deceive, mislead, beguile
2. antiquated, old, antique
3. pushy, assertive, goal-oriented
4. pathetic, unfortunate, touching
5. cheap, inexpensive, economical

EXERCISE 19.3 (p. 187)

Answers will vary. Here is one revision.

Part-time jobs I have held include waiting tables, landscaping, and selling stereo equipment. Each of these jobs requires strong communication skills. In my most recent position, I sold automobile stereos.

EXERCISE 19.5 (p. 191)

Answers will vary. Here are some examples.

forefathers, ancestors
man-eating shark, carnivorous shark
manpower, workforce
workman's compensation, worker's compensation
men at work, workers
waitress, server
first baseman, first base
congressman, representative
manhunt, search

EXERCISE 21.1 (p. 205)

1. he; it is the subject of the sentence
2. me; it is the direct object

EXERCISE 21.2 (p. 207)

Answers will vary. Here are some examples.

1. Herb Ritts, who got his start by taking photographs of Hollywood stars, has photographed world leaders, leading artistic figures in dance and drama, and a vanishing African tribe.
2. Tim Green, who once played for the Atlanta Hawks and has a law degree, has written several novels about a fictional football team.

EXERCISE 21.3 (p. 209)

1. the expedition
2. Lewis and Clark

EXERCISE 22.1 (p. 213)

sold, sneaked

EXERCISE 22.2 (p. 213)

1. set
2. laying

EXERCISE 22.3 (p. 218)

1. give
2. have read
3. established
4. becoming
5. had made

EXERCISE 22.4 (p. 219)

performed, challenged, were, was

EXERCISE 22.5 (p. 221)

The Chinese invented rockets about AD 1000. They packed gunpowder into bamboo tubes and ignited it by means of a fuse. Soldiers fired these rockets at enemy armies and usually caused panic. In the thirteenth century, England's Roger Bacon introduced an improved form of gunpowder. As a result, soldiers used rockets as a common—although unreliable—weapon in battle.

EXERCISE 22.6 (p. 221)

Answers will vary.

The Regent Diamond is one of the world's most famous and coveted jewels. The 410-carat diamond was discovered by a slave in 1701 in an Indian mine. [Emphasis is on the diamond rather than on who discovered it.] Over the years, it was stolen and sold several times. [Emphasis is on what happened rather than on people.]

EXERCISE 23.1 (p. 223)

A popular self-help trend in the United States today is motivational podcasts. These podcasts, with titles like *How to Attract Love, Freedom from Acne,* and *I Am a Genius,* are intended to solve every problem known to modern society—quickly and easily. The podcasts are said to work because they contain "hidden messages" that bypass conscious defense mechanisms.

The listener hears only music or relaxing sounds, like waves rolling slowly and steadily.

EXERCISE 23.2 (p. 224)

Answers will vary. Here are some possibilities.

1. David seemed tired.
   Jerry was anxious.
   Lienne appeared happy.
   Maggie is depressed.
   Chris remained confident.

EXERCISE 23.3 (p. 226)

1. difficult/more difficult/most difficult
2. eccentric/more eccentric/most eccentric
3. confusing/more confusing/most confusing
4. bad/worse/worst
5. mysterious/more mysterious/most mysterious

EXERCISE 24.1 (p. 228)

1. F
2. F
3. CS
4. F
5. F

EXERCISE 24.2 (p. 230)

The drive-in movie came into being just after World War II, <u>when both movies and cars were central to the lives of many young Americans</u>. Drive-ins were especially popular with teenagers and young families during the 1950s, <u>when cars and gas were relatively inexpensive</u>. Theaters charged by the carload, <u>which meant that a group of teenagers or a family with several children could spend an evening at the movies for a few dollars</u>. In 1958, when the fad peaked, there were over four thousand drive-ins in the United States, <u>while today there are just a few hundred</u>.

EXERCISE 24.3 (p. 231)

Most college athletes are caught in a conflict <u>between their athletic and academic careers</u>. Sometimes college athletes' responsibilities on the playing field make it difficult for them to be good students. Often, athletes must make a choice <u>between sports and a degree</u>. Some athletes would not be able to afford college <u>without athletic scholarships</u>. Ironically, however, their commitments to sports (training, exercise, practice, and travel to out-of-town games, for example) deprive athletes <u>of valuable classroom time</u>. The role of college athletes is constantly being questioned.

EXERCISE 24.4 (p. 233)

Answers will vary. Here is one revision.

Many food products have well-known trademarks, <u>identified by familiar faces on product labels</u>. Some of these symbols have remained the same, while others have changed considerably. Products such as Sun-Maid Raisins, Betty Crocker potato mixes, Quaker Oats, and Uncle Ben's Rice use faces <u>to create a sense of quality and tradition and to encourage shopper recognition of the products</u>. Many of the portraits have been updated several times <u>to reflect changes in society</u>.

EXERCISE 24.5 (p. 234)

Answers will vary. Here is one revision.

Until the early 1900s, communities in West Virginia, Tennessee, and Kentucky were isolated by the mountains that surrounded them, <u>the great chain of the Appalachian Mountains</u>. Set apart from the emerging culture of a growing America and American language, these communities retained a language rich with the dialect of Elizabethan English and with hints of a Scotch-Irish influence. In the 1910s and '20s, the communities in these mountains began to long for a better future for their children. The key to that future, as they saw it, was education.

EXERCISE 24.6 (p. 235)

Answers will vary. Here is one revision.

As more and more Americans discover the pleasures of the wilderness, our national parks are feeling the stress. Wanting to get away for a weekend or a week, hikers and backpackers stream from the cities into nearby state and national parks. They bring with them a hunger for the wilderness <u>but very little knowledge about how to behave ethically in the wild</u>. They also do not know how to keep themselves safe. Some of them think of the national parks as inexpensive amusement parks. Without proper camping supplies and lacking enough food and water for their trip, they are putting at risk their lives and the lives of those who will be called on to save them. One family went for a hike up a desert canyon with an eight-month-old infant <u>and their seventy-eight-year-old grandmother</u>.

EXERCISE 25.1 (p. 239)

Answers will vary. To illustrate the various responses, each sentence below is followed with the four possible types of correction. You should balance the types of choices in a piece of writing rather than adhering to a single method of correction.

Entrepreneurship is the study of small businesses, college students are embracing it enthusiastically.

1. businesses. College students
2. businesses; college students
3. businesses, and college students
4. Entrepreneurship, the study of small businesses, is being embraced enthusiastically by college students.

Many schools offer one or more courses in entrepreneurship these courses teach the theory and practice of starting a small business.

  1. entrepreneurship. These courses
  2. entrepreneurship; these courses
  3. entrepreneurship, and these courses
  4. entrepreneurship, which teach the theory and practice of starting a small business.

Students are signing up for courses, moreover, they are starting their own businesses.

  1. courses. Moreover,
  2. courses; moreover,
  3. courses, and, moreover,
  4. Students who sign up for courses are even starting their own businesses.

One student started with a car-waxing business, now he sells condominiums.

  1. business. Now
  2. business; now
  3. business, and now
  4. One student, who started with a car-waxing business, now sells condominiums.

EXERCISE 25.2 (p. 239)

  1. Several recent studies indicate that many American high school students have a poor sense of history; this is affecting our future as a democratic nation and as individuals.
  2. Surveys show that nearly one-third of American seventeen-year-olds cannot identify the countries the United States fought against in World War II, and one-third think Columbus reached the New World after 1750.
  3. Several reasons have been given for this decline in historical literacy, but the main reason is the way history is taught.
  4. Although this problem is bad news, the good news is that there is increasing agreement among educators about what is wrong with current methods of teaching history.
  5. History can be exciting and engaging, but too often it is presented in a boring manner.

EXERCISE 26.1 (p. 244)

  1. C
  2. C
  3. Neither Western novels nor science fiction appeals to me.
  4. Stage presence and musical ability make a rock performer successful today.
  5. C

EXERCISE 26.2 (p. 246)

  1. The core of a computer is a collection of electronic circuits that is called the central processing unit.
  2. Computers, because of advanced technology that allows the central processing unit to be placed on a chip, a thin square of semiconducting material, have been greatly reduced in size.

3. No error

4. Pressing keys on keyboards resembling typewriter keyboards <u>generates</u> electronic signals that are input for the computer.

5. Computers have built-in memory storage, and equipment such as flash drives or portable hard drives <u>provides</u> external memory.

EXERCISE 27.1 (p. 248)

1. He wore his <u>almost</u> new jeans. [He wore his nearly new jeans.]

He <u>almost</u> wore his new jeans. [He decided at the last minute not to wear his new jeans.]

2. He had <u>only</u> three dollars in his pocket. [Besides the three dollars, he had nothing else in his pocket.]

<u>Only</u> he had three dollars in his pocket. [He alone had this amount of money in his pocket.]

EXERCISE 27.2 (p. 249)

1. The bridge <u>across the river</u> swayed <u>in the wind</u>.

2. The spectators <u>on the shore</u> were involved <u>in the action</u>.

3. <u>Mesmerized by the spectacle</u>, they watched the drama unfold.

4. The spectators were <u>afraid of a disaster</u>.

5. <u>Within the hour</u>, the state police arrived.

EXERCISE 27.3 (p. 249)

1. The lion, <u>watching Jack</u>, paced up and down in its cage, ignoring the crowd.

2. <u>In terror</u>, Jack stared back at the lion.

EXERCISE 27.4 (p. 250)

1. She realized after the wedding that she had married the wrong man.

2. *The Prince and the Pauper*, by Mark Twain, is a novel about an exchange of identities.

EXERCISE 27.5 (p. 251)

1. The people in the audience finally quieted down when they saw the play was about to begin and realized the orchestra had finished tuning up and had begun the overture.

2. Expecting to enjoy the first act very much, they settled into their seats.

EXERCISE 27.6 (p. 252)

1. Writing for eight hours every day, she publishes a lengthy book every year or so.
2. As an out-of-state student without a car, Joe had difficulty getting to off-campus cultural events.
3. To build a campfire, one needs kindling.
4. With every step we took upward, the trees became sparser.
5. Because I am an amateur tennis player, my backhand is weaker than my forehand.

EXERCISE 28.1 (p. 255)

Answers will vary. Here are some possibilities.

1. C
2. Women went to work in the textile mills of Lowell, Massachusetts, in the late 1800s; their efforts at reforming the workplace are seen by many as the beginning of the equal rights movement.
3. Farm girls from New Hampshire, Vermont, and western Massachusetts came to Lowell to make money and to experience life in the city.
4. The factories promised the girls decent wages and promised their parents that their daughters would live in a safe, wholesome environment.
5. Dormitories were built by the factories to ensure a safe environment for the girls.

EXERCISE 28.2 (p. 256)

Answers will vary. Here are some possibilities.

1. Implementing the "motor voter" bill has made it easier for people to register to vote.
2. They won the game because she sank the basket.

EXERCISE 28.3 (p. 257)

Answers will vary. Here are some possibilities.

1. Inflation is a decline in the purchasing power of currency.
2. Hypertension is elevated blood pressure.

EXERCISE 28.4 (p. 258)

1. Opportunities in technical writing are more promising than those in business writing. (illogical comparison)
2. Technical writing is more challenging than business writing. (incomplete comparison)

EXERCISE 29.1 (p. 264)

1. Julius Caesar was killed in 44 BC.
2. Dr. McLaughlin worked hard to earn his PhD.

EXERCISE 29.2 (p. 265)

1. He wondered whether he should take a nine o'clock class.
2. The instructor asked, "Was the Spanish-American War a victory for America?"

EXERCISE 30.1 (p. 266)

1. Pope Benedict did not hesitate to visit Cuba, nor did he hesitate to meet with former president Fidel Castro.
2. Advertisers place brand-name products in prominent positions in films, and the products are seen and recognized by large audiences.

EXERCISE 30.2 (p. 268)

1. Seals, whales, dogs, lions, and horses are all mammals.
2. C

EXERCISE 30.3 (p. 269)

While childhood is shrinking, adolescence is expanding. Whatever the reason, girls are maturing earlier, beginning puberty at increasingly younger ages. What's more, both boys and girls are staying in the nest longer. At present, it is not unusual for children to stay in their parents' home through their twenties or early thirties, delaying adulthood and extending adolescence.

EXERCISE 30.4 (p. 271)

The Statue of Liberty, which was dedicated in 1886, has undergone extensive renovation. Its supporting structure, whose designer was the French engineer Alexandre Gustave Eiffel, is made of iron.

EXERCISE 30.5 (p. 272)

1. Kermit the Frog is a Muppet, a cross between a marionette and a puppet.
2. The common cold, a virus, is frequently spread by hand contact, not by mouth.
3. C
4. C
5. The submarine *Nautilus* was the first to cross under the North Pole, wasn't it?

EXERCISE 30.6 (p. 274)

1. India became independent on August 15, 1947.
2. The UAW has more than 1,500,000 dues-paying members.
3. Nikita Khrushchev, former Soviet premier, once said, "We will bury you!"
4. Mount St. Helens, northeast of Portland, Oregon, began erupting on March 27, 1980, and eventually killed at least thirty people.
5. Located at 1600 Pennsylvania Avenue, Washington, DC, the White House is a popular tourist attraction.

EXERCISE 30.7 (p. 275)

1. According to Maria, Frank's computer is obsolete.
2. Da Gama explored Florida; Pizarro, Peru.
3. By Monday, evening students must begin preregistration for fall classes.
   OR
   By Monday evening, students must begin preregistration for fall classes.
4. Whatever they built, they built with care.

EXERCISE 30.8 (p. 277)

1. A book is like a garden carried in the pocket.
2. Like the iodine content of kelp, air freight is something most Americans have never pondered.

EXERCISE 31.1 (p. 278)

During the 1950s movie attendance declined because of the increasing popularity of television. As a result, numerous gimmicks were introduced to draw audiences into theaters. One of the first of these was Cinerama; in this technique three pictures were shot side by side and projected on a curved screen. Next came 3-D, complete with special glasses; *Bwana Devil* and *The Creature from the Black Lagoon* were two early 3-D ventures. *The Robe* was the first picture filmed in Cinemascope; in this technique a shrunken image was projected on a screen twice as wide as it was tall.

EXERCISE 31.2 (p. 279)

Answers will vary. Here are some possibilities.

1. The Aleutians lie between the North Pacific Ocean and the Bering Sea, where the weather is harsh; for example, dense fog, 100-mph winds, and even tidal waves and earthquakes are not uncommon.
2. These islands constitute North America's largest network of active volcanoes; still, the Aleutians boast some beautiful scenery, and they are relatively unexplored.

EXERCISE 31.3 (p. 280)

1. The history of modern art seems at times to be a collection of "isms": Impressionism, a term that applies to painters who attempted to depict contemporary life by reproducing an "impression" of what the eye sees; Abstract Expressionism, which applies to artists who stress emotion and the unconscious in their nonrepresentational works; and, more recently, Minimalism, which applies to painters and sculptors whose work reasserts the physical reality of the object.
2. Although the term *Internet* is widely used to refer only to the web and email, the Internet consists of a variety of discrete elements, including social media sites, which allow users to share images and videos on an unbelievably broad range of topics; interactive communication forums, such as blogs, discussion forums, and chat rooms; and FTP, which allows users to download material from remote computers.

EXERCISE 31.4 (p. 281)

Barnstormers were aviators who toured the country after World War I, giving people short airplane rides and exhibitions of stunt flying; in fact, the name *barnstormer* was derived from the use of barns as airplane hangars. Americans' interest in airplanes had all but disappeared after the war. The barnstormers helped popularize flying, especially in rural areas. Some were pilots who had flown in the war; others were just young men with a thirst for adventure.

EXERCISE 32.1 (p. 284)

1. Addams's
2. The popularity of *A Room of One's Own*

EXERCISE 32.2 (p. 285)

1. It's; you're
2. Who's
3. They're; their
4. Who's
5. its

EXERCISE 32.3 (p. 286)

1. *x*'s and *o*'s
2. *R*'s

EXERCISE 32.4 (p. 287)

1. Schaefers'; ours
2. colleges; outsiders
3. its
4. yours
5. favorites

EXERCISE 33.1 (p. 289)

1. Few people can explain what Descartes's words "I think, therefore I am" actually mean.
2. Gertrude Stein said, "You are all a lost generation."

EXERCISE 33.2 (p. 294)

1. "Kilroy was here" and "Women and children first" are two expressions *Bartlett's Familiar Quotations* attributes to Anon.
2. C; indirect quotation
3. "The answer, my friend," Bob Dylan sang, "is blowin' in the wind."
4. The novel was a real thriller, complete with spies and counterspies, mysterious women, and exotic international chases.
5. The sign said, "Road liable to subsidence"; it meant that we should look out for potholes.

EXERCISE 34.1 (p. 297)

1. Books about the late John F. Kennedy include the following: *A Hero for Our Time; Johnny, We Hardly Knew Ye; One Brief Shining Moment;* and *JFK: Reckless Youth.*
2. Only one task remained: to tell his boss he was quitting.

EXERCISE 34.2 (p. 298)

1. Tulips, daffodils, hyacinths, lilies—all these flowers grow from bulbs.

2. India—a country with a rich cultural history—gained independence after two hundred years of British rule.

EXERCISE 34.3 (p. 299)

1. During the Great War (1914–1918), Britain censored letters written from the front lines.
2. Those who lived in towns on the southern coast (such as Dover) could often hear the mortar shells across the channel in France.

EXERCISE 34.4 (p. 302)

Answers will vary. Some possibilities follow.

1. "When I was eighteen . . . my mother told me that when out with a young man I should always leave a half-hour before I wanted to."
2. "When I was eighteen or thereabouts, . . . I recognized the advice as sound, and exactly the same rule applies to research."

EXERCISE 34.5 (p. 303)

1. Mark Twain (Samuel L. Clemens) made the following statement: "I can live for two months on a good compliment."
2. Liza Minnelli, the actress/singer who starred in several films, is the daughter of legendary performer Judy Garland. [For emphasis, dashes may replace the commas.]
3. Saudi Arabia, Oman, Yemen, Qatar, and the United Arab Emirates—all these are located on the Arabian Peninsula.
4. John Adams (1735–1826) was the second president of the United States; John Quincy Adams (1767–1848) was the sixth.
5. The sign said, "No tresspassing [*sic*]."

EXERCISE 35.1 (p. 309)

1. rec ei pt
2. var ie ty
3. caff ei ne
4. ach ie ve
5. kal ei doscope

EXERCISE 35.2 (p. 310)

1. surprising
2. surely
3. forcible
4. manageable
5. duly

EXERCISE 35.3 (p. 310)

1. journeying
2. studied

3. carrying
4. shyly
5. studying

EXERCISE 36.1 (p. 318)

1. Two of the Brontë sisters wrote *Jane Eyre* and *Wuthering Heights*, nineteenth-century novels that are required reading in many English classes that study Victorian literature.
2. It was a beautiful day in the spring—it was April 15, to be exact—but all Ted could think about was the check he had to write to the Internal Revenue Service and the bills he had to pay by Friday.
3. Traveling north, they hiked through British Columbia, planning a leisurely return on the cruise ship *Canadian Princess*.
4. Alice liked her mom's apple pie better than Aunt Nellie's rhubarb pie, but she liked Grandpa's punch best of all.
5. A new elective, Political Science 30, covers the Vietnam War from the Gulf of Tonkin to the fall of Saigon, including the roles of Ho Chi Minh, the Viet Cong, and the Buddhist monks; the positions of Presidents Johnson and Nixon; and the influence of groups such as the Student Mobilization Committee and the Vietnam Veterans against the War.

EXERCISE 37.1 (p. 321)

1. I said Carol, not Darryl.
2. A *deus ex machina*, an improbable device used to resolve the plot of a fictional work, is used in Charles Dickens's novel Oliver Twist.
3. He dotted every i and crossed every t.
4. The Metropolitan Opera's production of Carmen was a tour de force for the principal performers.
5. C

EXERCISE 38.1 (p. 324)

1. One of the restaurant's blue-plate specials is chicken-fried steak.
2. Virginia and Texas are both right-to-work states.
3. He stood on tiptoe to see the near-perfect statue, which was well hidden by the security fence.
4. The five-and-ten-cent store had a self-service make-up counter and many up-to-the-minute gadgets.
5. The so-called Saturday night special is opposed by pro-gun-control groups.

EXERCISE 39.1 (p. 328)

1. The committee meeting, attended by representatives from Action for Children's Television (ACT) and the National Organization for Women (NOW), Senator Putnam, and the president of ABC, convened at 8 a.m. on Monday, February 24, at the YWCA on Germantown Avenue.

2. An economics professor was suspended after he encouraged his students to speculate on securities issued by a corporation under investigation by the Securities and Exchange Commission (SEC).
3. Benjamin Spock, who wrote *Baby and Child Care*, was a respected doctor known throughout the United States.
4. C [if this sentence can be defined as "technical writing"]
5. The Reverend Dr. Martin Luther King Jr., leader of the Southern Christian Leadership Conference (SCLC), led the famous Selma, Alabama, march.

EXERCISE 40.1 (p. 331)

1. C [*1984* is a book title.]
2. C
3. In a control group of 247 patients, almost 3 out of 4 suffered serious adverse reactions to the new drug.
4. Before the Thirteenth Amendment to the Constitution, slaves were counted as three-fifths of a person.
5. The intensive membership drive netted 2,608 new members and additional dues of over five thousand dollars.

EXERCISE 42.1 (p. 373)

You are encouraged to try to find the information in more than one source. Here are some possibilities.

1. *Academic Search Elite, LexisNexis Academic Universe, Expanded Academic ASAP*
2. *Monthly Catalog of U.S. Government Publications* or *Catalog of U.S. Government Publications* will list available publications
3. *American National Biography, Encyclopedia Americana, International Who's Who of Authors and Writers*
4. Library catalog or discovery service
5. *The Encyclopedia of Associations* lists organizations by subject; there are several with the word *wolves* in the title

EXERCISE 43.1 (p. 383)

1. Old but classic source. Information may establish role of women before they were given the right to vote. Note importance of author in history of women's suffrage.
2. While this reference work provides useful background information, it is not acceptable for college-level research.

EXERCISE 49.1 (p. 497)

1. asked
2. had
3. decided
4. travels
5. spent

6. do

7. decide

EXERCISE 49.2 (p. 503)

1. months

2. C

3. C

4. C

5. rules

EXERCISE 49.3 (p. 505)

1. The

2. the

3. C

4. C

5. C

6. C

7. C

8. C

9. C

10. C

EXERCISE 49.4 (p. 508)

The young couple seated across from Daniel at dinner the night before were newlyweds from Tokyo. The young couple and Daniel ate together with other guests of the inn at long, low tables in a large dining room with straw mat flooring. The man introduced himself immediately in English, shook Daniel's hand firmly, and, after learning that he was not a tourist but a resident working in Osaka, gave him a business card. The man had just finished college and was working at his first real job, clerking in a bank. Even in a sweatsuit, the man looked ready for the office: chin closely shaven, bristly hair neatly clipped, nails clean and buffed.

EXERCISE 49.6 (p. 512)

1. delete *of*

2. in

3. on

4. in

5. in

This page constitutes an extension of the copyright page. We have made every effort to trace the ownership of all copyrighted material and to secure permission from copyright holders. In the event of any question arising as to the use of any material, we will be pleased to make the necessary corrections in future printings. Thanks are due to the following authors, publishers, and agents for permission to use the material indicated.

Text

p. 5–6: "The Consumer: A Republic of Fat" from *The Omnivore's Dilemma* by Michael Pollan, copyright © 2006 by Michael Pollan. Used by permission of The Penguin Press, a division of Penguin Group (USA) Inc.

p. 10: Richard Rodriguez, *Aria: Memoir of a Bilingual Childhood.*

p. 11: "English Comes First" by Richard D. Lamm from the *New York Times*, July 1, 1986. Copyright © 1986 by Richard D. Lamm. Reprinted by permission of the author.

p. 11: Source: Alexander Petrunkevitch, "The Spider and the Wasp."

p. 11: Review of *A Dance with Dragons* by George R. R. Martin. Random House, 2011. May 16, 2015.

p. 13: From the *New York Times*, June 29, 2003, © 2003 The New York Times. All rights reserved. Used by permission and protected by the copyright laws of the United States. The printing, copying, redistribution, or retransmission of the material without express written permission is prohibited.

p. 22: © Cengage Learning.

pp. 22–23: © Cengage Learning.

p. 37: © Cengage Learning.

P. 37–38: © Cengage Learning.

p. 42: © Cengage Learning.

p. 46: © Cengage Learning.

p. 48: © Association for the Sociology of Religion. Used by permission of Association for the Sociology of Religion, Inc.

p. 56–61: © Cengage Learning.

p. 68–70: "Questioning the Motives of Home-Schooling Parents" by Froma Harrop as appeared in the *Seattle Times*, June 28, 2001. Reprinted by permission of The Providence Journal Company.

p. 82: ©2017 Cengage Learning.

p. 91–92: © Cengage Learning.

p. 93–95: "The True Blue American" by Delmore Schwartz, from *Selected Poems: Summer Knowledge*, copyright © 1959 by Delmore Schwartz. Reprinted by permission of New Directions Publishing Corp.

p. 95–97: © Cengage Learning.

p. 122: © Cengage Learning.

p. 123: © Cengage Learning.

p. 124: © Cengage Learning. Data © US Department of Education.

p. 126: © Cengage Learning.

p. 127: © University of West Florida Students.

p. 127: © University of West Florida Students.

p. 137: Richard Rodriguez, *Aria: Memoir of a Bilingual Childhood.*

p. 137–38: Rachel Carson, "The Obligation to Endure," *Silent Spring.*

p. 140: Norman Mackenzie, *The Escape from Elba.*

p. 143: Victoria Fromkin and Robert Rodman, *An Introduction to Language.*

P. 143: Loren Eiseley, *The Night Country.*

p. 146: Jonathan Kozol, *Illiterate America.*

p. 146: Annie Dillard, "In the Jungle."

p. 147: Anthony Lewis, *Gideon's Trumpet.*

p. 147–48: Benjamin Spock, *Baby and Child Care.*

p. 148: J. William Fulbright, *The Arrogance of Power.*

p. 148: Garrett Hongo, "Kubota."

p. 149: Merrill Markoe, "Men, Women, and Conversation."

p. 149: Morton Hunt, *New York Times Magazine.*

p. 150: Source: Smithsonian.

p. 151: Isaac Asimov, "The Case against Man."

p. 152: Mary Gordon, "Mary Cassatt."

p. 153: Ellen Mansoor Collier, "I Am Not a Terrorist."

p. 153: John Pheiffer, "Seeking Peace, Making War."

p. 153–54: Henry Louis Gates Jr., "One Internet, Two Nations."

p. 154: Amy Tan, "Mother Tongue."

p. 154: Peshe Kuriloff, "If John Dewey Were Alive Today, He'd Be a Webhead."

p. 170: Rebecca Hill, *Blue Rise.*

p. 172: Richard Rodriguez, *Aria: Memoir of a Bilingual Childhood.*

p. 172: Adapted from *Newsweek.*

p. 177: Adapted from Jane Brody's *Nutrition Book.*

p. 185: Charles Darwin, *The Origin of Species.*

p. 282: Adapted from William Goldman, *Adventures in the Screen Trade.*

p. 290: Alexander Pope.

p. 290: Wilfred Owen.

p. 302: Thomas Hood, "The Song of the Shirt," 1843.

p. 384: Source: June Foley, "Women 1982: The Year That Time Ran Out."

p. 384: Source: Eleanor Clift and Tom Brazaitis, *Madam President.*

p. 384: Source: Susan B. Anthony.

p. 385: Republished with permission of Tribune-Review Publishing Co., from "Women's Impact Grows" by Salena Zito, *Pittsburgh Tribune-Review,* Sunday, May 22, 2011, © 2011; permission conveyed through Copyright Clearance Center, Inc.

p. 390: From *Scholastic Update,* 1992. Copyright © 1992 by Scholastic Inc. Reprinted by permission of Scholastic Inc.

p. 392: Turkle, Sherry. *The Second Self: Computers and the Human Spirit.* New York: Simon & Schuster, 1984. 83–84.

p. 394: Courtesy Landon Y. Jones, *Great Expectations: America and the Baby Boom Generation,* © 1980.

p. 403: Excerpt from Lindner, Katharina. "Images of Women in General Interest and Fashion Magazine Advertisements from 1955 to 2002." *Sex Roles* 51 (2004): 409–421.

p. 404: Excerpt from *Can't Buy My Love: How Advertising Changes the Way We Think and Feel* by Jean Kilbourne.

p. 405: Excerpt from *The Beauty Myth: How Images of Beauty Are Used against Women* by Naomi Wolf.

p. 408: Source: Conkling, John A. "Pyrotechnics" *Scientific American,* July 1990: 96.

p. 410: Source: Irving Howe, "The Value of the Canon."

p. 412: Source: Alison Gregg, "Planning and Managin an Oral History Collection," *APLIS* 13.4 [2000]: 174.

p. 412: Source: Freeman, Jean R., "Never Underestimate the Power of a Bus: My Journey to Oral History," *Oral History Review* 29:2 [2002]: 30.

p. 413: Source: Honig, Emily, "Getting to the Source: Striking Lives: Oral History and the Politics of Memory." *Journal of Women's History* 9.1 [1997]: 139.

p. 427: From "The Reception of Reader Response Theory" by Patricia Harkin from *CCC* 56:3, February 2005, p. 410. Copyright © 2005 by the National Council of Teachers of English, Reprinted with permission.

p. 428 (both): From Kleiner, *Gardner's Art Through the Ages,* 13E. © 2011 Cengage Learning.

p. 431: Source Info: https://ebscohost.com.

p. 437: © Cengage Learning.

p. 469: © Association for the Sociology of Religion. Used by permission of Association for the Sociology of Religion, Inc.

p. 471: From Straubhaar/Larose/Davenport, *Media Now,* 7e, © 2012 Cengage Learning.

p. 472: From Straubhaar/Larose/Davenport, *Media Now,* 7e, © 2012 Cengage Learning.

p. 482: © Cengage Learning.

p. 491: © Cengage Learning.

Index

Note: Page numbers in blue type indicate definitions.

Correction Symbols

abbr	Incorrect abbreviation: **39a–c**; *editing misuse*, **39d**	**p**	Punctuation error: **Pt. 5**
adj	Incorrect adjective: **20d; 23a–b**; *comparative/superlative forms*, **23d**	**par** *or* **¶**	New paragraph: **13a–e**
		no ¶	No paragraph: **13a–e**
		¶ coh	Paragraph not coherent: **13b**
adv	Incorrect adverb: **20e; 23a; 23c**; *comparative/superlative forms*, **23d**	**¶ dev**	Paragraph not developed: **13c**
		¶ un	Paragraph not unified: **13a**
		plan	Lack of planning: **3a–e; 7a; 9a; 45b**
agr	Faulty agreement: *subject/verb*, **26a**; *pronoun/antecedent*, **26b**	**purp**	Purpose not clear: *determining purpose*, **2b; 12a**; *purpose checklist*, **p. 12**
aud	Audience not clear: *identifying audience*, **2c; 12a**		
awk	Awkward: **28a–d**	**ref**	Incorrect pronoun reference: **21c**
ca	Incorrect case: **21a**; *case in special situations*, **21b**	**rep**	Unnecessary repetition: *eliminating*, **17b**
cap	Incorrect capitalization: **36a–e**; *editing misuse*, **36f**	**rev**	Revise: **5b–c; 7d; 9c; 41k**
		run-on	Run-on sentence: *correcting*, **25b**
coh	Lack of coherence: *paragraphs*, **13b**	**shift**	Unnecessary shift: **28a**
con	Be more concise: **17a–c**	**sl**	Inappropriate use of slang: *level of diction*, **19a2**
cs	Comma splice: *correcting*, **25b**		
d	Inappropriate diction: *appropriate words*, **19a**; *inappropriate figures of speech*, **19c**; *inappropriate language*, **19d**; *offensive language*, **19e**	**sp**	Spelling error: **35a–b**
		sxt	Sexist or biased language: **19e2**
		thesis	Unclear or unstated thesis: **4a–c; 41d; 41h**
		var	Lack of sentence variety: **15a–b**
dead	Deadwood: **17a1**	**w**	Wordiness: *eliminating*, **17a; 17c4–5**
det	Use concrete details: **19b3–4**		
dev	Inadequate development: **13c**	**ᵛ**	Apostrophe: **32a–c**; *editing misuse*, **32d**
dm	Dangling modifier: **27c**		
doc	Incorrect or inadequate documentation: *MLA*, **47a**; *APA*, **48a**	**[ ]**	Brackets: **34d**
		:	Colon: **34a1–3**; *editing misuse*, **34a4**
emp	Inadequate or unclear emphasis: **16a–e**	**ᶺ**	Comma: **30a–f**; *editing misuse*, **30g**
		—	Dash: **34b**
exact	Use more exact word: **19b**	**. . .**	Ellipsis: **34f**
fig	Inappropriate figure of speech: **19c**	**!**	Exclamation point: **29c**
frag	Sentence fragment: *correcting*, **24b–d**	**//**	Faulty parallelism: *using parallelism*, **16c; 18a**; *revising*, **18b**
fs	Fused sentence: *correcting*, **25b**		
ital	Use italics: **37a–c**; *for emphasis or clarity*, **37d**	**-**	Hyphen: **38a–b**
		( )	Parentheses: **34c**
lc	Use lowercase: *editing misuse of capitals*, **36f**	**.**	Period: **29a**
		?	Question mark: **29b1–2**; *editing misuse*, **29b3**
log	Incorrect or faulty logic: **6a–f; 28d**		
mix	Mixed construction: **28b**	**" "**	Quotation marks: **33a–d**; *with other punctuation*, **33e**; *editing misuse*, **33f**
mm	Misplaced modifier: **27a**		
ms	Incorrect manuscript form: *MLA*, **47b**; *APA*, **48b**	**;**	Semicolon: **31a–c**; *editing misuse*, **31d**
num	Incorrect use of numeral or spelled-out number: **40a–b**	**/**	Slash: **34e**

Contents

about fifty with rouge on her cheekbones and no eyebrows"
(239). Other customers are characterized in equally negative
terms—for example, "houseslaves in pin curlers" (240) and
"an old party in baggy gray pants" (241). Unlike the other
customers, the leader of the three girls is described as a
"queen":

> She came down a little hard on her heels, as if she didn't
> walk in her bare feet that much, putting down her heels
> and then letting the weight move along to her toes as if
> she was testing the floor with every step, putting a little
> deliberate extra action into it. (239)

It seems clear that Sammy realizes that Queenie and her
friends come from farther away than just the beach. They have
come to test the floors of a store patronized by the less well-
off and do it openly, in defiance of social rules. In a sense,
they are "slumming."

Long prose quotation (more than four lines) is set off from text and introduced by a colon. Quotation is indented 1/2" from left margin; no quotation marks are used.

Westmoreland 6

Works Cited

Oates, Joyce Carol. "John Updike's American Comedies." *Joyce Carol Oates on John Updike*, U of San Francisco, 5 Apr. 1998, www.usfca.edu/fac-staff/southerr/onupdike.html.

Steiner, George. "Supreme Fiction: America Is in the Details." *The New Yorker,* 11 Mar. 1996, p. 105.

Updike, John. "A&P." *Compact Literature: Reading, Reacting, Writing*, edited by Laurie G. Kirszner and Stephen R. Mandell, 9th ed., Cengage, 2016, pp. 39-43.

---. Interview by Donald Murray. *The Heinle Original Film Series in Literature,* directed by Bruce Schwartz. Thomson, 2004.

---. "Still Afraid of Being Caught." *The New York Times,* 8 Oct. 1995, www.nytimes.com/1995/10/29/magazine/l-still-afraid-of-being-caught-095796.html.

Wells, Walter. "John Updike's 'A&P': A Return Visit to Araby." *Studies in Short Fiction,* vol. 30, no. 2, 1993, pp. 127-33. *Questia,* www.questia.com/library/journal/1G1-14081343/john-updike-s-a-p-a-return-visit-to-araby.